House of Lords Reform: A History

House of Lords Reform: A History

1971-2014:
The Exclusion of Hereditary Peers

Book Two: 2002-2014

Peter Raina

PETER LANG

Oxford · Bern · Berlin · Bruxelles · Frankfurt am Main · New York · Wien

Bibliographic information published by Die Deutsche Nationalbibliothek
Die Deutsche Nationalbibliothek lists this publication in the Deutsche Nationalbibliografie;
detailed bibliographic data is available on the Internet at http://dnb.d-nb.de.

A catalogue record for this book is available from the British Library.

Library of Congress Control Number: 2015935021

Cover illustration includes portraits of Dame Margaret Becket MP (reproduced by
permission of the editor of the Andrew Marr Show, BBC1); Baroness D'Souza (reproduced
by permission of the House of Lords, 2014); Baroness Hayman (reproduced by permission
of the Baroness Hayman); the 7th Marquess of Salisbury (reproduced by permission of the
7th Marquess of Salisbury); Baroness Jay of Paddington (reproduced by permission of the
House of Lords, 2014); Lord Plant of Highfield (reproduced by permission of ActiveShot/
Winchester Cathedral); Lord Lloyd of Berwick (reproduced by permission of Photoshot.
com); Lord Falconer of Thoroton (reproduced by permission of the Palace of Westminster
Collection, WOA 6560 www.parliament.uk/art); Lord Irvine of Lairg (reproduced by
permission of the Palace of Westminster Collection, WOA 6272 www.parliament.uk/
art) and Bernard Weatherill MP (reproduced by permission of the Palace of Westminster
Collection, WOA 3578 www.parliament.uk/art).

ISBN 978-3-0343-1856-3 (print)
ISBN 978-3-0353-0707-8 (eBook)

© Peter Lang AG, International Academic Publishers, Bern 2015
Hochfeldstrasse 32, CH-3012 Bern, Switzerland
info@peterlang.com, www.peterlang.com, www.peterlang.net

This publication has been peer reviewed.

Printed in Germany

Contents

List of Illustrations

The Rt Hon. the Lord Lloyd of Berwick *by Photoshot.com*
Reproduced by permission of Photoshot.com

The Rt Hon. Dan Byles MP *by Danielle King*
Reproduced by permission of the Rt Hon. Dan Byles

The Baroness D'Souza *by Chris Moyse*
Reproduced by permission of the House of Lords, 2014

Rt Hon. the Lord Falconer of Thoroton *by Michael Tylor*
Reproduced by permission of the Palace of Westminster Collection, WOA 6560
www.parliament.uk/art

The Rt Hon. the Baroness Hayman *by Anita Corbin*
Reproduced by permission of the Baroness Hayman

Rt Hon. the Earl Ferrers *by an unknown artist*
Reproduced by permission of Annabel, Countess of Ferrers

Rt Hon. the Lord Richard QC *by an unknown artist*
Reproduced by permission of the Lord Richard

David Martin Scott Steel, Baron Steel of Aikwood *by Bassano & Vandyk Studios*
Reproduced by permission of the National Portrait Gallery, London

The Rt Hon. Jack Straw MP *by an unknown artist*
Reproduced by permission of the Ministry of Justice/Open Government Licence v.1.0

While every effort has been made to trace copyright holders, if any have been inadvertently overlooked, the author will be happy to acknowledge them in future editions.

CHAPTER TEN

2002–03. The Joint Committee on House of Lords Reform

On 13 May 2002 the president of the Council and leader of the Commons, Robin Cook, announced in the Commons that the government had listened carefully to the wide range of views expressed in the recent debates on Lords reform in both Houses of Parliament and had heeded responses to the White Paper. The government had also taken account of a report from the Public Administration Committee advising that the issue of reform should be considered by a Joint Committee of both Houses, so as to reconcile differences and seek a 'principled consensus' on the way forward.[1]

Eric Forth, for the Opposition, welcomed the government statement. His party, he said, had seen clearly, some time ago, that a 'joint parliamentary approach would be needed'. He pledged that 'we will play our full and positive part in the deliberations of the Joint Committee'.

A short debate followed. Paul Tyler asked the government if it could give a 'more precise indication' of what timetable it would like. Robin Cook replied that it would be wrong to predetermine a specified date by which the Joint Committee had to respond. Regarding the size of the Committee, he said that any joint committee that was set up had to be divided equally between the two chambers – 'only half the membership comes from here'. It was, he said, appropriate to proceed by a free vote. Different views existed on both sides of the chamber, so 'it would be wrong to try to proceed on a party political basis, with the Whip applied. It is right that both sides

---

[1]   *Parliamentary Debates*, House of Commons, vol. 385, 13 May 2002, cols 516–33.

be able to cast their votes freely, so that we can establish where the centre of gravity lies.'[2]

The Joint Committee was composed of 24 members, 12 from the House of Lords and 12 from the House of Commons. The Committee delivered two reports. The minutes of these reports give us a detailed insight into how the Committee worked. The first report was published in December 2002.[3]

First Report of the Committee

HOUSE OF LORDS REFORM: FIRST REPORT

The Joint Committee was first appointed in July 2002:

(1) to consider issues relating to House of Lords reform, including the composition and powers of the Second Chamber and its role and authority within the context of Parliament as a whole, having regard in particular to the impact which any proposed changes would have on the existing pre-eminence of the House of Commons, such consideration to include the implications of a House composed of more than one 'category' of member and the experience and expertise which the House of Lords in its present form brings to its function as the revising Chamber; and

---

2   *Ibid.*, col. 532. A similar statement was made in the House of Lords by the lord chancellor, Lord Irvine of Lairg. A Joint Committee, he said, would 'help reconcile differences and seek a principled consensus on the way forward'. See *Parliamentary Debates*, House of Lords, vol. DCXXXVI, 13 May 2002, col. 12–13.

3   See *Joint Committee on House of Lords Reform: First Report*. Ordered by the House of Lords to be printed 9 December 2002. HL Paper 17. Ordered by the House of Commons to be printed 10 December 2002. HC 171.

(2) having regard to paragraph (1) above, to report on options for the composition and powers of the House of Lords and to define and present to both Houses options for composition, including a fully nominated and fully elected House, and intermediate options;

and to consider and report on –

(a) any changes to the relationship between the two Houses which may be necessary to ensure the proper functioning of Parliament as a whole in the context of a reformed Second Chamber, and in particular, any new procedures for resolving conflict between the two Houses; and

(b) the most appropriate and effective legal and constitutional means to give effect to any new Parliamentary settlement;

and in all the foregoing considerations, to have regard to –

(i)   the Report of the Royal Commission on House of Lords Reform (Cm 4534);
(ii) the White Paper *The House of Lords – Completing the Reform* (Cm 5291), and the responses received thereto;
(iii) debates and votes in both Houses of Parliament on House of Lords reform; and
(iv) the House of Commons Public Administration Select Committee report *The Second Chamber: Continuing the Reform*, including its consultation of the House of Commons, and any other relevant select committee reports.

The twelve Lords members, appointed on 4 July 2002, are:

Lord Archer of Sandwell
Viscount Bledisloe
Lord Brooke of Alverthorpe
Lord Carter
Lord Forsyth of Drumlean
Baroness Gibson of Market Rasen
Lord Goodhart

Lord Howe of Aberavon
Lord Oakeshott of Seagrove Bay
Baroness O'Cathain
The Earl of Selborne
Lord Weatherill

The twelve Commons members, appointed on 19 June 2002, are:

Janet Anderson
Mr James Arbuthnot
Mr Chris Bryant
Mr Kenneth Clarke
Dr Jack Cunningham
Mr William Hague
Mr Stephen McCabe
Joyce Quin
Mr Terry Rooney
Mr Clive Soley
Mr Paul Stinchcombe
Mr Paul Tyler

At its first meeting, on 9 July 2002, the Committee elected Dr Jack Cunningham as its Chairman.

Background

In this report we set out, for consideration by both Houses, an inclusive range of seven options for the composition of a reformed House of Lords. We do so against a background of broad agreement on the role, functions and powers of a reformed second chamber. The aim of maintaining the effectiveness and increasing the legitimacy of the second chamber has become common ground.

Our terms of reference called upon us to consider a wide range of documents and evidence, and so we have not felt it necessary to call for further evidence. In this report we have sought to inform the debates and votes in both Houses by clarifying what we believe should be the future role, powers and nature of the second chamber and identifying the implications of our conclusions for its composition.

Place of the second chamber in Parliament

We envisage a continuation of the present role of the House of Lords, and of the existing conventions governing its relations with the House of Commons. These conventions, which are of a self-restraining nature, impact profoundly on the relations between the Houses and need to be understood as a vital part of any future constitutional settlement. When the views of the Houses on composition are made known, we will return to the detailed matter of how these important conventions should be maintained in a new constitutional settlement between the Houses.

Powers of the second chamber

We do not recommend, at this stage, that any new or additional powers be given to the House. However, we recognise that more consideration needs to be given to the best way of ensuring that the reformed House can act effectively in respect of secondary legislation. When the Houses' views on the matter of composition are known, we shall consider whether any change is needed in the powers of the House in this area. Subject to satisfactory assurances that carry-over arrangements could not be used to erode the powers of the House, we do not consider at this stage that the provisions of the Parliament Acts need to be altered.

The nature of a reformed second chamber

We consider five qualities desirable in the makeup of a reformed second chamber:

- legitimacy
- representativeness
- no domination by any one party
- independence
- expertise

The existing House of Lords meets several of these criteria, namely lack of domination by one party, independence and expertise. If these existing qualities, bolstered by a greater representativeness, can be transferred to the reformed House, we believe that a new legitimacy, which we have already highlighted in considering the House's role, will naturally develop.

Composition of a reformed second chamber

We propose that the reformed House should comprise about six hundred members. This represents little change from the present House without the 92 hereditary peers, but we recognise that transitional arrangements may necessitate an increase in size before equilibrium is reached. A tenure for all members of some twelve years is about right. While members should be able to resign their seats earlier, members who do so should not thereby be able to stand for election to the House of Commons at least for a certain period, perhaps three years. There should be a new Appointments Commission established. But that should not exclude the possibility of nomination by the Prime Minister of the day, nor proposals by party leaders and members of the public. Such nominations would be scrutinised by the new Appointments Commission. Only the Prime Minister would have the right to have nominations confirmed.

Transitional arrangements may, depending on the composition chosen, need to be spread over a substantial period. At this stage we have concluded only that we are not attracted by the idea of compulsory retirement for existing life peers. The membership of the law lords and the bishops and other religious representatives will need to be considered in the light of the composition chosen. The judicial function of the House of Lords is worthy of independent inquiry and expert attention.

We consider it essential that some detailed work should be done on costing options.

The options

We recommend that there should be votes on seven options, set out in paragraphs 63 to 74:

1. Fully appointed
2. Fully elected

3. 80 per cent appointed/20 per cent elected
4. 80 per cent elected/20 per cent appointed
5. 60 per cent appointed/40 per cent elected
6. 60 per cent elected/40 per cent appointed
7. 50 per cent appointed/50 per cent elected

The next stage

We hope that there will first be debates on this report in both Houses, with the opportunity to vote on the options coming later, after members have had time to study both debates. We are convinced that it is essential that both Houses follow the same procedure in voting on options. We recommend that a series of motions, each setting out one of the seven options we have identified, be moved successively in each House notwithstanding the normal practice in regard to questions. Members would be free to vote in favour of as many of the options as they considered acceptable. After both Houses have expressed views, we shall resume our deliberations and seek to develop, in our second report, a single set of proposals for reform.

PART 1: INTRODUCTION

The opportunity

1. Over the past century attempts at reform of the House of Lords have failed principally because of a lack of agreement on what was needed to replace the existing House. Each attempt generated wide debate both in and outside Government and parliamentary circles; opinion ranged from complete abolition of the second House to preservation of the status quo which, until 1999, included a dominant hereditary element. That position was changed by the House of Lords Act 1999 and the announcement by Government of its intention to remove the hereditary element entirely at the next stage of reform.

2. There is now much greater agreement about the role, functions and powers of a reformed second chamber. Whilst there

remain differences about how the reformed House should be composed, the aim of maintaining the effectiveness and enhancing the legitimacy of the second chamber has become common ground. A re-balancing of parliamentary institutions, which reform implies, is something that can only evolve over time. Nevertheless we believe that there is now an historic opportunity to enact a reform which will enable the second chamber to continue to play an important and complementary role to the Commons, with its future at last secure.

3. By identifying this wide area of agreement in our report and describing the conditions in which we consider a reformed House can realistically operate, our aim is to help the Houses consider the range of options on composition which are set out in our terms of reference. Once both Houses have had the opportunity to debate and vote on the options which we set out here, we shall, as we said in our Special Report, need to consider such differences as may exist between the expressed views of the two Houses and the means by which, and extent to which, they might be brought closer to each other, if not actually reconciled. We shall then develop a full set of proposals to take the reform forward. In this report we will also identify issues which we will need to consider in more detail at that later stage, when it will be essential to develop workable proposals that command the widest possible support within and outside Westminster.

Background

4. The Committee met for the first time on 9 July 2002, three working days after the House of Lords agreed, on 4 July, to a Resolution concurring with the Commons in the setting up of a Joint Committee.

5. At our first meeting, we elected the Rt Hon. Jack Cunningham MP as our Chairman and began to consider how to fulfil our remit. The deliberation was continued at a second meeting in the following week when we considered a Special Report, agreed to on 16 July.

6. In that Special Report of 16 July, we outlined our method of proceeding, which was to consider carefully what amounted to a library of material, including a Government White Paper and supporting documents, a Royal Commission Report, a Select Committee Report and the evidence appended to these papers and debates in both Houses. The evidence referred to us contains a very wide range of views from members of both Houses and includes opinions from outside experts as well as from the general public. We have therefore not felt it necessary to call for further evidence. Analysing it and applying our collective parliamentary experience to it has enabled us to fulfil our first task of setting in context, and presenting to both Houses, an inclusive range of options on the interrelated matters of role and composition. The Committee was reappointed in the current session on 28 November 2002.

7. We have carried out our examination in a series of deliberative meetings and have been assisted in our task by our two Clerks, Malcolm Jack, Clerk of the Journals in the House of Commons and David Beamish, Clerk of the Journals in the House of Lords, both with long experience of Parliament.

Structure of Report

8. We concluded at an early stage in our deliberations that we needed to consider the roles, functions and powers of a second chamber whilst we were considering the options on composition. Accordingly our conclusions and recommendations are set out as follows:

Part 2 – roles, conventions, functions and powers of a second chamber
Part 3 – the kind of members needed: the issues of legitimacy, representativeness, party balance, independence and expertise
Part 4 – considerations affecting composition, including tenure and transitional arrangements
Part 5 – the options on composition.

The historical background to our work is described in Appendix 1.

PART 2: ROLES, CONVENTIONS, FUNCTIONS AND POWERS

Role in relation to the Commons

9. It is generally recognised that reform of the House of Lords would have a significant effect on its role in relation to the House of Commons. That is a key constitutional issue, which needs to be considered in the context of existing conventions, which we consider, on the whole, to work well. But there are other roles for the new House, including the way in which it can better represent society as a whole, as well as the nations and regions of our country.

10. One of the principal arguments for having second chambers – and we find little support in the evidence we have examined for uni-cameralism in the United Kingdom – is that such chambers provide an opportunity for second thoughts. The revising role of the existing House of Lords has been progressively strengthened by the arrival of Life Peers since 1958 (bringing specialist knowledge in many fields including the public service, science and medicine, academic life, the voluntary sector, business and industry, etc.) and by the increase in the numbers and importance of the Cross-benchers, who do not take any party whip, and add an invaluable independent approach to scrutiny. Under both Conservative and Labour governments, the House of Lords has played a significant role in amending legislation, sometimes in considerable detail, throughout the period from 1970 to the present. The value of the Lords revising and advisory role is widely acknowledged, for example by the Commons Select Committee on Public Administration, which noted that the House is regarded as 'very effective in carrying out a range of scrutiny and legislative work'. That role does not challenge the convention that, in the last resort, the House of Commons has the final word.

The Existing Conventions

11. Whilst this role of revision is identified in all the papers referred to us, insufficient attention has been paid to the conventions that

actually govern how the Lords conducts its business and behaves towards the Commons. We consider that these existing conventions, which are of a self-restraining nature, impact profoundly on the relations between the Houses and need to be understood as a vital part of any future constitutional settlement.

12. The two most significant conventions are that the House of Commons shall finally have its way and that the Government is entitled to have its business considered without undue delay. The first of these understandings is embodied, in relation to manifesto bills, in the Salisbury Convention, formulated by the then Viscount Cranborne (when he was Leader of the Conservative Opposition from 1945–51) whereby the Opposition (of whichever party is in Government) refrains from voting against the second reading of any Government Bill which had been part of that party's election manifesto. The second convention, that the Government should have its business, also implies, as the Royal Commission noted, that such business should be considered within a reasonable time.

Other more pragmatic practices (including, for example, the end of session procedures known as 'ping pong') relate to the point at which the Lords will give way in a struggle over amendments. Taken together, these conventions govern the day-to-day relations between the Houses during a parliamentary session, contributing in a significant way to the overall effectiveness of Parliament as a place where business is transacted efficiently. The House of Lords could depart from any of these conventions at any time and without legislation, and might well be more inclined to do so if it had been largely (and recently) elected. But the continuing operation of the existing conventions in any new constitutional arrangement will be vital in avoiding deadlock between the Houses – which could all too easily become an obstacle to continuing good governance. We therefore strongly support the continuation of the existing conventions. When the views of the Houses on composition are made known, we will return to the detailed matter of how these important conventions should be maintained in a new constitutional settlement between the Houses.

OTHER ROLES

Constitutional long stop

13. The Royal Commission Report stated that one of the most important roles of a reformed second chamber would be to act as a 'constitutional long stop'. In other words it should ensure that changes of a constitutional nature are not made without full and open debate and without awareness of the consequences. One existing constitutional check is the Lords' veto over the dismissal of office holders, including, for example, High Court judges, the Comptroller and Auditor General and the Information Commissioner. It is an important way of ensuring, as the Royal Commission noted, their independence from the Executive.

14. Another constitutional check is contained in the provision of the Parliament Act 1911 which limits the life of Parliament to five years. The Lords can thereby prevent a Government, with its control of the Commons, from legislating to extend its own existence.

15. The Royal Commission supported the retention of existing powers in this general area of what might be called constitutional guardianship, but resisted any further extension of the Lords' constitutional role – such as an absolute veto on all 'constitutional' bills or the extension of the suspensory veto for two years in the case of such bills, whether they were to be defined by a Speaker's certificate or by the Lords itself. Nor did it support recourse to a referendum when there was a clash between the Houses over a constitutional bill. The Commons' Select Committee, for its part, suggested that the matter of how to deal with constitutional bills might be further considered by the House of Lords Constitution Committee, which was set up following the Royal Commission's recommendation. We intend to return to the matter of the constitutional role of the Lords in the later stages of our work but we underline its importance here.

Role in relation to the public: a new legitimacy

16. The lack of representativeness of the hereditary House gradually diminished its authority in the twentieth century. This

perhaps had a greater long-term impact than the formal curtailment of the powers of the House by the Parliament Act 1911. Whilst the House subsequently developed its role as a revising chamber after 1945, the continuation of the hereditary element, perceived as inherently unrepresentative, and the massive imbalance of the political parties in the House, called into question its authority. The problem of the House's legitimacy was considered by the Royal Commission. Its view was that insofar as the House became more representative of society as a whole, it would gain legitimacy and with it, confidence. Its recommendations included ensuring that people with particular expertise, for example in human rights or with special spiritual knowledge, as well as representatives of professional and vocational groups (many of whom would not want to stand for election), were among the membership of a reformed House. The composition of the House should take into account gender balance and social characteristics such as the pattern of ethnic groups and different faiths: together these various changes would enhance the legitimacy of the Lords. It will be important to ensure that the reformed House is as inclusively representative as possible. We concur with the conclusions of the Royal Commission that increased representativeness will enhance the legitimacy of the House of Lords. We will consider methods to achieve that end when we deal with getting the right membership of the House later in this report but it is also a matter that will need further careful attention in future.

Role in relation to the regions and nations: representing the United Kingdom

17. A body of opinion envisages the reformed House serving as a Parliamentary focus for the regions and nations of the United Kingdom, rather in the way that upper Houses operate in some of the Commonwealth parliaments or the Senates in the USA or in France. The relationship of a newly reformed House to the devolved bodies is clearly relevant to the perception of that role. The Joint Committee has received a joint representation from the presiding officers of the Scottish Parliament, the National

Assembly of Wales and the Northern Ireland Assembly, who are all members of the House of Lords, suggesting that in a reformed House their successors should be *ex officio* members. The presiding officers say that their membership has not only enabled them to keep abreast of affairs in Parliament, but has also given them a chance to represent the views of Wales, Scotland and Northern Ireland in Parliament.

18. In its report the Commons Public Administration Select Committee dealt with the wider aspects of the relations a reformed House might have with the devolved bodies. It considered the proposal (supported by the Leader of the House of Commons in his evidence to that Committee) that indirect election by the devolved assemblies might be one route of entry to the second chamber, bringing the United Kingdom more in line with the model of second chambers of Europe. The Royal Commission, for its part, did not recommend membership of the devolved assemblies as qualifying for membership of the reformed House. Instead it talked of a new 'category of people within Parliament' who would provide a 'voice in Parliament' for the regions and nations. We are convinced that a reformed House should contain an appropriate number of members from all parts of the country and later in this report we will consider how this might be achieved. It is difficult to see at the moment structures which are parallel to those to be found in fully federal countries like the USA and Germany upon which to base this representation, although we note in the recent Queen's Speech the Government's intention to hold referendums on the issue of regional governance in England.

FUNCTIONS

Legislative functions

19. One important fact to make clear in discussing the legislative function of the Lords is that much legislation actually begins in the Lords. Although its role as a revising chamber is well known and supported in the documents referred to us, it needs to be

understood that a considerable part of the Government's programme, normally about one-third, is introduced in the Lords. Its role as a revising chamber, giving a chance for second thoughts, is, of course important, as we have already said. The Anti-terrorism, Crime and Security Bill considered in November and December 2001 provides a good recent example. Despite its accelerated passage, the House spent 53 hours examining the bill and made substantial and important amendments, which were accepted by Government and Commons alike.

20. The Government has announced that it proposes no change in the legislative powers of the Lords. We do not consider it likely that any Government will be able or wish to change the practice of introducing legislation in the second House but the balance of business between the Houses is something that may need closer parliamentary supervision in future. If both Houses are to act more efficiently as legislative chambers, there will need to be greater co-ordination between them over workloads, as the Commons Modernisation Committee has recently pointed out. We consider that a co-ordination of the legislative loads between the Houses is a practical but important part of any new constitutional settlement.

Pre-legislative scrutiny

The Government is also committed to extending the role of both Houses in the process of pre-legislative scrutiny. It has reasserted its view of the importance of that scrutiny in the recent Queen's Speech, announcing that legislation in draft will be published in three different areas – housing, nuclear liabilities and corruption. Joint Committees have considered the draft Financial Services and Markets Bill, the draft Local Government (Organisations and Standards) Bill and most recently the draft Communications Bill. The Royal Commission supported this practice, recommending that 'pre-legislative scrutiny of draft bills should become an established feature of Parliamentary business'. The Lords Group on Working Practices has recommended that 'virtually all major government bills should, as a matter of course, be subject in draft to pre-legislative scrutiny'. The Select Committee on the Modernisation of the House of Commons attaches 'the highest importance' to pre-legislative scrutiny. Recognising the practical realities of parliamentary programmes, we nevertheless consider that pre-legislative scrutiny is an important aspect of making the legislature function more effectively and we welcome the proposals announced in the recent Queen's Speech.

Secondary legislation

22. There is a greater diversity of views about the treatment of secondary legislation. The Royal Commission first recommended a change in the status quo (whereby the Lords, like the Commons, can reject statutory instruments). It proposed that if the second chamber votes to annul an instrument, the annulment would not take effect for three months and could in the meantime be over-ridden by the Commons. The Government, in its White Paper, accepted the Royal Commission's recommendation, arguing that the change would increase the influence of the Lords by enabling it to call the Commons to recast the instrument. Most members who spoke in debate in the House of Commons were against the Government proposals and the Commons Select Committee on Public Administration pointed out that Lord Wakeham has himself expressed second thoughts. The Commons Select Committee itself was unconvinced of the Government proposal and recommended continuance of the existing veto.

23. Affirmative instruments present a more straightforward case since the Lords have almost always refrained from voting on such instruments. It may be that a reformed House might feel reinvigorated enough to act differently, as has happened on one occasion in the recent past. The present veto is a less drastic weapon than it might appear, because it is open to the Government to lay another instrument. When the Houses' views on the matter of composition are known, we shall consider whether any change is needed in the powers of the Lords in this area.

Scrutiny of policy

24. The scrutiny function of the House of Lords is an important and distinctive part of the parliamentary process of making Government accountable. It is carried out by the whole House as well as by Select Committees. Cross-bench members add an element to the scrutiny process which is less noticeable in the Commons, something mentioned in the debates in both Houses. Whilst the House has developed certain Select Committees with notable success (Science and Technology, European Union, and Delegated Powers and Regulatory Reform Committees are usually cited), several members in the debate in the House of Lords expressed the view that the committee system needed improvement in order to maintain its success. We assert the importance of the scrutiny function of the House. At a later stage in our work, we will return to consider how that scrutiny might be made even more effective.

Judicial function

The existing House acts through its Appellate and Appeals Committees (composed of the Lords of Appeal in Ordinary and other judicially qualified Lords) as the highest court of appeal. There is a current discussion about whether this function should be separated and a United Kingdom Supreme Court be established. This is a complex matter which has divided opinion even within the judiciary. Although we may return to it later in our deliberations, we consider the judicial function of the House of Lords to be a matter worthy of independent inquiry and expert attention. Even if a separation takes place it does not need to entail the ending of membership of the House by the law lords.

POWERS

Parliament Acts

26. Until the twentieth century there was little formal definition of the powers of either House. By various resolutions and under

the terms of the Bill of Rights (1689) both Houses had articulated privileges reserved to them, the Commons in particular asserting its control in financial matters more frequently during the seventeenth century. It was with the passing of the Parliament Act 1911 that the Lords' legislative power was first restricted by statute.

27. The most important provisions of the Parliament Act 1911 were to:

(i)   restrict the Lords' power to reject 'money bills' to a month;

(ii) allow a public bill introduced in the Commons to pass into law, though not agreed by the Lords, if passed in the Commons in three successive sessions, with not less than two years elapsing between the second reading in the House of Commons in the first session and the passing of the bill in the House of Commons in the Third Session; and

(iii) alter the provision of the Septennial Act 1715, setting five-year Parliaments.

By the provisions of the Parliament Act 1949, the period of time that needed to elapse (under (ii)) was reduced to one year.

28. Although the Parliament Acts have curtailed the power of the Lords, they have done so in quite narrow circumstances, that of a dispute between the Houses over a particular bill. By virtue of the provision of the 1911 Act of a two-year period between a second reading in the Commons and Royal Assent without Lords concurrence, the practical reality is that a Government could only effectively use it in the first two sessions of a five-year Parliament. The narrowing of the necessary time between stages by the 1949 Act does not seem to have made it a much more attractive tool for Government. Between 1949 and 1997 the Parliament Act was invoked only once (the War Crimes Act 1991) and twice between 1997 and 2002 (the European Parliamentary Elections Act 1999 and the Sexual Offences (Amendment) Act 2000). Two of the three Acts (War Crimes and Sexual Offences) were the subject of

a free vote in both Houses. But even though the Parliament Act procedure has only seldom been used, its existence is powerful as a factor in the relations between the Houses and as a constraint on the exercise of the legal powers of the Lords.

29. Despite the terms of the Parliament Acts, the House of Lords, for practical purposes, has retained considerable legislative power. But it has exercised its power responsibly, if at times critically. Because it has kept within the constraints of the conventions we have already described, the Lords has managed to avoid usurping the role of the Commons or causing undue delay or deadlock. We have already concluded, from the actual experience of the relationship between the Houses, that similar arrangements will need to be in place in any new constitutional settlement if the system is to work as well as it has done in the past. The current provision for carry-over of bills from one session to the next has clear implications for the handling of the legislative programme.

We do not imagine that a government would wish controversial legislation to be treated in this way. Subject to satisfactory assurances that carry-over arrangements could not be used to erode the powers of the House of Lords, we do not consider at this stage that the provisions of the Parliament Acts need to be altered. Together with our conclusions about maintaining the existing conventions, we therefore recommend (subject to what we say about secondary legislation in paragraph 23 above) that no new or additional powers are given to the House of Lords at this stage.

PART 3: WHAT SORT OF MEMBERSHIP?

30. Having identified the appropriate roles, functions and powers of the second chamber, we turn to the question what sort of membership is desirable to undertake these roles and perform those functions. We consider five qualities desirable in the makeup of a reformed House, namely (not in any order of importance):

- legitimacy
- representativeness

- no domination by any one party
- independence
- expertise

Legitimacy

31. We have referred above (in paragraph 2) to a general desire to increase the legitimacy of the second chamber and (in paragraph 16) to the lack of legitimacy which has in the past beset the House of Lords and to the view of the Royal Commission that greater representativeness would confer a new legitimacy on the House. The Royal Commission Report talked of the new 'confidence' that a reformed House would have.

The Commons Public Administration Committee Report also considers the question of legitimacy. Some maintain that only a democratically elected second chamber can be truly legitimate, others that there are other routes to legitimacy, including in particular the other qualities which we discuss below.

Representativeness

32. Before the introduction of life peerages the House of Lords could be said to have been unrepresentative of almost any group other than landowners. It is now a much more representative body, though the manner in which its members are appointed has continued to sustain some doubts about its legitimacy.

33. Nevertheless, of the desirable qualities we have listed, the present House is weakest in respect of representativeness. It is overwhelmingly male (84 per cent). It includes few young members (the average age is almost 68). It has a disproportionate number of members from the south-east and too few from the English regions. And, although more representative of ethnic minorities than the House of Commons (over 20 members), it still falls short of properly representing the UK's ethnic diversity. We consider that all these elements of representation must be improved and that better balances can be achieved either by a new appointment system or, with appropriate checks in place, by various methods of election.

No domination by any one party

34. The Royal Commission considered that it was crucial that no one political party should be able to dominate the second chamber: 'If it were to be controlled by the party of Government it might become nothing more than a rubber stamp. If the main Opposition party were to gain control, it could be used to produce legislative deadlock ...'. This view was endorsed by the Government in its White Paper and accepted by the Commons Public Administration Committee. We note that this is a characteristic of the present House: no party has more than one-third of the members of the House (and this would continue to be the case with the departure of the 92 excepted hereditary peers). We therefore conclude that any arrangements for the reformed House must take account of the importance of maintaining the principle that no one political party should be able to be dominant in it.

Independence

35. We have identified independence as an important characteristic of the present House of Lords in keeping the executive to account. That independence arises from the fact that the House contains a substantial number of Cross-bench members who do not take a party whip. But equally important is an independence that arises from membership of a House where the party whips do not influence party-affiliated members in the same way as they do in the Commons. The fact that members of the present House do not face election or some form of reselection is an important element in underpinning that independence. It is our view that any new system of getting members into the House needs to ensure that independence, whether arising from non-party affiliation or from less attention to the requests of the Whips, is not jeopardised or diminished.

The independent members

36. Of the 681 members of the House of Lords on 9 December, 210 (31 per cent) were not members of one of the three main

political parties. They comprised 24 bishops, 9 members with no affiliation and 177 Cross-benchers. The term 'Cross-bencher' is used to describe those members who belong to a group which represents the interests of members who do not take a party whip, and which meets weekly under a Convenor to discuss matters of common interest, but not matters of political controversy (which are for individual members). Since 1999 the Convenor has received public funds to enable him to employ assistance.

37. Among the Cross-benchers are 12 serving Lords of Appeal in Ordinary, several members of minor political parties and several members with definite political affiliations who sit on the Cross-benches because of the office or position which they hold or have held, or for other reasons. By custom, law lords, former Speakers and former public servants normally join the Cross-benchers. Many others such as industrialists and scientists choose to do so, including some but not all politicians from minority parties with no party organisation in the Lords. The fifteen non-party political life peers so far nominated by the Independent Appointments Commission have all joined the Cross-benchers.

38. The impact of the Cross-benchers on voting in the House of Lords is less frequent than their numbers might suggest, because as un-whipped members they usually vote only when they have heard the arguments. On the other hand it is this very ability to listen to argument and vote accordingly that makes the contribution of the Cross-benchers particularly valuable in specialised areas such as medical ethics, or areas of special sensitivity or importance such as anti-terrorism measures. In the last session, 2001–02, 3355 votes out of a total of 39,007 cast in 172 divisions (8.6 per cent) were cast by Cross-benchers. The role of Cross-benchers is often particularly significant in relation to participation in debates and committees and the quality they bring to these deliberations.

Independence among party members

39. It is much more common in the Lords than in the Commons for party members to speak and vote against their party's line.

This is particularly true of supporters of the governing party. This may result from the fact that, on the whole, the Opposition parties choose the issues on which they decide to challenge the Government; it is hardly surprising that they should thus choose issues on which their supporters are united and Government supporters are not. The fact that members almost all have seats for life and that the whips have few sanctions available other than withdrawal of the whip contributes to independence among members of the House who are party members. Furthermore, in an unpaid part-time House it is easy for members unsympathetic to their party's line to absent themselves when they do not wish to go to the extent of voting against the party line.

Implications for a reformed House of Lords

40. The presence of a substantial number of independent members, and the fact that almost all the members of the House have seats for life, crucially ensure a valuable degree of independence which is so important to the effectiveness of the present House. Such independence would be significantly reduced in a substantially elected House. We consider this independence an important element in any reconstituted House.

Expertise

41. It has often been said that in the House of Lords an expert may be found on any subject. The nominations made by successive prime ministers have brought into the House, as well as a very significant proportion of politicians, a wide range of people who have achieved distinction in many fields. It can be argued that, because membership is for life, there is a risk that some older members' expertise may sometimes be out of date. On the other hand the part-time nature of the present House enables members with contemporary knowledge and skills in a wide range of disciplines to participate in the work of the House. There is no doubt that the quality of debates can be very high as a result of the range of expertise to be found in the House. While many of

those concerned are Cross-benchers, there are also others with specialist knowledge who take a party whip. It is unlikely that many of them would wish to fight an election to gain membership of the House, nor to accept a commitment to more or less full-time membership.

42. We consider the expertise which is evident in the existing House to be something of considerable importance which we would wish to see preserved in the new House.

Conclusion

The existing House of Lords meets several of the criteria which we have been considering, namely lack of domination by one party, independence and expertise. If these existing qualities, bolstered by a greater representativeness, can be transferred to the reformed House, we believe that a new legitimacy, which we have already highlighted in considering the House's role, will naturally develop.

PART 4: WHAT SORT OF COMPOSITION?

44. Composition needs to be understood against a number of interrelated factors which encourage the qualities of membership we have been discussing.

Number of members

45. We envisage that in order to retain the benefits of a House whose members are not necessarily full-time salaried party politicians, the reformed House will have to remain at about the same size as the present House.

46. In the second stage of our inquiry we shall give further consideration to the exact eventual size of the House – something which will in any case depend on the number of spaces, if any, required for *ex officio* members such as law lords and bishops. At this stage we propose simply that the House should comprise about six hundred members. This represents little change from the present House without the 92 hereditary peers, but we recognise

that transitional arrangements may necessitate an increase in size before equilibrium is reached.

Tenure

47. The present system of life membership encourages a high degree of independence, because members do not need to think at all about reappointment or re-election. A short tenure, by contrast, would limit the independence of all those members other than those with no wish for reappointment or re-election. That is not to say that all the arguments are in the direction of a very long tenure. At the end of a very long term, elected members might be seen to have lost the representativeness and legitimacy which they had at the time of their election. Members appointed on account of their particular background or expertise might have lost touch as a result of their service in the House.

48. A balance has to be struck, and our view is that a tenure for all members of some twelve years is about right. While members should be able to resign their seats earlier, we consider that members who do so should not thereby be able to stand for election to the House of Commons at least for a certain period, perhaps three years.

Appointment and election

49. Some of the options we set out below involve a mixed House of appointed and elected members, on the basis that neither arrangement on its own would produce the right blend of members. Some commentators have feared difficulties with a 'mixed' House on account of certain members appearing to have greater 'legitimacy' than others, but the House has for a considerable time been a mixture of appointed and hereditary peers. However, we do recognise that a significant element of elected, full-time members is likely to demand support and facilities which have not been sought in the past by members of the existing House.

50. One difficulty which may have been underestimated in the course of recent debate is that of gaining the interest of the

electorate at a time of disappointing turnouts at all elections. Recent experience of, for example, elections to the European Parliament makes it doubtful whether there would be a substantial turnout, even for an election of the whole House. Consideration should be given to having full postal ballots and/or combining the elections with other elections – for example the elections to devolved institutions. Moreover, while it is one thing to ask the electorate to decide the entire membership of a second chamber, it is another to ask it to decide on only a proportion of the membership. Especially if the proportion is a small one, there is likely to be a feeling that the election does not matter much, and there must be a risk of very small turnouts and high votes for fringe candidates, both of which could imperil the reputation, legitimacy and effectiveness of the reformed second chamber.

An appointments commission

51. Getting the right balance in the matter of appointments is a difficult but vitally important matter. The Royal Commission opposed the use of political patronage: 'Precluding any scope for political patronage is a basic element of our scheme for the composition of the second chamber. The abolition of such patronage is essential if the chamber is to have the legitimacy and confidence required.' But we do not take the view that all power should be removed from the Prime Minister and party leaders. There are cases – such as the appointment of a new member to serve as a Minister – where the exercise of prime ministerial nomination is perfectly justified. Equally it is important to ensure that appointments are made on an independent and widely respected basis.

52. The present arrangements do not, in our view, achieve the balance which we consider necessary and legitimate. There should be a new Appointments Commission established on a statutory basis, as the Royal Commission originally proposed. However, that should not exclude the possibility of nomination by the Prime Minister of the day, nor proposals by party leaders and members of the public. All these nominations would be scrutinised by the

new Appointments Commission. Only the Prime Minister would have the right to have nominations confirmed.

Methods of election

53. Most opinion concludes that, if the second chamber is to be different from the first – and we believe that it should – then the method of election needs to be different, and elections should be held on different dates from general elections. The context should not be the election of a government, and, in any case, without fixed-term Parliaments there would be practical difficulties. For example, the electoral systems recommended by the Commons Public Administration Committee (open regional lists or Single Transferable Vote) both have the advantages that they provide for much larger constituencies than for MPs, minimising the risk of overlap. 'First-past-the-post', especially if applied to a smaller percentage of a smaller sized House, would both rule out minor parties and independents, and give an undue preponderance to the largest party.

Transitional arrangements

54. Since the nature of the reformed second chamber which we envisage is similar to the present House of Lords, it is desirable that there should be a smooth transition. It is generally accepted that the 92 hereditary peers should cease to be members, but it is equally generally accepted that transitional arrangements are needed to avoid an immediate exodus of the remaining members. The Royal Commission proposed that existing life peers should be able to continue in membership of the reformed House for life. The Government, in *Completing the Reform*, accepted this recommendation, but noted (in the *Supporting Documents* which accompanied the White Paper) that this would lead to significant difficulties in the process of transition to a reformed House.

55. We are conscious that retaining life membership for all existing life peers would mean that for some years a substantial (though decreasing) proportion of the House comprised an

increasingly elderly group of survivors from the present House of Lords. On the other hand it would be difficult to devise a fair and workable means of removing existing members, who have been led to believe that their membership will be allowed to continue, and many of whom have planned their lives around a long-term commitment to membership. In the second stage of our inquiry we shall consider possible means of encouraging voluntary retirement and smoothing the transition. At this stage we have concluded only that we are not attracted by the idea of compulsory retirement for existing life peers.

OTHER MATTERS

Law lords and bishops

56. There are a number of issues which will need to be resolved regardless of decisions taken on the numbers of appointed and elected members in a reformed House of Lords. Prominent among these are the future membership of the law lords and of the Church of England bishops (and perhaps other religious representatives). We have already said that the question of a separation of the judicial role from the Lords is a complex matter worthy of an inquiry of its own. Since decisions on these issues could complicate the process of choosing between different options, we have chosen to defer these matters until the second stage of our inquiry. This has the practical advantage of sparing us from answering a range of hypothetical questions, as the handling of the question of *ex officio* membership would vary with the numbers of appointed and elected members (and would not even arise if all the members were to be elected).

Financial consequences

57. The level of financial support for members of a reformed House is another important question which can appropriately be left until the broad outline of its composition is settled. We believe that elected members (inevitably with some representative role) would

understandably expect better facilities and support than those which currently exist. It was only in 2001, following the acquisition of office space in Millbank House, that it became possible for all peers wishing to do so to have a desk. In most cases those desks are tightly packed with several in each room. Unless the number of members were to fall substantially, this situation could be significantly improved only by the acquisition or construction of additional office space in the vicinity of the Palace of Westminster.

58. There is provision for members to recover expenditure on secretarial help and research assistance, but the amount is linked to attendance and even for a member attending every sitting the annual limit would be under £10,000, far too little to permit the employment of a secretary or assistant. The level of research support offered by the Library is modest – a total of six research staff and three supporting staff at present. In both respects reform is likely to lead to pressure for change.

59. We note that there is little sign in the reform proposals produced by the Royal Commission, the Government or the Public Administration Committee that any work has been undertaken on the costing of those proposals. The present House costs under £60 million annually (some £85,000 per member as against some £380,000 per member of the House of Commons). A reformed House could cost substantially more, mainly because of the need for better support and facilities for members. We consider it essential that some detailed work should be done on costing options.

The name of the House and its link with the peerage

60. Finally, the name of the reformed House, and its link (if any) with the concept of a peerage, are issues to which we will return at the next stage.

PART 5: THE OPTIONS

61. In our terms of reference we were required to report on the options for composition from a fully nominated to a fully elected

House and on intermediate options. We were also required to consider the implications of these options in terms of the role and authority of the reformed House in Parliament as a whole, taking into account the experience and expertise of the existing House. In this part of the Report we focus more closely on the options and their implications, though the observations and conclusions we have come to throughout this Report must be taken into account when considering that narrower focus.

62. We identify seven options. We have marshalled these options so that the two complete models – appointed and elected – are first considered and then decreasing proportions of each in turn until the exact balance is reached in Option 7. The proportion of elected members of a mixed House could be phased in over a period of twelve years rather than fixed at a particular time. This would ease transitional arrangements and ensure that a House with experienced members continued over a number of years. The options are:

1. Fully appointed
2. Fully elected
3. 80 per cent appointed/20 per cent elected
4. 80 per cent elected/20 per cent appointed
5. 60 per cent appointed/40 per cent elected
6. 60 per cent elected/40 per cent appointed
7. 50 per cent appointed/50 per cent elected

Option 1: A fully appointed House

63. A fully appointed House would most closely resemble the existing House of Lords, with the remaining hereditary element removed. Although the legitimacy of such a House would be challenged, this could be mitigated if a new independent and respected Appointments Commission was set up by statute. We have said that we consider that there is a place for political appointments to the House but, to ensure the integrity of the process, all such appointments should be scrutinised by the Appointments Commission.

64. An appointed House could more easily be made representative both of sections of society (ethnic groups, sexes, etc.) and of the regions. It would be the responsibility of the new statutory body, the Appointments Commission, to ensure that such representativeness was achieved. It is essential that a revamped Appointments Commission should itself be seen to be independent and to gain widespread support for its difficult but important work.

65. A fully appointed House could also provide a method for the inclusion of independent members and experts. It could continue to provide part-time members who could bring contemporary professional experience to bear on the duties of scrutiny and the passing of legislation. The matter of the length of tenure and any conditions attaching to renewal and eligibility for entering the Commons would need detailed investigation.

66. A fully appointed House suggests a larger House, particularly during the transitional period, than a fully elected House.

Option 2: A fully elected House

67. The principal argument in favour of a fully elected House is that it would have greater legitimacy and accountability. That view rests upon the premise that legitimacy and accountability are conferred by election. On the other hand the existing House, in exercising independence and in applying expertise, has contributed significantly to the process of parliamentary scrutiny. That may also be considered a basis of legitimacy, important but different from legitimacy conferred by election. Legitimacy based entirely on election may well result in a House which is more assertive. While a reformed second chamber could not unilaterally increase its formal powers, it is a matter for consideration just how far it might feel disposed, by more vigorous use of its existing powers, to challenge the House of Commons and the Government. Such developments could represent a significant constitutional change. A further advantage of a fully elected House is that it provides representation from across the United Kingdom.

68. An elected House is also likely to have few if any independent members, although, as we have said, independence is a quality that can be found among members from party backgrounds as well as from those not affiliated to any party. Nevertheless the domination of the House by elected party politicians would irrevocably change the nature of the House and the attitude and relationship of the House to the Commons and to the Government. In a fully elected House there could be no question of continuing membership for the law lords or Church of England bishops (or other religious representatives). A fully elected House suggests a smaller House since members might be expected to be largely full-time.

69. Even so, the cost is likely to be greater because elected members will expect to be salaried and will expect facilities on a par with those in the House of Commons. The transitional arrangements – i.e. getting from the present House to a fully elected House – will also be more complex and will need to include detailed provisions with respect to existing members. The matters of the length of tenure and any conditions attaching to renewal and eligibility for entering the Commons would need to be spelt out. Some consideration also needs to be given to the method of election. One concern which we have expressed in our Report is to build upon the representative quality of the existing House in terms of ethnicity, gender distribution and regional representation. A first-past-the-post system would seem to us to be likely to lead to replication of the Commons, particularly if elections were held at the same time. It would not be possible to ensure that there was sufficient balance between parties in the second chamber. We are aware of the difficulties of various methods of indirect election in a country like ours where there is no federal structure on which to base it. Nevertheless some form of indirect election might possibly be a better way of achieving the aims of representativeness and regional balance in a second chamber. It will in any case be necessary for further detailed work to be done on the methods and timing of such elections once the

opinion of the Houses on composition is known. We do, however, recognise that turnout at any proposed election is likely to be higher if it coincides with another election.

Option 3: 80 per cent appointed/20 per cent elected

70. We do not share the view that a House of mixed composition is necessarily undesirable. Indeed, in certain senses the House of Lords has always been a mixed House (comprising hereditary peers by succession, hereditary peers of first creation, *ex officio* members, and in recent times life peers). However, although this model would ensure the entry to the House of a sufficient number of independents, we can foresee difficulties in holding a direct election for only twenty per cent of the second House. Turnout in all elections has fallen to a worryingly low level. We cannot see an election for a small proportion of the new House raising any enthusiasm or contributing to a sense of the importance of the reformed House in the eyes of the electorate.

Option 4: 80 per cent elected/20 per cent appointed

71. We have said that there may be virtue in a mixed House. Nevertheless, if the appointed element is pitched as low as 20 per cent, difficulties will arise. The current working House consists of 300 or so members but it is a frequently changing 300, depending on the business being considered. The independent element and the element of expertise need to have a sufficiently wide base to provide opinion on a vast range of subjects as they arise in the course of the House's business. With a smaller appointed element in an elected House of reduced size, that provision is unlikely to be sufficient or satisfactory. The law lords and the bishops (or other religious representatives) could not easily be retained. Moreover, a House of largely elected members is bound to change the culture of the second House, making it less attractive for those who wish to remain unaffiliated to party. It will also make it difficult for part-time members with valuable specialist knowledge to participate.

Option 5: 60 per cent appointed/40 per cent elected

72. This balance of composition would provide a more reasonable basis of independent members and experts who do not wish to stand for election. It would, on the other hand, provide a significant elected element, to go some way to meet the demands of legitimacy. The replacement of a large number of existing members would imply a long transitional period and a large interim House. The proportion of elected members could be established over a period of twelve years rather than at one particular time, easing transitional arrangements.

Option 6: 60 per cent elected/40 per cent appointed

73. This model retains the advantages of a mixed House. Nevertheless, it is a matter of judgement as to whether a 40 per cent appointed House is sufficient to provide the necessary diversity of expertise. Two important considerations affecting this judgement are the size of the new House and the nature of the transitional arrangements i.e. what happens to the existing members. This option would imply that the House would be substantially larger than 600 for a lengthy transitional period.

Option 7: 50 per cent elected/50 per cent appointed

74. The above arguments broadly apply to this option as well. However, the exact halfway House may have some appeal on grounds of mathematical neatness. It would provide an apparently sufficient balance of electoral legitimacy on the one hand and of independence and expertise from appointment on the other.

Independent members and the appointment process

75. If any option other than 2 or 4 above is chosen, it will be necessary to specify the quota of independent members within the appointed element so as to ensure that they form about 20 per cent of the House. The appointed element should be nominated by a

new independent statutory Appointments Commission whose principal function would be to ensure a quality of representativeness and regional balance in the reformed House.

How shall the Houses decide?

76. Finally, we have considered the matter of how the Houses should proceed in deciding on the options. We hope that there will first be 'take-note' debates on this report in both Houses, with the opportunity to vote on the options coming later, after members have had time to study both debates. We are convinced that it is essential that both Houses follow the same procedure in voting on options. If they do not, the task which we identified in our Special Report, of establishing how the respective views of each House might be brought closer together if they differ, will be made a great deal more difficult.

77. Having considered various possible methods of approaching the voting, including the possibility of a ballot, we conclude that the best way of getting an accurate measure of views in both Houses would be to have a series of motions put on the different options one after the other, notwithstanding the normal practice of the Houses in dealing with substantially similar questions and questions disagreed to. This follows the precedent used in the case of the Motions on Hunting with Dogs in both Houses in March 2002. Accordingly we recommend that a series of motions, each setting out one of the seven options we have identified, be moved successively in each House notwithstanding the normal practice in regard to questions. Members would be free to vote in favour of as many of the options as they considered acceptable, after a separate debate on the issues raised in this Report.

78. We suggest that the form of the motions should be on the following lines:

House of Lords Reform – [Name of mover] to move, That this House approves Option 1 (fully appointed) in the Report from the Joint Committee on House of Lords Reform.

House of Lords Reform – [Name of mover] to move, That this House approves Option 2 (fully elected) in the Report from the Joint Committee on House of Lords Reform.

House of Lords Reform – [Name of mover] to move, That this House approves Option 3 (80 per cent appointed/20 per cent elected) in the Report from the Joint Committee on House of Lords Reform.

House of Lords Reform – [Name of mover] to move, That this House approves Option 4 (80 per cent elected/20 per cent appointed) in the Report from the Joint Committee on House of Lords Reform.

House of Lords Reform – [Name of mover] to move, That this House approves Option 5 (60 per cent appointed/40 per cent elected) in the Report from the Joint Committee on House of Lords Reform.

House of Lords Reform – [Name of mover] to move, That this House approves Option 6 (60 per cent elected/40 per cent appointed) in the Report from the Joint Committee on House of Lords Reform.

House of Lords Reform – [Name of mover] to move, That this House approves Option 7 (50 per cent appointed/50 per cent elected) in the Report from the Joint Committee on House of Lords Reform.

SUMMARY OF CONCLUSIONS AND RECOMMENDATIONS

(i) The existing conventions, which are of a self-restraining nature, impact profoundly on the relations between the Houses and need to be understood as a vital part of any future constitutional settlement. (paragraph 11)

(ii) We strongly support the continuation of the existing conventions. When the views of the Houses on composition are made known, we will return to the detailed matter of how these important conventions should be maintained in a new constitutional settlement between the Houses. (paragraph 12)

(iii) We intend to return to the matter of the constitutional role of the Lords in the later stages of our work but we underline its importance here. (paragraph 15)

(iv) We concur with the conclusions of the Royal Commission that increased representativeness will confer a new legitimacy on the House of Lords. We will consider methods to achieve that end when we deal with getting the right membership of the House later in this report but it is also a matter that will need further careful attention in future. (paragraph 16)

(v) We are convinced that a reformed House should contain an appropriate number of members from all parts of the country and later in this report we will consider how this might be achieved. It is difficult to see at the moment structures which are parallel to those to be found in fully federal countries like the USA and Germany upon which to base this representation, although we note in the recent Queen's Speech the Government's intention to hold referendums on the issue of regional governance in England. (paragraph 18)

(vi) We consider that a co-ordination of the legislative loads between the Houses is a practical but important part of any new constitutional settlement. (paragraph 20)

(vii) Recognising the practical realities of parliamentary programmes, we nevertheless consider that pre-legislative scrutiny is an important aspect of making the legislature function more effectively and we welcome the proposals announced in the recent Queen's Speech. (paragraph 21)

(viii) When the Houses' views on the matter of composition are known, we shall consider whether any change is needed in the powers of the Lords in relation to secondary legislation. (paragraph 23)

(ix) We assert the importance of the scrutiny function of the House. At a later stage in our work, we will return to consider how that scrutiny can be made more effective. (paragraph 24)

(x) Although we may return to it later in our deliberations, we consider the judicial function of the House of Lords to be a matter worthy of independent inquiry and expert attention. Even if a separation takes place it does not need to entail the ending of membership of the House by the law lords. (paragraph 25)

(xi) Subject to satisfactory assurances that carry-over arrangements could not be used to erode the powers of the House of Lords, we do not consider at this stage that the provisions of the Parliament Acts need to be altered. Together with our conclusions about maintaining the existing conventions, we therefore recommend (subject to what we say about secondary legislation in recommendation viii above) that no new or additional powers are given to the House of Lords at this stage. (paragraph 29)

(xii) We consider that the lack of representativeness of the House must be improved and that better balances can be achieved either by a new appointment system or, with appropriate checks in place, by various methods of election. (paragraph 33)

(xiii) Any arrangements for the reformed House must take account of the importance of maintaining the principle that no one political party should be able to be dominant in it. (paragraph 34)

(xiv) It is our view that any new system of getting members into the House needs to ensure that independence, whether arising from non-party affiliation or from less attention to the requests of the Whips, is not jeopardised or diminished. (paragraph 35)

(xv) We consider this independence an important element in any reconstituted House. (paragraph 40)

(xvi) We consider the expertise which is evident in the existing House to be something of considerable importance which we would wish to see preserved in the new House. (paragraph 42)

(xvii) The existing House of Lords meets several of the criteria which we have been considering, namely lack of domination by one party, independence and expertise. If these existing qualities, bolstered by a greater representativeness, can be transferred to the reformed House, we believe that a new legitimacy, which we have already highlighted in considering the House's role, will naturally develop. (paragraph 43)

(xviii) At this stage we propose simply that the House should comprise about six hundred members. This represents little change from the present House without the 92 hereditary peers, but we recognise that transitional arrangements may necessitate an increase in size before equilibrium is reached. (paragraph 46)

(xix) A balance has to be struck, and our view is that a tenure for all members of some twelve years is about right. While members should be able to resign their seats earlier, we consider that members who do so should not thereby be able to stand for election to the House of Commons at least for a certain period, perhaps three years. (paragraph 48)

(xx) The present arrangements do not, in our view, achieve the balance which we consider necessary and legitimate. There should be a new Appointments Commission established on a statutory basis, as the Royal Commission originally proposed. However, that should not exclude the possibility of nomination by the Prime Minister of the day, nor proposals by party leaders and members of the public. All these nominations would be scrutinised by the new Appointments Commission. Only the Prime Minister would have the right to have nominations confirmed. (paragraph 52)

(xxi) At this stage we have concluded only that we are not attracted by the idea of compulsory retirement for existing life peers. (paragraph 55)

(xxii) We consider it essential that some detailed work should be done on costing the options before the Houses. (paragraph 59)

(xxiii) We hope that there will first be 'take-note' debates on this report in both Houses, with the opportunity to vote on the options coming later, after members have had time to study both debates. We are convinced that it is essential that both Houses follow the same procedure in voting on options. (paragraph 76)

(xxiv) Accordingly we recommend that a series of motions, each setting out one of the seven options we have identified, be moved successively in each House notwithstanding the normal practice in regard to questions. (paragraph 77)

[...]

APPENDIX 3: *Memorandum from the Presiding Officers of the Devolved Assemblies*

We refer to the Committee's inquiry into House of Lords Reform, and should be grateful if you would take the terms of this memorandum into account in your considerations. It is a happy coincidence that the three current presiding officers of the devolved assemblies are members of the House of Lords. During the three years in the role so far, we have each found a number of benefits from this situation. Not only has such membership provided us with regular opportunities to meet together informally and share advice and support, but it has also facilitated the establishment of a closer network of officials of the three institutions. Very significantly, it has also allowed us to keep up-to-date with the thinking and actions of the UK Parliament. One of the key advantages of this has been to put us in the position of being able to contribute to the thinking on matters that are before the House of specific interest to Wales, Scotland and Northern Ireland. The presiding officers of Scotland and Northern Ireland are not intending to stand at the next elections and, given the very limited number of peers in both institutions, it seems unlikely that the presiding officers next time will be members of the House of Lords. Given the obvious advantages we have so far found, we would ask the Committee to consider if there is merit in ensuring that future presiding officers of the devolved institutions are members of the upper chamber. We would be grateful if you would give this matter your consideration.

Lord Steel of Aikwood
Presiding Officer, the Scottish Parliament

Lord Alderdice
Speaker, the Northern Ireland Assembly

Lord Elis-Thomas
Presiding Officer, the National Assembly for Wales

17 July 2002

Proceedings of the Committee

PROCEEDINGS OF THE COMMITTEE RELATING TO THE REPORT SESSION 2001–02

1

DIE MARTIS, 9° JULII 2002

Present:
Lord Archer of Sandwell
Viscount Bledisloe
Lord Brooke of Alverthorpe
Lord Carter
Lord Forsyth of Drumlean
Baroness Gibson of Market Rasen
Lord Goodhart
Lord Howe of Aberavon
Lord Oakeshott of Seagrove Bay
Baroness O'Cathain
The Earl of Selborne
Lord Weatherill
Mr James Arbuthnot
Mr Chris Bryant
Mr Kenneth Clarke
Dr Jack Cunningham
Mr William Hague
Mr Stephen McCabe
Joyce Quin
Mr Terry Rooney
Mr Clive Soley
Mr Paul Stinchcombe
Mr Paul Tyler

The Orders of Reference are read.

It is moved that the Rt Hon. Jack Cunningham do take the Chair (the Earl of Selborne).

The same is agreed to.

The Joint Committee deliberate.

Ordered, That the Joint Committee be adjourned to Tuesday 16 July at half-past Ten o'clock.

2

DIE MARTIS, 16° JULII 2002

Present:
Lord Archer of Sandwell
Viscount Bledisloe
Lord Brooke of Alverthorpe
Lord Carter
Lord Forsyth of Drumlean
Baroness Gibson of Market Rasen
Lord Goodhart
Lord Howe of Aberavon
Lord Oakeshott of Seagrove Bay
The Earl of Selborne
Lord Weatherill
Janet Anderson
Mr James Arbuthnot
Mr Chris Bryant
Mr Kenneth Clarke
Mr William Hague
Joyce Quin
Mr Terry Rooney
Mr Clive Soley
Mr Paul Stinchcombe
Mr Paul Tyler
Dr Jack Cunningham, in the Chair.

The Order of Adjournment is read.

The Proceedings of Tuesday 9 July are read.

A draft Special Report is proposed by the Chairman, brought up and read.

Ordered, That the draft Report be read a second time, paragraph by paragraph.

Paragraphs 1 to 7 read and agreed to.

Resolved, That the Report be the Special Report of the Joint Committee to each House.

Ordered, That the Chairman do make the Report to the House of Commons and that the Lord Howe of Aberavon make the Report to the House of Lords.

Ordered, That such Reports be laid upon the Table of each House.

Ordered, That the Joint Committee be adjourned till Tuesday 17 September at half-past Ten o'clock.

3

DIE MARTIS, 17° SEPTEMBRIS 2002

Present:
Lord Archer of Sandwell
Viscount Bledisloe
Lord Brooke of Alverthorpe
Lord Carter
Lord Forsyth of Drumlean
Baroness Gibson of Market Rasen
Lord Goodhart
Lord Howe of Aberavon
Lord Oakeshott of Seagrove Bay
Baroness O'Cathain
The Earl of Selborne
Janet Anderson
Mr James Arbuthnot

Mr Chris Bryant
Mr Kenneth Clarke
Mr William Hague
Mr Stephen McCabe
Joyce Quin
Mr Clive Soley
Mr Paul Stinchcombe

In the absence of the Chairman it is moved that Lord Howe of Aberavon do take the Chair (Kenneth Clarke).

The Order of Adjournment is read.

The Proceedings of 16 July are read.

The Joint Committee deliberate.

Ordered, That the Joint Committee be adjourned to Tuesday 8 October at half-past Ten o'clock.

4

DIE MARTIS, 8° OCTOBRIS 2002

Present:
Lord Archer of Sandwell
Lord Brooke of Alverthorpe
Lord Carter
Lord Forsyth of Drumlean
Baroness Gibson of Market Rasen
Lord Goodhart
Lord Howe of Aberavon
Lord Oakeshott of Seagrove Bay
Baroness O'Cathain
The Earl of Selborne
Lord Weatherill
Mr James Arbuthnot
Mr William Hague

Joyce Quin
Mr Clive Soley
Mr Paul Stinchcombe
Mr Paul Tyler
Dr Jack Cunningham, in the Chair.

The Order of Adjournment is read.
 The proceedings of 17 September are read.
 The Joint Committee deliberate.
 Ordered, That the Joint Committee be adjourned till Tuesday
15 October at half-past Ten o'clock.

5

DIE MARTIS, 15° OCTOBRIS 2002

Present:
Lord Archer of Sandwell
Viscount Bledisloe
Lord Brooke of Alverthorpe
Lord Carter
Lord Forsyth of Drumlean
Baroness Gibson of Market Rasen
Lord Goodhart
Lord Howe of Aberavon
Lord Oakeshott of Seagrove Bay
Baroness O'Cathain
The Earl of Selborne
Lord Weatherill
Mr James Arbuthnot
Mr Chris Bryant
Mr Kenneth Clarke
Mr William Hague
Joyce Quin

Mr Terry Rooney
Mr Clive Soley
Mr Paul Tyler
Dr Jack Cunningham, in the Chair.

The Order of Adjournment is read.
    The proceedings of 8 October are read.
    The Joint Committee deliberate.
    Ordered, That the Joint Committee be adjourned till Tuesday
29 October at Ten o'clock.

6

DIE MARTIS, 29° OCTOBRIS 2002

Present:
Lord Archer of Sandwell
Viscount Bledisloe
Lord Brooke of Alverthorpe
Lord Carter
Lord Forsyth of Drumlean
Baroness Gibson of Market Rasen
Lord Goodhart
Lord Howe of Aberavon
Lord Oakeshott of Seagrove Bay
Baroness O'Cathain
The Earl of Selborne
Lord Weatherill
Janet Anderson
Mr James Arbuthnot
Mr Chris Bryant
Mr Kenneth Clarke
Mr William Hague
Mr Stephen McCabe

Joyce Quin
Mr Terry Rooney
Mr Clive Soley
Mr Paul Tyler
Dr Jack Cunningham, in the Chair.

The Order of Adjournment is read.
    The proceedings of 15 October are read.
    The Joint Committee deliberate.
    Ordered, That the Joint Committee be adjourned *sine die*.

7

SESSION 2002–03
DIE MARTIS, 3° DECEMBRIS 2002

Present:
Viscount Bledisloe
Lord Brooke of Alverthorpe
Lord Carter
Lord Forsyth of Drumlean
Baroness Gibson of Market Rasen
Lord Howe of Aberavon
Lord Oakeshott of Seagrove Bay
Baroness O'Cathain
The Earl of Selborne
Lord Weatherill
Janet Anderson
Mr James Arbuthnot
Mr Chris Bryant
Dr Jack Cunningham
Mr Stephen McCabe
Joyce Quin
Mr Terry Rooney

Mr Clive Soley
Mr Paul Tyler

The Orders of Reference are read.

    It is moved that the Rt Hon. Jack Cunningham do take the Chair (Lord Howe of Aberavon).

    The same is agreed to.

    The Joint Committee deliberate.

    Ordered, That the Joint Committee be adjourned to Monday 9 December at Four o'clock.

8

DIE LUNAE, 9° DECEMBRIS 2002

Present:
Lord Archer of Sandwell
Viscount Bledisloe
Lord Brooke of Alverthorpe
Lord Carter
Lord Forsyth of Drumlean
Baroness Gibson of Market Rasen
Lord Goodhart
Lord Howe of Aberavon
Lord Oakeshott of Seagrove Bay
Baroness O'Cathain
The Earl of Selborne
Lord Weatherill
Mr Chris Bryant
Mr Kenneth Clarke
Mr William Hague
Mr Stephen McCabe
Joyce Quin
Mr Terry Rooney
Mr Clive Soley
Mr Paul Stinchcombe

Mr Paul Tyler
Dr Jack Cunningham, in the Chair.

The Order of Adjournment is read.

The Proceedings of Tuesday 3 December are read.

A draft Report is proposed by the Chairman, brought up and read.

Ordered, That the draft Report be read a second time, paragraph by paragraph.

Paragraphs 1 to 47 were read and agreed to with amendments.

Paragraph 48 was read.

It was moved by Joyce Quin to leave out 'A balance has to be struck, and our view is that a tenure for all members of some twelve years is about right.' and insert 'A balance has to be struck, and our view is that a tenure for all members (elected and appointed) of 8 years, renewable once, is appropriate.'

Which being objected to, the question was put thereupon, and the Committee divided:

Contents 7

Mr Chris Bryant
Mr Kenneth Clarke
Lord Goodhart
Lord Oakeshott of Seagrove Bay
Joyce Quin
Mr Clive Soley
Mr Paul Tyler

Not-Contents 14

Lord Archer of Sandwell
Viscount Bledisloe
Lord Brooke of Alverthorpe
Lord Carter
Lord Forsyth of Drumlean
Baroness Gibson of Market Rasen

Mr William Hague
Lord Howe of Aberavon
Mr Stephen McCabe
Baroness O'Cathain
Mr Terry Rooney
The Earl of Selborne
Mr Paul Stinchcombe
Lord Weatherill

The amendment was disagreed to.
　　Paragraph 48 was agreed to.
　　Paragraphs 49 to 68 were read and agreed to with amendments.
　　Paragraph 69 was read.
　　It was moved by Mr Paul Tyler to leave out 'A first-past-the-post system would seem to us to be likely to lead to replication of the Commons, particularly if elections were held at the same time. It would not be possible to ensure that there was sufficient balance between parties in the second chamber. We are aware of the difficulties of various methods of indirect election in a country like ours where there is no federal structure on which to base it. Nevertheless some form of indirect election might possibly be a better way of achieving the aims of representativeness and regional balance in a second chamber.'
　　Which being objected to, the question was put thereupon, and the Committee divided:

Contents 8

Mr Chris Bryant
Mr Kenneth Clarke
Lord Forsyth of Drumlean
Lord Goodhart
Mr William Hague
Lord Oakeshott of Seagrove Bay
Joyce Quin
Mr Paul Tyler

Not-Contents 10

Lord Archer of Sandwell
Lord Brooke of Alverthorpe
Lord Carter
Lord Howe of Aberavon
Mr Stephen McCabe
Baroness O'Cathain
Mr Terry Rooney
The Earl of Selborne
Mr Clive Soley
Mr Paul Stinchcombe

The amendment was disagreed to.

Paragraph 69 was agreed to.

The remaining paragraphs were read and agreed to with amendments.

The summary, summary of conclusions and recommendations, and appendices were agreed to.

Resolved, That the Report as amended be the First Report of the Joint Committee to each House.

Ordered, That the Chairman do make the Report to the House of Commons and that the Lord Howe of Aberavon do make the Report to the House of Lords.

Ordered, That such Reports be laid upon the Table of each House.

Ordered, That the Joint Committee be adjourned to a date and time to be fixed by the Chairman.

Debate in the House of Commons

The First Report from the Joint Committee on House of Lords Reform was presented to the House of Commons by the chairman, Jack Cunningham, on 21 January 2003. He thanked the government for accepting the recommendation of the Committee that 'we should have the opportunity, both here and in another place, to debate the report fully before votes are taken on motions that may subsequently be tabled'.[4] Mr Cunningham then proceeded to explain the main objects of the Joint Committee. The report, he said, did not recommend maintaining the status quo. There was a historic opportunity to enact a reform that would enable the second chamber to 'continue to play an important role' that was complementary to that of the Commons. On composition, the report listed 'five desirable qualities'. It referred to 'improvements in the representative nature of the second Chamber and its legitimacy and representativeness, no domination by any one party, independence and the need to sustain expertise'. The present House of Lords was also weak in terms of gender and ethnicity. The report had offered various options: a fully appointed House; a fully elected House; but 'a hybrid' was also possible. There was an opportunity to reflect on the report before voting on options for change.

William Hague paid tribute to the Joint Committee for having delivered a valuable report. He gave credit to the leader of the House (Robin Cook) for introducing reforms designed to improve the scrutiny of government decisions. Mr Hague believed that an elected, or largely elected chamber would 'become a more assertive House, even under existing powers'. It would, however, enjoy 'greater legitimacy in using those powers'. He 'certainly' favoured the majority-elected option, and hoped that 'the vast majority will vote against the minority-elected option'.

Robin Cook (the leader of the Commons) then spoke for the government. There was, he said, broad agreement on the 'relative status' of the two chambers. It had been a feature of all reports on Lords reform that the House of Commons 'should remain pre-eminent'. The Commons 'must remain the crucible in which governments are forged and reputations are made or broken'. But the House of Lords needed to be reformed. The Joint Committee had given 'us options for a more representative second Chamber'. The government did not intend to 'express a collective view on which option should be chosen'. And, given that this 'issue has profound

4   *Parliamentary Debates*, House of Commons, vol. 398, 21 January 2003, cols 187–272.

implications for the future of Parliament, it is right it should be Parliament that resolves what a reformed second Chamber should look like'. All options were to be put to the vote, and voting would be free. Robin Cook only hoped that 'we achieve a commanding majority for one of those seven options'. If the current attempt was to succeed, it was essential that those who wanted reform 'show flexibility in supporting whatever option can command the greatest support as the centre of gravity'. He could not 'abide the prospect of continuing with the issue' into another Parliament: 'I want to get rid of it in this Parliament.'

Paul Tyler thought that the report was 'unique in the consideration of the issue'. The Committee had produced a 'unanimous' report. It was the first time that that had happened in the 'history of this long saga'. He welcomed it; and he did not agree with those who feared that strengthening the second House of Parliament would automatically weaken the first. That was a myth. One could create 'an improved situation for our House and for the other House if we see it as a total parliamentary improvement in our ability to scrutinise both the legislation and the executive action of the Government of the day'.

George Foulkes thought differently. He warned that any element of election to the second Chamber was 'inevitably a threat to the primacy of the House of Commons and will undermine the position of individual elected Members'. He urged the House not to be 'lured by the false and misleading argument that democracy would be enhanced by having two elected Chambers'. It would lead to a 'constant battle between the two Houses, with resultant constitutional chaos'.

Kenneth Clarke believed that a stronger upper House would 'complement this House', the Commons. He agreed with those who argued that a stronger upper House needed the legitimacy of democracy, but also accepted the argument that 'we must guard against the danger of the tyranny of the majority'. And yet we should not 'resent the suggestion of stronger competition between the two Houses. The problem facing us is that the necessary checks and balances that ought to exist in a modern constitution and parliamentary democracy are not at present strong enough in this country.'

Tony Wright said he preferred a system of indirect election. He suggested that the House of Commons should become an electoral college which might include members of the devolved legislatures in Scotland and Wales. 'that it would elect 75 per cent of the members of the House of Lords and that the other 25 per cent would come through a joint committee of the two Houses'.

Patrick Cormack 'strongly' believed that the country 'would be better served by a wholly nominated, all appointed second Chamber'.

George Howarth argued that the option of abolition of the Upper House should be a matter for consideration. He intended to table an amendment to 'enable that option to be expressed'.

George Young pleaded for flexibility. His judgement was that 'roughly one third of members in the new House of Lords should be non-political and appointed, and the balance of two-thirds should be political and elected'. He was not in favour of a chamber that was 100 per cent elected. Such a place would 'exclude many people who do not belong to a political party and do not want to stand for election, but who add enormous value to debates in the upper House'.

Joyce Quin said that she strongly believed in the principle of election. It conferred legitimacy. She would like to 'see a wholly elected House', but she was not against 'some kind of compromise'.

James Arbuthnot thought that the problem was 'that we have no idea where we are going'. The Joint Committee had strengthened in his 'mind the view that, in reforming the House of Lords, we run the risk of losing the great talent and experience that, through systems that have evolved through the ages, we have managed to build'.

Clive Soley asked members to look at 'the 60:40 option, and at the possibility of indirect election or appointments, so that we can establish a good hybrid second Chamber that acts as a effective safeguard for our constitution and our basic freedoms, but also has all the legitimacy that comes from such a structure'.

Norman Lamb argued that 'we need to strengthen the effectiveness of Parliament and its ability to hold the Government to account and pass good legislation'. The present second chamber lacked legitimacy and suffered from un-representativeness. A House 'wholly or substantially elected' was the 'essential precondition for legitimacy'.

Alan Howarth said that it was 'ever more important that we should have a second Chamber that is legitimate, capable and confident, and that can make some impact in mitigating the elective dictatorship'. There should be a second Chamber that was 'inclusively representative in terms of gender, race, faith, minorities and the regions'.

Robert Key believed that '60 per cent of the Members should be elected, with 20 per cent appointed and 20 per cent ex officio'. What mattered was 'legitimacy in the eyes of the electors'. A ratio of this kind would give the second chamber 'its strength'.

Malcolm Savidge urged that the supremacy of the House of Commons should 'apply in deciding the proportion of elected Members of the House of Lords'. 'We' should have a second chamber that created 'greater equity'. For that matter, party membership should 'aim to reflect party strengths in the country. The best way of doing that is proportional representation.'

Teddy Taylor warned that, if they went ahead with the Joint Committee's plan, 'we will simply create a costly nonsense that will further undermine our democracy'. Instead of 'proper direct elections, we will have party lists'. That would make 'things worse, not better, and less representative'.

Calum MacDonald believed that the solution lay in a system of indirect election, or 'genuinely independent appointment that is accountable to the House of Commons'.

John Maples said that he would like to see the Lords 'remain pretty much as it is, with pretty much the same powers as it has now'.

David Clelland argued that members of the second Chamber must be people who commanded respect and were generally 'recognised as having expertise and experience'. A composition of this kind could be achieved by 'widening the responsibility for making appointments, by calling for representatives from bodies such as the Confederation of British Industry, the Trades Union Congress, religious and voluntary organisations, devolved Assemblies, local government and political parties too – they are an important part of the national system'.

Simon Thomas said he preferred a 'completely elected' second chamber. Patronage and nomination were 'totally unacceptable in the 21st century'. The name of the chamber also needed to be changed. This 'is the House of Commons, and "Commons" means communes or communities'; the second chamber, he hoped, would become either 'the Senate' or 'the House of the Nations and Regions of the United Kingdom'.

Fiona Mactaggart said that it was important that 'we grab the opportunity to deliver a democratic reform of the second Chamber, not just
because it is in the Labour party's manifesto, but because it goes to our
sense of ourselves as a nation'.

Edward Leigh thought that the debaters were 'losing sight of an essential problem with our legislature. We should not spend so much time arguing about the mix between elected and appointed Members in the other
place. We should direct our attention to the quality of those Members, and
their ability and wish to hold the Executive to account.'

Win Griffiths said that he would like the second chamber 'to be 100
per cent elected, but I appreciate that, for the sake of consensus I may have
to settle for 80 per cent or, perhaps at worst, 60 per cent'.

Bill Wiggin argued that legitimacy was not the 'key to better government'. What we needed was 'wisdom'. If legitimacy was considered to be
more 'important than wisdom, it will not be long before the Parliament
Acts are repealed, and one political party could, after a landslide, occupy
both Houses. That would create a risk for the minorities in this country.'

Mark Lazarowicz said he supported a House of Lords that was 'elected
by a form of proportional representation'.

Winding up for the Opposition, Eric Forth said he intended to vote
for an 100 per cent elected House and an 80 per cent elected House, and
'probably vote against all other options'.

The parliamentary secretary, Ben Bradshaw, wound up for the government. The members of the government, he said, did not 'have a view on
the vote that we shall have in two weeks' time on composition, but they
are certainly of the view that they want to get Lords reform concluded
in this Parliament'. He hoped that their lordships would 'pay close attention to our proceedings today'. The Commons would return to the issue
on 4 February, when Members 'will have a chance to vote on the seven
options, and the Joint Committee will note what has been said and resume
its work'. He hoped that 'we can send both the Committee and the House
of Lords a good strong signal'.

It being now seven o'clock, the 'motion for the Adjournment of the
House lapsed without Question put'.

Debate in the House of Lords

The report was debated in the House of Lords for two days, on 21 and 22 January 2003. On 21 January, Lord Howe of Aberavon, as vice-chairman of the Joint Committee, rose to move 'that this House takes note of the first report of the Joint Committee of Lords reform'.[5] He briefly explained the vital points of the report. It set out seven options on which both Houses 'will be invited to express their opinions on 4th February. The interval between these debates and that date is intended to provide a time for mutual reflection by both Houses on views expressed in each House.' When questioned on why so many options were set out in the report, he answered that the Committee 'were required to do that by our terms of reference. We were required to consider an all-elected and an all-nominated House and opinions in between. The options effectively chose themselves.' The Committee, he assured his hearers, was 'notably free of rancour or partisanship', having a 'genuine sense of common purpose'. Many important questions still remained to be considered: the future of the law lords, the future of the bishops, the pattern of elections and their timing, and the financial implications of the various alternatives. The report had concluded that the existing role, functioning powers and conventions regulating the House of Lords in relation to the Commons should, in all essential respects, be maintained.

Lord Carter spoke next. He supported the Committee's conclusion that a proper system of appointment, backed by statute, would produce a House with the right balance of politics, regional representation, gender, ethnicity and occupation.

Baroness Williams of Crosby referred to the duties of the House of Lords. The first was, regardless of politics, to hold the executive – the government of the day – accountable to the people and to Parliament. The second was to scrutinize legislation, to mend it, and make it as good as it could possibly be.

5   *Parliamentary Debates*, House of Lords, vol. DCXLIII, 21 January 2003, cols 575–688.

Lord Craig of Radley favoured the adoption of a fully appointed House. That would allow the reformed House to 'continue to draw on the experience, knowledge and remarkable sense of duty to Parliament and the country' that existed in the Lords.

Lord Wakeham said that the Committee had shown a 'remarkable degree of objectivity and understanding'. The members still had a difficult, but not impossible, task. In his view, any solution must have two essential elements: first, a significant element of compromise; and secondly, a lengthy transitional period. The Lords, he said, had always been hybrid, and it 'can continue to be so successfully if care is taken in the way new Members are brought in as the old Members fade away. This has to be done over an adequate period of time.'

Lord Rea communicated that he was in favour of a majority elected House of Lords.

Lord Richard said that the argument that strengthening the Lords would weaken the Commons was out of place. The reality was that, 'if we get the composition, role and powers of the Upper House right, we can have a largely democratic second Chamber without challenging the supremacy of the House of Commons'. In a democratic Parliament, the second chamber 'should be the next most important democratic institution in the country after the House of Commons'. The objective of reform, and the test for its validity, was surely that it 'should strengthen the second Chamber to the point where it has legitimacy vis-à-vis the House of Commons to perform its functions without threatening the position of the Commons. If the second Chamber does not have that legitimacy, the constitution becomes unbalanced and has to be re modelled.'

The lord Bishop of Guildford said that the bishops shared in the 'widespread gratitude' he felt around him to the members of the Joint Committee for their report. It was 'clear, concise and balanced'. It gave 'us the opportunity to see whether, in the parliamentary process, there is another way of representing the people in a complementary way alongside the House of Commons'.

Baroness Goudie argued that the correct starting point should not be the composition of the House of Lords. Function and size must come first. The second chamber did not need to be elected. There could be no doubt that an entirely elected House would be 'massively expensive and exclude most sensible candidates'. An entirely elected House would not be a 'sensible' option. And a hybrid House was 'surely the worst of all worlds'. We 'should keep the existing appointed Peers and add to them, but with appropriate provisions in relation to appointment'.

Lord Oakshott of Seagrove Bay felt that if 'we support those options with a substantial elected element, we will be seen to be seeking common ground rather than confrontation with the House of Commons. We will be sending the Joint Committee into the final phase of its work with a realistic target and a real chance of a successful united outcome.'

Viscount Bledisloe believed that it to be very important that 'we ensure that Members come here, whether by election or appointment, for one, single long term with no prospect of reappointment. That will be necessary to ensure that this House retains its independence.'

Objecting to the word 'legitimacy', Earl Ferrers believed that there was 'nothing unlawful or lacking in legitimacy in the House of Lords as it is, or indeed as it was. It conforms with law. Hereditary Peers were here by law. The House was perfectly legitimate. It is here by law. So I do hope that we will stop using this wholly inappropriate and offensive word when what we really mean is *acceptable*, and that is, of course, a personal judgement.' It would, he argued, be wrong for the Upper House to be elected: there was 'one elected Chamber and that is the House of Commons', which was 'where the power lies and where it should lie. This House should not seek to vie with the House of Commons or to usurp its authority. If it is elected, it will do both.' Further, a partly elected and partly appointed House would be an 'impossible compromise, whatever the mix. The elected ones would always consider themselves to be the top dogs and the appointed ones to be their inferiors. The elected ones would always jump up and down at Question Time – heaven forbid, it would be worse than it is at the moment – to try to appear in the media. If a constituent wrote to a Member of Parliament about something over which he was aggrieved and he received no satisfaction, he would then write to his elected Peer. If he received satisfaction from the elected Peer – which he did not receive from the Member of Parliament – one can imagine the kind of relations which would exist between the House of Lords and the House of Commons.'

Lord Norton of Louth said that he would vote for the option of an all-appointed second Chamber. The accountability of the political system would be maintained, and the House would 'fulfil a vital function of legislative revision'.

Lord Lipsey rejected substantial election, thinking it would be a change for the worse, not for the better.

Lord Weatherill thought that in a fully elected House there would be no place for Cross-Benchers, and he could not support that option. An option for a partially elected House was also suspect. The present House was 'working well and performing its duty of scrutinising legislation'.

Lord Lloyd of Berwick thought that a hybrid House was not only workable but also desirable. A proportion of elected Members would 'give the reformed House that legitimacy, which it undoubtedly needs, especially if the elected House are elected to represent the regions, which seems to me to be important'. Also the balance of appointed peers 'would give the House the independence and expertise which is also needed and which is often regarded as one of the great glories of the existing House'.

Baroness Blatch said that her preferred option would be to 'leave well alone'; to 'give more time for earlier reforms to work; to create a truly independent appointments commission, which was underpinned by statute; to deal with the additional members; to encourage members of another place to be more courageous in holding the executive to account; and to leave Parliament to get on with considering those matters which affect the everyday lives of people in our country'.

Lord Parekh thought the House needed both elected and appointed members. The only question was the relative proportion. He felt that 'we should have both in broadly equal proportions'.

The Earl of Selborne felt that he was a 'bit cautious' about a large elected element. He would favour a large element of appointed members.

Lord Lea of Crondall argued that the Joint Committee must 'address, as one of its priorities, the question of striking a balance between allowing party leaders a degree of control and giving an appointments commission a degree of control'.

Lord Phillips of Sudbury felt that if 'we were to come to a radically different conclusion from our brethren in another place, why not contemplate a referendum of the British people so that they could decide what should happen to their second Chamber?'

Lord Ampthill said, that no matter what proportions they were in, the elected members in the second chamber 'will inevitably feel themselves to be superior beings to the rest. The remarkable effectiveness of the House over the centuries, and continuing to this day, will no longer be there.'

Lord Hughes of Woodside argued that 'we started the process and we cannot hold it back. We have to make a choice – and a hybrid Chamber is the worst of all.'

Lord Dixon-Smith believed that an elected House, or a House with a 'proportion of elected Members, will be in the greater interest of the British people'.

Lord Jopling strongly believed that if 'we had an elected House – whether all elected or largely elected – it would quickly become a clone of the House of Commons'.

Baroness Finlay of Llandaff supported the proposal that a statutory independent appointments commission be established. Such a commission 'must examine all nominations. Every one to be considered should complete the forms and be considered. They could be from any political party or be non-party and independent. They could be senior religious figures or even the occasional current hereditary, whose great expertise has much to offer a reformed Chamber. There should be no patronage and no party donation to influence the process. They must be open, transparent and subject to scrutiny.'

Lord Davies of Coity thought that a fully appointed Upper House was not 'anti-democratic, but is in the interest of the nation. A wholly appointed House will serve best the people, the country and its democratic structure.'

Lord Thomas of Swynnerton believed that 'we should go to very great trouble indeed to ensure that something that we currently have is preserved or at least improved'.

Lord Wolfson said he would like to 'envisage a House part-appointed including hereditary Peers and part-elected with representatives from each geographical region or county of the constituent parts of the United Kingdom'. There should 'normally be an age of retirement for legislators'. In order not to be controversial, he suggested his own current age. He was born in 1927.

The Duke of Montrose believed that a reformed House should be 'able to attract a membership with a sense of history and of the civic duty which is required in the modern world'.

Lord Sheldon observed that the question of appointment was the key to maintaining the 'important standing of this House'.

Lady Saltoun of Abernethy thought that an all-appointed House was the 'only sensible' option.

Lord Crickhowell hoped that those who cast their vote on 4 February 'will be careful not to destroy something that works and replace it with something much worse, on a basis of ignorance or prejudice, or create the *super elective dictatorship*'.

Baroness Seccombe believed that a hybrid would be a disaster, and that eminent people would not stand for election, and the country would be the loser.

Lord Barnett observed that the idea of a hybrid House remained a 'nonsense', and an elected House would 'create a nightmare scenario'.

The lord Bishop of Worcester criticized the Joint Committee for having presented 'us with a choice between election and appointment without considering the possibility of indirect election'.

Baroness Carnegy of Lour thought that the only kind of second chamber able to 'counterbalance the present-day House of Commons would be a wholly appointed Chamber'.

Lord Winston said that he was strongly in favour an unelected second chamber.

Baroness Strange observed that 'we are all agreed that we need two Houses of Parliament. On that point, perhaps the colours of the carpets are significant. The Sovereign's carpet is blue, representing the sky and the heavens above; the carpet in the Commons is green, representing growing things and the grass roots of our people; and the carpet of the Lords is red, not so that you cannot see blood spilt on it, but because it is the colour of our hearts and the life blood of our people.' She believed that 'we are a good mix at the moment', that 'we love each other, and we love this House'.

Lord Gray of Contin said that, if non-elected, the new House could be 'completely independent and could complement the work of the Commons'.

Baroness Knight of Collingtree said that she was a 'little disappointed' that many peers seemed to be 'going down the track of asking for a fully elected House of Lords'. She believed that, if 'we go down that path, we shall destroy the character, competency and independence of this place'.

Lord Hoyle thought that the present House was outdated and out of touch. There was need for major reform: 'We must have a new start, a new name and be more democratic.'

Lord Palmer said that he was against any [elected] element in the House, and Lord Forsyth of Drumlean said he would vote for a fully appointed House.

Lord Birt thought that introducing an elected element into the chamber without materially changing its role risked 'unbalancing, and unsettling our constitution'.

Lord Swinfen felt the House should be wholly appointed, not wholly elected. A partially elected House would not work properly.

Lord Sewel said that Parliament would be best served by arriving at a position in which the House of Lords, because of its 'lack of democratic legitimacy, cannot and will not challenge the supremacy of the House of Commons'.

Lord Skidelsky said that his instincts were in favour of a wholly appointed House. The system of appointment had to be much more open, transparent and publicly accountable than it had been in the past.

The Earl of Caithness felt disappointed that there was not an option allowing a right to vote for the status quo.

Lord Lucas suggested that 'we should elect the Cross-Benchers and appoint the politicians'.

It was past 11 p.m. when the debate ended. Lord Grocott begged to move that the debate be adjourned and his motion was agreed to.

The debate resumed on 22 January 2003 and was opened by Baroness Jay.[6] She congratulated the Joint Committee on 'its excellent report', welcoming the degree of cross-party consensus. The Committee had 'helpfully formulated and crystallised a basis of positive consensus' and broken the

6   *Ibid.*, 22 January 2003, cols 720–838.

'log jam'. She herself preferred option 5: 60 per cent appointed, 40 per cent elected Members. Appointed members should be selected by an independent statutory Appointments Commission. There were, she said, omissions in the report. The most important were: the question of how to achieve a workable size of the new House; the question of costs; the issue of how any elected member should reach the House – whether they, or any nominated members, would have a link with the peerage. She thought that membership should be decoupled from the peerage. The award of a life peerage should continue to be high honour, but should not automatically confer a seat in Parliament.

Lord Higgins said that 'this House' was not 'here to be democratic'; this House was an 'effective revising' chamber. Hybridity would be the 'worst of all possible worlds'.

Lord McNally argued that legitimacy, representativeness, no domination by one party, independence and expertise could 'all be delivered, given the kind of voting system, regionally based constituencies and length of term envisaged'.

Lord Elder believed that, in an 'ideal world, we should have a unicameral system'. But he would support a wholly appointed chamber.

The Earl of Sandwich thought that a hybrid House would be 'unequal and unworkable'. The interim House had worked well. 'We should feel content with what we have achieved.'

Lord Beaumont of Whitley took the view that if 'something is bust, you mend it, but you do not think it necessary to replace it entirely to stop it breaking in other ways'.

Lord Brooke of Alverthorpe agreed that 'we should have elected Members to represent the nations and regions'. He thought that, if 'we had elected people, we would get them in, but under an appointments system I do not believe that there is any more guarantee that people who have accepted appointment to the House would necessarily come in and do the daily grind of work that is required.'

Lord MacGregor of Pulham Market said that he was 'clearly' in favour of Option 1.

Lord Desai thought that the report 'makes an awful muddle of the options. The proposed voting procedure is the daftest I have seen in a long time and will not result in a decision being arrived at'. He believed that 'we really ought to use a system of ranking alternatives, adding up the rankings and reaching a decision on the rank order criterion'.

Lord Rix observed that 'this House still has a great deal to offer to the business of government. Of course, like all ancient institutions it could do with a bit of tidying up and spring cleaning, but it would be tragedy if, in pursuing change for change's sake, all that was to disappear from the Mother of Parliaments.'

Lord Rodgers of Quarry Bank said that having two classes – elected and appointed – could do more harm than good. He was 'uncomfortable' about his decision, but would vote for Option 1, abstain on Option 2, and vote against the others.

The lord Bishop of Portsmouth argued that 'we need to think wider and deeper if we are to avoid going around on what feels like a rather self-regarding merry-go-round which, with best intentions, can give way to slogans and ideological trench warfare, disguised, at this stage, as a series of mathematical options'.

Lord Archer of Sandwell felt that 'we shall have to ensure that the qualities which your Lordships' House already contributes do not go out with the bath water. [...] We shall need to leave room to build on existing practices and conventions, where they serve our purpose. Free elections are a vitally important way of choosing governments, but at this moment, I do not believe that I detect a very wide demand for even more elections.'

Viscount Goschen said that the 'strongest argument that could be deployed today is that the current House works. It is effective at scrutinising legislation and, indeed, in holding the Government to account.'

Lord Dubs wished that the Joint Committee had 'given us fewer and more manageable options'. The Upper House had an 'enormous contribution to make. Changing its composition would not lessen that contribution; it would enhance it and give us more legitimacy than we now have.'

Earl Peel observed that the fact that the second Chamber was not subjected to an electoral process was a 'real positive', 'enhancing informed debate, enacting better legislation and, therefore, enhancing the whole process of democratic responsibility'.

Baroness Darcy de Knayth believed that the Lords was the 'only Chamber in the world in which one can survive and operate effectively without the backing of a political party. That is precious and must be preserved.' She found herself increasingly favouring an all-appointed chamber. An elected House would be more political and have less expertise and experience.

Lord Selsdon suggested that, if 'we want to be representative, we must be all appointed. If we want to be democratic, we must be all elected. However, if we are to be representative, let us work out who we are meant to represent.'

Lord Gordon of Strathblane said the truth was that the 'only thing that will give full legitimacy in some people's eyes is 100 per cent elected Members'. But 'do not let us pretend that any half-way House will stop short of that'.

Lord Butler of Brockwell argued that an element of the House with the function of injecting regional opinion into the debates should be elected.

Lord Rees supposed that 'we could survive with a very small elected proportion of Members'.

Lord Mackenzie of Framwellgate said that the House worked 'extremely well and does the job that it is designed to do of scrutinising, revising and improving legislation sent to this House form another place'. By all means, 'let us change' – 'but without throwing out the baby with the bath water'. That would be constitutional disaster.

Lord Armstrong of Ilminster suggested that it would be 'advantageous for the Standing Orders in this House to be amended so that a Cabinet Minister or Minister in charge of a Department who is a Member of another place could be permitted, by leave of both Houses, to attend and speak but not vote within the House when business warranted it'.

Lord Renton of Mount Hary declared that he did not think that Option 1, for a fully appointed House, was a 'practical alternative'. He would vote for the 50–50 option 'at the start'.

Viscount Tenby hoped that the Lords would vote for the first option, because to vote for other options, 'no doubt for the best intentions', would 'irreparably damage a system which, despite all logic, has served this country well over the centuries'.

Lord Harrison suggested adopting a 'team system', built on the Wakeham Commission's suggestion that the composition of the Lords 'should reflect in its political proportions the results of the most recent general election'. This was how the system would work: 'Each party is given a team of Peers from which it will draw its voting strength. The numbers in each party's team will be decided by an appropriate independent body such as the appointments commission, which will meet regularly to take account of changing political patterns and strengths. Each Peer will serve 10 years, un-renewable.'

Baroness Miller of Hendon was firm in her belief that the House should 'never be tinkered with to turn it into a rubber stamp for the government of the day'.

Lord Plant of Highfield suggested that 'ideally the House should be replaced by a small, wholly elected chamber that is elected regionally using a form of proportional representation'. The size would be, say, half the size of the House of Commons. Difference in its representative base and difference in the electing system would increase the legitimacy of this second chamber. At the same time, legitimacy would not be increased so much that it would be a rival to the House of Commons: the size of the Commons and its own established constituency basis would ensure its primacy. Moreover, the degree of proportionality of elections set for the second chamber would make it most unlikely that one party would have an overall majority in the House. Also, if the PR system had a low threshold, that would mean that 'a wide range of parties would be able to have a voice in the House'.

Lord Campbell of Alloway said that, at the age of 86, he had a 'somewhat tenuous interest which may end all too soon, and not only by the Grace of God. Nonetheless, I care very much about the place and I am concerned with the retention of its continued role.' He would vote for Option 1, and oppose all election options.

Lord Graham of Edmonton said that he was in favour of democracy, and 'I equate democracy with election'.

Lord Mayhew of Twysden wanted to secure a new statutory Appointments Commission and 'a less haphazardly representative second Chamber', wholly appointed by it.

Lord Faulkner of Worcester said that he would be voting for Option 1 and against the remaining options, provided that 'I get an assurance that the heredity by-election procedure will be abolished' and a more transparent appointments system 'will be implemented to avoid the accusations of patronage that would result from an open system'.

Lord Bowness supported the concept of the statutory Appointments Commission.

The Earl of Onslow suggested giving 'this House more authority so that it can be beastly to the government or to any government. That, in turn, would make the House of Commons do its job better.'

Lord Monson said that the present House 'works extremely well'. It 'ain't broke' and should not therefore 'be fixed', unless one could be 'absolutely certain that the patched-up version would be an improvement on what we have now'.

Lord Marlesford suggested that there was 'one precedent on which I should like to build. The convention is that the House of Commons nominates the retiring Speaker to come to the House of Lords. That is entirely free from prime ministerial patronage. I believe that system could be extended, with Members of the House of Commons nominating and, if necessary, electing a limited number of distinguished parliamentarians for membership of the House of Lords.'

Lord Howell of Guildford said that he accepted that a strong Parliament must be the aim of all democrats. But to try to achieve that by creating a second elected chamber 'is utterly misguided'.

Lord Dean of Harptree noted that, given the 'enormous variety of views' expressed in the House, not only between parties but within them, he doubted whether consensus was likely to emerge.

The lord Bishop of Southwark suspected that the bishops, this 'bevy of Episcopal cats will find themselves heading for different options when they are finally put before us. But that, to its credit, has been the long tradition of the Bench of Bishops.'

Lord Moran believed that there was a need to keep the party-political aspects of the House to 'a minimum'. The 'less political, the more useful is the work of the House'.

Lord Gilbert said he favoured Option 1. He was 'fervently' against all others.

Lord Elton argued that one could belong to the House of Commons 'only with the consent and support of one's party at the general election'. That gave the whips 'inordinate power over the behaviour of the Members of another place. All that flows from the electoral system. That, coupled with our social and economic organisation, has undermined the efficiency of the democratic process in defending the public from the operation of an over-mighty executive. We are being asked to introduce the same system here to protect the public by having more elected people and, perhaps, a wholly elected House. That really is to stand logic on its head.'

Lord Goodhart warned that, if 'we are seen to reject democracy, we will end up increasingly as an irrelevant and ineffective body'.

Lord Strathclyde conceded that the executive was 'too strong' and Parliament 'too weak'. What was needed was a 'stronger Parliament and a stronger House that is able to exercise its authority and work with another place in holding the executive in account. [...] We should accept no reduction in the powers of this House. We should seek more influence over secondary legislation.'

The lord chancellor, Lord Irvine of Lairg, wound up the debate. The dominant view, he registered, was in favour of an all-appointed House. A free vote would reflect that reality. Yet, despite disagreement within the parties, there seemed to be consensus that the House's main role should be to continue to be a revising, scrutinising and deliberative assembly with the power to delay, but not to veto, legislation; and that the House of Commons should retain its role as the pre-eminent chamber. The government's ultimate objective, he assured the House, was to secure a second chamber that was broadly representative of contemporary Britain, a chamber 'which will complement the other place by reinforcing Parliament's ability to conduct scrutiny and hold the executive to account'; that has a distinctive composition, so that it is neither a rival to the House of Commons nor a pale imitation of it; that 'is not dominated by the political parties either collectively or singly'; that 'brings to its deliberations distinctive expertise and experience'.

It had now passed 11 p.m. Before adjournment, Lord Howe closed the debate, appreciating the advice the Joint Committee had received to 'guide us in our further deliberations'.

Both Houses voted on the main motion put before them on 4 February 2003. The voting revealed how divided members in both places were in their opinions. There was anything but the 'principled consensus on the way forward' the government had hoped to achieve.[7]

Voting in the House of Commons, 4 February 2003

The leader of the House of Commons begged to move 'That this House approves Option 1 (fully appointed) in the First Report from the Joint Committee on House of Lords Reform'.

An amendment to the motion for Option No. 1 had been put by George Howarth: 'in line 1, leave out from "House" to end and add: "declines to approve Option 1 as it does not accord with the principle of a unicameral Parliament"'.

A four-hour debate followed.[8] Members of the House spoke about the First Report, expressing their various views. The parliamentary secretary, Ben Bradshaw, wound up the debate, stating that there would be eight votes, including the amendment on abolition, which 'will be taken first'. Members, he said, could 'vote for, abstain on, or vote against as many of the Options as they wish[ed]': it was a 'free vote'. The Joint Committee was to 'reconvene later this month to consider the results of this Chamber and in the other place, and it will then produce a second, more detailed report.'

The House then divided on the amendment: Ayes 172; Noes 390. The question was accordingly negatived.

Next, 'Main Question put: that this House approves Option 1 (fully appointed) in the First Report from the Joint Committee on House of Lords Reform.' The House divided: Ayes 245; Noes 323. Question accordingly negatived.

---

7   For a critical evaluation of the voting, see Iain McLean, Arthur Spirling and Meg Russell, 'None of the Above: The UK House of Commons Votes on Reforming the House of Lords, February 2003', *Political Quarterly*, 14 July 2003.

8   *Parliamentary Debates*, House of Commons, vol. 399, 4 February 2003, cols 152–243.

Then, 'Question put: that this House approves Option 2 (fully elected) in the First Report from the Joint Committee on House of Lords Reform.' The House divided: Ayes 272; Noes 289. Question accordingly negatived.

And so it went on.

'Motion made: that this House approves Option 3 (80 per cent appointed/20 per cent elected) in the first Report from the Joint Committee on House of Lords Reform.' Question put and negatived.

Question put: 'that this House approves Option 4 (80 per cent elected/20 per cent appointed) in the First Report from the Joint Committee on House of Lords Reform.' The House divided: Ayes 281, Noes 284. Question accordingly negatived.

'Motion made: that this House approves Option 5 (60 per cent appointed, 40 per cent elected) in the First Report from the Joint Committee on House of Lords Reform.' Question put and negatived.

'Question put: that this House approves Option 6 (60 per cent elected, 40 per cent appointed) in the First Report from the Joint Committee on House of Lords Reform.' The House divided: Ayes 253; Noes 316. Question accordingly negatived.

'Motion made: that this House approves Option 7 (50 per cent appointed/50 per cent elected) in the First Report from the Joint Committee on House of Lords Reform.' Question put and also negatived.

After the voting ended, with these extraordinary results, the shadow leader of the Opposition rose to say: 'Now that the House has put itself in an interesting position, and the Government in an even worse position, in that the commitments made in the Government's manifesto look as if they are now in shreds, and the option that got the closest vote was my party's policy, can we expect an immediate statement from the Leader of the House as to where he expects us now to go?'

The leader of the House commented thus: 'The view expressed by hon. Members was wise. We should go home and sleep on this interesting position. That is the most sensible thing that anyone can say in the circumstances. As the right hon. Gentleman knows, the next stage in the process is for the Joint Committee to consider the votes in both Houses. Heaven help the members of the Committee, because they need it.'

Voting in the House of Lords, 4 February 2003

The First Report from the Joint Committee was debated in the House of Lords on 4 February 2003 as well. The lord privy seal and the leader of the House, Lord Williams of Mostyn, begged to move 'that this House approves Option 1 (fully appointed) in the report from the Joint Committee on House of Lords Reform'.[9] It was possible, he said, that the debate might be decisive and 'will determine the broad shape of the House in the future'. Members were free to vote 'Content' or 'Not Content'.

Lord Strathclyde, leader of the Opposition, confirmed that 'it will be a genuinely free vote'.

The Lords voted differently from the members of the Commons. On question, 'whether the said Motion (Option 1: fully appointed) shall be agreed to', their lordships divided: 'Contents 335; Not Contents 110. Resolved in the affirmative, Motion agreed to accordingly.'

When Lord Williams moved 'that this House approves Option 2 (fully elected)'. The House divided: 'Contents 106; Not-Contents 329. Resolved in the negative, and the Motion disagreed to accordingly.'

The other options were turned down with equal determination.

On question 'whether this House approves Option 3 (80 per cent appointed, 20 per cent elected)', the House divided: 'Contents 39; Not-Contents 375. Resolved in the negative, and Motion disagreed to accordingly.'

On question 'whether this House approves Option 4 (80 per cent elected, 20 per cent appointed)', their lordships divided: 'Contents 93, Not-Contents 338. Resolved in the negative, and Motion disagreed to accordingly.'

On question 'whether this House approves Option 5 (60 per cent appointed, 40 per cent elected)', their lordships divided: 'Contents 60; Not-Contents 358. Resolved in the negative, Motion disagreed to accordingly.'

9　　*Parliamentary Debates*, House of Lords, vol. DCXLIV, 4 February 2003, cols 115–38.

On question 'whether this House approves Option 6 (60 per cent elected, 40 per cent appointed)', their lordships divided: 'Contents 91, Not-Contents 317. Resolved in the negative, and Motion disagreed to.'

On question 'whether this House approves Option 7 (50 per cent appointed, 50 per cent elected)', their lordships divided: 'Contents 84; Not-Contents 322. Resolved in the negative, and Motion disagreed to accordingly.'

The Lords had voted overwhelmingly for Option 1 (a fully appointed House).

The Joint Committee's Second Report

The Joint Committee met again to consider the results of the debate in both Houses. It published its Second Report on 29 April 2003. Here are the minutes:[10]

HOUSE OF LORDS REFORM: SECOND REPORT

The Joint Committee on House of Lords Reform has agreed to the following Report:

INTRODUCTION

1. In December 2002 we said in our First Report that although the re-balancing of parliamentary institutions is something that can only evolve over time, we believed that there was an historic opportunity to enact reform of the House of Lords based on the need for a second Chamber which would continue to play an important and

---

10   See *Joint Committee on House of Lords Reform: Second Report*. Ordered by the House of Lords to be printed 29 April 2003. HL Paper 97. Ordered by the House of Commons to be printed 29 April 2003. HC 668.

complementary role to the Commons. However, for the present at least, the scale and nature of that opportunity has now changed.

2. For not only has there been predictable disagreement between the two Houses. There has also been the lack of decision on the matter of composition in the House of Commons – and indeed, at a late stage, the absence of a clear lead from the Government itself. The effect of these decisions (or lack of them) has been to reduce the pressure for change in any direction. Even if the engines have not actually fallen off the train, their thrust has been diminished.

3. Even so, this Committee remains unanimous in its view that simply to maintain the status quo is undesirable. The differences between us as to the long-term future structure of the second Chamber inevitably reflect those in Parliament and Government alike. Some of us may have been tempted to believe that the best way to promote the case for radical change is to leave things as they are – and thus be exposed to continuing criticism. Others could have been tempted, in the opposite direction, to regard 'no change' as an acceptable prescription for an enduring quiet life. Collectively, however, we do not accept either of these views.

4. Whatever may or may not be decided later – perhaps some considerable time ahead, perhaps not – about the long-term composition of the second Chamber, there are possible changes affecting the effectiveness, representative quality and credibility of the House that can and should be considered and decided now. Things should not simply be left as they are. So in this Report we emphasise the importance of reasserting the case for reform and for regaining at least some part of the momentum which was recognised by the Commons Public Administration Select Committee in its Report. And we seek from Government, and subsequently from Parliament, a clear response to this Report.

PART 1: THE PRESENT POSITION

5. Our first remit as a Joint Committee was to examine the composition and powers of the Second Chamber in the context of

Parliament as a whole and to put forward, for consideration of both Houses, a set of options on composition ranging from a fully appointed to a fully elected House.

6. We decided early in our deliberations that it was essential to establish the nature of the roles, functions and powers of a reformed House and how it operated in respect of the Commons, before we went on to the matter of composition. Accordingly in our First Report we considered what a reformed House should do as well as setting out our conclusions about the kind of membership that was most desirable. That analysis was based on a clear understanding of how the present House performs its roles and functions and how the best and most successful features of it might be continued in a newly constituted Chamber. We then identified other important matters – such as tenure, appointment methods, methods of election – as issues we would have to return to once we had had decisions on composition from the Houses.

7. We put seven options before the Houses, suggesting that a wide debate on a take note motion should precede any vote on them. When it came to the method of voting on the options, we recommended a departure from the usual practice of putting questions so that questions could be put successively on each option and Members could vote on any number of options they wished to. We stressed that the same procedure should be followed in each House.

8. Our recommendation on having a separate debate prior to a vote on the options was followed in each House. We consider that the contributions to the debates in both Houses benefited from that process since it allowed time for reflection and it made it possible for Members to read the debate in the other House before proceeding to vote in their own House. In the Lords, the initial debate was on a take-note motion; in the Commons the motion was to adjourn.

The votes on the seven options

9. The votes on the options on 4 February provided no endorsement of any one option in the Commons and a clear endorsement of appointment rather than election in the Lords.

10. The votes on the options did not follow an identical pattern in each House. In the Commons a reasoned Amendment to the first option, on a fully appointed House, was put to the vote. The Amendment, which declined to approve the option because 'it does not accord with the principle of a unicameral Parliament', was negatived by 390 to 172 votes. The first option itself was then defeated by 323 votes to 245. No other option out of the remaining six was agreed to. Three were disagreed to without a division.

11. In the Lords the first option, for a fully appointed House, was agreed to by 335 votes to 110. All the other six options were disagreed to. The voting figures in both Houses are set out in the following table. The options were:

Option 1 Fully appointed
Option 2 Fully elected
Option 3 80% appointed, 20% elected
Option 4 80% elected, 20% appointed
Option 5 60% appointed, 40% elected
Option 6 60% elected, 40% appointed
Option 7 50% appointed, 50% elected

Lords
For
Option 1: 335; Option 2: 106; Option 3: 39; Option 4: 93; Option 5: 60; Option 6: 91; Option 7: 84.

Against

Option 1: 110; Option 2: 329; Option 3: 375; Option 4: 338; Option 5: 358; Option 6: 317; Option 7: 322.

Commons
For
Amendment: 172; Option 1: 245; Option 2: 272; Option 4: 281; Option 6: 253.

Against

Amendment: 390; Option 1: 323; Option 2: 289; Option 4: 284; Option 6: 316.

12. In our Special Report to both Houses we recognised the possibility of differences in outcome in the votes in the two Houses and understood that we would need to consider the differences that existed between the two Houses and the means by which they might be brought closer together. One way in which we had considered that that might be done, and a way forward thus found, was to take stock of what was actually agreed by Members of both Houses across a broad front. But we acknowledge that the lack of a vote, in the House of Commons in favour of any of the options for composition requires the reform process to be given more time and consideration.

13. We also note that support for uni-cameralism turned out to be greater than expected, although of the 172 Commons Members who supported that amendment 160 went on to vote for one or more of the options.

PART 2: PROGRESS ON REFORM: A NEW CONSENSUS

14. We consider that, if it is the wish of the Houses, it would be possible for the Committee to contribute to the progress of the reform process by investigating and reporting on certain specific issues, which will have to be resolved as part of an overall reform. This should facilitate future decisions on these matters and it would be possible, if thought desirable, to bring into effect some specific changes on the road to overall reform. Our conclusion that further progress can be made is based on the much wider acceptance than at any previous time of the roles, functions and powers that a reformed House should have and of the kind of qualities desirable in it. The debates in both Houses on our First Report have reinforced our view on this matter.

Roles and Conventions

15. In our First Report we identified a number of significant roles that a reformed House does and could in future fulfil. In the case of some of these roles, for example in its role in relation to the Commons, we believe that the way forward is to recognise

the existing conventions that govern how the Lords conducts its business and behaves towards the Commons, and examine ways of defining them in a new constitutional settlement between the Houses. In the debate in the House of Commons, the Leader of the House rightly said that these conventions 'buttress the relative status of each House'. The two most important conventions, both of a self-restraining nature, are the recognition on the part of the House of Lords that the Commons should eventually have its way, and its acceptance that the Government of the day is entitled to have its business considered without undue delay. We noted in our First Report that the House of Lords could depart from these conventions at any time, since they have no basis in law. A reformed House might look upon its relations with the Commons with a fresh, more assertive stance. We therefore consider that the manner of maintaining these conventions requires careful attention and could form one part of the continuing programme of reform.

Constitutional Long-stop

16. A second important role, already performed by the Lords, is that of a constitutional long-stop or check on the ability of the Commons to make constitutional changes without full debate and an awareness of the consequences. This role was well understood by the Royal Commission in its report. The House of Lords has accepted the Royal Commission proposal that a Constitution Committee should be established; the Committee was appointed in February 2001. The exact significance of the constitutional role of the Lords needs to be carefully assessed in the further programme of reform.

Representativeness

17. Other roles which we identified in our First Report, in respect of the public on the one hand and the regions and nations of the UK on the other, are areas in which the substantial work already done by the Royal Commission needs to be carried forward. As

one Member in the Lords debate put it, 'this House is seen as too male, too old and too much from the south-east of England, with insufficient ethnic diversity'. In these areas, it is not so much a matter of consolidation of what the present House does, but of thinking afresh and in the overall context of parliamentary activity. On the one hand, there is a need to consider how the Lords can be made more legitimate, more directly representative of social groups (gender-wise, racially and in respect of religions) without significantly affecting its relations with the Commons. On the other, there is a need to work out what role a reformed House should have in relation to the nations and regions of the UK and how that might be achieved.

Functions

18. We also identified, in our First Report, functions at present performed by the Lords which need to continue and be enhanced in a reformed House. These include the overridingly important function of the House as a legislative body in which some Government business can be initiated and the task of revision taken on in a serious manner. Up to one-third of public bills are actually introduced into the Lords. Recent Governments of all political complexions would not have been able to achieve their legislative programmes without this facility. The Lords' revising role is widely acknowledged and attested to by the levels of activity in amending legislation over a long period, with well known results. We emphasised in our First Report that co-ordination of legislative loads between the Houses would be an important part of any new constitutional settlement, something already noted by the Commons Modernisation Committee.

Scrutiny

19. Other functions of the Lords include its important scrutiny function – carried out in the House and through select committees. There are issues here, for example, to do with the effectiveness of the select committees which need to be looked at carefully so

that the present, already significant, scrutiny role can be expanded
and enhanced.

Judicial function

20. The judicial function of the Lords is a uniquely important
area of its own. There is still the need for a full, public discussion
about whether there should be a separate Supreme Court and that
might best arise from the work of an independent inquiry which
can call on expert advice and evidence. We have heard nothing
in the debates in both Houses to change our view that this is a
separate matter that needs an inquiry of its own.

Powers

21. We did not envisage any significant change in the powers of
the Lords as defined in the Parliament Acts, although we reserved
our position on the matter of powers in the area of secondary
legislation and we expressed concern at the use of carry-over provisions for public bills.

The Five Desirable Qualities

22. In putting forward our views on reform of the House of
Lords, we identified five qualities which we consider essential to
a reformed House. The five qualities are tests to be applied to the
composition of a House which is to perform its role effectively.

23. The five qualities are:

- legitimacy
- representativeness
- no domination by one party
- independence
- expertise

24. We do not want to rehearse here in detail our discussion of
these matters in our First Report but we stress that we were unanimous in agreeing to their importance. Nor has anything which
has been said in the debates in both Houses seriously challenged

this conclusion. Many Members emphasised the need for lack of domination by one party and worry was expressed about the degree of political patronage in the existing system of appointments. In his remarks on the second day of the debate in the House of Lords, the Lord Chancellor said that reform of the Lords should produce a House which was not 'a rival nor a pale imitation' of the Commons and one that is not 'dominated by the political parties either collectively or singly; that brings to its deliberations distinctive expertise and experience'. The five qualities we have enumerated and discussed in our First Report are designed to produce exactly that.

25. In both Houses, the need for a strong independent element in a reformed second chamber was voiced by supporters of every position on composition.

PART 3: WHAT IS THE WAY FORWARD?

26. We have already noted (paragraphs 2–4 above) the absence of common ground on which to found proposals for change in the long-term composition of the second chamber. There is, however, a range of inter-related matters which need to be examined carefully if the case for reform is to be taken forward. Progress can be made and has been made already on an incremental basis. Further consideration of these matters does not in any way entrench the present composition of the House since they would have had to be examined even if there were no proposals to reform the composition of the House. The matters we highlight in this Report would have had to be the object of detailed scrutiny whatever the outcome of the votes on composition in the two Houses. We made these issues quite clear in our First Report, including among them the question of the size of a reformed House, tenure, the appointments system, the position of the law lords and the bishops and the financial consequences of reform. On many of these questions, the way ahead has been foreshadowed in the Royal Commission Report and subsequent documents. At least some

parts of this agenda can, moreover, be carried forward without the need for primary legislation.

Size/Tenure

27. Our views on the size of the House and on tenure were challenged in the debates preceding the votes on the seven options, particularly in the House of Commons. There was a broad opinion that a House of six hundred Members, with an appreciably larger House during the transitional period, was too high. The Leader of the House of Commons urged us to 'think more boldly about the eventual reduction in size of the second chamber'. Other Members also spoke in favour of a smaller House. The question of size must be linked to that of tenure, frequency of attendance as well as to the need for flexibility to secure appropriate political 'balance' and an independent 'base' as we said in our First Report. Nevertheless we would enter the second phase of our deliberations with an awareness that a reduction in size (from 600 as the eventual number) is widely considered desirable. However, the question of size is inevitably linked to decisions as to whether existing life peers should be subject to compulsory retirement, what proposals should be made for voluntary retirement, whether members should regard membership as a full-time commitment, consequent provisions relating to remuneration, and procedural reforms such as the degree of delegation to committees.

28. The matter of the length of tenure was raised in debate, when it was suggested that the 12-year term proposed in our First Report might be too long. This was one of only two matters on which the Committee divided, an amendment to allow an 8-year term, once renewable, being defeated. This is another matter to which the Committee can return in its further deliberations.

Appointment

29. There was less criticism of our stance on the important matter of the Appointments Commission (which would be necessary

for every possible future prospect, save that of an 100 per cent elected House). The importance that we attached to getting the right balance between allowing for *some* nominations to be made by the Prime Minister of the day and others by party leaders and otherwise delivering an open and fair system of appointment was not seriously challenged in the debates in either House although disquiet about patronage was expressed. The need for independence and integrity of the appointments system was recognised by the Royal Commission in its Report. We agree with the Royal Commission that much the best way of achieving this is to reformulate the existing Commission and put it on a statutory basis. But much work needs to be done on exactly what is needed to produce a widely respected and viable method of appointment.

30. Meantime, and in the possible absence of primary legislation, this is not an issue that can be neglected for long. Two years have passed since the appointment of the last group of new life peers. There is, therefore, a growing need to top up the stock of expertise and of younger members. In order to handle this problem, consideration should, therefore, be given to the appointment of a new and manifestly independent Appointments Commission, and endorsed – as an interim alternative to primary legislation – by an Order in Council, approved by both Houses.

Bishops and the representation of other denominations and faiths

31. We have already indicated in our First Report that the position of the Church of England bishops would need to be considered in a reformed House. We believe that such reforms, aimed at making the House more representative of British society as a whole, must entail examining the merits of religious representation. We would wish to consider that matter carefully, on the basis of evidence from various religious and spiritual communities.

Financial matters

32. The financial consequences of reform are something that should be costed. Parliament should not consider itself above

an exercise that would be routinely part of inquiry into changing the structure of any other organisation in the land. There are implications here about the requirements which Members of a reformed House would demand. They include accommodation, secretarial services and research support. The size and composition of the reformed House will be decisive in setting figures on these demands but in any case they merit serious inquiry. There would also need to be a review of the present system of offering no remuneration to Members but only reimbursing expenses within daily limits.

Two remaining issues

33. There are two remaining issues of particular importance which we now consider need to be tackled. The first is that of the position of the remaining 92 hereditary peers; the second is whether we should begin to examine systems of indirect election to a reformed House.

The Hereditaries

34. The 92 hereditary peers (including *ex officio* Members) have continued to participate effectively in the affairs of the House. The Government White Paper *Completing the Reform* confirmed the Government's intention that the remaining 92 hereditary peers would leave the House as part of the next stage of reform.

An indirectly elected House?

35. We note the view expressed by a number of Members of the House of Commons that the possibility of indirect elections to the House of Lords should be considered. Various possibilities exist for moving towards an indirectly elected House. The main problem so far identified is the lack of a regional structure, especially in England, from which to draw membership. Nevertheless things are developing in this direction – the Government remains committed to taking forward measures to

introduce regional assemblies. Members of a reformed House could be indirectly elected by these new bodies together with the Scottish Parliament and the Welsh Assembly. Another possible approach involves a 'secondary mandate' whereby votes in elections to the House of Commons are also used to elect Members of the House of Lords using a regional list system. These are complex matters which would need careful scrutiny in an ongoing programme of reform.

Response from the Government

36. We have identified in this report the area of consensus that has been achieved in the matter of reform. So far as recognition of the roles, functions and powers of a reformed House are concerned, that consensus is considerable. It is accepted by almost all Members of the House of Commons who spoke, including the uni-cameralists who, once their preferred option had been defeated, divided almost equally into supporters of a fully appointed and a fully elected House. It is also a view shared by almost all Members of the House of Lords who spoke in the debates.

37. Agreement about those matters is, in our view, a strong basis for continuing the reform. We have identified areas where work needs to be done – namely in respect of the issues of the hereditary peers, the appointments system and such matters as the size and conditions of tenure of the House. As a longer-term matter there is the possibility of indirect election to the House. If these reforms can be carried through in a sustainable way, then the fundamental issue will remain to be resolved, namely whether the Lords should be wholly appointed, wholly or partly directly elected or wholly or partly indirectly elected. We look forward to a reply from Government within the customary two months and then acceptance by both Houses that our work should continue on the lines we have set out.

The Committee's Struggle for Survival

Drafting a Plea

PROCEEDINGS OF THE COMMITTEE RELATING TO THE REPORT
SESSION 2002–03

DIE MARTIS, 25° FEBRUARII 2003

Present:
Lord Archer of Sandwell
Viscount Bledisloe
Lord Brooke of Alverthorpe
Lord Carter
Lord Goodhart
Lord Howe of Aberavon
Lord Oakeshott of Seagrove Bay
Baroness O'Cathain
The Earl of Selborne
Lord Weatherill
Mr James Arbuthnot
Mr Chris Bryant
Mr Kenneth Clarke
Dr Jack Cunningham
Mr William Hague
Joyce Quin
Mr Clive Soley
Mr Paul Stinchcombe
Mr Paul Tyler

The Joint Committee deliberate.
    Ordered, That the Joint Committee be adjourned to Tuesday
1 April at Ten o'clock.

DIE MARTIS, 1° APRILIS 2003

Present:
Lord Archer of Sandwell
Viscount Bledisloe
Lord Brooke of Alverthorpe
Lord Carter
Lord Forsyth of Drumlean
Baroness Gibson of Market Rasen
Lord Goodhart
Lord Howe of Aberavon
Lord Oakeshott of Seagrove Bay
Baroness O'Cathain
The Earl of Selborne
Lord Weatherill
Janet Anderson
Mr James Arbuthnot
Mr Chris Bryant
Dr Jack Cunningham
Mr William Hague
Mr Stephen McCabe
Joyce Quin
Mr Terry Rooney
Mr Clive Soley
Mr Paul Stinchcombe
Mr Paul Tyler
Dr Jack Cunningham, in the Chair.

The Order of Adjournment is read.
    The Proceedings of Tuesday 25 February are read.
    The Joint Committee deliberate.
    Ordered, That the Joint Committee be adjourned to Tuesday
29 April at Ten o'clock.

DIE MARTIS, 29° APRILIS 2003

Present:
Lord Archer of Sandwell
Viscount Bledisloe
Lord Brooke of Alverthorpe
Lord Carter
Lord Forsyth of Drumlean
Baroness Gibson of Market Rasen
Lord Goodhart
Lord Howe of Aberavon
Lord Oakeshott of Seagrove Bay
Baroness O'Cathain
The Earl of Sclborne
Lord Weatherill
Janet Anderson
Mr James Arbuthnot
Mr Chris Bryant
Mr Kenneth Clarke
Dr Jack Cunningham
Mr William Hague
Mr Stephen McCabe
Joyce Quin
Mr Terry Rooney
Mr Clive Soley
Mr Paul Stinchcombe
Mr Paul Tyler
Dr Jack Cunningham, in the Chair.

The Order of Adjournment is read.

The Proceedings of Tuesday 1 April are read.

A draft Report is proposed by the Chairman, brought up and read.

A draft Report is proposed by Mr Paul Stinchcombe, brought up and read as follows:

PART ONE: HOW TO RESPOND TO THE VOTES OF 4TH FEBRUARY 2003

Introduction

1. We began our First Report by reminding ourselves why, over the past century, all attempts at reform of the House of Lords have failed – it was because of the lack of agreement on what was needed to replace the existing House. We went on, however, to state our firm resolve to play our part in avoiding the repetition of that history:

'...(W)e believe that there is now an historic opportunity to enact a reform which will enable the second chamber to continue to play an important and complementary role to the Commons, with its future at last secure.'

2. And yet despite our early optimistic protestations to the contrary, history is clearly in danger of repeating itself.

3. In particular, by our First Report this Committee put before the Houses of Parliament seven options for the composition of a reformed House of Lords ranging from an all appointed second chamber to one which was all-elected, with intermediate possibilities of a hybrid House of Lords part-elected, part-appointed in different proportions.

4. On 4 February 2003, however, the House of Commons rejected each and every one of the options that was put before them. The votes were as follows:

1. Fully appointed: Rejected by 323 votes to 245
2. Fully elected: Rejected by 289 votes to 272
3. 80 per cent appointed/20 per cent elected: No division
4. 80 per cent elected/20 per cent appointed: Rejected by 284 votes to 281
5. 60 per cent appointed/40 per cent elected: No division
6. 60 per cent elected/40 per cent appointed: Rejected by 316 votes to 253
7. 50 per cent appointed/50 per cent elected: No division.

5. So it is that, despite our early optimism, despairing voices have urged this Committee to give in and give up.

6. There is, however, a serious inhibition on the powers of the Joint Committee to dissolve itself by its own motion. In particular, the reform of the House of Lords is a matter for Parliament, not for the Joint Committee (and not for the Executive either). Through resolutions of both Houses, it was Parliament that established the Joint Committee as the vehicle to report to it on models of potential reform of the second chamber. Having created the Joint Committee by resolution, neither House of Parliament has yet resolved to wind it up.

7. The Joint Committee firmly believes that it does not have the capacity to wind itself up. The Committee was established by the Houses of Parliament and not by itself. Accordingly, it is not for us but for the Houses of Parliament to determine the Committee's fate.

The options: wind-up the Joint Committee or give it a renewed mandate.

8. There are two options for the future of the Joint Committee which Parliament could decide upon – winding the Joint Committee up or asking it to continue and complete its work.

Four reasons for giving the Joint Committee a renewed mandate.

9. For the following four reasons we believe that if Parliament were to accede to counsels of despair and dissolve the Joint Committee, that would amount to a lamentable failure of Parliamentary resolve. Indeed, it would mean that Parliament had either colluded with – or surrendered to – a divided executive and an obstructionist House of Lords to prevent the latter's reform, when its reform was the sole purpose for which Parliament actually established the Joint Committee.

1. Restoring the credibility of Parliament

10. Commentators have already noted the unusual voting patterns of certain Honourable and Right Honourable Members as

highlighted by Early Day Motions 686 and 689. As those Early Day Motions reveal, several Honourable and Right Honourable Members of the House of Commons appear to have voted in an inconsistent fashion, leading – perhaps – to a contrived rejection by the Commons of certain democratic models put before them on 4th February. In addition, commentators have also noted the fact that some Right Honourable Members of our own Joint Committee spoke powerfully in debate in the House of Commons in favour of a largely elected second chamber and then conspicuously failed to vote for it.

11. Such behaviour inevitably adds to the political cynicism in the country, to the growing belief that there never was a firm intention on the part of Parliament to take the reform of the House of Lords remotely seriously.

12. If Parliament were to confirm this impression by resolving to wind the Joint Committee up, the credibility of Parliament itself would be seriously undermined. Moreover, there could not be a worse time for Parliament to play so dangerous a game with the public's confidence in our democratic processes – the people's disengagement with politics is already such that mayoral candidates have been elected on joke platforms. Turnout is at an all-time low – down from 77.7% in the 1992 General Election to 59.4% in 2001, a loss of some 7 million voters in under a decade. Turnout in other elections is already far lower. The risk must be very real that turnout at the next General Election will be less than 50%. If it is, the legitimacy of democratic government itself will be in question. The opportunity for reforming the House of Lords is one which could reverse that trend, and to opt instead to undermine yet further the public's confidence in Parliament would be an act of monumental folly.

13. The first reason for Parliament asking the Joint Committee to continue its work is that to do otherwise would reinforce the cynicism that the public already feels in our Parliamentary processes. Indeed, if Parliament were to vote to wind the Joint

Committee up it would undermine the credibility of Parliament itself. That would be a very grave mistake to make.

2. *Filling the leadership void*

14. As earlier indicated, the reform of the House of Lords is a matter for Parliament not the executive. Nonetheless the Joint Committee cannot help but note that despite the governing party's manifesto commitment at the last General Election,

'to complete the House of Lords reform and make it more representative and democratic, while maintaining the House of Commons' primacy',

the votes on 4th February – and the comments made in the run-up to the debate – reveal that the cabinet itself is deeply divided as to the best way forward.

15. In addition, analysis of the votes cast in the House of Commons on 4th February reveals that these divisions run right through both the governing party and the official opposition.

16. The second reason for Parliament asking the Joint Committee to continue its work is that with the executive split, with the major political parties deeply divided, and with the governing party thereby in danger of not being able to deliver on a firm manifesto commitment, there is an absence of political leadership on the issue of the reform of the House of Lords. This is a void that only the Joint Committee is positioned to fill. We believe that if the Joint Committee were to fail to fill that void it would be abdicating the responsibilities vested in it by Parliament.

3. *Preventing an unacceptable constitutional settlement*

17. The Joint Committee is – as stated immediately above – the only vehicle by which the reform of the House of Lords can currently be progressed. If it were wound-up by Parliament that vehicle for reform would thereby be abolished. We would then be left with the status quo – a hybrid second chamber whose membership was very largely appointed, but in smaller part there by accident

of birth. This model is universally condemned and has been made to look even more absurd by the recent election by the second chamber of a replacement hereditary peer from a candidate list of 81 former hereditary peers. It was precisely because the status quo was thought repugnant that the Houses of Parliament established the Joint Committee to preside over its reform, and to allow the status quo to stay by default will serve only to bring the second chamber into further disrepute.

18. The third reason for Parliament asking the Joint Committee to continue its work is that the Joint Committee believes that to surrender our responsibilities now would leave the nations and regions of the United Kingdom with a constitutional status quo which is not remotely acceptable – a hybrid second chamber with the majority there only through the exercise of patronage and the minority there only by reason of the accident of their birth. The Joint Committee does not believe that it should condemn the constitution of the United Kingdom to such a settlement.

4. Fulfilling the original mandate

19. The Joint Committee notes, also, that it has not yet fulfilled the mandate it was originally given. In particular, the Joint Committee was established by the Houses of Parliament:

'... to report on options for the composition and powers of the House of Lords and to define and present to both Houses options for composition, including a fully nominated and fully elected House, and intermediate options'.

In purported fulfilment of the above, the Joint Committee has – so far – presented to both Houses certain options. As we have noted above, none of these have commanded the support of the House of Commons. There are other options – however – which the Joint Committee has not yet even considered nor allowed either House of Parliament to vote upon. In particular, we have not given any consideration whatsoever to any option of either indirect election or election by secondary mandate.

20. In the premises it is evident that the remit for which Parliament first established the Joint Committee has not yet been fulfilled. In these circumstances it would be obviously premature to dissolve the Joint Committee.

21. The fourth reason for Parliament asking the Joint Committee to continue its work is that despite the breadth of our remit 'to report on options for composition (...) of the House of Lords', we have conspicuously failed to report to either House in respect of any option of indirect election or election by secondary mandate.

Conclusions on the options for the Joint Committee

22. For all of these reasons, the Joint Committee invites the Houses of Parliament not to wind the Joint Committee up but to give it instead a renewed mandate to continue to consider options for the reform of the House of Lords which might reconcile the differences of opinion which the recent votes in the House of Commons dramatically exposed.

PART TWO: THE PREFERRED NATURE OF THE RENEWED MANDATE

The options: minor revision or radical reform

23. The Joint Committee appreciates, however, that the votes on 4 February 2003 in the House of Commons indicate the scale of the task that now confronts it. If all past attempts at reform of the House of Lords have been broken by the failure to agree on its replacement, the rejection by the House of Commons of every single option for reform that we proposed by our First Report shows that disagreement still continues.

24. Indeed, the scale of the apparent disagreement inevitably tempts us to ask the Houses of Parliament to invite the Joint Committee to consider first those areas in which the recent debates indicate the disagreements to be less serious – removing the remaining hereditary peers, improving the current system of appointment,

considering the size of the second chamber, the age at which Lords might retire, and whether they should be remunerated.

Three reasons for favouring radical reform

25. However, the Joint Committee believes that – for the following three reasons – it would be a grave mistake for the Joint Committee to continue to meet only to tinker with minimalist measures, not properly to debate radical reform.

1. Legitimising the illegitimate

26. The first reason is that any Bill which simply addressed issues of peripheral concern would run the risk of legitimising the illegitimate, leading to the greater longevity of the Lords as it is currently and unacceptably composed. Whilst perfection should never be the enemy of the good, it must always be the enemy of the bad.

2. Practical difficulties

27. The second reason is that there would be real difficulties in getting a minimalist Bill through either House of Parliament. The Commons would likely reject the reforms as insufficient and the Lords reject any Bill that expelled the remaining hereditary peers. Moreover, even if such a Bill could be enacted, a real question has to be asked as to whether it would be worth the Parliamentary time taken to pass it.

3. Fulfilling the original mandate

28. The third, and perhaps most important, reason is that minor tinkering with the more obvious failings of the status quo would not remotely address our wholesale failure to fulfil our original mandate properly to consider and report upon the options for potential reform of the House of Lords – not the least of which are the models of indirect election or election by secondary mandate which we have thus far ignored.

The Joint Committee's responsibility for past failure

29. The Joint Committee accepts its share of responsibility for the current state of affairs. In our First Report we should have

addressed the principled objections which Honourable and Right Honourable Members held against direct election, appointment and hybridity and endeavoured to develop constitutional models which might meet those concerns. We avoided that entire debate. Rather than attempt to reconcile the differences of Honourable and Right Honourable Members, we simply afforded them the opportunity to restate their previous positions.

30. We were wrong to narrow the debate as we did, reducing a complex series of constitutional issues to the two alternatives of an all-elected and all-appointed second chamber (which we were obliged to present in any event) and a baffling series of arbitrary arithmetic options in-between. The Houses of Parliament should have been asked to debate not numbers but principles – legitimacy, primacy, expertise and, above all, participation. We needed to give Parliament the chance to do more than choose between *varying proportions* of members elected and members appointed, we needed to afford them the opportunity to consider the potential *means* of election to the second chamber. We failed to do so.

31. We accept that our First Report will have left many Honourable and Right Honourable Members confused when they addressed those options on 4th February. In particular, through failing in our First Report to deal explicitly or at all with the issue of indirect election or election by secondary mandate, the Joint Committee denied those who supported such options any chance to vote for them. Moreover, some in this position – perhaps many – voted for an appointed second chamber instead of one which was elected, either in the mistaken belief that indirect election and/or election by secondary mandate was in fact a method of appointment; or because they feared that a vote for an elected chamber might yield a *directly* elected chamber with which they strongly disagreed. We accept that we should not have put Honourable and Right Honourable Members is so invidious a position.

The way forward

32. For all of the above reasons, the Joint Committee believes that Parliament should give it a fresh mandate to do the job it should

have done the first time – to report on options for the reformed composition of the House of Lords which have not thus far been considered, including the options of indirect election and election by secondary mandate.

PART THREE: THE OBJECTIONS IN PRINCIPLE TO APPOINTMENT, DIRECT ELECTION AND HYBRIDITY

The context for further consideration: the objections to past options

33. The context within which the Joint Committee must proceed to consider the options of indirect election and election by secondary mandate is necessarily provided by the objections in principle which were raised by Honourable and Right Honourable Members against the options which previously we reported to the House.

34. The Joint Committee accepts, therefore, that it must take proper cognisance of the votes of the House of Commons on 4th February when it conducts its future work. In particular, the Joint Committee acknowledges that the options of 100% direct election, 100% appointment, and the range of hybrid chambers in-between have all been rejected.

35. The Joint Committee believes that – in the light of those votes – it must investigate the detailed reasons why the House of Commons rejected all of the above options and consider whether, and if so how, those objections might best be accommodated. After all, it is those objections which lie behind the position we are in. Even if – as individuals – we do not agree with all of those objections, it is incumbent upon us at least to understand them. Otherwise we will never bridge the divisions of principle which separate us, so to achieve a broad consensus on reform.

1. The objections to direct election

36. Those Honourable and Right Honourable Members who object to a directly elected second chamber do so – principally – because they believe that a directly elected second chamber would fundamentally undermine our bicameral system of Parliament, one which only works if one House has primacy over the other.

37. In particular, they note that for centuries the Lords had primacy over the Commons because the landed aristocracy were perceived to be superior to the lower social orders. They note – further – that it was only with the advent of democracy that the Commons attained its primacy. They therefore conclude that democracy conferred upon the Commons a legitimacy with which the unelected Lords could never compete, and that this democratic legitimacy was the source of primacy. From this analytical premise they argue that history compels the view that if the second chamber was to be directly elected it would have legitimacy equal to that of the Commons and would one day assert itself against the Commons, challenging its primacy.

2. The objections to appointment

38. Those Honourable and Right Honourable Members who object to an appointed second chamber also believe that it is democracy which brings legitimacy. However, they argue that this cannot possibly justify a second chamber being composed by appointment for that would make the second chamber illegitimate by design – a constitutional settlement which is absurd. They assert, moreover, that an appointed second chamber will be illegitimate however expert its members and however they are appointed: if the power of appointment is placed in the hands of an independent Appointments Commission we will have patronage by the great and the good; if that power is placed in the hands of political parties we will have cronyism.

39. They argue – moreover – that there is no point in reforming the House of Lords unless it is to make it more democratic: it was because the hereditary peers were an affront to democracy that they were removed; and we now have to deal with the equally undemocratic life peers. They accept that democracy does not equal legitimacy but assert that it does confer it, that it affords two vital constitutional protections – government by consent and government by representatives. They conclude that in the democratic age it is simply inconceivable that we should now turn away from democracy and embrace patronage instead.

3. The objections to hybridity

40. Those Honourable and Right Honourable Members who object to a hybrid chamber – part-directly elected, part-appointed – do so because they consider that constitutional stability demands that all members have the same standing, that none is more legitimate than others.

41. They point to the fact that, at present, all members of the House of Lords owe their presence to patronage – their mandate is by appointment: not one peer has the legitimacy which democratic election confers. They therefore argue that introducing a directly elected element into the second chamber will create a chamber of conflicting mandates and that such a chamber would be fatally unstable.

Summary of objections

42. In summary, it has been argued that all three of the principal options are objectionable in principle – that direct election will threaten the supremacy of the House of Commons; that appointment will not be a democratic expression of the will of the people; and that a hybrid House will be a fudged compromise which is constitutionally unstable. Moreover, the votes cast in the House of Commons – whereby all of the options were rejected – indicate that a majority of that House attribute real weight to all of these objections.

PART FOUR: WIDENING THE DEBATE – INDIRECT ELECTION AND ELECTION BY SECONDARY MANDATE

Responding to the objections by widening the debate

43. The Joint Committee considers that in the light of these objections and their reflections in the votes cast on 4th February, we must now recast this entire debate. Our purpose must be to wrestle with the objections to the past options we have put forward and endeavour to devise an electoral model which meets them – one which is democratic, which will lead to a membership which

will make it both effective and legitimate, but which will ensure
that the second chamber neither duplicates the composition of
the Commons nor receives a mandate from the electorate which
allows it to challenge the Commons' primacy. This – indeed – is
the course of action we expressly anticipated in paragraph 3 of
our First Report:

*'Once both Houses have had the opportunity to debate and vote
on the options which we set out here, we shall ... need to consider
such differences as may exist between the expressed views of the two
Houses and the means by which, and the extent to which, they might
be brought closer together.'*

44. In order to take this bold agenda forward the Joint
Committee will – firstly – need to look to models of indirect
election to the second chamber and/or of election by secondary
mandate, models which – as we have already noted – are not even
canvassed in our First Report.

45. Moreover, in reporting to the Houses of Parliament on
the possible models of indirect election or election by secondary
mandate, we must continue to be guided by the five qualities
which the Joint Committee has always considered to be desirable
in a reformed second chamber:

- Legitimacy
- Representativeness
- No domination by any one party
- Independence
- Expertise

46. In addition, however, the Joint Committee must also bear in
mind the need to re-engage the electorate so that they not only
participate in our democracy more fully but begin once more to
trust it, own it, and even cherish it. In particular, at a time of falling
voter turnout, the Joint Committee believes that Lords reform is
the only issue presently before Parliament which has the ability
to re-engage the public in our democratic process. We must take
full advantage of the opportunity this affords us.

Models of indirect election and of election by secondary mandate

47. There are at least three models of indirect election and election by secondary mandate which the Joint Committee could consider: functional constituencies; indirect regional elections; and election by secondary mandate. We briefly describe those models below.

1. Functional constituencies

48. Under the functional constituency model, members would be elected to the second chamber by discrete representative groups (Local Authorities, TUC, CBI, small business, banks, doctors, teachers, lawyers, environmentalists, the disabled, ethnic minorities, faith groups, etc.), so ensuring democratically elected members in the second chamber with real expertise (and a greater likelihood of independence) covering the range of departmental responsibilities.

2. Indirect regional elections

49. Under the indirect regional election model, members would be elected by those already elected to Local Authorities and Regional Assemblies so that the second chamber would have democratic roots and be geographically representative, but with members who would not have the prime mandate of directly elected MPs.

3. Election by secondary mandate

50. Under the model of election to the second chamber by secondary mandate, MPs would continue to be elected by the first past the post system but each vote cast at the general election would carry with it a secondary mandate for the second chamber, adding additional weight to the votes cast at those elections. Members would then be elected to the second chamber according to regional lists and in proportion to the votes cast within each of the 12 regions and nations of the United Kingdom.

Preliminary thoughts on the models of indirect election

51. The first two of the above three options have already been criticised in some quarters, including in the debates on 4th February. In particular, it has been argued that the functional constituency model would narrow the electoral base to the vested interests so that we would create a Parliament of lobbyists. Likewise, the model of indirect regional elections has been criticised because the regional agenda is too undeveloped and because – again – it does not encourage participation on the part of the electorate.

52. Notwithstanding the evident strength of the objections to the first two of the options, we believe they should not be dismissed out of hand and that the Joint Committee should at least be invited to consider whether they merit more detailed analysis.

Preliminary thoughts on the model of election by secondary mandate

53. We also believe that the Joint Committee should consider the merits of the alternative option of election by secondary mandate. Indeed, our preliminary view is that this model passes successfully and comprehensively our guiding tests of legitimacy, representativeness, no domination by any one party, independence and expertise.

54. In particular:

Legitimacy – Since the second chamber would be elected by a genuine expression of the will of the people, it would be legitimate. However, its legitimacy would be one step removed from that conferred by the direct election of MPs so that the primacy of the Commons would be preserved.

Representativeness – Members elected by secondary mandate would be elected by regional lists and would therefore be geographically representative.

No domination by any one party – As the secondary mandate would be proportional, the Government of the day would not be able to command a majority in both Houses of Parliament.

Independence – Since the secondary mandate would be proportional, smaller parties would be able to secure election to the second chamber. In addition, and as we canvassed in our First Report, independence could further be secured by regulating such matters as the ability to stand for re-election either to the Commons or the Lords, length of tenure, and the capacity of members of the Lords to be made a Minister.

Expertise – Experts, often unwilling to stand for direct election, would be far more likely to stand if they could be elected from Regional Lists and pursuant to a secondary mandate. Depending upon the rules of the various political parties, they could be voted onto lists by party activists in local primaries.

55. Moreover, the model of election by secondary mandate carries with it the possibility of reinvigorating our democracy – by adding weight to the votes we already cast instead of imposing another tier of elections on an electorate already suffering from election fatigue. Currently, the only votes that count in the General Election are those that are cast for the winning candidate. Under the secondary mandate system all votes would count. That could be a critical advantage in times of rapidly declining electoral turnout and falling public confidence in the democratic process. In addition, it also addresses – and in terms – the critical issue: how to maintain the primacy of the Commons whilst ensuring the democratic legitimacy of the Lords.

56. We note – moreover – that we have received a letter expressly asking the Joint Committee to put this option before Parliament for debate – alongside other methods of indirect election – from a number of individuals and think tanks with a long-standing interest in constitutional reform: Billy Bragg; Karen Bartlett (Director, Charter 88); Matthew Taylor (Director, IPPR, in a personal capacity); Will Hutton, Chief Executive, The Work Foundation; Tom Bentley (Demos); Karen Chouhan (Director, 1990 Trust); Nicholas Boles (Director, Policy Exchange); Anthony Rowlands (Chief Executive, Centre for Reform); Martin McIvor (Director, Catalyst, in a personal capacity);

Ed Mayo (New Economics Foundation); Anthony Barnett (Open Democracy, in a personal capacity); and Dan Plesch.

Incremental radicalism

57. We note – finally – that although this solution would amount to a radical reform of the existing constitution, it is incremental in its radicalism. In particular, it requires no new elections to be held. Indeed, it would be possible to re-establish the House of Lords within a very short period of time according to this model since we already know the results from the last General Election and, therefore, the proportions of votes cast in favour of each of the political parties in each of the regions and nations of the United Kingdom.

PART FIVE: CONCLUSIONS

The opportunity that remains

58. For all of the above reasons the Joint Committee believes that – despite the inevitable cloud of pessimism cast by the votes on 4th February – it may yet be possible to agree a broad consensus on the best way forward. In particular, it is conceivable that we might meet the concerns of those who fear a challenge to the supremacy of this House by making sure that the second chamber does not have the mandate to make that challenge; meet the concerns of those opposed to patronage by ensuring that places in the second chamber derive from votes cast by the electorate; and meet the concerns of those opposed to a hybrid House by indirectly electing the entire membership of the second chamber or by electing them all by secondary mandate.

59. There remains before us an historic opportunity to enact a reform which will enable the second chamber to continue to play an important and complementary role to the Commons, with its future at last secure. Parliament can – if it has the will – rescue reform of the House of Lords from the long grass. Moreover, for so long as this is possible and options for reform remain which have not yet been considered and which might

command support, the Joint Committee must be ready to consider and report upon them.

60. Parliament – and especially the democratically elected Commons which is supreme – must now assert itself against the unworthy coalition of those who would not reform the House of Lords at all. History will not look kindly upon our efforts if we fail that test of our resolve. Rather, we will appear willing players in a pathetic Parliamentary farce. That is an outcome we must do everything in our power to avoid.

61. We therefore ask the Houses of Parliament to give us a renewed mandate, so that the reform of the House of Lords might finally be completed.

SUMMARY OF CONCLUSIONS AND RECOMMENDATIONS
PART ONE: HOW TO RESPOND TO THE VOTES OF 4TH FEBRUARY 2003

(i) The Joint Committee firmly believes that it does not have the capacity to wind itself up. The Committee was established by the Houses of Parliament and not by itself. Accordingly, it is not for us but for the Houses of Parliament to determine the Committee's fate.

(ii) There are two options for the future of the Joint Committee which Parliament could decide upon – winding the Joint Committee up or asking it to continue and complete its work.

(iii) For the following four reasons we believe that if Parliament were to accede to counsels of despair and dissolve the Joint Committee, that would amount to a lamentable failure of Parliamentary resolve. Indeed, it would mean that Parliament had either colluded with – or surrendered to – a divided executive and an obstructionist House of Lords to prevent the latter's reform, when its reform was the sole purpose for which Parliament actually established the Joint Committee.

(iv) The first reason for Parliament asking the Joint Committee to continue its work is that to do otherwise would reinforce the cynicism that the public already feels in our Parliamentary processes. Indeed, if Parliament were to vote to wind the Joint Committee up, it would undermine the credibility of Parliament itself. That would be a very grave mistake to make.

(v) The second reason for Parliament asking the Joint Committee to continue its work is that with the executive split, with the major political parties deeply divided, and with the governing party thereby in danger of not being able to deliver on a firm manifesto commitment, there is an absence of political leadership on the issue of the reform of the House of Lords. This is a void that only the Joint Committee is positioned to fill. We believe that if the Joint Committee were to fail to fill that void it would be abdicating the responsibilities vested in it by Parliament.

(vi) The third reason for Parliament asking the Joint Committee to continue its work is that the Joint Committee believes that to surrender our responsibilities now would leave the nations and regions of the United Kingdom with a constitutional status quo which is not remotely acceptable – a hybrid second chamber with the majority there only through the exercise of patronage and the minority there only by reason of the accident of their birth. The Joint Committee does not believe that it should condemn the constitution of the United Kingdom to such a settlement.

(vii) The fourth reason for Parliament asking the Joint Committee to continue its work is that despite the breadth of our remit 'to report on options for composition of the House of Lords', we have conspicuously failed to report to either House in respect of any option of indirect election or of election by secondary mandate.

(viii) For all of these reasons, the Joint Committee invites the Houses of Parliament not to wind the Joint Committee up but to give it instead a renewed mandate to continue to consider options for the reform of the House of Lords which might reconcile the differences of opinion which the recent votes in the House of Commons dramatically exposed.

PART TWO: THE PREFERRED NATURE
OF THE RENEWED MANDATE

(ix) The Joint Committee appreciates, however, that the votes on 4 February 2003 in the House of Commons indicate the scale of the task that now confronts it.

(x) Indeed, the scale of the apparent disagreement inevitably tempts us to ask the Houses of Parliament to invite the Joint Committee to consider first those areas in which the recent debates indicate the disagreements to be less serious – removing the remaining hereditary peers, improving the current system of appointment, considering the size of the second chamber, the age at which Lords might retire, and whether they should be remunerated.

(xi) However, the Joint Committee believes that – for the following three reasons – it would be a grave mistake for the Joint Committee to continue to meet only to tinker with minimalist measures, not properly to debate radical reform.

(xii) The first reason is that any Bill which simply addressed issues of peripheral concern would run the risk of legitimising the illegitimate, leading to the greater longevity of the Lords as it is currently and unacceptably composed. Whilst perfection should never be the enemy of the good, it must always be the enemy of the bad.

(xiii) The second reason is that there would be real difficulties in getting a minimalist Bill through either House of Parliament. The Commons would likely reject the reforms as insufficient and the Lords reject any Bill that expelled the remaining hereditary peers. Moreover, even if such a Bill could be enacted a real question has to be asked as to whether it would be worth the Parliamentary time taken to pass it.

(xiv) The third, and perhaps most important, reason is that minor tinkering with the more obvious failings of the status quo would not remotely address our wholesale failure to fulfil our original mandate properly to consider and report upon the options for potential reform of the House of Lords – not the least of which are the models of indirect election or election by secondary mandate.

(xv) For all of the above reasons, the Joint Committee believes that Parliament should give it a fresh mandate to do the job it should have done first time – to report on options for the reformed composition of the House of Lords which have not thus far been considered, including the options of indirect election and election by secondary mandate which we have thus far ignored.

PART THREE: THE OBJECTIONS IN PRINCIPLE TO APPOINTMENT, DIRECT ELECTION AND HYBRIDITY

(xvi) The context within which the Joint Committee must proceed to consider the options of indirect election and election by secondary mandate is necessarily provided by the objections in principle which were raised by Honourable and Right Honourable Members against the options which previously we reported to the House.

(xvii) In summary, it has been argued that all three of the principal options are objectionable in principle – that direct election will threaten the supremacy of the House of Commons; that appointment will not be a democratic expression of the will of the people; and that a hybrid House will be a fudged compromise which is constitutionally unstable.

PART FOUR: WIDENING THE DEBATE – INDIRECT ELECTION AND ELECTION BY SECONDARY MANDATE

(xviii) The Joint Committee considers that in the light of these objections and their reflections in the votes cast on 4th

February, we must now recast this entire debate. Our purpose must be to wrestle with the objections to the past options we have put forward and endeavour to devise an electoral model which meets them – one which is democratic, which will lead to a membership which will make it both effective and legitimate, but which will ensure that the second chamber neither duplicates the composition of the Commons nor receives a mandate from the electorate which allows it to challenge the Commons' primacy.

(xix) In order to take this bold agenda forward the Joint Committee will – firstly – need to look to models of indirect election to the second chamber and/or of election by secondary mandate, models which – as we have already noted – are not even canvassed in our First Report.

(xx) Moreover, in reporting to the Houses of Parliament on the possible models of indirect election or election by secondary mandate, we must continue to be guided by the five qualities which the Joint Committee has always considered to be desirable in a reformed second chamber:

- Legitimacy
- Representativeness
- No domination by any one party
- Independence
- Expertise

(xxi) There are at least three models of indirect election and election by secondary mandate which the Joint Committee could consider: functional constituencies; indirect regional elections; and election by secondary mandate.

(xxii) The first two of the above three options have already been criticised in some quarters, including in the debates on 4th February.

(xxiii) Notwithstanding the evident strength of the objections to the first two of the options, we believe they should not be dismissed out of hand and that the Joint Committee should at least be invited to consider whether they merit more detailed analysis.

(xxiv) We also believe that the Joint Committee should consider the merits of the alternative option of election by secondary mandate. Indeed, our preliminary view is that this model successfully and comprehensively passes our guiding tests of legitimacy, representativeness, no domination by any one party, independence and expertise.

(xxv) Moreover, the model of election by secondary mandate carries with it the possibility of reinvigorating our democracy – by adding weight to the votes we already cast instead of imposing another tier of elections on an electorate already suffering from election fatigue. In addition, it also addresses – and in terms – the critical issue: how to maintain the primacy of the Commons whilst ensuring the democratic legitimacy of the Lords.

(xxvi) We note – moreover – that we have received a letter expressly asking the Joint Committee to put this option before Parliament for debate – alongside other methods of indirect election – from a number of individuals and think tanks with a long-standing interest in constitutional reform.

(xxvii) We note – finally – that although this solution would amount to a radical reform of the existing constitution, it is incremental in its radicalism. In particular, it requires no new elections to be held. Indeed, it would be possible to re-establish the House of Lords within a very short period of time according to this model since we already know the results from the last General Election and, therefore, the proportions of votes cast in favour of each of the political parties in each of the regions and nations of the United Kingdom.

PART FIVE: CONCLUSIONS

(xxviii) For all of the above reasons the Joint Committee believes that – despite the inevitable cloud of pessimism cast by the votes on 4th February – it may yet be possible to agree a broad consensus on the best way forward.

(xxix) There remains before us an historic opportunity to enact a reform which will enable the second chamber to continue to play an important and complementary role to the Commons, with its future at last secure. Parliament can – if it has the will – rescue reform of the House of Lords from the long grass. Moreover, for so long as this is possible and options for reform remain which have not yet been considered and which might command support, the Joint Committee must be ready to consider and report upon them.

(xxx) Parliament – and especially the democratically elected Commons which is supreme – must now assert itself against the unworthy coalition of those who would not reform the House of Lords at all. History will not look kindly upon our efforts if we fail that test of our resolve. Rather, we will appear willing players in a pathetic Parliamentary farce. That is an outcome we must do everything in our power to avoid.

(xxxi) We therefore ask the Houses of Parliament to give us a renewed mandate, so that the reform of the House of Lords might finally be completed.

APPENDIX 1

Letter sent to members of the Joint Committee by Billy Bragg and others

We, the undersigned, call upon the Joint Committee on House of Lords Reform to give further consideration to methods of composition, specifically indirect election by secondary mandate. This model, recommended by the Royal Commission of the House of Lords (Recommendation 76, paragraph 12.26, 12.27, 12.28), involves counting all of the votes cast for every candidate in the first past the post contest for seats in the Commons and accumulating them at regional level. Parties would secure the number of seats in the second chamber in proportion to their share of the vote, drawing names from a previously published regional list. In its first report dated 11 December 2002, the joint committee stated the five qualities it considered to be desirable in the makeup of a reformed second chamber:

- legitimacy
- representativeness
- no domination by any one party
- independence
- expertise

We believe that the secondary mandate deserves to be considered because:

> As a genuine expression of the will of the people, it is legitimate, yet its legitimacy is one step removed from that conferred by the direct election of MPs and so the primacy of the Commons is preserved.
>
> Members elected by secondary mandate will be representative of the regions and nations of the UK.
>
> As the secondary mandate is proportional, the government of the day will not be able to command a majority in both chambers.
>
> Fixed single terms and an absence of ministers in the second chamber will encourage independence.

Experts, often unwilling to stand for election, can be voted onto lists by party activists in local primaries. At a time of falling voter turnout, we believe that Lords reform is the only issue presently before parliament which has the ability to engage the public in our democratic process. Significantly, the secondary mandate actively encourages participation in the General Election and it is for this reason that we call upon the joint committee to put this option before parliament for debate, alongside other methods of indirect election.

Signatories:

Billy Bragg
Karen Bartlett, Director, Charter 88

Matthew Taylor, Director, IPPR (personal capacity)
Will Hutton, Chief Executive, The Work Foundation
Tom Bentley, Demos
Karen Chouhan, Director, 1990 Trust
Nicholas Boles, Director, Policy Exchange
Anthony Rowlands, Chief Executive, Centre for Reform
Martin McIvor, Director, Catalyst (personal capacity)
Ed Mayo, New Economics Foundation
Anthony Barnett, Open Democracy (personal capacity)
Dan Plesch

Amends to the Draft

18 March 2003

It was moved by the Chairman that the Chairman's draft Report be read a second time, paragraph by paragraph.

It was moved by Mr Paul Stinchcombe, as an amendment to the motion, to leave out the words 'Chairman's draft Report' and insert the words 'draft Report prepared by Mr Paul Stinchcombe'.

Which being objected to, the question was put thereupon, and the Committee divided:

Contents 1:
Mr Paul Stinchcombe

Not-Contents 19:
Janet Anderson
Mr James Arbuthnot
Lord Archer of Sandwell
Viscount Bledisloe
Lord Brooke of Alverthorpe
Lord Carter
Mr Kenneth Clarke
Dr Jack Cunningham
Baroness Gibson of Market Rasen

Lord Goodhart
Mr William Hague
Lord Howe of Aberavon
Mr Stephen McCabe
Lord Oakeshott of Seagrove Bay
Baroness O'Cathain
Mr Terry Rooney
The Earl of Selborne
Mr Clive Soley
Mr Paul Tyler

The amendment was disagreed to.

Then the main Question was put and agreed to.

Ordered, That the draft Report be read a second time, paragraph by paragraph.

Paragraph 1 was read as follows:

> '1. In December 2002 we said in our First Report that although the re-balancing of parliamentary institutions is something that can only evolve over time, we believed that there was an historic opportunity to enact reform of the House of Lords based on the need for a second Chamber which would continue to play an important and complementary role to the Commons. Our opinion has not changed, although we recognise that the lack of decision on the matter of composition in the House of Commons needs to be resolved. The Committee was unanimous that the status quo is undesirable. Things should not be left as they are; in this Report we emphasise the importance of reasserting the case for reform and regaining the momentum which was recognised by the Commons Public Administration Select Committee in its Report but we also seek a view from the Government about the way forward.'

It was moved by Lord Howe of Aberavon to leave out paragraph 1 and insert:

'*Introduction*

1. In December 2002 we said in our First Report that although the re-balancing of parliamentary institutions is something that can only evolve over time, we believed that there was an historic opportunity to enact reform of the House of Lords based on the need for a second Chamber which would continue to play an important and complementary role to the Commons. However, for the present at least, the scale and nature of that opportunity has now changed.

1A. For not only has there been predictable disagreement between the two Houses. There has also been a lack of decision on the matter of composition in the House of Commons – and indeed, at a late stage, the absence of a clear lead from the Government itself. The effect of these decisions (or lack of them) has been to reduce the pressure for change in any direction. Even if the engines have not actually fallen off the train, their thrust has been diminished.

1B. Even so, this Committee remains unanimous in its view that simply to maintain the status quo is undesirable. The differences between us as to the long-term future structure of the second Chamber inevitably reflect those in Parliament and Government alike. Some of us may have been tempted to believe that the best way to promote the case for radical change is to leave things as they are – and thus exposed to continuing criticism. Others could have been tempted, in the opposite direction, to regard 'no change' as an acceptable prescription for an enduring quiet life. Collectively, however, we do not accept either of these views.

1C. Whatever may or may not be decided later – perhaps some considerable time ahead, perhaps not – about the long-term composition of the second Chamber, there are possible changes affecting the effectiveness, representative quality and credibility of the House that can and should be considered and decided now. Things should not simply be left as they are. So in this Report we emphasise the importance of reasserting the case for reform and for regaining at least some part of the momentum which was recognised by the Commons Public Administration Select Committee in its Report. And we seek from Government a clear response to this Report.'

Which being objected to, the question was put thereupon, and the Committee divided:

Contents 14
Janet Anderson
Lord Archer of Sandwell
Viscount Bledisloe
Lord Brooke of Alverthorpe
Lord Carter
Dr Jack Cunningham
Lord Forsyth of Drumlean
Baroness Gibson of Market Rasen
Lord Howe of Aberavon
Mr Stephen McCabe
Baroness O'Cathain
Mr Terry Rooney
Mr Clive Soley
Mr Paul Stinchcombe

Not-Contents 8
Mr James Arbuthnot
Mr Chris Bryant
Mr Kenneth Clarke
Lord Goodhart
Mr William Hague
Lord Oakeshott of Seagrove Bay
The Earl of Selborne
Mr Paul Tyler

The amendment was agreed to.
    Paragraph 1C (*now 4*) was amended.

Paragraphs 2 to 8 (*now 5 to 11*) were read and agreed to.

Paragraph 9 (*now 12*) was read.

It was moved by Mr Paul Tyler to leave out paragraph 9 and insert:

> 'We note that a total of 332 MPs (more than half the House of Commons) voted for a directly elected component of some sort. 299 voted for one or other of the so-called 'hybrid' options (i.e. a mixed composition of elected and appointed membership). In any case, we consider that it would be a direct negation of the will of the predominant House now to develop proposals to give effect to a fully appointed Second Chamber.'

Which being objected to, the question was put thereupon, and the Committee divided:

Contents 6

Mr James Arbuthnot
Mr Kenneth Clarke
Lord Goodhart
Mr William Hague
Lord Oakeshott of Seagrove Bay
Mr Paul Tyler

Not-Contents 15

Janet Anderson
Lord Archer of Sandwell
Viscount Bledisloe
Lord Brooke of Alverthorpe
Mr Chris Bryant
Lord Carter
Lord Forsyth of Drumlean
Baroness Gibson of Market Rasen
Lord Howe of Aberavon
Mr Stephen McCabe
Baroness O'Cathain

Mr Terry Rooney
The Earl of Selborne
Mr Clive Soley
Mr Paul Stinchcombe

The amendment was disagreed to.

Paragraph 9 was agreed to with amendments.

Paragraph 10 (*now 13*) was read and amended.

It was moved by Mr Chris Bryant, at the end of paragraph 10, to insert 'and that support for a fully elected Second Chamber in the House of Lords was also higher than expected, at 106 or one in four of voting members'. Which being objected to, the question was put thereupon, and the Committee divided:

Contents 9
Mr James Arbuthnot
Mr Chris Bryant
Mr Kenneth Clarke
Lord Forsyth of Drumlean
Lord Goodhart
Mr William Hague
Lord Oakeshott of Seagrove Bay
The Earl of Selborne
Mr Paul Tyler

Not-Contents 12
Janet Anderson
Lord Archer of Sandwell
Viscount Bledisloe
Lord Brooke of Alverthorpe
Lord Carter
Baroness Gibson of Market Rasen
Lord Howe of Aberavon
Mr Stephen McCabe
Baroness O'Cathain
Mr Terry Rooney
Mr Clive Soley
Mr Paul Stinchcombe

The amendment was disagreed to.

Paragraph 10 was agreed to as amended.

Paragraph 11 (*now 14*) was read.

It was moved by Viscount Bledisloe to leave out the first sentence ('Since we are arguing in this Report for the continuation of the reform process, we consider it necessary to spell out the basis on which this can be taken forward.') and insert 'We consider that, if it is the wish of the Houses, it would be possible for the Committee to contribute to the progress of the reform process by investigating and reporting on certain specific issues, which will have to be resolved as part of an overall reform. This should facilitate future decisions on these matters and it would be possible, if thought desirable, to bring into effect some specific changes on the road to overall reform.'

Which being objected to, the question was put thereupon, and the Committee divided:

Contents 13
Janet Anderson
Lord Archer of Sandwell
Viscount Bledisloe
Lord Brooke of Alverthorpe
Lord Carter
Lord Forsyth of Drumlean
Baroness Gibson of Market Rasen
Lord Howe of Aberavon
Mr Stephen McCabe
Baroness O'Cathain
Mr Terry Rooney
Mr Clive Soley
Mr Paul Stinchcombe

Not-Contents 7
Mr James Arbuthnot
Mr Kenneth Clarke
Lord Goodhart
Mr William Hague

Lord Oakeshott of Seagrove Bay
The Earl of Selborne
Mr Paul Tyler

The amendment was agreed to.
    Paragraph 11 was further amended and agreed to.
    Paragraph 12 (*now 15*) was read and amended.
    It was moved by Mr Chris Bryant, at the end of paragraph 12, to insert 'We recognise that more work may need to be done on how those conventions might need to be codified in, for instance, a new Parliament Act.' Which being objected to, the question was put thereupon, and the Committee divided:

Contents 6
Mr Chris Bryant
Mr Kenneth Clarke
Lord Goodhart
Lord Oakeshott of Seagrove Bay
Mr Paul Stinchcombe
Mr Paul Tyler

Not-Contents 15
Janet Anderson
Mr James Arbuthnot
Lord Archer of Sandwell
Viscount Bledisloe
Lord Brooke of Alverthorpe
Lord Carter
Lord Forsyth of Drumlean
Baroness Gibson of Market Rasen
Mr William Hague
Lord Howe of Aberavon
Mr Stephen McCabe
Baroness O'Cathain
Mr Terry Rooney
The Earl of Selborne
Mr Clive Soley

The amendment was disagreed to.

Paragraph 12 was agreed to as amended.

Paragraphs 13 to 21 (*now 16 to 24*) were read and agreed to with amendments.

Paragraph 22 (*now 25*) was read and amended.

It was moved by Mr Paul Tyler to leave out all after the first sentence ('Even the Member moving the amendment to support the principle of unicameralism, Mr George Howarth, acknowledged that some of the deficiencies he detected in the House of Commons arose from its inability to hold the executive to proper account or to "scrutinise legislation well enough" because of the very lack of qualities we are saying are essential in a reformed House of Lords. In the Lords debate the link was made by Lord Winston between the expertise that could be brought to their scrutinising tasks and Members' outside experience, in his own case, of medicine. The matter of expertise by independent Members is also addressed by the five qualities we have identified. We read these suggestions and others made in the debates as bolstering us in a view that reform of the Lords must be undertaken to improve overall parliamentary scrutiny of the executive.').

Which being objected to, the question was put thereupon, and the Committee divided:

Contents 12
Mr James Arbuthnot
Viscount Bledisloe
Mr Chris Bryant
Mr Kenneth Clarke
Lord Forsyth of Drumlean
Lord Goodhart
Mr William Hague
Lord Oakeshott of Seagrove Bay
Baroness O'Cathain
Mr Paul Stinchcombe
Mr Paul Tyler
Lord Weatherill

Not-Contents 10
Janet Anderson
Lord Archer of Sandwell
Lord Brooke of Alverthorpe
Lord Carter
Baroness Gibson of Market Rasen
Lord Howe of Aberavon
Mr Stephen McCabe
Mr Terry Rooney
The Earl of Selborne
Mr Clive Soley

The amendment was agreed to.

Paragraph 22 as amended was agreed to.

Paragraph 23 (*now 26*) was read and amended.

It was moved by Lord Goodhart, at the end of paragraph 23 to insert 'However, the absence of any consensus on the future composition of a reformed House of Lords makes it impracticable for us to make further progress at this time on these issues because of the extent to which they are inextricably linked to the composition of the House. We would need a fresh mandate before we could proceed further on resolving these issues.'

Which being objected to, the question was put thereupon, and the Committee divided:

Contents 7
Mr James Arbuthnot
Mr Kenneth Clarke
Lord Goodhart
Mr William Hague
Lord Oakeshott of Seagrove Bay
The Earl of Selborne
Mr Paul Tyler

Not-Contents 16
Janet Anderson
Lord Archer of Sandwell

Viscount Bledisloe
Lord Brooke of Alverthorpe
Mr Chris Bryant
Lord Carter
Lord Forsyth of Drumlean
Baroness Gibson of Market Rasen
Lord Howe of Aberavon
Mr Stephen McCabe
Baroness O'Cathain
Joyce Quin
Mr Terry Rooney
Mr Clive Soley
Mr Paul Stinchcombe
Lord Weatherill

The amendment was disagreed to.

Paragraph 23 was further amended and agreed to.

Paragraph 24 (*now 27*) was read.

It was moved by Viscount Bledisloe to leave out 'There was a broad opinion that a House of' and insert 'As was made plain in the debates in both Houses, any conclusion on the proper size of a reformed House is directly connected with the decision on its composition. There is general agreement that for a wholly or largely elected House'.

Which being objected to, the question was put thereupon, and the Committee divided:

Contents 3
Mr James Arbuthnot
Viscount Bledisloe
Mr Paul Tyler

Not-Contents 19
Janet Anderson
Lord Archer of Sandwell
Lord Brooke of Alverthorpe

Mr Chris Bryant
Lord Carter
Mr Kenneth Clarke
Lord Forsyth of Drumlean
Baroness Gibson of Market Rasen
Lord Goodhart
Mr William Hague
Lord Howe of Aberavon
Mr Stephen McCabe
Baroness O'Cathain
Joyce Quin
Mr Terry Rooney
The Earl of Selborne
Mr Clive Soley
Mr Paul Stinchcombe
Lord Weatherill

The amendment was disagreed to.

Paragraph 24 was amended and agreed to.

Paragraph 25 (*now 28*) was read.

It was moved by Lord Goodhart to leave out the last sentence ('This is another matter to which the Committee can return in its further deliberations.').

Which being objected to, the question was put thereupon, and the Committee divided:

Contents 6
Mr James Arbuthnot
Mr Kenneth Clarke
Lord Goodhart
Mr William Hague
The Earl of Selborne
Mr Paul Tyler

Not-Contents 16
Janet Anderson
Lord Archer of Sandwell

Viscount Bledisloe
Lord Brooke of Alverthorpe
Mr Chris Bryant
Lord Carter
Lord Forsyth of Drumlean
Baroness Gibson of Market Rasen
Lord Howe of Aberavon
Mr Stephen McCabe
Baroness O'Cathain
Joyce Quin
Mr Terry Rooney
Mr Clive Soley
Mr Paul Stinchcombe
Lord Weatherill

The amendment was disagreed to.

Paragraph 25 was agreed to.

Paragraph 26 (*now 29*) was read and amended.

It was moved by Lord Goodhart to leave out the last two sentences ('We agree with them that the only way of achieving this is to put the Appointments Commission on a statutory basis. But much work needs to be done on exactly what is needed to produce a widely respected and viable method of appointment.'') and insert 'But these matters also could only be considered once it has been decided whether there should be appointed members and, if so, how many of them.'

Which being objected to, the question was put thereupon, and the Committee divided:

Contents 9
Mr James Arbuthnot
Mr Chris Bryant
Mr Kenneth Clarkc
Lord Goodhart
Mr William Hague
Joyce Quin
The Earl of Selborne

Mr Paul Stinchcombe
Mr Paul Tyler

Not-Contents 13
Janet Anderson
Lord Archer of Sandwell
Viscount Bledisloe
Lord Brooke of Alverthorpe
Lord Carter
Lord Forsyth of Drumlean
Baroness Gibson of Market Rasen
Lord Howe of Aberavon
Mr Stephen McCabe
Baroness O'Cathain
Mr Terry Rooney
Mr Clive Soley
Lord Weatherill

The amendment was disagreed to.

Paragraph 26 was further amended.

It was moved by Mr Chris Bryant, at the end of paragraph 26, to insert 'and we note that the least popular option in the House of Commons, apart from unicameralism, was for a wholly appointed Second Chamber'.

Which being objected to, the question was put thereupon, and the Committee divided:

Contents 9
Mr James Arbuthnot
Mr Chris Bryant
Mr Kenneth Clarke
Lord Goodhart
Mr William Hague
Joyce Quin
Mr Paul Stinchcombe
Mr Paul Tyler
Lord Weatherill

Not-Contents 13
Janet Anderson
Lord Archer of Sandwell
Viscount Bledisloe
Lord Brooke of Alverthorpe
Lord Carter
Lord Forsyth of Drumlean
Baroness Gibson of Market Rasen
Lord Howe of Aberavon
Mr Stephen McCabe
Baroness O'Cathain
Mr Terry Rooney
The Earl of Selborne
Mr Clive Soley

The amendment was disagreed to.

    Paragraph 26 was agreed to as amended.

    It was moved by Lord Howe of Aberavon, after paragraph 26, to insert a new paragraph: '26A. Meantime, and in the possible absence of primary legislation, this is not an issue that can be neglected for long. Two years have passed since the appointment of the last group of new life peers. There is, therefore, a growing need to top up the stock of expertise and of younger members. In order to handle this problem, consideration should, therefore, be given to the appointment of a new and manifestly independent Appointments Commission (composed as recommended by the Royal Commission), and endorsed – as an interim alternative to primary legislation – by an Order in Council, approved by both Houses.'

    Which being objected to, the question was put thereupon, and the Committee divided:

Contents 14
Janet Anderson
Lord Archer of Sandwell

Viscount Bledisloe
Lord Brooke of Alverthorpe
Lord Carter
Lord Forsyth of Drumlean
Baroness Gibson of Market Rasen
Lord Howe of Aberavon
Mr Stephen McCabe
Baroness O'Cathain
Mr Terry Rooney
The Earl of Selborne
Mr Clive Soley
Lord Weatherill

Not-Contents 8
Mr James Arbuthnot
Mr Chris Bryant
Mr Kenneth Clarke
Lord Goodhart
Mr William Hague
Joyce Quin
Mr Paul Stinchcombe
Mr Paul Tyler

The amendment was agreed to.

Paragraphs 27 to 30 (*now 31 to 34*) were read and agreed to with amendments.

Paragraph 31 (*now 35*) was read and amended.

It was moved by Mr Paul Tyler to leave out the last sentence and insert 'The Leader of the House made it clear during the Commons debate that if the options for an elected component were defeated it would follow that the method of election – direct, indirect or secondary mandate – inevitably would be irrelevant. We do not feel that we are entitled to examine these further options without a clear statement from both Houses that, despite the votes on 4 February, we are instructed to do so.'

Which being objected to, the question was put thereupon, and the Committee divided:

Contents 7
Mr James Arbuthnot
Mr Kenneth Clarke
Lord Goodhart
Mr William Hague
Joyce Quin
The Earl of Selborne
Mr Paul Tyler

Not-Contents 15
Janet Anderson
Lord Archer of Sandwell
Viscount Bledisloe
Lord Brooke of Alverthorpe
Mr Chris Bryant
Lord Carter
Lord Forsyth of Drumlean
Baroness Gibson of Market Rasen
Lord Howe of Aberavon
Mr Stephen McCabe
Baroness O'Cathain
Mr Terry Rooney
Mr Clive Soley
Mr Paul Stinchcombe
Lord Weatherill

The amendment was disagreed to.

Paragraph 31 was agreed to as amended.

Paragraph 32 (*now 36*) was read and agreed to with an amendment.

It was moved by Mr Clive Soley, after paragraph 32, to insert a new paragraph:

> '32A. The Committee recognises the duty on the Government to respond to this Report, but also takes the view that such fundamental reforms of our Parliamentary structure should be led by Parliament. It is for Parliament, and not

Government, to decide the final shape and form of our two Houses. We therefore recommend that this Committee continues to examine proposals for the reform of the second chamber, and from time to time reports with recommendations to each House.'

Which being objected to, the question was put thereupon, and the Committee divided:

Contents 8
Janet Anderson
Lord Archer of Sandwell
Lord Brooke of Alverthorpe
Lord Carter
Baroness Gibson of Market Rasen
Mr Stephen McCabe
Mr Clive Soley
Mr Paul Stinchcombe

Not-Contents 13
Mr James Arbuthnot
Viscount Bledisloe
Mr Chris Bryant
Mr Kenneth Clarke
Lord Forsyth of Drumlean
Lord Goodhart
Mr William Hague
Lord Howe of Aberavon
Baroness O'Cathain
Joyce Quin
The Earl of Selborne
Mr Paul Tyler
Lord Weatherill

The amendment was disagreed to.

Paragraph 33 (*now 37*) was read.

It was moved by Mr Paul Tyler to leave out all except the last sentence.

Which being objected to, the question was put thereupon, and the Committee divided:

Contents 9
Mr James Arbuthnot
Mr Chris Bryant
Mr Kenneth Clarke
Lord Forsyth of Drumlean
Lord Goodhart
Mr William Hague
Joyce Quin
The Earl of Selborne
Mr Paul Tyler

Not-Contents 12
Janet Anderson
Lord Archer of Sandwell
Viscount Bledisloe
Lord Brooke of Alverthorpe
Lord Carter
Baroness Gibson of Market Rasen
Lord Howe of Aberavon
Mr Stephen McCabe
Baroness O'Cathain
Mr Clive Soley
Mr Paul Stinchcombe
Lord Weatherill

The amendment was disagreed to.
Paragraph 33 was amended.
It was moved by Lord Carter to insert at the end of paragraph 33 'and then acceptance by both Houses that our work should continue on the lines we have set out.'
Which being objected to, the question was put thereupon, and the Committee divided:

Contents 14
Janet Anderson
Lord Archer of Sandwell
Viscount Bledisloe
Lord Brooke of Alverthorpe
Lord Carter
Lord Forsyth of Drumlean
Baroness Gibson of Market Rasen
Lord Howe of Aberavon
Mr Stephen McCabe
Baroness O'Cathain
Mr Terry Rooney
Mr Clive Soley
Mr Paul Stinchcombe
Lord Weatherill

Not-Contents 8
Mr James Arbuthnot
Mr Kenneth Clarke
Lord Goodhart
Mr William Hague
Lord Oakeshott of Seagrove Bay
Joyce Quin
The Earl of Selborne
Mr Paul Tyler

The amendment was agreed to.

Paragraph 33 as amended was agreed to.

Resolved, That the Report as amended be the Second Report of the Joint Committee to each House.

Ordered, That the Chairman do make the Report to the House of Commons and that the Lord Howe of Aberavon make the Report to the House of Lords.

Ordered, That such Reports be laid upon the Table of each House.

Ordered, That the Joint Committee be adjourned to a date and time to be fixed by the Chairman.

The Government Response

The government responded to the Second Report of the Joint Committee later in July 2003. In a letter dated 16 July 2003 the secretary of state for constitutional affairs and Lord Chancellor, Lord Falconer of Thoroton wrote to the chairman of the Joint Committee, Jack Cunningham that the government had found the report 'very helpful and constructive', but since the Joint Committee had demonstrated that there was 'no consensus about the best composition for the second chamber', the government would, 'for the time being', concentrate on 'making the House of Lords work as effectively as possible in fulfilment of its role'.

The full government response read as follows:[11]

JOINT COMMITTEE ON HOUSE OF LORDS REFORM:
SECOND REPORT
GOVERNMENT RESPONSE

Introduction

1. The Government is grateful for the work which the Joint Committee has undertaken in considering the issues raised by further reform of the House of Lords, and which is reflected in both this Report and their First Report on December 2002 (*HL Paper 17; HC 171*). This is the Government's response to the specific issues raised by the Joint Committee.

    2. The two Reports are the product of a careful analysis of the many and fundamental issues which are raised by the question of the reform of the UK's second chamber. They provide a useful synthesis of the arguments to date, and identify a number of areas where there is wide agreement on the objectives of reform, for example over the role and functions of the House of Lords. They

11   See *Joint Committee on House of Lords Reform: Government Reply to the Committee's Second Report*. Ordered by The House of Lords to be printed 16 July 2003. HL Paper 155. Ordered by The House of Commons to be printed 16 July 2003. HC 1027.

provide a fitting summary of the debate which has taken place since the establishment in January 1999 of the Royal Commission chaired by Lord Wakeham.

3. Consistently with the Joint Committee's original remit, its First Report proposed a number of different possible compositions for the House of Lords, with varying numbers of elected members. The Government had hoped, in seeking the establishment of the Joint Committee, that consideration of these options by both Houses of Parliament would give an indication of a way forward that would be acceptable to both Houses. The options were debated in the House of Commons on 21 January 2003 and in the House of Lords on 21 and 22 January. These debates were followed on 4 February by votes in each House.

4. Those votes resulted in a clear decision in the House of Lords in favour of a wholly appointed House. There was, however, no such clear decision from the House of Commons, which voted against every one of the Joint Committee's proposed configurations. These votes, as the Joint Committee has recognised in this Second Report, have made it difficult for it to continue with the second part of its original remit, to work up a detailed proposed blue-print for reform. That failure is no reflection on the quality of the work the Joint Committee has done up to now.

5. The Government agrees with the Joint Committee's view that the Parliamentary votes have shown that there is no consensus about introducing any elected element in the House of Lords.

6. The Joint Committee states in paragraph 3 of its Report that 'simply to maintain the status quo' is undesirable. The Government agrees with that view. If the present configuration of the House is to become a medium-term rather than a short-term settlement, then some changes will be needed. The Joint Committee has itself noted a number of areas where there might usefully be further work around the re-configuration of a wholly appointed House.

Government proposals

7. The Government strongly welcomes the Committee's views on the role and powers of the House of Lords. In particular, the Government agrees with the Joint Committee that there should be no significant change in the powers and functions of the House. The House of Commons must remain pre-eminent. The Government shares the Joint Committee's concern to ensure proper co-ordination of the legislative loads between the two Houses. It supports the Joint Committee's view that a consensus has now been established around the proper role, functions and powers of the House of Lords, and that all proposals for further reform must respect that consensus.

8. The Government also endorses the Joint Committee's analysis, in paragraph 23 of its Report, of the five qualities which need to be applied to the composition of a House which can perform the functions assigned to it. Those five qualities of legitimacy; representativeness; no domination by one party; independence; and expertise must remain the touchstone against which all reforms, whether major or minor, are measured.

9. The Government has already announced a further major reform of the House of Lords, with its decision to establish a separate Supreme Court. That will lead to the removal of the Law Lords. The Joint Committee report calls (paragraph 20) for full public discussion of this issue. The Government published on 14 July a consultation paper designed to facilitate precisely this debate with a request for comments by 7 November.

10. In addition, the Government has invited the House to consider establishing a Speakership independent of the executive. The House has appointed a Select Committee to consider this matter.

11. The key issue in establishing the present House of Lords in a stable state for the medium term is the appointments process for new members. The Joint Committee discusses this issue in paragraphs 29–30 of its report. The Government agrees that the

appointments process must display 'independence and integrity' and must be 'respected and viable' and that the Government should examine the present arrangements with a view to seeing where they might be strengthened. The Government therefore proposes to consider this issue further over the course of the summer, and will consult in the autumn on proposals for a revised Appointments Commission.

12. This consultation on the role of the Appointments Commission will give the opportunity for looking at a number of the other issues highlighted by the Joint Committee. Foremost among these are the optimum and maximum size of the House (paragraph 27 of the Committee's Report); how to ensure that the House is as representative as possible on a broad range of measures, including ethnicity, gender, and making sure the nations and the regions are properly represented (paragraph 17 of the Report); and how to widen the basis for religious representation (paragraph 31).

13. The Joint Committee highlights the position of the remaining hereditary peers. It remains the Government's policy, as set out in its White Paper in November 2001, that the remaining hereditary peers should be removed from the House.

Conclusion

14. The Government is grateful to the Joint Committee for the work that they have done, and their efforts to take forward the question of House of Lords reform. It agrees with the Joint Committee that its work, and that of the Royal Commission and the Government itself before it, have produced a considerable degree of consensus on the roles, functions and powers of the House of Lords. They have demonstrated, in contrast, that there is no consensus about the best composition for the second chamber. For the time being, the Government will concentrate on making the House of Lords work as effectively as possible in fulfilment of its important role.

The government had not only lost patience, but also heart. Indeed, observers could have been forgiven for thinking that any further Lords reform might be wholly given up.

This was not the case. Realizing how difficult it was to achieve consensus about the composition and powers of the House of Lords, the government indeed decided to postpone the idea of 'Completing the Reform' as originally envisaged. But instead it resolved to abolish the appellate jurisdiction of the House of Lords and to establish a new 'Supreme Court'. This was a major constitutional reform; and the government was determined to carry it out during its second term – in the parliament of 2001–05.

CHAPTER ELEVEN

2005. Constitutional Reform: The Lord Speaker

The office of lord Speaker is a recent one. It came into existence in 2005 as a result of the constitutional reform of that year. We must elucidate the background.

Proposed Changes in the Judiciary

After the Joint Committee on House of Lords Reform had delivered its Second Report (on 9 May 2003), the government felt it should, for the time being, proceed no further with legislation.[1] The reports of the Joint

1   Although no government bill was presently forthcoming, discussion on reform continued outside government circles. In one way or another, this discussion did influence the opinion of those officially concerned with reform. Some of the valuable contributions are worth noting here: Lord Carter, 'The Powers and Conventions of the House of Lords', *Political Quarterly*, 14 July 2003; Meg Russell, 'Is the House of Lords Already Reformed?', *Political Quarterly*, 14 July 2003; Lord Norton of Louth, *Reforming the House of Lords: A View from the Parapets* (Representation, 2004); Paul Tyler et al., *Reforming the House of Lords: Breaking the Deadlock* (The Constitution Unit, February 2005); Emma Crewe, *Lords of Parliament* (Manchester: Manchester University, 2005); Meg Russell, *Views from Peers, MPs and the Public on the Legitimacy and Powers of the House of Lords* (The Constitution Unit, 12 December 2005); Alexandra Kelso, 'Reforming the House of Lords: Navigating Representation, Democracy and Legitimacy at Westminster', *Parliamentary Affairs*, 3 June 2006; Meg Russell and Maria Sciara, *The House of Lords in 2005: A More Representative and Assertive Chamber?* (The Constitution Unit, February 2006); Joseph Rowntree, *Power: An Independent Inquiry into Britain's Democracy* (Foundation, March 2006).

Committee had brought into prominence how difficult it was going to be to achieve all-party consensus over the House of Lords – especially with regard to the House's composition. Yet the government was not prepared to back down totally. It embarked on another major constitutional reform, and planned to force it through the current Parliament. The reform concerned the establishment of a separate Supreme Court, the removal of the law lords from the House of Lords and the abolition of the office of lord chancellor. The office at 10 Downing Street made this decision public on 12 June 2003. The announcement came as a complete surprise – it had not been a manifesto commitment. But it is wrong to mark it out, as Lord Henley did, as a measure 'brought forward to deal with a botched ministerial reshuffle',[2] although a cabinet reshuffle did indeed take place on 12 June.

In the afternoon of this same day, news came out that Lord Irvine of Lairg, the lord chancellor, was leaving the government, and Lord Falconer of Thoroton was going to succeed him. The sudden departure of Lord Irvine aroused speculation that there must have been some strong difference of opinion between him and the prime minister on the proposed constitutional reform. This conjecture seems highly plausible. Though Lord Irvine may have disagreed with the prime minister, it would be unfair to say that he was traditional and conservative. The stance he took in the debate on the removal of the hereditary peers from the House of Lords in 1999 proved without doubt that he was, at heart, a great reformer. But he believed very firmly that the office of lord chancellor should be retained and that the law lords should continue to sit in the Upper House. He made no secret about his views. In a speech to the Third Worldwide Common Law Judiciary Conference in Edinburgh (on 5 July 1999) he had aired his convictions strongly:[3] '[W]ith our doctrine of Parliamentary sovereignty, and the powerful influence of the executive, the judicial arm is not as strong, yet it must ensure that the executive is kept subject to the rule of law.'

---

2   *Parliamentary Debates*, House of Lords, vol. DCLVIII, 8 March 2004, col. 1104.
3   Lord Irvine, 'Lord Chancellor's Views': *Third Worldwide Common Law Judiciary Conference, 5 July 1999*. As Delivered. Parliamentary Archives WHE/1/1/13.

Especial care, he said, had to be taken to guarantee 'our judicial independence'. There were various means of ensuring this. Sticking to convention was one of them. Judicial independence did not depend on the law. It had to be nourished by a 'political and a professional culture'. And yet another 'important bulwark of judicial independence in our system is the office of Lord Chancellor'. As lord chancellor, Lord Irvine explained, he was a senior member of the cabinet and a minister of justice. He was also, like his predecessors over many centuries, a judge. In this capacity he was also the president of the Appellate Committee of the House of Lords. This body was a 'significant part of our constitutional arrangements to protect the independence of the judiciary'. The office of lord chancellor dated back to the eleventh century at least. It was older than 'our Parliament, older than our democratic system'. The value of having a lord chancellor in the government was that he 'upholds judicial independence and can mediate between the executive and judiciary when need be'. There were those, he continued, who thought the time had come to 'dismantle' the office of lord chancellor, basing their arguments 'in part on a purist view of the separation of powers – which if pursued with purity would lead them to drive every Cabinet Minister from the House of Commons or the House of Lords'. He could not be persuaded that such a view was correct. Indeed his experience of the office had 're-enforced' his conviction that the role of the lord chancellor was 'to compensate for the fusion of powers elsewhere'. Lord Irvine then defended the place of the law lords in the House of Lords. The Appellate Court was an 'organic part of our legislature' – an example of 'our flexible approach to the separation of powers'. It was, however, important to appreciate that the appellate function was not exercised by the peers at large, but 'by a small and highly professional court', and although this court sat in the Parliament building, it consisted only of law lords. These senior figures in the judiciary were full members of the House of Lords.

> They may take part in the House's legislative activities, under certain conventions. They are 'cross-benchers' who have no connection with any political party. In particular, they avoid making any comment in the House on any issue that is, or may come, before them judicially. Within these conventions, the Law Lords

make a distinctive contribution to the work of the House of Lords in debates on the administration of justice, and in the valuable specialist contributions they make to many Select Committees. Their knowledge in these areas is unequalled and the House would be the loser without them. Therefore, to the question whether the House of Lords in its legislative capacity must lose the benefits the Law Lords confer because of the doctrine of the separation of powers, I say 'no' for two reasons: first, because we do not apply the doctrine strictly; and, secondly, provided their role in the legislature does not prejudice their primary role as our final appellate judges, there is no need to change a beneficial system.

Some suggest that Article 6 of the European Convention, which is entitled 'right to a fair trial', requires Britain, by a side wind from the guarantee of that right, to change our long-settled constitutional arrangements. But Article 6 requires a fair and impartial hearing, not a strict separation of powers. Provided a Law Lord hearing a case in the House of Lords has abstained from expressing a concluded view in the legislative chamber, on an issue coming before him judicially, then there will be no breach in my view of Article 6 if he sits.

With such entrenched views, Lord Irvine could hardly have been expected to carry on as a member of the cabinet, which had decided to pursue a course of radical judicial reform.

Two underlying factors, we believe, caused the government to undertake the major constitutional reform it had now announced. First, the cabinet seems to have been discouraged by the reports of the Joint Committee on Reform of the Lords: the prospects of reform legislation getting successfully through Parliament appeared decidedly meagre. But secondly the triumph of the 1999 Reform Act spurred an urge to strive for further glory. If the government could carry out the judiciary-related reforms just announced, that would be as historic an achievement as the abolition of the rights of hereditary peers to sit in the House of Lords.

This second factor was, perhaps, the decisive element behind the proposed judicial reform.

The government was strengthened in its decision by the pronouncements of two senior law lords, Lord Bingham and Lord Steyn. Lord Bingham had advocated the separation of the final court of appeal from the second chamber in a lecture, 'A New Supreme Court for the United Kingdom', which he had delivered at the UCL Constitution Unit in the spring of 2000. Lord Steyn had expressed similar views in a lecture given in March 2002 at All Souls College, Oxford, which had the title, 'The Case for a Supreme Court'.

On 8 July (2003), the prime minister upheld his decision of 12 June before the Commons Liaison Committee. He said he felt it was important that there should be changes. He also referred to the fact that 'discussions about these type of changes had been around for a considerable period of time'.

In the meantime Lord Falconer's Department for Constitutional Affairs had been drafting a series of proposals, and these were made public on 14 July.[4] It was obvious from these proposals that the new Supreme Court would have the same powers and jurisdiction as the Appellate Committee of the House of Lords had had. A few changes alluded to 'devolution issues'; but, in general, the proposals were anything but radical. Nevertheless they incited 173 responses, chiefly from people with legal experience. The law lords were divided in their opinions. Lords Bingham, Steyn, Saville, and Walker supported the government proposals; Lords Nicholls, Hoffmann, Hope, Hutton, Milett, and Rogers expressed dissent.[5]

---

4   See *Constitutional Reform: A Supreme Court for the United Kingdom*, 14 July 2003 (CP 11/03).

5   See <www.dca.gov.uk/consult/supremecourt/scresp.htm>. On the constitutional reform issue under discussion, I have learnt a great deal from the very thorough and valuable article by Andrew Le Sueur, 'From Appellate Committee to Supreme Court: A Narrative' in Louis Bloom-Cooper, Brice Dickson and Gavin Drewry, *The Judicial House of Lords, 1876–2009* (Oxford: OUP, 2009), pp. 64–94.

A Committee and Its Opponents

The government now felt it would be opportune to appoint a joint Commons Constitutional Affairs Committee to enquire into the judicial reforms. The Committee was established in November 2003. The following were its members:

Alan Beith MP, Chairman (Liberal Democrat)
Peter Bottomley MP (Conservative)
James Clappison MP (Conservative)
Ross Cranston MP (Labour)
Anne Cryper MP (Labour)
Jim Cunningham MP (Labour)
Hilton Dawson MP (Labour)
Andrew Rosindell MP (Conservative)
Clive Soley MP (Labour)
Keith Vaz MP (Labour)
Alan Whitehead MP (Labour)
Mark Field MP (Conservative)

The Committee met seven times, inviting experts to give evidence. It published its report on 3 February 2004.[6] The report analysed the various views the experts had put forward and suggested its own recommendations. The primary objective of the government was to separate the highest court of appeal in the United Kingdom from Parliament. Its main argument for this change was that it was wrong in principle to have judges sitting as members of the legislature. The Human Rights Act, especially in relation to Article 6 of the European Convention on Human Rights, required a stricter view to be taken not only of anything which might undermine the independence or impartiality of a judicial tribunal, but even of anything which might appear to do so. Thus the fact that the law lords were a committee of the House of Lords could raise issues about

6   See *Judicial Appointments and a Supreme Court (Court of Final Appeal)*. HC 48–1 of 2003–04.

the judiciary's independence from legislation, even if (as the Committee thought) such issues were based on the *appearance* of partiality rather than the *substance*.

The counter-argument advanced by a number of serving law lords run thus. They believed that, on 'pragmatic' grounds, the proposed change was unnecessary and would 'be harmful'. The present arrangements worked well. The House of Lords, these law lords argued, was a well established court which was dispensing justice in an 'effective and efficient way'. Appeals were heard in 'a unique, suitably prestigious, setting for this country's court of final appeal. The House of Lords as a judicial body is recognised by that name throughout the common law world. Overall, it is believed, it has a fine record and reputation.'

Other legal experts thought differently. They believed the functional separation of the judiciary (at all levels) from the legislature and the executive to be a cardinal feature of a modern, liberal, democratic state governed by the rule of law. They considered it important, as a matter of constitutional principle, that this functional separation should be reflected in the major institutions of the State, of which the final court of appeal was certainly one.

The Committee came to the conclusion that the government's consultation process had been too short and the legislative timetable too restrictive to deal with changes which were far-reaching in their effects. The reason for haste seemed to the Committee to be primarily political. It therefore recommended that the government should proceed with the Constitution Bill on the basis of its being *draft* legislation. If this course of action were followed, it was likely that many of the arrangements could be agreed on consensus. As the plan was to create a court of appeal to last for centuries, sufficient time needed to be spent on thinking it through.

Announcement in the House of Lords

On 26 January 2004 – before the Constitutional Affairs Committee made its report public – the lord chancellor, Lord Falconer of Thoroton, made a statement in the House of Lords, saying that he had reached an understanding with the lord chief justice, Lord Woolf, on judicial reform.[7] The 'concordat', as it came to be known, would be conditional upon parliamentary approval.[8] It was agreed that, in making changes, 'we must secure embedded, enduring judicial independence; a good working relationship between the judiciary and the executive; high quality judges and high public confidence in the judiciary'; that there should be a 'separate specific duty falling on the Secretary for Constitutional Affairs to defend and uphold the independence of the judiciary'. In the forthcoming bill, Lord Falconer said that the government intended to define the 'respective responsibilities of the Secretary of State for Constitutional Affairs and those of the Lord Chief Justice'. The secretary of state would be responsible for the administration of the courts, for supporting the judiciary in enabling it to fulfil its functions, and accountable to Parliament for the efficiency and effectiveness of the court system. The lord chief justice would lead the judges. He would be responsible for 'ensuring that the views of the judiciary are effectively represented; he will be responsible for the education and training of judges and for the decisions on deployment of individual members of the judiciary'. The lord chief justice 'will be given the title of President of the courts of England and Wales'. In addition, there would be a judicial appointments commission to ensure that the judges were 'strictly' appointed on merit.

Lord Kingsland, shadow chancellor, and Opposition spokesperson for justice, objected to the fact that matters of such importance as the independence of the judiciary and the selection of judges should have been 'conducted in negotiations in confidence between the executive and the judiciary without any participation by either House [as to] the legislation'. The government, he said, must hold a *pre-legislative review*. The concordat could form the basis of such a review.

Lord Goodhart, speaking for the Liberal Democrats, welcomed the government statement. The concordat 'will get the new system off to a better start'.

Lord Woolf said that, before consenting to the agreement, he had consulted the Judges' Council, the judiciary of the High Court and the

7   For details see: <www.dca.gov.uk/consult/lcoffice/judiciary.htm>.
8   *Parliamentary Debates*, House of Lords, vol. DCLVI, 26 January 2004, cols 12–30.

Court of Appeal. It was with 'their agreement' that he welcomed the lord chancellor's statement. The concordat was the result of detailed discussions between the lord chancellor and himself. If the proposals were accepted by Parliament, 'their implementation will have my firm support'. However, Lord Woolf made it clear that the package of proposals did not deal with the question of the creation of a new Supreme Court, nor the question of whether senior judges should continue to sit in the House of Lords. He had not sought to address the question whether the office of lord chancellor should be abolished. It seemed to the judiciary that that was a matter for Parliament.

Various other lords spoke in this short debate. They asked for clarification on certain points. The lord chancellor, ending the debate, promised that the House would 'get an opportunity to consider the proposals in detail'.

The House did get this opportunity on 9 and 12 February.[9] The secretary of state for Constitutional Affairs and lord chancellor, Lord Falconer, opened the debate on 9 February, stating that the government believed the time had 'come to make a clear change and transparent separation between the judiciary and the legislature. By creating a Supreme Court we will separate fully the final court of appeal from Parliament.' The government planned to 'sustain and enhance the vital independence of the judiciary'. The present position was 'no longer sustainable'. The time had come for the United Kingdom's highest court to 'move out from under the shadow of the legislature'. The government would bring forward legislation to create a Supreme Court. It would replace the existing system whereby the law lords operated as a committee of the House of Lords. The new Supreme Court would exercise the same appellate jurisdiction as the Appellate Committee presently exercised, in terms of both of the courts from which appeals might lie and be reviewed by appellate petition. There would be no changes to the rules governing leave to appeal. The Supreme Court would also take over the jurisdiction of the Judicial Committee of the Privy Council in respect of devolution issues under the Scotland Act 1998, the Government of Wales

---

9 *Parliamentary Debates*, House of Lords, vol. DCLVI, 9 and 12 February 2004, cols 926–41, 1253–324.

Act 1998 and the Northern Ireland Act 1998. The creation of a separate Supreme Court did not in any way imply the creation of a new body of United Kingdom law. Judges of the Supreme Court would be known as 'Justices of the Supreme Court'. They, as well as other holders of all-time judicial offices, would no longer be entitled to sit or to vote in the House of Lords or to participate in the work of Parliament as long as they held their judicial appointments. An Appointments Commission would guarantee the independence of the judges. The government also proposed that the first twelve justices would be 'those holding office as Lords of Appeal in Ordinary at the commencement of the new Supreme Court'.

Lord Kingsland spoke. He said that the Opposition believed that the government was intending to 'weaken the judicial arm of the constitution', and suggested that it proceed first to a pre-legislative review of the bill.

Lord Goodhart, speaking next, welcomed the government initiative. The Liberal Democrats had, he said, advocated the creation of a separate Supreme Court long before the government had become converted to this idea.

The debate on 9 February was a short one, but it was resumed on 12 February. Lord Craig of Radley spoke first. He thought that the abrupt removal of the law lords would weaken the House of Lords. The government proposals were too fundamental to be enacted suddenly by a 'here today, gone tomorrow' administration.

The Earl of Onslow believed that the current lord chancellor did not have the right to abolish an a-thousand-year-old office, the one he presently held. It was a 'sad day for the understanding of a liberal democracy, for the rule of law and the high court of Parliament'.

Lord Hoffmann thought it was a 'remarkable' change of policy, made 'in such a haste'. It did not 'allow time even for private consultation with someone who understood the constitutional position of the Lord Chancellor'. One of the 'glories of this country's constitution, unique in the world, has been its continuity. Institutions such as the Lord Chancellor have adapted themselves over centuries to new constitutional roles without having to make a new start.'

Lord Borrie said he agreed there was need for some of the government's proposals. But he did not see the need for, or the 'desirability' of, the abolition of the office of lord chancellor.

Lord Lloyd of Berwick said that, if he was asked whether it was in the public interest that the office of lord chancellor should continue to exist, his answer was an 'unhesitating Yes'.

Lord Hobhouse of Woodborough said the concordat was 'redolent with statements about how the Government – the executive – will keep their hand in the pie; not even a finger, a whole hand'.

Lord Norton of Louth said that the 'case for change has all the qualities of a lemon meringue pie: superficially attractive but, when you bite it, there is nothing there'.

Lord Rees-Mogg argued that 'we would be better to stay with a system that has preserved the ultimate supremacy of Parliament and of democracy'.

Lord Morris of Aberavon, referring to the office of lord chancellor, said that he believed in the transfer of functions, but did not 'necessarily believe in the abolition of the title'.

Lord Phillips of Sudbury argued that, on 'common sense grounds', when 'institutions, arrangements and offices have served so effectively for so many centuries and are so deeply etched into the public consciousness, so far as they ever can be, it is folly to destroy the reputation, familiarity and public ownership that attaches to them'.

Lord Ackner argued that it was difficult to 'follow that an office which had survived centuries could be abolished on the Prime Minister's say-so'.

Baroness Kennedy of the Thaws thought it was important to 'embrace constitutional change, but that it should be done properly'.

Baroness Howe of Idlicote warmly congratulated the government on their plans to establish a Judicial Appointments Commission; but some of the government's other proposals – 'particularly the proposal to abolish the office of Lord Chamber and to remove the Law Lords from your Lordships' House – cannot command even my most grudging support'.

Lord Mayhew of Twysden called for a draft bill. He did so because 'we all agree that this legislation will be of monumental constitutional importance'.

The Lord Bishop of Portsmouth supported the report of the Constitutional Affairs Committee.

Lord Woolf said that the House should take into account the 'thoughtful recommendations' of the Constitutional Affairs Committee. A Joint Committee of both Houses, he thought, 'might have some merit'.

Lord Millett said that he advocated the creation of a Supreme Court, but he was 'appalled at the proposal to abolish the office of Lord Chancellor'.

Lord Mackay of Clashfern suggested that the present bill should proceed as a draft bill, which could be the 'subject of rather more mature consideration'.

Lord Hope of Craighead believed that the 'preservation of the quality of our legal system at the highest level is the first priority'. As a lord of appeal in ordinary, he could say that 'the judicial function that we perform is, in my experience, not in the least inhibited by pressure of any kind from the executive. Our independence from that pressure is complete.'

Lord Brennan thought that the concordat that had been reached was a good sign for cooperation.

Lord Donaldson of Lymington thought that there was 'an enormous case for some degree of pre-legislative review, from which enormous advantages would follow'.

Lord Goodhart said that he supported the ending of the office of lord chancellor and the creating of a Supreme Court.

Lord Henley wanted to underline the desirability of some degree of pre-legislative scrutiny.

Lord Falconer wound up the debate. He agreed that, in relation to the abolition of the office of lord chancellor, there must be a 'positive case, not just a theoretical reference to the separation of powers, for the abolition of that important role'. He thanked their lordships for contributing to the debate and begged to move the motion. This was agreed to.

The Constitutional Reform Bill in the Lords

The government now acted rather foolishly, ignoring the advice from the Lords that the bill be first printed in draft so that there could be a pre-legislative review. Instead, on 24 February 2004, the lord chancellor introduced a bill into the House of Lords to:

make provision for replacing the office of Lord Chancellor and to abolish that office; to establish a Supreme Court of the United Kingdom and to abolish the appellate jurisdiction of the House of Lords; to make provision about the jurisdiction of the Judicial Committee of the Privy Council and the judicial functions of the president of the Council; to make other provisions about the judiciary; their appointment and discipline, and for connected purpose.

He begged to move that this bill be read for the first time.

Why did the government refuse to pay attention to the calls for a pre-legislative review of the bill? Was it simply because, Lord Falconer, the lord chancellor, desired it so? He had been variously characterized in comments in the House. Lord Lloyd had said that he did not understand the historical significance of the lord chancellor's post, and that he was 'nothing but a politician'. Lord Mayhew had said that, though he had many 'enviable qualities' he had 'often thought that they engagingly include the quality of a motor tyre which, no matter how grievously punctured, nevertheless of its own resources manages to reseal itself and roll on un-deflated'.[10] Both these indictments seem rather severe. Lord Falconer was only carrying out the policy of the government, and he did this with dedication and determination.

When a bill is introduced the first time, it is recorded in the House, but not debated. When the bill is read a second time the members have an opportunity to consider its clauses. This happened, in the House of Lords, on 8 March 2004. The secretary of state for Constitutional Affairs and lord chancellor, Lord Falconer, rose to say that he had it 'in command from Her Majesty the Queen to acquaint the House that Her Majesty, having been informed of the purport of the Constitutional Reform Bill, has consented to place her prerogative and interest, so far as are reflected by the Bill, at the disposal of Parliament for the purposes of the Bill'.[11] He moved that the

---

10   *Parliamentary Debates*, House of Lords, vol. DCLVI, 12 February 2004, col. 1286.
11   *Ibid.*, vol. DCLVIII, 8 March 2004, col. 979.

bill be read a second time, and that it 'be committed to a Committee of the Whole House'. Lord Lloyd of Berwick had tabled an amendment in his name on the Order Paper to the motion – to leave out 'Committee of the Whole House' and insert 'Select Committee'. The debate began at 3 p.m.

The lord chancellor outlined the main features of the Constitutional Reform Bill. It had 'two main strands', the first of which was abolition of the office of lord chancellor, and the second the creation of a Supreme Court. The bill allowed the 'statutory functions' of the lord chancellor in his capacity as Speaker of the House of Lords to be exercised by 'whoever fills that role'. The current role of the lord chancellor would be divided between the lord chief justice and the secretary of state for Constitutional Affairs. The bill provided for the establishment of a new Supreme Court, separate from Parliament, and for the 'transfer to that court of the appellate jurisdiction of the House of Lords'. The bill restricted the right of members of the House of Lords to sit and vote for so long as they held full-time judicial office. A Judicial Appointments Commission would also be created to ensure the independence of the judges.

A large number of lords had put their names on the list to speak. The debate that ensued was a very long one, which ended well after 11 p.m. We propose to cite only a few speakers in order to register the main arguments for and against the bill.[12]

Lord Kingsland said that the bill had 'confirmed our worst suspicions about the Government's constitutional intentions'. He believed that the establishment of a Supreme Court was 'pointless and extravagant'. The bill needed to be reviewed, and therefore the proposed amendment was timely and should be supported.

Lord Lester of Herne Hill also supported the amendment. A Select Committee would be 'able to receive evidence and scrutinise the details of the bill and make recommendations to remove its undoubted defects'.

Lord Lloyd of Berwick thought that the government intended to make fundamental changes in the constitution 'without any mandate from the people'. The bill was of major importance, yet there had been no 'proper

---

12   *Ibid.*, cols 980–1107.

consultation'. The bill was 'an obvious candidate for pre-legislative scrutiny'. What exactly was the 'alleged benefit' of having a new Supreme Court? He thought that the 'only benefit so far identified by the Government is the removal of a so-called perception in the mind of the public: a perception that the Law Lords are not independent; a perception that their decisions are politically motivated; and a perception that they are operating under the shadow of Parliament. These are not my words; they are the words of the Government in their consultation paper. I find it very difficult to take those words seriously.'[13] He understood that judicial changes were necessary. What he could not understand was the 'need to hurry'. He could not share the anxieties of those who thought the amendment would cause the disappearance of the bill altogether. The Select Committee would not need more than three months to gather evidence and to 'form a view'. The Committee could report by the end of July, which meant that the bill could go through the House of Lords by the end of October, and then be carried over to the Commons. Lord Lloyd believed that the learned Lords Bingham and Steyn were 'constitutional purists'. Lord Woolf was spared this allusion, perhaps out of respect for a lord chief justice. But he himself, Lord Lloyd said, was a 'realist'.

Lord Carter, a former Labour chief whip in the Commons, argued that to send a 'major Government Bill to a Select Committee is completely unprecedented and the procedure of such a committee is singularly inappropriate for the consideration of a major Bill'. If the House, Lord Carter maintained, were to 'accept this amendment, it would be setting a very dangerous precedent. It is clear that the Bill could not be completed this Session. The House would be ignoring a very powerful convention that the Government of the day are entitled to get their business through without unreasonable delay.'

---

13 We must note here that Lord Lloyd has had a very distinguished legal career: QC 1967; bencher 1976; attorney-general to the Prince of Wales 1969–77; judge of the High Court of Justice, Queen's Bench Division 1978–84; lord justice of appeal 1984–93; lord of appeal in ordinary 1993–98.

This last argument did not impress many of their lordships. The House of Lords *did* have power to call a Select Committee, convention or no.

Lord Woolf once more emphasized the fact that the judiciary considered 'highly desirable' those parts of the bill that reflected the sections of the concordat. They were designed to ensure the continued independence of the judiciary. He thought delay could be accommodated; but he would be 'very concerned' if the bill did not pass.

Lord Brennan confessed to being 'a constitutional purist'. The bill, he said, demanded 'the fullest parliamentary attention, impartiality wherever possible, and an apolitical approach'. If the House accepted the amendment, it faced two consequences: 'First, will confidence in our ability to accept and undertake major and sometimes controversial legislation as the first Chamber remain as it is now? I wonder. Secondly, do we not run the risk of being seen unreasonably to be obstructing reasonable reform?'

Lord Waddington said that he felt 'a sense of outrage at the cavalier way in which the Government determined to do away with an office older than Parliament itself, and to do so without even informing the Queen of their intention. We are talking about an office the holder of which has precedence over the Prime Minister himself.'

Viscount Bledisloe said the bill was 'thoroughly ill thought out' and required further scrutiny before it came before the full body of either House.

Baroness Jay of Paddington thought that, from a political and parliamentary perspective, the abolition of the office of lord chancellor seemed to her a 'positive and an important opportunity' for creating a vacancy for the presiding officer in the House of Lords.

Lord Desai said that for a long time he had been in favour of the removal of the post of lord chancellor. With the European Convention on Human Rights on the statute book, it was an 'anomaly to have the head of the judiciary sitting in the Cabinet and sitting in this House'.

Lord Crickhowell did not think that a Select Committee would be as good as full pre-legislative scrutiny, but it would 'provide an opportunity for evidence to be taken on key issues'.

Lord Morgan believed that the proposals in the bill were 'logical and wholly defensible'. The post of lord chancellor was a 'historic anomaly'. It seemed to him that a Committee of the Whole House would 'be active and constructive' and 'will improve' the bill.

Lord Donaldson of Lymington said that his own experience of Committees of the Whole House had *not* been 'fortunate': the bill must 'receive very careful scrutiny'.

Lord Clinton-Davis regretted that the debate had been 'tarnished by two matters'. First the amendment moved by Lord Lloyd was, 'behind all the camouflage, untenable and inconsistent with the traditions and procedures of this House. If he were to succeed, it would, inevitably, delay reform, and indeed, as I think is his wont, destroy the Bill altogether.'

Lord Alexander of Weedon supported the concept of a Supreme Court. He also believed that the functions of the lord chancellor could not 'long continue in their present form'. But he supported a Select Committee, though not with a 'view to killing this Bill'. It was possible, he thought, for the House to 'give instruction to a Select Committee to report within three months'.

Lord Plant of Highfield said that he was a 'constitutional purist', and offered his full support to the basic principles of the bill. The establishment of a Supreme Court and the separation of powers that it would embody were 'rather overdue'.

Earl Ferrers said that the abolition of the office of the lord chancellor was not 'modernisation', but rather 'destruction'. It was, 'in effect, a virtual rape of the constitution'.

Further speeches continued, with much repetition. The wind-up speech was delivered by the lord chancellor, Lord Falconer. He did not, he said, think that it would be sensible to proceed with a Select Committee in relation to a bill 'of this importance'. He strongly urged the House not to be 'drawn into what is political mischief-making by the party opposite'. Commending the bill to their lordships, Lord Falconer moved that it be committed to a Committee of the Whole House.

However, Lord Lloyd persisted, and moved his amendment to the motion – to leave out 'Committee of the Whole House' and insert 'Select Committee'. The House divided on the question whether 'the said amendment shall be agreed to'. Result: 'Contents, 216; Not-Contents, 183. Resolved in the affirmative, and amendment agreed to accordingly.'

The 'realists' had won, and the 'purists' were defeated – at least for the moment. The government's feeling of frustration was voiced by Baroness Amos. The House, she feared, had taken 'a very serious step'. By this vote, she said, 'this House – the unelected House – has made it impossible for the democratically elected House of Commons to receive this Bill promised in the Queen's Speech in November in time to consider it this Session. That is very serious indeed, and the Government will consider what the consequences my be.'

Lord Strathclyde thanked the baroness for her 'short statement', but she had not, he pointed out, been 'able to tell us what the consequences might be, this evening'.

Baroness Williams of Crosby also regretted the result of the division. Speaking for the Liberal Democrats, she declared that her party would consider 'very carefully' any way that 'we can rescue the Bill and the essential amendments that should be made to it. We feel that that has been made more difficult, not more easy, by the vote of this House.' The House adjourned at 'thirteen minutes before midnight'.

The Select Committee

The Lords Select Committee consisted of 16 members, representing Labour, Conservative, Social Democrat and Cross-Bench members of the House of Lords. The selection of members was made on the basis of their considerable legal and government experience.

The Labour members were: Lord Richard (who acted as chairman of the Committee), Lord Falconer, Lord Carter, Lord Elder and Baroness Gibson of Market Rasen.

The Conservatives were represented by: Lord Carlisle of Bucklow, Lord Howe of Aberavon, Lord Kingsland, Lord Crickhowell and Lord Windlesham.

The Liberal Democrats were represented by: Lord Holme of Cheltenham, Lord Goodhart and Lord Maclennan of Rogart.

The Cross-Bench members were: Viscount Bledisloe, Lord Craig of Radley, and Lord Lloyd of Berwick.

The Select Committee met twice a week between 24 March and 24 June 2004.[14] It took evidence from 32 witnesses, sitting publicly, and received 80 written proposals. It considered the bill, clause by clause, behind closed doors and made 400 amendments. The members of the Committee were evenly divided in their opinions, and the government was satisfied with the proceedings. Objections from the Scottish judges had also been removed. Lord Falconer agreed later that the Committee had indeed improved the bill.

The Improved Bill in the Lords and Commons

The bill returned to the House of Lords on 13 July 2004, where it was again debated at length. The Opposition now accepted its 'new architecture'.

On 11 October, after the summer recess, the bill reached the Committee stage in the Lords. Here further amendments were tabled. Lord Goodhart described them as 'wrecking amendments'.

The Report stage debate took place on 7 December. Further amendments were tabled. The lord chief justice, Lord Woolf, was disheartened. If this went on, he feared, the bill might never reach the statute book. He believed that the bill was 'a piece of great reforming legislation' and, if it was 'given life, it will rank in importance with the great constitutional instruments of the past'.

The debate was continued on 14 December and a third reading of the bill took place on 20 December, with the government tabling 14 pages of amendments. These included the retention of the title and formal office of the lord chancellor, though he would not be a member of the House of Lords. His new powers were specified. After further debate the House passed the bill and then sent it to the House of Commons.

Thus, on 17 January 2005, the Commons read the bill a second time. The government was supported by the Liberal Democrats. On division, it won by 329 votes to 126.

14   For more details, see Andrew Le Sueur, 'From Appellate Committee to Supreme Court: A Narrative', *op. cit.* I have heavily drawn on this article.

The Committee stage debate followed on 31 January. Any amendments by the Lords that went against the intentions of the government were rejected by the Commons.

The Committee of the Whole House debated the bill on 1 March, and this was followed by a third reading, when it was again passed. The bill now journeyed between the two Houses. The Lords debated it on 15 March, reintroducing certain amendments but agreeing to others made by the Commons. The bill then returned to the Commons on 16 March, where the Government suggested compromise amendments. These were considered by the Lords on 21 March, and finally accepted by them.[15] Thus ended what has rightly been termed the political 'ping-pong'.[16]

The bill received Royal Assent on 24 March 2005.

The Lord Speaker

The Constitutional Reform Act 2005 was indeed a major achievement in reforming the House of Lords.[17] The 'purists' had fought a hard, but just battle, and had finally won, but the 'realists' had not lost everything – they had, at least, achieved the retention of the traditional title of lord chancellor. But his office was now modified, and provisions were made relating to the functions of this office. Since he was no more a member of the House of Lords, the new post of 'lord Speaker' was created. It is this post we must now describe in some detail.

---

15   *Parliamentary Debates*, House of Lords, vol. DCLXXI, 21 March 2005, cols 13–42. Lord Kingsland tried to block the bill at the last moment by tabling an amendment. However, after debate, the Lords rejected it (Contents, 191; Not-Contents, 203).

16   See Andrew Le Sueur, 'From Appellate Committee to Supreme Court: A Narrative', *op. cit.*, p. 88.

17   The full text of the Act is printed in *The Public General Acts and General Synod Measures 2005, Part I* (London, 2005).

Recommendations Concerning the Role and Elections to the Post

The day after the Downing Street announcement on 12 June 2003, the lord president, Lord Williams of Mostyn moved in the House of Lords that it was 'expedient' that a Select Committee of 11 lords be appointed to 'consider the future arrangement for the Speakership of the House in the light of the Government's announcement that it is intended to reform the office of Lord Chancellor, and to make recommendations'. An amendment tabled by Lord Elton was withdrawn, and the motion was agreed to. On 9 July the Lords' Committee of Selection named the following to be members of the suggested Select Committee:

Lord Alexander of Weedon
Lord Ampthill
Lord Carter
Lord Desai
Lord Freeman
Baroness Gould of Potternewton
Lord Lloyd of Berwick (chairman)
Lord Marsh
Baroness Miller of Chilthorne Domer
Lord Tordoff
Lord Trefgarne

The Select Committee had power to appoint advisers, and had leave to report 'from time to time'. The reports were to be printed. The Committee held its first meeting on 15 July. It then met regularly, inviting views in writing from members of the House of Lords. About 60 Members replied. At four meetings oral evidence was heard. The Committee published its First Report on 18 November 2003.[18] This report lay dormant, and there could be no further progress until the bill on Constitutional Reform received Royal Assent in March 2005.

---

18   See *Speakership of the House – First Report.* HL Paper 199.

The question of the Speakership did not therefore come before the House of Lords until 12 July 2005, when it was resolved 'That this House should elect its own presiding officer'. A new Select Committee was appointed to implement this resolution, with 'full regard to the House's tradition of self-regulation'. This Committee consisted of the following members.

Lord Ampthill
Lord Carter
Bishop of Chelmsford
Lord Desai
Lord Freeman
Baroness Gould of Potternewton
Lord Higgins
Lord Lloyd of Berwick (chairman)
Lord Marsh
Baroness Miller of Chilthorne Domer
Lord Tordoff
Lord Trefgarne

The new Select Committee was required to report by 20 December 2005. It published its report on 19 December.[19] The Committee members were unanimous in their recommendations. We cite below some of the most significant of these.[20]

The Role of the Speaker in the Chamber[21]

1. The primary role of the Speaker is to preside over the proceedings in the Chamber, including the Committee of the Whole of House. The Speaker seeks the leave of the House for any necessary absence of a full sitting day or more.

---

19 See *The Speakership of the House of Lords: Report with Evidence*, 19 December 2005. HL Paper 92.
20 See 'Third report of session 2005–06 from the Procedure Committee'.
21 The functions of the Speaker were 'clearly and strictly codified' in the *Companion*.

2. The Speaker has no power to act in the House without the consent of the House.

3. The role of assisting the House at question time rests with the Leader of the House, not the Speaker.

4. At other times of day the Lord on the Woolsack or in the Chair may assist the House by reminding members of the relevant parts of the *Companion*. Such assistance is limited to procedural advice and is usually given at the start of business in hand, for example how time is to be divided between the front and back benches in response to a statement, the correct procedure at Report stage, the handling of grouped amendments, and the procedure to be followed in the case of amendments to amendments. Assistance may be helpful at other stages when procedural problems arise.

5. The Government Chief Whip advises the House on speaking times in debates. Enforcing such time limits is handled by the front benches rather than the Speaker. Timed debates are brought to an end (if necessary) by the Speaker on an indication from the Table.

6. Interventions, in particular those calling attention to the failure of an individual Member to comply with the rules, may come from the front benches or other Members. This would be the case, for example, when arguments deployed in committee were repeated at length on report. Such interventions would not normally come from the Speaker.

7. The Speaker observes the same formalities as any other Member of the House. He addresses the House as a whole, and not an individual Member. He does not intervene when a Member is on his feet. His function is to assist, and not to rule. The House does not recognise points of order. Any advice or assistance given by the Speaker is subject to the view of the House as a whole.

Election of Lord Speaker

1. The first election of the Lord Speaker shall be held no later than 30 June 2006. Thereafter elections shall be held (a) no more than

five years after the previous election, or (b) within three months of the death of the Lord Speaker, or his giving notice of resignation, if sooner. If, after a date has been set in accordance with (a) or (b), a Dissolution of Parliament is announced, the applicable deadline shall be extended to one month after the opening of the next Parliament.

2. All members of the House shall be entitled to stand for election and to vote, save that (a) Lords who have not taken the Oath in the current Parliament, or who are on Leave of Absence, may not stand or vote and (b) a Lord who has been successful in two previous elections may not stand. Before they can stand, candidates shall require a proposer and a seconder, who must themselves be eligible to stand.

3. The election shall be conducted in accordance with arrangements made by the Clerk of the Parliaments. The Clerk of the Parliaments may refer any question concerning the propriety of the electoral process to the Committee of Privileges.

4. In the event of a tie between two or more candidates, the matter (if not resolved by the electoral arrangements adopted by the House) shall be decided by the drawing of lots.

5. The result of the election shall be subject of the approval of Her Majesty The Queen.

6. The Chairman of the Committees may act during any vacancy in the office of Speaker.

7. The Lord Speaker may resign at any time by giving written notice to the Leader of the House.

8. If the House passes a motion for an Address to Her Majesty seeking the Lord Speaker's removal from office, the Lord Speaker shall be deemed to have resigned.

We also recommend the following Code of Conduct for the election. It is based closely on the code for the election of hereditary peers in 1999, and for by elections:

a) Ballot papers will not indicate any qualification or reason why a candidate should be elected.

b) Candidates may not offer hospitality, entertainment or financial inducements to electors intended to influence their votes or likely to have that effect.

c) Candidates may not engage in any activity intended or likely to discredit other candidates in the election.

d) Candidates may not solicit votes near the room where the election is taking place.

e) If the Clerk of the Parliaments suspects, on reasonable grounds, that some material irregularity or improper conduct may have occurred in the electoral process, he may refer the matter to the Committee of Privileges. The Committee may, if it thinks fit, recommend the disqualification of a successful candidate if their election appears to have been influenced by material irregularity or improper conduct.

f) In this code of conduct, 'candidate' includes an agent or supporter acting on behalf of the candidate.

We recommend the following procedure for the announcement of the result:

(i) The Lord Chancellor will process in for Prayers.

(ii) After Prayers, the Clerk of the Parliaments will announce the result.

(iii) The Lord Chancellor will signify Her Majesty's approval from the Despatch Box.

(iv) The new Lord Speaker will take over the Woolsack from the Lord Chancellor.

(v) Speeches will be made to mark the occasion.

We recommend that polling day for the election should be Wednesday 28 June and that the result should be announced on Tuesday 4 July.

Other aspects of the election process will be governed by the report of the Select Committee on the Speakership, to which the House has agreed, and by the arrangements to be made by the Clerk of the Parliaments, which will be set out in a Lords Notice.

We endorse the proposed amendments to existing Standing
Orders in Appendix 4 to the report of the Select Committee on
the Speakership, with the following modifications:

(A) Standing Order 17: Recall of the House

In Standing Order 17(3), on recall of the House for judicial business, the words 'The Lord Chancellor or, in his absence' should
be deleted. This should be done at the next opportunity, since
the Lord Chancellor will cease to have a judicial role on 3 April.

(B) Standing Order 63: Committees of the Whole House

The words 'Whenever the House resolves itself into a Committee,
the Lord Chancellor leaves the Woolsack and the Lord Chairman
of Committees presides over the Committee' should not be left
out, but should be amended to read 'Whenever the House resolves
itself into Committees, the Lord Speaker leaves the Woolsack
and he or the Lord Chairman of Committees presides over the
Committee from the Chair'.

(C) Standing Order 87: Appellate and Appeal Committees

In Standing Order 87(4), on the chairmanship of appellate and
appeal committees, the words 'by the Lord Chancellor or, in
his absence' should be deleted. This should be done at the next
opportunity, since the Lord Chancellor will cease to have judicial
role on 3 April.

It was further recommended that the lord Speaker should wear a gown,
but not a wig. On ceremonial occasions he (she) should wear his (her) parliamentary robes. The lord Speaker should have precedence immediately
after the Speaker of the House of Commons. He (she) should be appointed
a privy councillor. The lord Speaker should take over from the lord chancellor as one of the three 'key-holders' of Westminster Hall, together with
the Speaker of the House of Commons and the lord great chamberlain.
The lord Speaker should also have a wide role in representing the House,
acting where appropriate as an apolitical spokesman, attending Speakers'

conferences abroad, and taking over the lord chancellor's former duties of entertaining visiting Speakers and parliamentarians from abroad.

On 31 January 2006 Baroness Amos, president of the Council, introduced a motion in the House of Lords that the final Report of the Select Committee on the Speakership of the House of Lords be approved.[22] The baroness argued that the Committee had given the House a 'workable solution', and she hoped that the House would accept it in its entirety. Various amendments were tabled by Lord Strathclyde, Lord Barnett, Lady Gould and Lord Geddes. In the debate, which lasted for three hours, 65 speeches were made. The amendments were either withdrawn or rejected. The Lords subsequently approved the Report in its entirety. It was also agreed that the first election should be held not later than at the end of June 2006.

The Elections

On 6 June 2006 a list of nine candidates for election to the post of (first) lord Speaker was published. The candidates were:

> Lord Boston of Faversham (Cross-bench)
> Lord Elton (Conservative)
> Baroness Fookes (Conservative)
> Lord Grenfell (Independent)
> Baroness Hayman (Labour)
> Countess of Mar (Cross-bench)
> Lord Richard (Labour)
> Lord Redesdale (Liberal Democrat)
> Viscount Ullswater (Conservative)

The election, held on 28 June, was conducted using the Alternative Vote method.[23] The result was announced on 4 July 2006.

---

22   *Parliamentary Debates*, House of Lords, vol. DCLXXVIII, 31 January 2006, col. 134.
23   This is a preferential voting system where the voter has the chance to rank candidates in order of preference.

Candidate	Count							
	1	2	3	4	5	6	7	8
Baroness Hayman	201	201	209	215	229	236	248	263
Lord Grenfell	109	103	106	109	129	147	170	236
Viscount Ullswater	74	78	79	83	84	103	135	–
Countess of Mar	55	56	59	64	66	79	–	–
Lord Elton	52	57	58	60	65	–	–	–
Lord Richard	45	46	46	46	–	–	–	–
Lord Boston of Faversham	22	22	22	–	–	–	–	–
Lord Redesdale	17	17	–	–	–	–	–	–
Baroness Fookes	12	–	–	–	–	–	–	–

Electorate:702
Turnout: 582
Valid: 581
Spoilt: 1

Baroness Hayman was thus elected the first lord Speaker in the history of the House of Lords. She was also the first woman Speaker. She replaced the lord chancellor, Lord Falconer of Thoroton, on the Woolsack immediately. The lord chamberlain, Lord Luce, 'was on hand to confirm the assent of the Queen to the election'.

Baroness Hayman wonderfully fulfilled her obligations during her period of office. On 9 May 2011 she announced that she would not seek election to a second term. Thereupon six members of the House of Lords announced their candidature on 27 June 2011. These were:

Lord Colwyn (Conservative)
Baroness D'Souza (Cross-bench)
Lord Desai (Labour)
Lord Goodlad (Conservative)
Baroness Harris of Richmond (Liberal Democrat)
Lord Redesdale (Liberal Democrat)

The election took place on 13 July 2011.[24] The results were announced on 18 July:

Candidate	*Count*				
	1	*2*	*3*	*4*	*5*
Baroness D'Souza	186	188	202	240	296
Lord Colwyn	166	167	193	213	285
Lord Goodlad	145	145	150	168	–
Lord Desai	78	79	92	–	–
Baroness Harris of Richmond	62	65	–	–	–
Lord Redesdale	7	–	–	–	–

Electorate:770
Turnout: 644
Valid: 644

Baroness D'Souza was duly elected. She has performed her duties to the highest standard possible. So both the first and the second of the lord Speakers have enhanced the grace and intensified the lustre of the House of Lords.

---

24 Amendments made on 3 May 2011 provided that elections must be held by 15 July in the final year of a term, with the new term beginning on 1 September.

CHAPTER TWELVE

2005. Voices From Outside and From Across the Parties

Reform of the Lords was not entirely reserved to the government alone nor kept simply within parliamentary debates. The delay in accomplishing reform caused anxiety elsewhere, and this expressed itself in private correspondence as well as in public expostulations. 'Heaven knows when, if ever, we shall finally have a reformed House of Lords established!' wrote Sir Patrick Nairne, one-time Master of St Catherine's College, Oxford.[1] He certainly wanted a second chamber ('with its own name'), but did not 'want any longer a House of Lords with its historical position in the constitution and all the pomp and ceremonial that still accompanies that. In particular, the Queen should in future open Parliament (with the Queen's speech, drafted by the Government) in the pre-eminent House of Commons'.[2] Nairne also believed 'strongly' that 'it will continue to be essential to have a significant number of members nominated, rather than elected, because of the expertise and experience such members (with which the House of Lords continues to be well stocked at present) can offer, in particular for the revision of legislation coming up, poorly drafted, from the Commons'. As to the future size of the Lords, he 'would favour an eventual total size of 400–450 rather than the 600 proposed by the Government'; and, to this end, he 'would have far fewer politically nominated members and more directly elected members, while having at least 120 independent members appointed by the proposed independent Appointments Committee'. Yet

---

1   Sir Patrick Nairne, 'Reform of the House of Lords', personal letter to the author, dated 11 July 2002.
2   *Ibid.*

the eventual composition of the second chamber should not be 'such as to challenge the House of Commons'.[3]

A paper written by two distinguished scholars gave a comprehensive view of how Lords reform ought to be accomplished.[4] The authors criticized the government proposals in the 2003 White Paper and offered their own response. We quote some of the suggested recommendations:

(i) The proposal to maintain the link between membership of the upper house and the peerage is surprising, given the government's previous rejection of this approach. Maintaining the link is potentially both confusing and damaging to the House, whilst there is no good argument for its retention.

(ii) Removing the hereditary peers will deprive the House of almost half its most active cross-bench members. If the government wants to maintain an active independent presence in the House, serious efforts will need to be made to counteract this loss. This implies appointment of a sizeable new group of cross-bench members, with an immediate emphasis on appointing those who will play an active part in proceedings.

(iii) One of the paper's most dangerous suggestions is that party balance in the chamber could take account of shares of House of Commons seats as well as general election votes cast. Even a modest implementation of this proposal threatens to send the size of the House spiralling out of control, and could see effective control handed to the governing – or even opposition – party. With party balance based on vote shares, it will already be hard to keep the size of the House within the proposed 600 member limit. Any formula including share of seats would make the proposals unworkable.

---

3   *Ibid.*
4   See Meg Russell and Robert Hazel, *Next Steps in Lords Reform: Response to the September 2003 White Paper* (London: The Constitution Unit, November 2003).

(iv) The commitment to retain a sizeable independent group in the House is welcome. However, these members are always likely to vote less, and probably attend less, than political members. To retain the independent element at its current level would demand that independents made up 25% (rather than the 20% proposed) of appointees.

(v) The government is right to emphasise the importance of improving representativeness amongst the upper house members. This should include gender and ethnic balance, and crucially regional balance and balance of expertise, to enable the chamber to do its job effectively. However, these objectives cannot be reached if the Appointments Commission controls only the independent members. The commission need not have power to choose representatives of the political parties, but must be able to direct them about the overall balances required and to vet and reject lists of nominees submitted if they do not meet representativeness criteria.

(vi) The proposal to put the Appointments Commission on a statutory footing, allowing its objectives to be set out, is welcome. So too is the proposal that it be accountable to parliament. However, this will need handling carefully, and it is desirable that the commission reports either to an existent committee, or new committee with additional duties, as in practice the role of monitoring its work will be small. Its accountability beyond parliament is also important.

(vii) If the Appointments Commission is made accountable to parliament, parliament must have full responsibility for appointing its members from the start. Members should be appointed on rolling fixed terms, as was done with the Electoral Commission. The chair is a high profile post and should be recruited separately. Independent commissioners should be drawn from outside parliament, and none should be eligible for membership of the House until 10 years after they have left the commission.

(viii) The proposal that various groups continue to be appointed to the chamber directly by the Prime Minister undermines the Appointments Commission, and will make its job of maintaining balance and size limits in the house more difficult. As far as possible the Appointments Commission should have sole control over appointments to the House, and all members should be considered on their merits. Such an arrangement would be easier if the peerage link were broken.

(ix) The suggestion that members of the upper house could renounce their peerages and immediately stand for the House of Commons is potentially very damaging. As the Royal Commission proposed, there should be a bar on members standing as MPs until at least 10 years after they have left the chamber. This difficulty could however usually be avoided if members were appointed for fixed 15 year terms rather than for life. This would also help with managing size and party balance.

The government White Paper (2003) did not move change any further. The removal of the law lords from the House of Lords was indeed a major reform. Yet, it could not be considered a second-stage reform of the Lords as such. A general election was approaching, and any immediate expectation of an agreement seemed far away.

A Cross-Party 'Reform Package'

A small group of cross-party members of Parliament, however, still believed that consensus was possible. With the help of the Constitution Unit, they composed a draft to 'kick-start the Lords reform process'. This bid was chiefly initiated by Kenneth Clarke MP (Conservative), Robin Cook MP (Labour), Paul Tyler MP (Liberal Democrat) Tony Wright MP (Labour) and George Young MP (Conservative). The other supporters of the initiative came from both Houses of Parliament: Lord Baker (Conservative), Alan Beith MP (Liberal Democrat), John Bercow MP (Conservative), Roger Berry MP (Labour), Richard Burden MP (Labour), Anne Campbell MP (Labour),

David Curry MP (Conservative), Lord Dholakia (Liberal Democrat), Stephen Dorrell MP (Conservative), Lord Goodhart (Liberal Democrat), Damien Green MP (Conservative), Win Griffiths MP (Labour), William Hague MP (Conservative), Lord Kinnock (Labour), Archy Kirkwood MP (Liberal Democrat), Andrew Mackinlay MP (Labour), Francis Maud MP (Conservative), Michael Meacher MP (Labour), Gordon Prentice MP (Labour), Joyce Quin MP (Labour), Lord Richard (Labour), Joan Ruddock MP (Labour), Chris Smith MP (Labour), Gisela Stuart MP (Labour), John Thurso MP (Liberal Democrat), Andrew Tyrie MP (Conservative), Alan Whitehead MP (Labour) and Shirley Williams MP (Liberal Democrat).

The comprehensive 'reform package'[5] was completed at the beginning of February 2005 and was introduced as a draft bill in the House Commons on 23 February 2005 by Robin Cook. It was over 50 pages long. We confine ourselves to its main recommendations.

The Functions and Powers of the Second Chamber

1. The second chamber should continue to operate as a House of review, scrutiny and deliberation. However, the chamber should seek to complement, rather than duplicate, the work of the House of Commons.

2. There should be no immediate reform to the Parliament Acts, or to the second chamber's power over secondary legislation.

3. At the heart of our parliamentary system is the convention that governments must maintain the confidence of the House of Commons, but not of the House of Lords. Such a convention should continue after the second chamber is reformed.

4. In order to resolve disputes between the chambers on legislation more constructively, a joint committee system should be established, where members are charged with proposing compromise amendments on which both chambers should vote. Initially such arrangements should be implemented through standing

---

5   K. Clarke, R. Cook, P. Tyler, T. Wright and G. Young, *Reforming the House of Lords: Breaking the Deadlock* (London: The Constitution Unit, 2005).

orders, but should be reviewed as part of the general review of the legislative process, and might later be made statutory.

Principles of Composition

5. We believe that the second chamber should have a mixed membership, including both elected and appointed members.

6. We believe that a majority of second chamber members should be elected.

7. Elected members should make up 70% of the reformed chamber.

8. We believe that the second chamber should be significantly smaller than it is now.

9. No party should have a majority in the second chamber.

10. The precise balance between the parties should be determined by the elections to the second chamber, which should be based on a proportional system.

11. Elected and appointed members of the second chamber should serve longer terms of office than MPs. We recommend terms equivalent to three House of Commons terms, which would normally amount to 12–14 years.

12. Members of the second chamber should be renewed in parts, in order that there is continuity in the chamber's membership. We recommend that one third of members are renewed at the time of each general election.

13. Although there are strong arguments for removing ministers from the second chamber, we do not believe that this move is justified at the present time.

14. Most cabinet ministers should continue to be drawn from the House of Commons.

15. The prime minister should retain the right to appoint up to four members of the house per parliament, to serve as ministers.

16. We propose for the moment, that the Bishops should remain in the chamber, but their number should be reduced from 26 to 16. In the future a separate short bill might end their formal representation altogether.

17. In future, retired senior judges may continue to make valuable members of the reformed House, but should be considered on their merits for appointments rather than gaining automatic seats.

18. We propose that the chamber should have up to 385 members in total, 270 of whom should be elected and 87 of whom should be appointed by an independent commission. In addition the Bishops would continue to hold 16 seats and there would be up to 12 places for prime ministerial appointees. Thus elected members would make up 70–72% of the total, and independently appointed members roughly 23%.

Elected Membership

19. The elected members of the chamber should be directly chosen by the people, rather than result from any kind of 'indirect' election.

20. The boundaries used for elections to the second chamber should be the established nations and regions of the UK, as used for European Parliament elections.

21. We believe that the electoral system for the second chamber should maximise voter choice, and we therefore reject the idea of closed party lists. We thus propose that elections should be carried out using either open lists or STV.[6] On balance we believe that STV is more in keeping with the needs of the second chamber.

22. We believe that as far as possible the tradition of selecting high profile and experienced members for the second chamber should continue. The political parties should make this a priority in their selections for elected seats. In addition existing members of the House should have the entitlement to stand, from the first election onwards.

23. Elections for the second chamber should be held on general election day.

6   STV = single transferable vote.

24. Second chamber members should normally serve three House of Commons terms. However, if two general elections are held within two years there would not normally be a requirement to hold a second chamber election. The exception would be if the previous parliament had also been a short one, and the two parliaments together added up to more than two years.

25. There should be no system of by-elections for the second chamber. Nor should there be a mechanism whereby people are automatically replaced by others from party lists. On the rare occasions when vacancies arise, an additional seat should be elected from that region at the next second chamber election, for the remainder of the original term.

26. Members of the second chamber should be able to be elected only once, for one long term.

27. Members of the second chamber should be free to retire before the end of their term. However, they should not immediately be able to stand for the House of Commons. A five-year bar should apply to standing for the Commons, starting at the date that the member's term in the second chamber was due to end.

Appointed Members

28. There should be a statutory Appointments Commission, with responsibility for choosing all appointed members of the chamber (except for the small number that the Prime Minister appoints as ministers). Some, but not a majority of members of the Commission should be Cross-bench members of the House. The members of the Commission should be appointed by parliament, on the recommendation of a joint committee of both Houses. This committee should also have responsibility for overseeing the Commission's work.

29. The main responsibility of the Appointments Commission should be to identify individuals of outstanding ability who have an important contribution to make to the second chamber. In doing so the Commission should be required to have regard to the current makeup of the House, and any gaps that need to be filled.

30. There should be no automatic inclusion of ex office holders in the reformed second chamber, though the Appointments Commission should be free to consider these members on their merit.

31. There should be an expectation that most individuals appointed by the Appointments Commission have no strong link to the political parties, and the Commission should seek to ensure that at least 20% of members take no party whip. However the Commission should not be barred from appointing people with a history of political activism, where they are independent minded and have other important qualities to offer.

32. The prime minister should be entitled to a maximum of four appointees per parliament, on the condition that they are made ministers straight away. These members should serve roughly the same terms as others in the chamber, and not be required to leave if they cease holding ministerial office.

33. Appointed members should serve the same terms of office as elected members. This means that one third should be appointed at the same time as each second chamber election, and these members should leave the chamber at the same time as the members elected at that election.

34. The balance between political party members in the chamber should be determined by the last three second chamber elections. Where there are any political appointees, the Appointments Commission should have a duty to ensure that this balance is maintained. In particular it should have the power to counterbalance prime ministerial appointments with appointees allied to other parties, if necessary.

35. Like elected members, appointed members of the second chamber should be free to leave the chamber before the end of their term, but be barred from standing for the House of Commons until five years after their term was due to end.

36. If a vacancy is created amongst appointed members, the normal practice should be for the Appointments Commission to fill it, within a maximum of six months. However the new

member would serve only to the end of the term of the member they have replaced.

The Appointments Commission should have the discretion to appoint members to the chamber for a single additional second chamber term. This applies whether they first entered the chamber by election or by appointment, but the expectation is that this would be rare.

Peerage

38. The automatic link between the peerage and membership of the second chamber should end.

The Name of the House

39. We believe that it would be somewhat anachronistic for the House to maintain the title the House of Lords. We therefore propose that it should be referred to as the Second Chamber, and its members as Members of the Second Chamber of Parliament.

Administrative Matters

40. Once the principles of composition in the reformed second chamber are agreed, the issue of salaries and allowances for members should be referred to the Senior Salaries Review Body for consideration. We believe that resources to members should be better than they are now but should be lower than those payable to MPs – particularly in terms of availability of staff.

The Transit from Here to There

41. We do not propose a 'big bang' reform to establish a largely elected second chamber overnight. Instead we believe that it is more practical and desirable to make a gradual transition to the new chamber so that continuity and tradition is maintained.

42. Existing members should leave the chamber in three tranches, as new members are added. This transition would begin at the general election after next.

43. For the purpose of the transition, life peers and hereditary peers should be treated equally. There should be no automatic

requirement for the hereditary peers to leave first. However, by-elections amongst hereditary peers should end immediately.

44. In order to encourage members to volunteer to leave the House, and to provide justice to those that depart, a generous retirement package should be offered, based on age, length of service and attendance.

45. If there are insufficient voluntary retirements from the chamber the decision on who remains at each round should be decided by the party groups, through election. At the first stage one third of each group should be required to depart, and at the second stage half of the remainder, and at the last stage all of the rest.

46. The number of Bishops should also be gradually reduced over three elections, from 26 to 16.

47. Existing members of the House should be free to stand for public election to the reformed second chamber, with no restriction. In order that such members are not disadvantaged, elections internally to choose who should remain during the transition should be held immediately after the first two public elections.

48. Departing members of the House of Lords should be able also to stand for election to the House of Commons. At the same time as the first second chamber elections, they should be able to do this without restriction. Any members who remain in the chamber after the first elections, however, should be subject to a five-year delay after leaving the House if they later decide to stand as an MP.

The proposals were not entirely new. Presenting them to the Commons on 23 February, Robin Cook told the House that he did not have a 'lively expectation' that the bill would be passed 'in this Parliament', but he was introducing it as a 'contribution to the debate'.[7] The debate was a very short one, lasting only an hour and a half. The Deputy Speaker then ordered that 'we must turn our attention to the next topic'. And that was the end of this cross-party 'reform package'.

7   *Parliamentary Debates*, House of Commons, vol. 431, 23 February 2005, col. 71WH.

CHAPTER THIRTEEN

2006. Conventions of the British Parliament

Great Britain has no written constitution. Instead there is convention – or, rather, a set of conventions. These customs or conventions, as F.W. Maitland makes amply clear, 'derive their force, a force which is often felt to be quite as strong as the force of law, from the fact that they are so much mixed up with law that they could hardly be violated without a violation of law'.[1] But no matter how strong the force of law may be, these constitutional practices, customs or conventions are not themselves rules of law. In the circumstances of 2005–6, it was necessary to ask whether departure from 'sound constitutional precedent' would serve any useful purpose. This question deserved careful consideration. Both Houses of Parliament decided to appoint a Joint Committee to make a study of the conventions that governed the relationship in matters of legislation between the two Houses.

The Joint Committee on Conventions

The House of Commons appointed its members of the Committee on 17 May 2006; the House of Lords did so on 22 May 2006. The Committee held its first meeting on 23 May 2006 and appointed Lord Cunningham of Felling to be the chairman. Parliament agreed to extend the Committee's life from 21 July to the end of the current session of Parliament.[2]

---

1   See F.W. Maitland, *The Constitutional History of England* (London: Cambridge University Press, 1911), p. 342.
2   The Commons did this on 20 June 2006 and the Lords on 4 July.

The membership of the Joint Committee was as follows:

HOUSE OF LORDS

Viscount Bledisloe
Lord Carter
Lord Cunningham of Felling
Lord Elton
Lord Fraser of Carmyllie
Lord Higgins
Lord McNally
Baroness Symons of Vernham Dean
Lord Tomlinson
Lord Tyler
Lord Wright of Richmond

HOUSE OF COMMONS

Mr Russell Brown
Mr Wayne David
Mr George Howarth
Mr Simon Hughes
Ms Sarah McCarthy-Fry
Mr Andrew Miller
Sir Malcolm Rifkind
Mr John Spellar
Ms Gisela Stuart
Mr Andrew Tyrie
Sir Nicholas Winterton

The Joint Committee's report was published on 3 November 2006 by authority of the House of Lords and the House of Commons.[3] We highlight below only the principal sections of the report.

The Joint Committee on Conventions was appointed with the following terms of reference:

---

3   See *House of Lords/House of Commons Joint Committee on Conventions of the UK Parliament*. First Report of Session 2005–06, vol I. HL Paper 265-I HC 1212-I.

That, accepting the primacy of the House of Commons, it is expedient that a Joint Committee of the Lords and Commons be appointed to consider the practicality of codifying the key conventions on the relationship between the two Houses of Parliament which affect the consideration of legislation, in particular –

(A) the Salisbury-Addison convention that the Lords does not vote against measures included in the governing party's Manifesto;

(B) conventions on secondary legislation;

(C) the convention that Government business in the Lords should be considered in reasonable time;

(D) conventions governing the exchange of amendments to legislation between the two Houses;

that the committee have leave to report from time to time;

that the committee have power to appoint specialist advisers;

that the committee have power to adjourn from place to place within the United Kingdom.

The Committee's Conclusions and Recommendations

The following were the conclusions and recommendations of the Joint Committee.

Primacy of the Commons, role of the Lords, and Lords reform

1. We were instructed to accept the primacy of the House of Commons. None of our witnesses has questioned it, and neither do we (paragraph 59). The primacy of the Commons is a present fact, requiring no codification (paragraph 283a).

2. Our conclusions apply only to present circumstances. If the Lords acquired an electoral mandate, then in our view their role as

the revising chamber, and their relationship with the Commons, would inevitably be called into question, codified or not. Given the weight of evidence on this point, should any firm proposals come forward to change the composition of the House of Lords, the conventions between the Houses would have to be examined again. What could or should be done about this is outside our remit (paragraph 63).

Salisbury-Addison convention

3. The Salisbury-Addison convention has changed since 1945, and particularly since 1999 (paragraph 99). Its provisions are:
In the House of Lords:
A manifesto Bill is accorded a Second Reading;
A manifesto Bill is not subject to 'wrecking amendments' which change the Government's manifesto intention as proposed in the Bill; and
A manifesto Bill is passed and sent (or returned) to the House of Commons, so that they have the opportunity, in reasonable time, to consider the Bill or any amendments the Lords may wish to propose (paragraph 101).

4. It would be practical for the Lords to debate and agree a resolution setting out the terms of the Convention as it has evolved, and to communicate it by message to the Commons, which could then debate a motion to take note of the message (paragraphs 116, 283c).

5. We do not recommend any attempt to define a manifesto Bill (paragraph 115). Without such a definition, it will be clear that the resolution is flexible and unenforceable (paragraph 283d).

6. We recommend that in future the Convention be described as the Government Bill Convention (paragraph 117).

7. In addition the evidence points to the emergence in recent years of a practice that the House of Lords will usually give a Second Reading to any government Bill, whether based on the manifesto or not (paragraph 102).

Reasonable time

8. There is undoubtedly a convention that the House of Lords considers Government business in reasonable time (paragraph 153). A statement to that effect could be adopted by the House of Lords by resolution and included in the *Companion* (paragraph 283e).

9. There is no conventional definition of 'reasonable', and we do not recommend that one be invented (paragraph 154). Without such a definition, it will be clear that the resolution is flexible and unenforceable (paragraph 283f).

10. It would however be possible for a new symbol to appear on the Lords order paper, to indicate a Bill which has spent more than a certain period in the House (paragraph 156). If there is to be a number of sitting days as an indicative measure, for this purpose, of when a Bill may have spent long enough in the Lords, then 80 days is more appropriate than 60 (paragraph 157). This would be a matter for the Lords Procedure Committee (paragraph 283g).

11. When the Government criticise the Lords for making slow progress with a Commons Bill, they are on firmer ground when they can point to full scrutiny in the Commons (paragraph 161).

12. There is scope for better planning of the parliamentary year as a whole, possibly involving greater use of pre-legislative scrutiny and carry-over. If the Government can even out the workload in both Houses throughout the Session, this should reduce time problems on individual Bills (paragraph 166).

'Ping-pong'

13. The exchange of Amendments between the Houses is an integral part of the legislative process that is carried on within the context of the primacy of the House of Commons and the complementary revising role of the House of Lords. It is not a convention, but a framework for political negotiation (paragraph 188). We find no scope for codification (paragraph 283h).

14. It would facilitate the exchange of Amendments between the two Houses if the convention that neither House will in

general be asked to consider Amendments without notice was more rigorously observed, i.e. if reasonable notice was given of consideration of Amendments from the other House (paragraph 189).

Secondary legislation

15. Neither House of Parliament regularly rejects secondary legislation, but in exceptional circumstances it may be appropriate for either House to do so (paragraph 227). A statement to that effect could be adopted by either House, or both (paragraph 283i).

16. Although we offer below a list of examples of exceptional circumstances, we do not recommend defining them further. Without such a definition, it will be clear that the statement is flexible and unenforceable (paragraph 283j).

17. There are situations in which it is consistent both with the Lords' role in Parliament as a revising chamber, and with Parliament's role in relation to delegated legislation, for the Lords to threaten to defeat an SI.[4] For example:

   a. where special attention is drawn to the instrument by the Joint Committee on Statutory Instruments or the Lords Select Committee on the Merits of SIs,
   b. when the parent Act was a 'skeleton Bill', and the provisions of the SI are of the sort more normally found in primary legislation,
   c. orders made under the Regulatory Reform Act 2001, remedial orders made under the Human Rights Act 1998, and any other orders which are explicitly of the nature of primary legislation, and are subject to special 'super-affirmative' procedures for that reason,
   d. the special case of Northern Ireland Orders in Council which are of the nature of primary legislation, made by the Secretary of State in the absence of a functioning Assembly,

---

4   SI = statutory instrument.

   e. orders to devolve primary legislative competence, such as those to be made under section 95 of the Government of Wales Act 2006,

   f. where Parliament was only persuaded to delegate the power in the first place on the express basis that SIs made under it could be rejected (paragraph 229).

18. This list is not prescriptive. But if none of the above, nor any other special circumstance, applies, then opposition parties should not use their numbers in the House of Lords to defeat an SI simply because they disagree with it (paragraph 230).

   19. The most constructive way for the Lords, as the revising chamber, to reject an SI is by motion (or amendment) incorporating a reason (paragraph 232).

   20. If the Government lose a vote on a non-fatal motion[5] about a Statutory Instrument, they should respond to the House in some way, at least by Written Statement (paragraph 232).

Financial privilege

21. When the Lords Economic Affairs Committee scrutinises the Finance Bill, it should continue to respect the boundary between tax administration and tax policy, to refrain from investigating the incidence or rates of tax, and to address only technical issues of tax administration, clarification and simplification. Provided it does so, we believe there is no infringement of Commons financial privilege, and no need to reopen the issue. If the House of Commons believe that their primacy or their privileges are being infringed, it is for them to act to correct the situation (paragraph 244).

   22. If the Government are prepared to describe National Insurance as a tax, then they can seek to bring it within the scope of financial privilege (paragraph 249).

---

5 When a member tables a motion to criticize a negative Statutory Instrument but not overturn it, it is a 'non-fatal' motion.

23. If the Commons have disagreed to Lords Amendments on grounds of financial privilege, it is contrary to convention for the House of Lords to send back Amendments in lieu which clearly invite the same response (paragraph 252). This matter could be considered by the House of Lords on the basis of a report from the Procedures Committee, with a view to adding to the guidance in the *Companion* (paragraph 283k).

Codification

24. All recommendations for the formulation or codification of conventions are subject to the current understanding that conventions as such are flexible and unenforceable, particularly in the self-regulating environment of the House of Lords. Nothing in these recommendations would alter the present right of the House of Lords, in exceptional circumstances, to vote against the Second Reading or passing of any Bill, or to vote down any Statutory Instrument where the parent Act so provides (paragraph 281).

25. The courts have no role in adjudicating on possible breaches of parliamentary convention (paragraph 285).

The Government Response

The government's response to the Joint Committee's report was presented to Parliament by the leader of the House of Commons and lord privy seal in December 2006.[6]

---

6   *Government Response to the Joint Committee on Conventions' Report of Session 2005–06: Conventions of the UK Parliament*. December 2006. Cm 6997.

Introduction

1. The Government is very grateful for the work which the Joint Committee has undertaken in considering the conventions governing the relationship between the two Houses of Parliament. The evidence it has collected, both oral and written, provides a valuable source of information on the origins, development and meaning of the various conventions which give life to the relationship between the two Houses of Parliament. Not only will this work inform the current debate, it will also be an important source for future reference. The Government is also grateful to the Committee for producing its report to the tight timetable which was set.

2. The complex issue of the relationship between the two Houses sits at the core of the arrangements through which Parliament holds the Government to account. The House of Lords has a crucial part to play in the process, through its role as the revising chamber. But it is clear that in our constitutional arrangements the House of Commons retains primacy. Only the Commons has the power to grant or withhold supply, and, linked to this, it is only the Commons whose confidence a government must maintain in order to remain in office. These arrangements mean that there is a very different relationship between the Government and the two Houses of Parliament. They ensure that the party which secures a majority through a general election has the right to form a government and to carry through the programme set out in its election manifesto.

3. The House of Lords must be equipped with the power to perform its role as a revising chamber effectively, but it must not exercise this power in a way which undermines the position of the House of Commons. The constitutional backstops of Commons' primacy are the Parliament Acts and the rules on supply. However, there are other elements which underline this those which govern the day-to-day relationship between the two Houses. These are the kinds of conventions that the Committee was asked to investigate.

4. We accept the Joint Committee's analysis of the effect of all the conventions, and the Joint Committee's recommendations and conclusions. Its report accurately defines the current relationship between the Lords and the Commons.

5. The conventions, as defined, will provide an essential point of reference in the months to come, as the Government works to build a consensus on further reform of the House of Lords.

6. This is the Government's response to the specific issues raised by the Joint Committee.

Primacy of the Commons, role of the Lords, and Lords reform (page 76, paras 1 & 2)

> 1. *We were instructed to accept the primacy of the House of Commons. None of our witnesses has questioned it, and neither do we. (Para 57) The primacy of the Commons is a present fact, requiring no codification. (Para 283 (a))*
> 2. *Our conclusions apply only to present circumstances. If the Lords acquired an electoral mandate, then in our view their role as the revising chamber, and their relationship with the Commons, would inevitably be called into question, codified or not. Given the weight of evidence on this point, should any firm proposals come forward to change the composition of the House of Lords, the conventions between the Houses would have to be examined again. What could or should be done about this is outside our remit. (Para 61)[7]*

7. The Government welcomes the Committee's view on the primacy of the House of Commons. We also note that the Committee recognises that the question of what the conventions should look like in a reformed House of Lords is outside its remit.

8. As the 2005 manifesto made clear, the Government believes that it is necessary for there to be further reform of the House

---

7   The texts that are indented and italicized are quotations from the Joint Committee's report and its evidence.

of Lords, removing the remaining hereditary peers and offering Parliament the chance to decide on whether there should be further changes to make the Lords more effective, legitimate and representative. The Government agrees with the Committee that such reform will raise the question of whether or not the current conventions should be carried forward to a differently constituted House.

9. Our answer to that question is that further reform should not alter the current role of the Lords as a revising chamber, and that the conventions governing its relationship with the Commons are fit for that purpose. We believe the relationship the Joint Committee describes is one which should apply to any differently composed chamber.

10. Effective and robust scrutiny of policies and proposals by the House of Lords is essential to good governance. We recognise that changes to the composition of the Lords could make it more assertive in performing this function, just as the 1999 reforms have done. We have no difficulties with this. Indeed overall our reforms have been designed to make Parliament as a whole more effective. Greater activity by the Lords, including more intense scrutiny of legislation, is not, of itself, disruptive of a settled and stable relationship between the two Houses, provided this is not taken to a point where it may threaten the primacy of the Commons. Indeed the Government's general election manifesto called for reform which allows the Lords to be effective 'without challenging the primacy of the House of Commons'.

11. Previous reforms to the House of Lords – such as the introduction of life peers and the removal of most of the hereditary peers – have, over time, altered the House in significant ways. As the Government said in evidence to the Committee:

> *the Government recognises that in respect of the particular constitutional and political environment in the UK that, as the Lords moved to becoming 'more representative' new members especially those elected could well be more assertive about the*

powers of the Lords, and this in turn could appear to challenge the essential primacy of the Commons. The Leader of the House of Commons put it thus in the debate on the establishment of the Joint Committee:

'any change in the composition of the [Lords] will inevitably change its appetite for its role in legislation and therefore in practice its sense of power' (Official Report, 10 May 2005, column 446).

Indeed, there has been a foretaste of this in the changed behaviour of the Lords since the first reforms were introduced seven years ago, with a rebalancing of its membership to ensure that no party has a majority.

For its part, the Government welcomes the active scrutiny which the Lords undertake of both primary and secondary legislation. The Leader of the House of Commons put it that this was 'not a zero-sum matter' either between the Lords and the Commons or the Lords and the Government (Official Report, 10 May 2005, column 472). But in the Government's view it is fundamental to the effective working of our democratic constitutional arrangements that the primacy of the Commons – as described in this paper – is maintained, and that increases or changes in activity by the Lords have to be subject to that constraint.

12. The Committee's report shows that there is general agreement about the current role of the Lords in Parliament. The Government believes that whatever further reform of the Lords takes place, that role is the right one. The question of composition of the House of Lords does not dictate its role. Function does not follow form. The questions of powers and composition certainly impact on each other, but are in fact separate.

13. As the Government made clear in its evidence, international comparisons bear out this point. There is a range of models of second chambers across the world, each constituted differently with varying degrees of power. There is no consistent correlation

between the nature of a chamber's composition and its degree of power relative to the primary chamber. It does not follow, for example, that directly elected chambers necessarily have more power than appointed chambers, or that because their members have democratic legitimacy, they have a greater say over legislation.

14. For example, the Canadian Senate is wholly appointed but has extensive powers in relation to legislation. Although, as the Clerk of the Canadian Senate pointed out to the Joint Committee, conventions have emerged there which have served to restrain the use of those powers, there nevertheless exists no formal mechanism, as there is in the UK, through which the Canadian House of Commons can exercise primacy. Legislation can shuttle between the two Houses indefinitely until agreement is reached. In contrast, the Czech Republic, Japan, and Poland all have wholly directly elected second chambers, which may be thought to correlate with extensive powers, yet in each case the primary chamber is able to override second chamber amendments.

15. Useful examples can be found in the federal systems of Austria and Germany, which have similar indirect methods of election for their second chambers, but quite different powers. In Austria, members of the Bundesrat (the second chamber) are elected by the Austrian provincial assemblies. In Germany, the state legislatures elect some of their own members to serve in their Bundesrat.

16. In Austria, Bills are usually introduced in the Nationalrat (the first chamber), which is the primary chamber. The Bundesrat has the right to submit Bills under certain conditions and can present motions and enquiries to the Nationalrat. In most cases, the Bundesrat has eight weeks to scrutinise a Bill. It may suggest amendments or veto it, but in most cases the Nationalrat can refuse to accept Bundesrat amendments or override a veto. However, when Bills affect the rights of the provinces or the powers of the Bundesrat, a Bundesrat veto is absolute (it cannot be overridden). Such a veto is rarely used.

17. In Germany, by contrast, many financial Bills and all Bills including details on administration (a state prerogative) can be finally vetoed by the Bundesrat. Only for the other 40–50% of Bills, can the veto be overridden by the first chamber.

18. Significantly, our view that the current powers of the House of Lords would be broadly fit for purpose in a reformed House is shared by previous reports on the issue:

The Royal Commission on the Reform of the House of Lords (the Wakeham Commission), chaired by the Rt Hon Lord Wakeham, concluded in 2000 that the overall convention of Commons' primacy and the provisions of the Parliament Acts should remain, were the House to be reformed. This was subject to two important provisos:

> *First, that the reformed second chamber should maintain the House of Lords convention that all Government business is considered within a reasonable time ... Second, we agreed with those that argue that the principles underlying the Salisbury Addison Convention remain valid and should be maintained ... where the Government has chosen a party to form a Government, the elements of that party's general election manifesto should be respected by the second chamber. More generally, the second chamber should think very carefully before challenging the clearly expressed views of the House of Commons on any issue of public policy.*

The Public Administration Select Committee (PASC), in its fifth report of the 2001–2002 session, examined the powers of the Lords in the context of the Government's proposals on Lords reform at that time. They concluded that:

> *There is no proposal for any major change to the role and functions of the House of Lords. This is one of the fundamentals on which there is broad agreement, and it is one of the firm foundations on which reform must build.*

While it considered that the effectiveness of the Lords in its main functions could be improved, PASC nevertheless concluded that:

We agree with the Government that no major change is required to the role or functions of the second chamber. It should continue to be a revising, scrutinising and deliberative assembly.

The previous Joint Committee on House of Lords Reform, also chaired by Lord Cunningham, which was specifically asked to look at composition, came to similar conclusions as the Wakeham Commission, (and PASC when it reported in 2002 and 2003) and strongly supported the continuance of the existing conventions. In its first special report it said:

We envisage a continuation of the present role of the House of Lords, and of the existing conventions governing its relations with the House of Commons. These conventions, which are of a self-restraining nature, impact profoundly on the relations between the Houses and need to be understood as <u>a vital part of any future constitutional settlement</u>. [emphasis added]

This was in the context of a number of different proposals on the future composition of the House of Lords – from an all appointed House right through to a fully elected House. The Committee's conclusions were to stand in any reformed House. The previous Joint Committee shared four members with the Joint Committee on Conventions – Viscount Bledisloe, the Rt Hon. Lord Carter and Lord Tyler (then Paul Tyler MP), as well as the Chair, the Rt Hon. Lord Cunningham (then Jack Cunningham MP).

The cross-party proposals set out in *Reforming the House of Lords – Breaking the Deadlock* recommended in 2005 that no immediate change should be made to the powers of a reformed second chamber, suggesting that 'the current settlement on Lords powers has served us well for more than half a century, and should not be altered without careful thought'.

19. The crucial point is that these reports, all of which advocated an elected element or suggested that this was a viable option, suggested that the role and powers of the Lords should remain the same, no matter what method of composition was decided on.

20. Commons' primacy, as the Government argued in its evidence to the Joint Committee, is based on a number of factors. The most important are the constitutional longstop of the Parliament Acts, and, linked with the Parliament Acts, the Commons' financial privilege and the ability to dismiss the Government of the day. There are no proposals to remove these fundamental aspects of Commons' primacy. The Parliament Acts are the legal framework which underpin this. It is a fact that, in a dispute between the two chambers concerning primary legislation, the Commons has the final say, albeit at the cost of delay.

21. Changes to composition must take account of the current role of the Lords and should be designed to make the Lords more effective at performing that role, rather than undermining or radically altering it. We should not assume that change means that the current conventions are not the right ones for the future. Quite the opposite: the continued application of these conventions should define the powers of a reformed House.

22. As a government, therefore, we support the application of the existing conventions, as described in the Joint Committee report, to any newly composed House. The extent to which there need to be additional steps to secure that would need to be addressed if there was any suggestion that the major parties did not support this approach in the context of a new House.

The Lords since 1999

23. The Committee states: 'At the risk of over-simplifying, the opposition parties are broadly happy with the Lords' behaviour since 1999; the evidence we have received suggests that the public at large feel the same. The Government do not.' This comment could be held to suggest that the Government objects to proper Parliamentary scrutiny of its actions. This is far from the case. The Government welcomes scrutiny of its policies, proposals and legislation, and believes it is essential in our democracy for Parliament to hold the Government properly to account. However, the Government believes that it is entitled on occasion

to question whether or not the correct balance is struck, to use the Committee's words, 'between enabling the Government to do things and holding them to account'. That is part of a healthy tension between Government and Parliament, and, in part, is one of the reasons for seeking the establishment of the Joint Committee on Conventions. As we stated in our evidence: 'For its part, the Government welcomes the active scrutiny which the Lords undertake of both primary and secondary legislation.'

Salisbury-Addison convention (page 76, para 3)

> *3. The Salisbury-Addison convention has changed since 1945, and particularly since 1999 (paragraph 97). Its provisions are:*
> *In the House of Lords:*
> *A manifesto Bill is accorded a Second Reading;*
> *A manifesto Bill is not subject to 'wrecking amendments' which change the Government's manifesto intention as proposed in the Bill; and*
> *A manifesto Bill is passed and sent (or returned) to the House of Commons, so that they have the opportunity, in reasonable time, to consider the Bill or any amendments the Lords may wish to propose (paragraph 99).*
> *4. It would be practical for the Lords to debate and agree a resolution setting out the terms of the Convention as it has evolved, and to communicate it by message to the Commons, which could then debate a motion to take note of the message (paragraphs 114, 283c).*
> *5. We do not recommend any attempt to define a manifesto Bill (paragraph 113). Without such a definition, it will be clear that the resolution is flexible and unenforceable (paragraph 283d).*
> *6. We recommend that in future the Convention be described as the Government Bill Convention (paragraph 115).*
> *7. In addition the evidence points to the emergence in recent years of a practice that the House of Lords will usually give a Second Reading to any government Bill, whether based on the manifesto or not (paragraph 100).*

24. We accept all of these conclusions and recommendations, although we make one further suggestion in relation to recommendation 6 above in recognition of the Committee's work in this area (see paragraph 27 below).

25. The Government welcomes the Committee's view that the Salisbury-Addison convention, as evolved, remains. This convention is fundamental in supporting the primacy of the Commons, and the Government believes that it should remain in place in a reformed House of Lords.

26. The Government welcomes the Committee's recognition in its conclusions that the Lords will usually give a Second Reading to any government Bill, whether based on the manifesto or not.

27. The Committee has set out very clearly how the convention that started off as the Salisbury-Addison convention has evolved. The Government agrees with the Committee's description of how the convention works at the present time. It also agrees that, in recognition of the developments which have taken place over the last 60 years, the time has come to change the name of the convention. We accept the Committee's proposed new name of the 'Government Bills Convention'. However, we are aware of some concern that the name might imply that the same, more restrictive, conventions apply to the Lords handling of non-manifesto government Bills as apply to manifesto legislation (the Committee has in fact noted that all government Bills get a second reading, and manifesto legislation substantially more). We would therefore be receptive to other suggestions on the name of this convention. For example, successful conventions frequently have, as a short title, the name of the individual or individuals who were particularly responsible for formulating them. So, in this case, the convention could become known as the 'Cunningham Convention' in recognition of the work of the Committee and a sign that it was defined by the Committee.

28. The Government also believes that the formulation settled on by the Joint Committee – that: *A manifesto Bill is not*

subject to 'wrecking amendments' which change the Government's manifesto intention as proposed in the Bill – will go a long way to helping address the difficulties, recognised by the Committee, in trying to specify in advance what a manifesto Bill is. The Government agrees with the Committee's view that any attempt to further define a manifesto Bill would make the convention more difficult to operate.

Reasonable time (page 77, paras 8–12)

> *8. There is undoubtedly a convention that the House of Lords considers Government business in reasonable time (paragraph 153). A statement to that effect could be adopted by the House of Lords by resolution and included in the Companion (paragraph 283e).*
>
> *9. There is no conventional definition of 'reasonable', and we do not recommend that one be invented (paragraph 154). Without such a definition, it will be clear that the resolution is flexible and unenforceable (paragraph 283f).*
>
> *10. It would however be possible for a new symbol to appear on the Lords order paper, to indicate a Bill which has spent more than a certain period in the House (paragraph 156). If there is to be a number of sitting days as an indicative measure, for this purpose, of when a Bill may have spent long enough in the Lords, then 80 days is more appropriate than 60 (paragraph 157). This would be a matter for the Lords Procedure Committee (paragraph 283g).*
>
> *11. When the Government criticise the Lords for making slow progress with a Commons Bill, they are on firmer ground when they can point to full scrutiny in the Commons (paragraph 161).*
>
> *12. There is scope for better planning of the parliamentary year as a whole, possibly involving greater use of pre-legislative scrutiny and carry-over. If the Government can even out the workload in both Houses throughout the Session, this should reduce time problems on individual Bills (paragraph 166).*

29. Again, we accept these conclusions and recommendations. In particular, the Government welcomes the Committee's recognition of the existence of the convention on reasonable time.

30. This may go some way to addressing the point made by the Committee, that Bills are taking longer to get through the Lords, and that, as they rightly note, this is having an effect on the management of business.

31. As stated in oral evidence by the Leader of the House of Commons, the purpose behind the Government's manifesto 60 days proposal was that the convention on reasonable time is respected. *What we are seeking is the outcome that is behind the manifesto commitment, which is the consideration of Bills here as a revising chamber and their timely return to the Commons, but we are not necessarily wedded to the method which is specified in the manifesto.* That being the case, the Government would support any efforts to ensure that the convention is adhered to, including the Committee's suggestion that an indication could appear on the Order Paper when a Bill has taken longer than half a session to be dealt with by the Lords. This would be helpful in indicating to members when there is a risk that the convention could be broken. We accept, as we have done throughout, that this would place as much discipline on the Government as on other parties and Members.

32. The Committee states that there is no conventional definition of 'reasonable', and recommends that there should not be an attempt to invent one, in part because this will reduce flexibility. The Lord Chancellor and Secretary of State for Constitutional Affairs recognised this point in oral evidence: *You do need flexibility. The question the 60 days raises is, is it helpful to have a starting point in relation to it?* The Committee's suggestion that 80 days may be a useful indicator of when a Bill may have spent long enough in the Lords is helpful in this respect.

33. The Government notes that the Committee does not seem to address our argument that, under present rules, the Lords has the ability to delay an entire programme in order to pursue its

opposition to one particular measure; or to threaten to do so in order to deter a government from bringing the measure forward in the first place. We take the implication of the report to be that this would infringe conclusion.

34. The Government notes the Committee's overall view on the reasonable time convention. We note and welcome the Committee's acceptance of the evidence of the then Clerk of the House of Commons, that the Lords should respect the Commons' use of its own time. The Government regularly looks at measures which can help smooth out the peaks and troughs of Parliamentary work, such as improved scrutiny and the use of carry-over. Such measures were discussed in the recent report of the Select Committee on Modernisation of the House of Commons on the Legislative Process, which made a number of recommendations relating to the better use of time. In its debate on 1 November 2006, the Commons welcomed the Committee's report and Government business managers will be seeking to take account of the relevant recommendations in their management of the legislative programme. The Government will wish to look at the impact of these and other factors over time, in both Houses, before deciding whether further steps need to be taken in this area.

'Ping-pong'

> *13. The exchange of Amendments between the Houses is an integral part of the legislative process that is carried on within the context of the primacy of the House of Commons and the complementary revising role of the House of Lords (paragraph 188). It is not a convention, but a framework for political negotiation. We find no scope for codification (paragraph 283h).*
>
> *14. It would facilitate the exchange of Amendments between the two Houses if the convention that neither House will in general be asked to consider Amendments without notice was more rigorously observed, i.e. if reasonable notice was given of consideration of Amendments from the other House (paragraph 189).*

35. The Government accepts the Committee's view on the nature of ping-pong, and notes the recommendation on the notice convention. As always, we will endeavour to give reasonable notice where possible. The Government believes, however, that continuation of the increase in the amount of ping-pong since 1997 could seriously disrupt any government's legislative programme.

Secondary legislation

> *15. Neither House of Parliament regularly rejects secondary legislation, but in exceptional circumstances it may be appropriate for either House to do so (paragraph 227). A statement to that effect could be adopted by either House, or both (paragraph 283i).*
>
> *16. Although we offer below a list of examples of exceptional circumstances, we do not recommend defining them further. Without such a definition, it will be clear that the statement is flexible and unenforceable (paragraph 283 j).*
>
> *17. There are situations in which it is consistent both with the Lords' role in Parliament as a revising chamber, and with Parliament's role in relation to delegated legislation, for the Lords to threaten to defeat an SI [Statutory Instrument]. For example:*
>
> *i. where special attention is drawn to the instrument by the Joint Committee on Statutory Instruments or the Lords Select Committee on the Merits of SIs,*
>
> *ii. when the parent Act was a 'skeleton Bill', and the provisions of the SI are of the sort more normally found in primary legislation,*
>
> *iii. orders made under the Regulatory Reform Act 2001, remedial orders made under the Human Rights Act 1998, and any other orders which are explicitly of the nature of primary legislation, and are subject to special 'super-affirmative' procedures for that reason,*
>
> *iv. the special case of Northern Ireland Orders in Council which are of the nature of primary legislation, made by the Secretary of State in the absence of a functioning Assembly,*

> *v. orders to devolve primary legislative competence, such as those to be made under section 95 of the Government of Wales Act 2006,*
>
> *vi. where Parliament was only persuaded to delegate the power in the first place on the express basis that SIs made under it could be rejected (paragraph 229).*
>
> *18. This list is not prescriptive. But if none of the above, nor any other special circumstance, applies, then opposition parties should n3ot use their numbers in the House of Lords to defeat an SI simply because they disagree with it (paragraph 230).*
>
> *19. The most constructive way for the Lords, as the revising chamber, to reject an SI is by motion (or amendment) incorporating a reason (paragraph 232).*
>
> *20. If the Government lose a vote on a non-fatal motion about a Statutory Instrument, they should respond to the House in some way, at least by Written Statement (paragraph 232).*

36. Again, we accept these conclusions and recommendations.

37. The Government welcomes the Committee's conclusion that the Lords should only threaten to reject Statutory Instruments (SIs) in exceptional circumstances. Indeed, the Government suggested in its supplementary evidence some limited circumstances in which we would see it as appropriate.

38. The Committee's view is consistent with our evidence that, though fatal motions are from time to time moved in the Lords, the House almost never chooses to approve such motions (twice in fifty years). The focus at such times is therefore more usually on requiring a government to meet the concerns expressed by Members, or to justify the proposed course of action.

39. The Government welcomes the Committee's conclusion that the opposition parties should not reject an SI simply because they disagree with it. It is important to remember that the power to create SIs, and the principles behind the primary legislation will already have been debated and considered by both Houses of Parliament. It goes without saying that it is at any time open to

Parliament to change the primary legislation. The Government believes this principle should apply even in relation to the types of SI referred to in the Committee's conclusion. Simply because a special procedure is required for particular SIs should not mean that the Lords can feel free to reject the Order on the grounds that it dislikes the policy, if the Order has in fact been properly made under the procedure set out.

40. In relation to the Committee's list of examples of the circumstances in which it could be appropriate for the Lords to reject an SI, the Committee may find it useful to be reminded that the Secretary of State for Northern Ireland has already agreed to consider different arrangements for scrutinising Northern Ireland Orders if devolution is not restored. Similarly, the Government has given a clear undertaking that Parliament will have the opportunity to give full and detailed pre-legislative scrutiny of Orders in Council transferring powers to the Welsh Assembly before they are laid. It is important to remember that these Orders do not make any substantive change to the law, but simply grant competence in a particular area to the National Assembly. The Assembly will arrange its own full scrutiny of resultant Measures, comparable to the scrutiny of primary legislation at Westminster.

41. The Committee's conclusion will be particularly important in relation to a reformed House because just as has been the case since the 1999 reforms, it would be very difficult for a single party to command a majority of the political Members of the House, much less of the whole House.

42. The Government does, as stated in its evidence, take very seriously the passing of non-fatal motions on SIs, but recognises that this is not always as apparent to Parliament as it could be. The Government therefore accepts the recommendation that it should respond to the House in some way if a non-fatal motion is passed.

43. We agree with the recommendation that in the very rare circumstances when the Lords actually reject an SI, rather than just threaten to, they should incorporate a reason for doing so.

44. The Government notes the Committee's comment that: *There is no consensus around the Wakeham proposal for a suspensory veto for the second chamber. As a change in law it is in any case outside our remit.*

45. The Wakeham Commission's proposal was as follows: '*where the second chamber votes against a draft instrument, the draft should nevertheless be deemed to be approved if the House of Commons subsequently gives (or, as the case may be, reaffirms) its approval within three months; and where the second chamber votes to annul an instrument, the annulment would not take effect for three months and could be overridden by a resolution of the House of Commons.*

46. The Wakeham Commission believed that the change to a suspensory veto would give the House of Lords: *greater scope to challenge Government proposals for secondary legislation and draw the issues to the attention of the House of Commons, who would take the final decision ... At the cost of weakening the formal power of the second chamber, in comparison with the present House of Lords, we believe it would actually strengthen its influence and its ability to cause the Government and the House of Commons to take its concerns seriously.*

47. The Government will consider carefully whether any legislative changes in relation to secondary legislation are necessary, but hopes that they are not.

Financial privilege

> *21. When the Lords Economic Affairs Committee scrutinises the Finance Bill, it should continue to respect the boundary between tax administration and tax policy, to refrain from investigating the incidence or rates of tax, and to address only technical issues of tax administration, clarification and simplification. Provided it does so, we believe there is no infringement of Commons financial privilege, and no need to reopen the issue. If the House of Commons believe that their primacy or their privileges are being infringed, it is for them to act to correct the situation (paragraph 244).*

22. If the Government are prepared to describe National Insurance as a tax, then they can seek to bring it within the scope of financial privilege (paragraph 249).

23. If the Commons have disagreed to Lords Amendments on grounds of financial privilege, it is contrary to convention for the House of Lords to send back Amendments in lieu which clearly invite the same response (paragraph 252). This matter could be considered by the House of Lords on the basis of a report from the Procedure Committee, with a view to adding to the guidance in the Companion (paragraph 283k).

48. Commons' financial privilege and the limitations on the powers of the House of Lords in this area are fundamental cornerstones of our Parliamentary system. Their erosion or undermining carry grave constitutional consequences.

49. The Government agrees with the Committee that it is of paramount importance that the Lords Economic Affairs Committee respects the boundary between tax policy and tax administration and refrains from investigating the rates or incidence of tax. In the Government's view, the Lords Committee should take the utmost care to ensure that possible breaches of both the spirit and the letter of Commons financial privilege do not arise.

50. The Government will continue to keep the activities of the Economic Affairs Committee and its Finance Bill Subcommittee under review and will take whatever steps may be necessary to defend Commons' financial privilege.

51. The Government welcomes the Joint Committee's view on amendments in lieu, and will support consideration of this matter by the Lords Procedure Committee.

52. The Government notes the views of the Joint Committee on National Insurance. It remains unpersuaded that financial privilege should not encompass National Insurance and may wish to examine this issue afresh at a later date.

Codification

> *24. All recommendations for the formulation or codification of conventions are subject to the current understanding that conventions as such are flexible and unenforceable, particularly in the self-regulating environment of the House of Lords. Nothing in these recommendations would alter the present right of the House of Lords, in exceptional circumstances, to vote against the Second Reading or passing of any Bill, or to vote down any Statutory Instrument where the parent Act so provides (paragraph 281).*
>
> *25. The courts have no role in adjudicating on possible breaches of parliamentary convention (paragraph 285).*

53. The Government agrees with the Committee's conclusion that the courts have no role in adjudicating on questions of breaches of convention, and will not introduce any proposal which would lead to this happening.

 54. The Government will support efforts in both Houses to provide time for debate to give effect to the Committee's recommendations.

 55. There will always be circumstances where Parliament will feel that it is necessary to depart from convention and usual practice. However, having a shared conception of what the conventions and usual practices actually are helps make clear when they are being departed from, and gives focus to discussions about whether it is right to do so. The Government agrees that the support of all three main parties will be essential to creating a shared understanding, and recognises too that the views of the Cross-bench peers will carry great weight.

The recommendations of the Joint Committee did come up in various debates. But on the whole both Houses stuck to the opinion that the existing conventions should remain conserved. The British constitution was to stand unwritten.

CHAPTER FOURTEEN

2007. A New White Paper on Reform: Jack Straw

The Labour Party's general election manifesto of 2005 promised to complete the reform of the House of Lords, so that 'it is a modern and effective revising Chamber'. Labour, it read, believed that a reformed Upper Chamber 'must be effective, legitimate and more representative without challenging the primacy of the House of Commons'. The process of modernization would include the removal of the remaining hereditary peers. The manifesto also declared that the promised plan would make allowance for a free vote on the composition of the reformed House.[1]

A Cross-Party Working Group on Lords Reform

The Labour Party won the election. Tony Blair, now prime minister for a third term, chose Mr Jack Straw, the leader of the House of Commons and lord privy seal to execute the promises of the manifesto. The choice could not have been better. Mr Straw was a great enthusiast for Lords reform. In addition to his other and various responsibilities, he devoted much of his energy and time to drawing up a plan to reform the House of Lords. Such a plan, he sincerely believed, would be effective, legitimate and balanced only if a cross-party group was mobilized to draft it. Mr Straw succeeded in bringing together such a group, which was composed of the following members:

---

1   See Labour Party manifesto: *Britain Forward Not Back* (2005).

The Rt Hon. Jack Straw MP
leader of the House of Commons and lord privy seal (chair)

The Rt Hon. Lord Falconer of Thoroton
lord chancellor and secretary of state for Constitutional Affairs (Labour)

The Rt Hon. Lord Strathclyde
shadow leader of the House of Lords (Conservative)

The Rt Hon. Theresa May MP
shadow leader of the House of Commons (Conservative)

Oliver Heald MP
shadow secretary of state for Constitutional Affairs (Conservative)

The Rt Hon. Lord McNally
leader of the Liberal Democrats in the House of Lords

Simon Hughes MP
Constitutional Affairs spokesman and shadow attorney-general (Liberal Democrat)

David Heath MP
member of the Commons (Liberal Democrat)

John Warren Gladwin
Bishop of Chelmsford

Lord Williamson of Horton
Convenor of the Cross-bench Peers

The Cross-Party Working Group on Lords Reform began its work in June 2006. It met eight times. During its 'invaluable discussions', the group 'worked with a high level of co-operation'. It recorded that a 'significant degree of consensus' had been found on 'several important aspects', but that there had not been 'unanimous agreement on all the issues'. Where agreement 'could not be reached', the concluding paper reflected 'the different arguments for and against particular options on reform in a balanced way'. There was agreement on:

(i)   the fundamental principle of the primacy of the Commons, and that the House of Lords should be a complement to the Commons, and not a rival to it;

(ii)　that a reformed House should consist of at least 20% non party-political members, and that it was essential that no political party should be able to hold a majority of the whole House or the party-political members of it;

(iii)　that effort should be made to ensure that the membership of the reformed House reflects the gender and racial diversity of the United Kingdom, and that the range of religious opinion in the country should also be reflected in the membership of the Lords;

(iv)　that the remaining number of the hereditary peers should come to an end;

(v)　that members of a reformed House should serve for a long, single term of office, with no prospect of re-election or re-appointment;

(vi)　that the elected element of the House should be elected through a form of direct election;

(vii)　that the reformed House should be hybrid House.

There was no agreement reached on:

(i)　the form of direct election, or timing to be used;

the future proportion of elected and appointed members of the reformed House (it was the government's intention that the free vote should provide a clear answer to this question).

Conclusions in the Group's White Paper

The conclusions of the Cross-Party Working Group formed the basis of a comprehensive government White Paper, which Jack Straw presented to Parliament in February 2007.[2] He introduced it by giving a lengthy

---

2　See *The House of Lords: Reform* (February 2007). Cm 7027. At this time various people made public their views on reform of the House of Lords. These proposals are worth

background of reform attempts from 1911 to 2003. He referred to current steps towards reform of the House of Lords and made international comparisons. These were contained in the first five chapters of the White Paper. Concrete reform proposals for the present day were recorded in chapters 6 to 12, and we present these below.[3] But we begin with Jack Straw's Foreword, which we think is highly instructive.

> Reform of the House of Lords has provoked intense debate and policy initiatives for over 100 years. The Lords is not a static institution. Like other key British institutions, it has changed and evolved through its history, and will continue to do so. This has never been more evident than in the last century, which saw major changes to the Lords – from the Parliament Acts to life peers and the introduction of the first women members of the House.
>
> In 1999, the Government enacted a significant, and overdue, reform by removing the right of the majority of the hereditary peers to sit and vote. As a result of this reform, a more assertive and effective House of Lords has emerged. The reform has improved the scrutiny of Government and in so doing, has improved British democracy overall. However, reform of the House of Lords remains unfinished business. There are still 92 hereditary peers sitting in the Lords. But ending this anomaly, in the Government's view, does not go far enough to ensure that Britain's second chamber is fit to meet the demands and expectations of this century.

---

    referring to: Lord Howe of Aberavon, Lord Carter and Lord McNally in Nicholas Baldwin, 'The House of Lords – Into the Future?', *Journal of Legislative Studies*, June 2007; Donald Shell, *House of Lords* (Manchester: Manchester University, 2007); Meg Russell and Maria Sciara, *The House of Lords in 2006: Negotiating a Stronger Second Chamber* (The Constitution Unit, January 2007); Meg Russell and Maria Sciara, 'Why Does the Government get Defeated in the House of Lords? The Lords, the Party System and British Politics', *British Politics*, 2007; Lord Howe of Aberavon, 'If it isn't Broke', *Journal of Legislative Studies*, June 2007; Andrew Partington and Paul Bickley, 'Coming off the Bench: The Past, Present and future of Religious Representation in the House of Lords', *Theos*, 2007.

3   The tables on pages 17 and 51 of the White Paper are not included in our text.

The legitimacy and authority of the second chamber continue to be called into question.

Significantly, the 2005 manifestos of the three main parties commit them to further reform of the Lords. If changes of the magnitude involved are to take place, broad agreement on some of the key issues and agreement that the changes should be introduced over a long period of time is, to say the least, highly desirable. The alternative is likely to be deadlock. Time and time again – in 1909, 1949, 1968 and 2003 – fundamental reform of the House of Lords has failed because, for some, the best became the enemy of the good. Deadlock would be easy to achieve; the prize of progress means moving forward gradually and by consensus. To reach the next stage of reform, our 2005 General election manifesto committed us to holding a free vote in Parliament on the composition of a reformed House of Lords. This reflects the fact that, despite parties' official positions on reform, there are strongly held and conflicting views on the future of the Lords. These will no doubt be reflected in the way in which the free votes are cast – including by Ministers. The paper therefore offers no prediction on the outcome of the votes: the future composition of the House is a matter for Parliament to decide.

However, to assist debate, and help progress, it is both practical and useful to offer an indication of a model around which consensus on the issue might be achieved. My own view is that a House where 50% of members are elected and 50% appointed is that point. This is also the model that the White Paper uses to illustrate how a hybrid House might work. The final outcome might well be different from this. Free votes are exactly that – free. But even then, the tangible proposals in this paper on transitional arrangements, on electoral systems and on a range of other matters should have focused debate and, hopefully, enabled Parliament to come to a clear view – something which was absent when a free vote on this issue was held in 2003. I believe that the approach outlined in this White Paper represents the best opportunity to make progress. It is, in my view, a unique opportunity to move forward with reform to make the House of Lords a more effective, legitimate and representative chamber, fully playing its part in a 21st century democracy.

What follows comes from later on in the Report:

6. A Reformed Chamber: Principles of Composition
6.1 The Government believes that there are certain principles that should underpin a reformed House of Lords, whatever its composition:

- Primacy of the House of Commons
- Complementarity of the House of Lords
- A More Legitimate House of Lords
- No Overall Majority for Any Party
- A Non Party-Political Element
- A More Representative House of Lords
- Continuity of Membership

Primacy of the House of Commons

6.2 The House of Commons has long been established as the pre-eminent authority in the United Kingdom's Parliamentary system. The party which secures a majority through a General Election has the right to form a Government and, subject to sustaining the confidence of the Commons, to carry through the programme set out in its election manifesto. Ministers are accountable to the House of Commons through debates and votes. Even during formal coalition Governments, the House of Commons has continued to perform its functions relating to the formation of a Government, enacting legislation and holding Ministers to account.

6.3 The primacy of the Commons rests on three clear factors. First, election of its members as the direct representatives of the people has meant the House of Commons has always had greater democratic legitimacy than the Lords, a factor which has grown in importance with the gradual introduction of universal adult suffrage.

6.4 Second is the Commons' power to grant or withhold supply (i.e. public expenditure), which has been asserted for over 300 years. This is the root of the Commons' ability to uphold or dismiss the Government. Without the consent of the House of Commons the Government cannot function. Government expenditure must be approved by those who have the power not just to hold the Government to account, but to withdraw their support so that the Government cannot govern. There is no case for giving the House of Lords the same power to grant or withhold supply, because there must be a single route through which the Government secures its authority to govern. Therefore, the House of Lords should have less power over the Government. And as discussed elsewhere, it is a strength of our current constitutional arrangements that the Lords can ask the Government to reconsider a proposal without calling into question its authority to govern.

6.5 Third, the principle of the primacy of the Commons is enshrined in the Parliament Acts, which limit the power of the Lords to veto legislative proposals, and contain specific provisions relating to Bills which deal with national taxation, public money or loans or their management. It is a fact that in a dispute between the two Houses on primary legislation, the Commons has the final say, albeit at the cost of delay. All major British political parties continue to support the principles of the Parliament Acts.

6.6 It is a common feature of many other bicameral legislatures for one House to have primacy over the other, and there does not seem to be any serious proposal that the primacy of the Commons in the United Kingdom's system should be challenged.

6.7 A reformed House should therefore not threaten the principle of primacy. It must not be a rival to the House of Commons. As the Royal Commission chaired by Lord Wakeham emphasised, *'The House of Commons, as the principal political forum, should have the final say in respect of all major public policy issues'* and *'it would be wrong to restore the fully bicameral nature of the Parliament'.*

Complementarity of the House of Lords

6.8 If a reformed House should not be a rival to the House of Commons, neither should it be a replica. There is general agreement that the House of Lords' role in revising and scrutinising legislation is best met by a chamber that is a complement to the primary chamber. Although there are examples of second chambers which effectively duplicate the functions of their primary chamber (e.g. the Italian Senate), much more often second chambers around the world provide a complementary function. That complementarity is usually reflected in both powers and composition.

6.9 They may, in a federal state, provide for a voice for the constituent states in the central legislature (e.g. the US Senate). They may, in unitary states, provide for collective regional or local representation at the centre (e.g. the French Sénat).

6.10 The House of Lords has traditionally provided a complementary function to the House of Commons through its composition; in the presence of a large contingent of non party-political members, and the fact that its members sit as individuals rather than representing a constituency, and through its powers and procedures. The United Kingdom's Parliamentary system is therefore built around the idea of a complementary second chamber.

6.11 The history of the development of our Parliamentary system shows that the United Kingdom has moved over time from a duplicatory system to the current complementary system. The Government believes that Parliament operates best with such a system. Therefore, a reformed House should continue to be different from the Commons and genuinely complementary.

A More Legitimate House of Lords

6.12 Although the House of Lords is less powerful than the House of Commons, it is a fundamental part of the United Kingdom's Parliament, and has an integral part to play in the creation of the laws that govern our country – it is not powerless. However, the authority of the Lords has been called into question over the last century. Recent concern over the allocation of seats in the House of Lords has once again brought this question to the forefront of debate. Despite a recognition that the House is working, its unelected basis means that, in many people's eyes, it still lacks the necessary legitimacy to carry out its current role.

6.13 The issue of legitimacy goes to the heart of the question of reform. In a modern democracy in the 21st century, it is increasingly difficult to justify a second chamber where there is no elected element. There is a strong case that the electorate should have a say in who is able to contribute to making the laws that govern it. A reformed House should be more accountable to the people of the United Kingdom than the current House. This greater democratic legitimacy would not just increase confidence in the second chamber, but strengthen Parliament as a whole.

6.14 As ever, the United Kingdom's constitutional arrangements must be a careful balancing act. The 'extent' of the reformed House's legitimacy needs to be balanced against the principles of primacy of the Commons and the complementarity of the second chamber outlined above. It is on the combination of these three fundamental principles that discussions about further reform of the Lords should be built.

6.15 If this is accepted, the following other key principles of composition should help deliver that.

No Overall Majority for Any Party

6.16 As shown in table 4 below, the House of Lords currently includes approximately an equal number of Labour and Conservative members. The third group by number is the non party-political members, and the fourth the Liberal Democrats. At 4 January 1999, 66% of the Lords taking a party whip were members of the Conservative Party. Since the 1999 reforms, no single party has been able to command a majority of the party-political members of the House of Lords. The largest party, the Labour Party, holds 42% of the party-political seats in the Lords. Overall, it makes up approximately 29% of the House.

6.17 This essential principle should remain in a reformed House. No single party should normally be able to command an overall majority of the political parties in the House of Lords. It may be that exceptional circumstances, such as a union of two parties, or very high public support over a long period of time for one party, could produce a House where a party has a majority over the other political parties. However, in the models discussed below, this is highly unlikely, and if at least 20% of the House is non party-political, public support for a party would have to be extraordinarily high for a long period of time to give a party a majority of the whole House. The principle that it should not normally be possible for a party to command a majority is crucial to maintaining the House of Lords' complementary role.

6.18 A balance between the parties would enable the House of Lords to continue to be relatively independent from the executive or any one political party, creating a clear distinction between the two Houses of Parliament. It would ensure that, within the House, the flow of work was generally negotiated, not imposed. The balance helps prevent any party, whether Government or opposition, from dominating the House of Lords either by blocking legislation or acting as a rubber stamp of the House of Commons.

Non Party-Political Element

6.19 As a result of the manner of their appointment, the powers of the Lords and above all their life term, the membership of the Lords is able to encompass a very wide range of views. A good many serving members of great distinction and expertise take a party whip, and this should be welcomed. But one of the distinct strengths of the current House of Lords is the presence of non party-political members. Their presence helps to focus debates on the merits of the argument in question, and away from partisan politics. This distinct feature should be preserved in a reformed House.

6.20 As to the proportion of non party-political members to form part of the reformed House, the Wakeham Commission suggested this should be at least 20%, and the Government agrees. This would be a large enough proportion to ensure, along with the other proposals in this White Paper, that no single party could achieve an overall majority in the House, and encourage the political parties to ensure they try to attract the support of the future non party members in presenting their position in debate.

6.21 This is not to suggest that the only reason for having the non party-political members is to block an overall majority. The non party-political peers currently play a very important role in the House, both in committee work and debates. This contribution should continue in a reformed House.

Table 4: Analysis Of Composition In The House Of Lords: As At February 2006

Party	Life Peers	Hereditary Elected by Party	Hereditary Elected Office Holder	Hereditary Royal Office Holder	Bishops
Conservative	157	38	9	0	0
Labour	207	2	2	0	0
Liberal Democrat	72	3	2	0	0
Crossbench	169	29	2	2	0
Bishops	0	0	0	0	26
Other	10	2	0	0	0
TOTAL	615	74	15	2	26

A More Representative House of Lords

Religious Representation

6.22 It is important that faith communities are represented in the House of Lords. The Church of England, as the established Church, enjoys a special status in social and political life in England and more widely around the United Kingdom. This has long been recognised even by people who are not themselves

Anglicans. Lords Spiritual have sat in the Lords since its inception. They are the only category of member whose term is limited to the holding of their office. There have in the past been arguments about the disestablishment of the Church of England. There is little steam behind such arguments today, and, in any event, any profound change in the status of the Church must be in the first instance for the Church itself. It is therefore right for there to continue to be special representation of the Church of England in the reformed Lords.

6.23 Whilst recognising the quality of work Lords Spiritual bring to the House, there remains a strong case for a more flexible approach which would allow the Church to determine, from among the Bishops, those who they consider would be able to make the best contribution, rather than appointment on seniority. Assuming the overall size of the House reduces, it would be difficult to justify retaining the current number of 26 Lords Spiritual.

6.24 It is equally important that a reformed House of Lords reflects the wider religious make-up of the United Kingdom, though the formal nominated representation of particular faith groups may not be possible. As the Wakeham Commission pointed out, 'It is clearly not possible to find a way in which all other faith communities could be formally represented on any kind of ex-officio basis. None of them has a suitable representative body.' The Government will look carefully at how the views of those of faith and those of none can be represented in a reformed House of Lords.

This will of course only be realistically possible if there is a significant appointed element in a reformed House.

Regional Representation

6.25 Before the 1999 reforms, as the Wakeham Commission indicated, membership of the House of Lords was heavily biased towards the south-east of England and Scotland in terms of the origin of its members. Although more members have joined the House from outside these regions since then, the potential for this bias remains. A reformed House of Lords should be set up to ensure that representation of the nations and regions is inbuilt, serving the interests of the whole of the United Kingdom, no matter what method of composition is chosen. Whilst members would not represent the interests and views of an individual constituency or assist with the problems of individual constituents as MPs do, their membership would as a whole be representative of the views held right across the nations and regions of the United Kingdom.

A Diverse Membership

6.26 It is vital that the diversity of interests and people are represented in a reformed House of Lords. One of the criticisms of Parliament as a whole, and of the Lords in particular, has been that it is not as representative as it could be of contemporary British society. Recent reforms – in particular the work of the House of Lords Appointments Commission – have made some progress in this direction, but work still remains to be done. The Government will look at how, under any system for choosing members of the House of Lords, the method of selection can best take account of the diverse population of the United Kingdom.

Continuity of Membership

6.27 One of the strengths of the current House of Lords is the continuity of its membership. Members serve for a long time, and new members make up a small proportion of the House. The Lords does not see the major changes in composition of the kind that the Commons experiences when there is a change of Government.

6.28 This is valuable for two reasons. First, the length of service helps ensure that members are able to take a long-term view of the issues before them, looking beyond election cycles and other relative short-term considerations. Second, it ensures that there is a great deal of experience of both the legislative process and the work of the House which can readily be passed on to new members when they become members of the House.

6.29 It seems desirable that a reformed House should try, as far as is possible, to retain this element of continuity, even if the terms of membership are unlikely to be as long as they are for current members.

6.30 Furthermore, if the Lords is to be wholly or partly elected, the terms of membership should be designed to maintain the current independence of the Lords. Long terms of office will help deliver this, as should the prevention of re-election or re-appointment. This will ensure that members are free to take potentially unpopular positions on issues without having to consider whether their standpoint makes it more or less likely that they would be returned to the House either by their party or the electorate.

7. A Reformed Chamber: Elected, Appointed, or Hybrid?

7.1 The question of how individuals obtain a seat in the House of Lords is the most hotly debated point in all discussions on Lords reform. The method of composition decided on for a reformed House must be able to deliver on the key principles outlined in the previous chapter. Broadly speaking, there are three main options, an all-appointed House, an all-elected House, or a hybrid of the two.

All-Appointed

7.2 A House made up of an all-appointed membership has the advantage of being the simplest way to ensure that the majority of the principles of composition set out above are met.

7.3 Appointment would mean that the composition of the Lords did not replicate the Commons at all. It would provide the maximum opportunity for those with sufficient experience of the outside world to gain a seat, and it would help ensure that the House properly reflects the diverse population of the United Kingdom.

7.4 However, an all appointed House fails to meet a crucial principle in a reformed chamber – that of legitimacy. It does little to meet the expectation of many that in a modern Parliament, the second chamber should have a degree of democratic legitimacy. Indeed, previous proposals for a fully or majority appointed House of Lords have been strongly criticised on these grounds, claiming that such composition would diminish the credibility and authority of the House in Britain's Parliamentary system.

All-Elected

7.5 Those who support a fully elected House believe that this is the best option because it is the most democratic model for a reformed House of Lords. It is often suggested that the limited, but still significant, power of the Lords to scrutinise, amend, and in some circumstances, delay legislation, should be justified by electoral authority. A fully elected Lords could also ensure that members were more obviously representative of the nations and regions of the United Kingdom.

7.6 However, a fully elected House could challenge a number of the other principles of composition set out in this paper. It is likely that such a House would become more overtly party political than the current House, which could well be detrimental to both its effectiveness and to the respect in which it is held. It is possible that such a House would find it difficult to avoid challenging the primacy of the Commons, undermining the principle of complementarity.

7.7 It would be very difficult in a fully elected House to ensure the desired degree of representation of non party-political members, because the political parties would be very likely to dominate any election process. Depending on the election system chosen, there is an increased likelihood that a single party could come to dominate the House, risking turning it into either a permanent block or a rubber stamp for the policies of the Government of the day.

7.8 Unless strict rules were in place about the individuals who were allowed to stand for election, it would be very hard to ensure that the principles of representation of the racial and gender mix of the United Kingdom, and the representation of religious opinion, were met. It would also be impossible, in a fully elected House, to see how representation of the Church of England could continue.

7.9 Additionally, some models of a fully elected House could pose a risk to the principle of continuity. The obvious way to ensure that the House is genuinely reflective of the political views of the United Kingdom is to elect the entire membership at once. This risks exposing the House of Lords to the kind of dramatic changes in membership that can be experienced by the Commons, and would mean the loss of valuable experience, expertise and continuity. Depending on when elections take place, it also risks creating a duplicate of the Commons both in terms of political balance, and in the behaviour of members.

7.10 There are also strong arguments that members should not be able to seek re-election to help preserve independent judgement and to ensure that they are not focused on seeking a second or third term. If this is accepted, then combining this with re-election of the whole House would mean the entire membership of the House changing at each election, which seems highly undesirable.

7.11 If members of a fully elected House entered through staggered elections, rather than all at once, this would safeguard a degree of continuity. However, staggered elections inevitably mean that the balance of the parties overall would not be the same as at the previous election, even if the relative votes for each party were similar.

7.12 This would undermine the legitimacy of a fully elected House (and the benefits to be expected from it), because two-thirds of the membership would not be reflective of current political opinion in the country. It would, however, go some way to mitigating concerns that a fully elected Lords would be a challenge to the Commons.

Hybrid

7.13 If a fully appointed House would lack the legitimacy necessary to make it effective, and a fully elected House might not deliver the necessary diversity of membership and sufficient presence of non-political members (as well as having other drawbacks), then the obvious alternative would seem to be a hybrid of the two.

7.14 All major cross-party proposals brought forward on Lords reform over the past 10 years have been for a hybrid House. Although they may have disagreed on the ratio of elected to appointed members, the Wakeham Commission, the Public Administration Select Committee (PASC) Report of 2002, and the more recent cross-party proposals, *Reforming the House of Lords – Breaking the Deadlock*, all proposed a hybrid House in one form or another.

7.15 The Wakeham Commission proposed a majority appointed House with a significant element of regional members. The Commission felt that a fully elected House would too readily be a potential source of challenge to the primacy of the Commons, and would not enable those with wider experience and expertise to enter the House easily; a fully appointed House would not allow the electorate any choice in the membership of the Lords and would not allow for adequate regional representation. The Commission offered three options for the elected element, ranging from approximately 12% to 35% of the House.

7.16 The report of the Wakeham Commission stated that each of the three options on an elected element 'has the support of different members of the Commission. Model B [87 regional members, elected at the same time as European Parliament elections] has the support of a substantial majority of the Commission.'

7.17 The PASC report analysed all the main options and concluded that a fully or majority appointed House would lack legitimacy and therefore authority, and a fully elected House: 'would leave little or no room for non-aligned people who are independent of party. And there is a fear that it could jeopardise some of the other principles set out above: that no party should have an outright majority (which cannot be precluded, even under proportional voting systems); that the House should be more diverse in a whole variety of ways (because this would be left to the hazards of party selection); and that the second chamber should include expertise and experience from people whose careers have lain outside politics.'

7.18 The Committee also argued in favour of retaining an element of party-political appointments:

> *We expect the parties to continue to nominate members of two kinds. First, former Prime Ministers, Cabinet Ministers, party leaders and other senior MPs who want to continue to serve in Parliament, but to retire from the House of Commons. In future such figures would have no routine expectation of a seat in the second chamber, but would have to take their chance within their party's quota. However, those who have served with distinction in Parliament and Government can and should be able to make a contribution in the second chamber. We do not subscribe to the denigration of party politicians and believe that they may have a valuable role to play in the reformed second chamber.*
>
> *Second, the parties will continue to nominate experts similar to those who sit on the cross benches, but who have a party affiliation. Not all experts are non-political: to take examples from three recent appointments, Lord Winston, professor of gynaecology (Labour), Lord Wallace of Saltaire, professor of international relations (Liberal Democrat), and Lord Norton of Louth, professor of Government (Conservative) are all distinguished experts in their respective fields who take the party whip.*

7.19 The Committee came down in favour of a predominantly elected House, proposing a split of 60% to 40%.

7.20 Breaking the Deadlock argued, for very similar reasons, that the House should be predominantly elected: 'A mixed chamber allows the strengths of both the elected and appointed models to be combined. It also helps ensure that whilst the chamber gains legitimacy, it can never challenge the primacy of the fully elected House of Commons. We believe that the diversity that a mixed chamber can bring should be celebrated.' The report argued for a 70% elected chamber.

7.21 In any model for a hybrid House, the appointed element, both non party and party-political members (should there be any) would be appointed by the Appointments Commission (as discussed at Chapter 8).

7.22 One objection to a hybrid House is that the differences in method of entry to the House would cause difficulties. It is argued by some that two classes of member would develop, with elected members claiming a greater degree of legitimacy, and therefore authority, than appointed members. How far this is a likely risk is questionable. The current House of Lords is, in some senses, a hybrid House. The House has long contained different categories of members – life peers, Lords Spiritual (who leave on retirement as Bishops), and hereditary members. Indeed, this objection ignores one of the strengths of the House of Lords (and one the Government would want to maintain in a reformed chamber) – the focus of its membership on the work they are there to do as members of the House, irrespective of how they got there.

7.23 If elections and appointment rounds are staggered, and appointments take account of the balance of support for the parties at the most recent General Election, then it would be difficult for particular individuals to claim that they have greater legitimacy than others. They would be one part of an institution embodying a number of different principles, all designed to deliver an effective second chamber of Parliament.

7.24 As to the correct proportion of elected and appointed members, the final decision rests, of course, with Parliament. However, the model for a reformed House set out here follows the PASC report's suggestion that there should be a rough balance between elected and appointed members. Rather than the 60/40 framework proposed by PASC, however, it envisages a 50/50 split. As mentioned in the Wakeham Report, systems of direct election sometimes tend not to provide a gender-balanced representation, or adequate representation for ethnic, religious and other minorities. That being the case, the White Paper illustrates a model of a hybrid House which, as well as non party-political appointments, allows for some party appointment within a framework which encourages greater diversity, to help ensure that the membership of the political parties within Parliament as a whole is more diverse than it might be under a system where the only party members of Parliament were elected.

7.25 A hybrid House of 50% elected, 50% appointed (20% non party-political and 30% party-political appointments) would allow for legitimacy through direct election, greater diversity within the political parties in Parliament, and a significant element of non party-political membership within the House of Lords. Models composed of a greater proportion of elected members would obviously include fewer party politically nominated members. A House with an 80/20 split, for example, would not contain any party politically appointed members at all.

7.26 If Parliament agrees that a hybrid House is the way forward, whatever proportion of elected to appointed members is eventually decided on, then there are two questions which need to be addressed: how do people get elected, and how do people get appointed?

Electing Members – Indirect or Direct Election?

Indirect Election

7.27 An indirect election system has been suggested by some, on the grounds that this would give legitimacy to the Lords while retaining some of the valuable aspects of an appointments system. Indirect election could also – it is argued – avoid any claims that the Lords had a different, and possibly more legitimate, mandate than the Commons, and should therefore have increased powers.

7.28 There is a range of options to deliver the idea within the overall heading of an indirect system, from electoral colleges made up of the main locally elected politicians and/or devolved assemblies, to direct representation of vocational and interest groups in the second chamber, and the so-called secondary mandate.

7.29 These options might offer a greater degree of democratic legitimacy than a fully appointed House, but the complexity of the systems, and the inevitable arguments about who would comprise the electoral colleges, or which organisations would be represented in the House of Lords are often seen as disadvantages to the proposals.

7.30 The simplest form of indirect election, which has been particularly suggested in the context of House of Lords reform, is the so-called secondary mandate proposal, where seats are allocated to nominated individuals on the basis of the proportion of votes cast at the General Election. Were it to be followed, it would probably be most appropriate on a regional basis.

7.31 Although very simple to operate, the secondary mandate proposal has significant disadvantages. The degree to which both it, and other indirect options, is more legitimate than a fully appointed House is open to question. Some argue that an indirectly elected House, where the general electorate casts no specific vote for its membership and has no say over the individuals who subsequently enter the House, is an all-appointed House by another name. The secondary mandate system leaves power almost entirely in the hands of the parties and may not meet public concerns about party control over who enters the House. It also counts votes cast for one purpose and uses them for a different purpose, which is unlikely to be regarded as satisfactory.

7.32 Such a system might also have consequences for voter behaviour at General Elections – acting as a distraction from the main purpose of electing MPs.

7.33 It can also be argued that the lack of any clear and transparent link in any indirect system between voters and the Lords would do little to increase the perceived legitimacy of the Lords.

7.34 The Wakeham Commission discounted any form of indirect election from the devolved institutions or United Kingdom MEPs to a reformed House. However, one of the three potential systems it put forward for electing its proposed regional element was what it called a 'complementary system', which was similar to the secondary mandate. Under this system, the votes cast for the parties' general election candidates would be accumulated at regional level and the parties would secure a number of regional members of each region proportional to their share of the vote in that region.

Direct Election

7.35 Direct election of individuals plainly would confer more legitimacy than an indirect system. Many other second chambers around the world use direct election as the method for selecting the whole or part of their membership, and it allows every voter in the country to have a say in who sits in the House of Lords.

7.36 If direct election is agreed as a principle, the next question is about the method of election to be deployed, and what constituencies should be used.

Direct Election – Electoral Method

7.37 Direct elections to the Lords could either be (a) first past the post, or (b) by one of the more proportional methods of election. There are two basic forms of the latter – list systems, or transferable or alternative vote systems.

First Past The Post

7.38 This system of voting is strongly linked to the idea of territorial representation, where an individual would stand for election and represent individual constituencies, rather than segments of opinion or political parties. The candidate who secured the most votes would be elected to Parliament and the chamber (or the elected element of it) would be comprised of all the individual representatives from the different constituencies.

7.39 The electorate is familiar with this method of voting. It would be simple and straightforward, and people would clearly understand how the voting would work. It also meets the legitimacy principle; voters would have a direct say in exactly which individual represented them in the reformed House of Lords, as they do in respect of the House of Commons.

7.40 It has also been argued that first past the post is better than list systems in allowing independent candidates to stand and be successful. A number of elected independents, as well as the appointed non party-political members, might further enhance the independent nature of the chamber.

7.41 The classic argument in support of first past the post is that it generally delivers majority Governments with a clear mandate, and that this benefit far outweighs the fact that the system is not proportionate. Supporters of first past the post also argue that no system of election is able to translate a proportionality of votes into a proportionality of power, and that first past the post does ensure that it is typically the largest minority of votes, not the smallest minority, which is able to exercise power, via a majority of seats. Although very strong, these arguments are only relevant to the chamber in Parliament which delivers the Government of the day. In the United Kingdom, that is the responsibility of the Commons. As a scrutinising and revising chamber, the Lords does not have any responsibility for delivering a Government. The argument in favour of using first past the post to elect its members therefore is considerably weaker than it is in respect of the Commons.

7.42 Those in favour of first past the post for the House of Commons cite the clear link between the member and the constituency as key strength – people would know which individual represented their area in a reformed House of Lords. And the personal accountability of that member would be transparent – people could see what 'their' member was voting for, and against.

7.43 For elections to the Lords however, this strength could easily become a weakness, as it poses a potential threat to the primacy of the House of Commons. Not only would the electoral mandate of the two Houses be identical, but it would also create the greatest potential for a rival focus to the constituency MP. A constituent who was, for example, unhappy with their MP's stance on an issue could try and get their member of the House of Lords to help them, thus creating a rivalry between the MP and the member of the Lords. Of course, such rivalry may exist between elected representatives covering the same area but in different democratic bodies (e.g. in the devolved legislatures, European Parliament, or local government) but rivalry within the same Parliament could pose a problem of quite a different order.

7.44 The importance of the current link between constituent and MP in the Commons cannot be overstated. At present, every citizen of the United Kingdom has a clearly identifiable point of contact for their issues and concerns, and a direct link to the legislature of the country. They also know that their MP is expected to represent their interests whether or not they happened to vote for the MP. Another person who might try and carve out a similar role would undermine the link between constituent and MP, and erode the clarity of the connection between citizen and Parliament, and the distinction in function between the two chambers.

7.45 Because of the way in which seats are allocated compared to proportions of votes cast, if first past the post were applied to the second chamber it makes acute the risk of the Lords becoming either a block or a rubber stamp for the policies of the Government of the day. A Government with a significant majority in the Commons could also have a large majority in the Lords too (even if, say, 20% of the seats were non political-party appointments). This would undermine the desired complementary role of the House of Lords, making it a more openly party political House, in competition with the Commons. It could also make it much more difficult to deliver a situation where no single party can under normal circumstances enjoy a majority in the Lords.

7.46 First past the post is criticised in some quarters for not delivering seats in proportion to votes cast. A variant could be to apply the alternative vote (where candidates are ranked in preference and votes are transferred until one candidate achieves more than half of the vote), which would deliver a more proportionate result within the individual constituencies. It can lead, however, to a less proportionate vote nationally, with first and second choice votes being split between two parties, squeezing out the first choice votes for the third.

7.47 Constituency size is a particularly important factor when considering any system of first past the post. If the same constituencies are used as for MPs, the risk of a competing role with the MP is heightened, and the size of the House increases beyond that proposed. If larger constituencies are used, then some of the advantages of first past the post (e.g. representativeness, connection with the constituency) carry less weight.

Regional Lists

7.48 In a regional list system voters are asked to choose between lists of candidates proposed by the political parties on a regional basis. Seats are then allocated to the parties in accordance with their proportion of the vote. This is the system which Parliament established in 1999 in respect of the European Parliamentary elections. Lists can be run on open or closed systems.

7.49 The advantage of the list system, whether open or closed, is that it produces a proportionate result, thus ensuring that more shades of political opinion in an area are represented. It also reduces the personal involvement of the member in the 'constituency', thus reducing the risk of the representative(s) of a particular area becoming a rival focus to the MP.

7.50 It emphasises that all the elected members represent the whole of the electoral area, and this wider-range of interests also helps to mitigate the risk of competition with the role of the MP.

7.51 In a closed list system, such as that used for elections to the European Parliament, voters simply select from the choice of parties, and the parties' ranking of the candidates is used to select the candidates who eventually take up a seat. Members who leave the House would be replaced by the next person on the list from that region, as is the case for European Parliament elections.

7.52 In a closed list system, the voter has a clear choice over the party for which they vote but no discretion over the identity of those elected. This gives a good deal of power to the political parties, allowing them to select and rank their candidates. It has been argued that this compromises the accountability and the independence of the candidates – dissenting voices are unlikely to be highly ranked within a list.

7.53 Partially open list systems go some way to overcoming the criticism levelled at closed lists by enabling the voter, if he or she wishes, to vote for an individual on the list, rather than for the party. The vote will still count towards the party's total in determining the number of seats to which it is entitled. Individuals on the list, however, may collect sufficient votes to entitle them to a seat within their party's quota, even if their original place on the list was too low to qualify.

7.54 As with a closed list, a partially open system would ensure that the relationship between the elected member and the electoral area is qualitatively different from that between the MP and his constituency. At the same time, it would give electors the opportunity to express support for an individual on the list, and therefore help them to connect better with the electoral process. It is more complicated to understand than a straightforward closed list system, and a method of election not presently used for other elections in the United Kingdom.

Single Transferable Vote

7.55 In a multi-member constituency, a Single Transferable Vote (STV) system would rank all (or some) of the candidates in preferential order. Seats within each constituency would then be allocated on the basis of a ranking of the proportion of votes cast for each candidate, with the least popular candidates dropping out of contention (and their votes transferring to the voters' alternative choices) until the seats are filled.

7.56 The advantage of such a system is that it produces a proportional result. It also allows the voter to nominate an individual, rather than a party, and thus it is claimed enhances accountability, and can give voters a feeling of ownership of at least one of the selected members. It can also allow voters to spread their votes among the parties and independent candidates.

7.57 This is a complicated system to operate, primarily in terms of counting the votes. It is the system of choice in some countries, e.g. Ireland, but it has been argued that such a complex system discourages voters.

7.58 The fact that individuals, rather than parties, have to campaign for votes may lead to individuals attempting to gain a higher public profile which could create a more political House. Individuals elected in this way may view themselves as having a more democratic mandate than in other systems, and could even argue that they have more of a mandate than MPs in the Commons, thus risking undermining the relationship between the Houses.

Constituencies

7.59 Because the existing Westminster constituencies would produce too large a House, and would risk competition between the role of the MP and the role of the member of the House of Lords, the only realistic options for the constituencies for Lords elections are as follows:

- (a) Those used for the European Parliament.
- (b) Cities and counties of the United Kingdom (the 'top-up' constituencies recommended by the 1998 Report of the Independent Commission on the Voting System).
- (c) Ad hoc groupings of Westminster constituencies.

(a) European Parliament Constituencies

7.60 European Parliament constituencies are coterminous with the nations and regions of the United Kingdom, and use of them would therefore emphasise the regional basis for membership of the House.

7.61 There is a political structure already in place in these constituencies, and election officials are used to operating within them. They are also large enough to deliver a proportional result when electing in staggered tranches of one-sixth of the whole House, within a total House of the size discussed later in the paper and on the basis of a 50/50 model (see Chapter 9).

7.62 The size of the European constituencies would also be large enough to diminish the risk of competition with the local MPs. However, some see their size as a disadvantage, arguing that they are too large and not easily identifiable, and therefore the regional link between voters and their elected representative in the Lords would be almost non-existent. That said, this may not be of crucial significance in the case of a reformed House as it is not envisaged that regional representatives will have the same role or visibility at a local level as an MP.

7.63 Another potential disadvantage is that constituency sizes vary quite widely, with small geographical but densely populated areas, like London, electing a higher number of members than, for example, a physically larger but sparsely populated region like the north-east.

(b) Cities and Counties of the United Kingdom

7.64 The 1998 Report of the Independent Commission on the Voting System (commonly known as the Jenkins Commission) suggested that for elections to the House of Commons, 80 special constituencies could be created to elect, by alternative vote, additional MPs as a top-up to the existing ones. These constituencies were based on the cities and counties of the United Kingdom, and there have been proposals to use these constituencies, or very similar ones, to elect representatives to the House of Lords.

7.65 The advantages are that these constituencies are readily identifiable for voters, they have more meaning and are more clearly linked to the area in which they live than the European Parliament regions. This would be particularly important if a first past the post electoral system were used, where one of the main benefits is a clear connection between constituent and representative.

7.66 The disadvantage is that, because of the number of constituencies, only a small number of representatives could be elected at each staggered election. Without this, the size of the eventual House becomes too large. For example, on a 50/50 model, electing 3 members per constituency per election means electing 240 members per election, and over a 3-election cycle this gives a House containing 720 elected members, with the possibility of some appointed members on top. Electing one or two members per constituency reduces the proportionality of the result within the constituency, and nationally, because only one person would represent the diverse range of views within an area.

7.67 The nature of these constituencies also makes it more likely that members will be drawn into local constituency work, creating competition between members and MPs.

7.68 Another drawback is that there would be no relevant political infrastructure to support these constituencies as there would be with the European constituencies. This would increase the cost of elections to the Lords.

(c) Ad hoc Groupings of Westminster Constituencies

7.69 A variation on the Jenkins Commission constituencies would be to devise new ones, of a size better suited to elections to the Lords. Careful selection would enable the constituencies to be the same size and return the same number of members, which may be seen to be fairer. Separating the constituencies from those used in other elections will also emphasise the importance in their own right of the elections to the House of Lords.

7.70 That said, these ad hoc groupings might not have any inherent identity and arguments about which areas should fall in which constituency could be complex. Voters would also be less likely to know which constituency they live in, and consequently who their representative in the Lords was. As with the criticisms levelled at the European constituencies, this is not necessarily a major problem given that there is not intended to be a constituency role.

7.71 Ad hoc groupings share similar problems with the cities and counties of the United Kingdom, in terms of their lack of political infrastructure.

7.72 For the system to allow a proportional result with only a proportion of members being elected at any one time, the constituencies would need to be quite large. In practice, they could therefore end up as little different from the regions used for European Parliament elections. It also seems unnecessary to design new constituencies when appropriate ones are already used for elections to the European Parliament.

Timing of Elections

7.73 There are several options for when elections and appointments to a reformed House of Lords could be held. All of the options discussed here are predicated on the idea that elections will be staggered, specifically, that a third of the elected element will be replaced at an election, and will sit for a term of three elections. This is to help ensure that the principle of continuity is not lost if there is an elected element in the Lords. Under the 50% elected, 50% appointed model, this will mean that one-sixth of the whole House will be chosen at each election.

(a) At the Same Time as a General Election

7.74 Holding elections to the House of Lords at the same time as elections to the House of Commons would be likely to give the highest turnout, thus enhancing the democratic accountability of the reformed House.

7.75 It would also emphasise the nature of the House of Lords as an important part of our Parliamentary system. Voters would be electing their regional representatives to it, as well as electing their local MP and helping to determine the party of Government.

7.76 Although some would argue that using two different voting systems at the same time may confuse voters, other combined elections already frequently require this.

7.77 The risk that Parliamentary terms under this timing system would be uneven and slightly uncertain (particularly if two General Elections were held quite close together) can be mitigated by having minimum terms of a specific number of years to compensate for any such circumstances, but these arrangements would be complex, and not readily understood. For example, the term of office could be until the dissolution of the Parliament in existence on the twelfth anniversary of the election to the reformed Lords. This would give terms of between 12 and up to just under 17 years, though in practice the term would be likely to be between 12 and 15 years. There would also need to be very detailed rules for determining whether elections to the reformed Lords should need to be held at all if a second General Election were held shortly after the first (as in 1964–66, and in 1974). It would also be inevitable that people would serve terms of differing lengths under this system.

7.78 However, elections at the same time as a General Election do not, unlike the other options, demonstrate that elections to the Lords are clearly different from the elections that deliver the Government.

(b) Alongside Elections to the European Parliament

7.79 The main advantage of elections at the same time as elections to the European Parliament is that the electoral cycle is fixed at 5 years, so it would be very straightforward to set the length of a member's term in a reformed House at 15 years.

7.80 It would also be more straightforward administratively if the same regions and electoral cycle were used for both European and House of Lords elections, and it could enhance the regional aspect of the elections.

7.81 Although turnout for European elections is historically much lower than that for General Elections, the prospect of elections to the House of Lords could boost turnout, enhancing the credibility of both elections.

7.82 It is likely that European elections would fall between General Elections, which creates a difficulty in respect of

Parliamentary procedure. If elections to a reformed Lords fell within sessions of Parliament, there is some risk that voting on individual pieces of legislation could be affected by the replacement of a third of the membership of the Lords part-way through consideration of legislation.

7.83 Similar arguments apply in respect of elections tied to those for the devolved administrations and to entirely freestanding elections, but these are not insurmountable difficulties.

(c) Alongside Elections to the Devolved Assemblies

7.84 There are two advantages of holding elections alongside elections to the devolved assemblies. First, there is a regular election cycle of four years, giving a fixed overall term for members of the Lords. Secondly, the coincidence of elections would help to bind the devolved elections more closely into the United Kingdom electoral system, and would mean that the whole of the United Kingdom, not just parts of it, were all voting on the same day.

7.85 The disadvantage is that there is at present no structure in England that is set up to hold major elections alongside elections to the devolved assemblies, as there is for the European Parliament elections.

7.86 Another drawback is that the electorate may be unhappy if elections to the Lords use different voting systems from those to the devolved assemblies.

By-election

7.87 There are different ways of replacing members of the Lords following resignation or death, but all are faced with the same difficulty. The term of office will be fixed, and entry and exit will only normally takes place at an election or at an appointment round. Therefore any entry or exit that takes place away from an election or appointment round causes difficulties in deciding how long an individual's term should be.

7.88 All options for replacement have their drawbacks. Some proposals lead to variable sizes of cohorts of Lords entering the

House at each election or appointment round. Some, such as not replacing members who leave the House, would require a very large House in order to cope with the effect of membership declining over time.

7.89 The simplest option, favoured by the Government, is to replace members as and when they leave (unless there was less than a year of their term remaining) with the incoming members serving the remainder of the term of the person they replaced.

7.90 The drawback of this option is that some individuals will serve very short terms, of perhaps as little as a year, with no prospect of re-election. Although it might seem at first that it would be difficult to find suitable candidates to serve shorter terms, in practice there are likely to be a good many people with the necessary abilities who would like to serve in the Lords but would prefer not to serve for a full term.

7.91 The question of whether a by-election is necessary will depend to a large extent on the method of election chosen. If first past the post is used, then a by-election will almost certainly be required. List systems allow the option of 'promoting' the next candidate willing to stand off the list of the party that won the seat. Under STV, it may well be that the next most popular candidate is someone of a different party, but since no party will be in the majority in the Lords, this may not be a serious consideration.

7.92 Appointed members who leave the House could, of course, simply be replaced by another appointment.

Government Proposals: Elections

7.93 The Government's overall judgement is that the most appropriate system of election for a reformed House of Lords is a partially open regional list system – which is the most consistent with the principles set out in Chapter 6. We will consider further the precise details of the list system to be used.

7.94 Under this kind of system, parties will wish to consider how they ensure that their lists are representative of the diversity of the United Kingdom. The Government will consult on and consider whether there is a case for making diversity a formal requirement for party lists, in respect of gender and/or ethnicity, and/or other factors.

7.95 In terms of constituency, the simplest approach is to use the regions used for elections to the European Parliament. Constituencies which are smaller and encourage a more direct constituency role could undermine both the position of MPs, and the role of the member of the House of Lords in a reformed chamber.

7.96 Overall, the advantages of holding elections to the Lords at the same time as elections to the European Parliament seem to outweigh the disadvantages. It is proposed therefore that elections should take place at the same time as elections to the European Parliament, giving a 15-year term for members of a reformed House. This approach also produces the simplest procedure for the electorate, who would vote at the same time, in the same area, for both their European representatives and the Lords. It is likely that parties would need to reach a minimum threshold of votes before they could gain entry to the Lords. The Government will consult further on this point.

7.97 Both appointed and elected members would sit for 15 years, and there would be no prospect of re-election or re-appointment. One-third of the elected members and one-third of the appointed members of a reformed House would be replaced at each election. Members who had been elected could not subsequently be appointed, nor could former appointees be elected.

8. A Reformed Chamber: a Statutory Appointments Commission

8.1 There seems to be general agreement that under any system with appointed members, party and non party-political appointments would be overseen and made by an independent Statutory Appointments Commission.

Pre 2000

8.2 Prior to the establishment of the current Appointments Commission in 2000, the arrangements for appointing life peers were somewhat haphazard. There was no system of inviting widespread nominations and no systematic machinery in place to identify appropriate candidates. The Prime Minister decided nominations from his or her own party, sometimes creating peerages to enable individuals to serve as Ministers. The Prime Minister invited recommendations from other party leaders to fill vacancies on their own benches. Non party-political appointments were in the control of the Prime Minister and the Political Honours Scrutiny Committee vetted all nominations for life peerages.

Current Appointments Commission

8.3 The House of Lords Appointments Commission, an independent, advisory, non-departmental public body, was established in May 2000 to assist with the transitional phase in reforming the House of Lords, to recommend non party-political appointments and vet all nominations of individuals to sit in the House of Lords. In February 2005, its remit was extended to take on the functions of the Honours Scrutiny Committee to scrutinise for propriety individuals added to the honours lists by the Prime Minister.

8.4 The Appointments Commission currently consists of six members, including the Chairman. Three members represent the main political parties and ensure expert knowledge of the House of Lords, and the other members, including the Chairman, are independent of Government and political parties. The current members of the Appointments Commission have been invited by the Prime Minister to continue to serve, pending further discussions on the House of Lords. The posts are part time, and the Cabinet Office provides the secretariat to the Appointments Commission.

8.5 Under the current arrangements, the Prime Minister retains the power to decide the overall number of new peers created and the balance between the parties. The appointment of party-political peers is a matter for the Prime Minister, in consultation with the other party leaders. The Appointments Commission is responsible for vetting the nominations but does not assess the suitability of those nominated by the political parties, which is a matter for the parties themselves. The Appointments Commission's role is to advise the Prime Minister of any concerns about propriety and it is the Prime Minister who then passes on the nominations from other parties to The Queen.

8.6 The responsibility for recommending non party-political appointments lies with the Appointments Commission. The Prime Minister then passes on these recommendations to The Queen and will not intervene, except in the most exceptional circumstances.

8.7 The Prime Minister has retained the power to nominate direct to The Queen a limited number of distinguished public servants on retirement and has agreed that the number of appointments under this arrangement will not exceed ten in any one Parliament. The Prime Minister also makes direct nominations to the Queen in respect of ministerial appointments.

8.8 The Appointments Commission role in vetting nominations does not extend to ministerial appointments, the Law Lords or the Lords Spiritual.

Performance of the Current Appointments Commission

8.9 As of May 2006, the Appointments Commission had appointed 36 individuals as non party-political members to the House of Lords, making up almost a fifth of the total number of non political-party members sitting in the House. Of these appointments, there are 9 from minority ethnic groups and 2 with disabilities. The Appointments Commission has appointed almost half of the female members sitting on the Cross-Benches.

8.10 Some of the members appointed by the Commission sit on Lords' committees. Many have made important contributions to discussions in the House on key matters of public interest, reflecting their own experience and expertise.

Proposed Statutory Appointments Commission

8.11 The current system of appointment cannot be retained in a reformed House. The establishment of the non-statutory

Appointments Commission was a temporary measure designed to assist with the transitional phase in reforming the House of Lords. Under any system with an appointed element in a reformed House, an independent United Kingdom body would need to oversee future appointments, as the Wakeham Commission recommended.

8.12 The proposals for the Appointments Commission set out here are broadly based on the Wakeham Commission's proposals, which envisaged that the Appointments Commission would have the only role in appointments to the reformed House:

> *The Appointments Commission should be charged by the Crown with a general duty to appoint members to the second chamber and empowered to appoint individual members on its own authority. (Recommendation 80).*

8.13 Whilst the Wakeham Commission acknowledged that there was no direct parallel for such a body in the United Kingdom or abroad, it argued that it was by no means an entirely new approach in the British constitution (Wakeham Commission report, paragraph 13.8). It identified several bodies in the United Kingdom that already had responsibility for sensitive elements of the relationship between the Government and Parliament – for example, the National Audit Office, the Parliamentary Commissioner for Standards and, more recently, the Electoral Commission. All these independent bodies play an important role in ensuring the smooth running of the Parliamentary system.

Legal Status

8.14 The role of the current Appointments Commission is limited to the appointment of non party-political appointments. Its only role in relation to party political appointments is to check nominations for propriety. Whilst it would be acceptable for the Appointments Commission to remain on a non-statutory basis if its current role were to continue, it would not be appropriate if its role were to increase significantly.

8.15 As it is envisaged that the new Statutory Appointments Commission would have power over both non-party and party-political appointments, the parameters of those powers would have to be laid down in statute. The body should be established by primary legislation. The Statutory Appointments Commission would be independent of Government and should be accountable to Parliament, rather than Ministers.

Membership of the Statutory Appointments Commission

8.16 It is envisaged that the Statutory Appointments Commission would consist of a total of 9 Commissioners to be formally appointed by The Queen on the address of both Houses of Parliament. There would be three members to represent the main political parties and the remaining six would be independent of Government and the political parties. The Commissioners would serve fixed but renewable terms of office.

Role of the Statutory Appointments Commission

8.17 The Statutory Appointments Commission would recommend people for appointment in two different classes:

- Political-party appointments (where nominations would be invited from the parties) and;
- Non party-political appointments (where individuals would be selected by the Statutory Appointments Commission).

8.18 It is envisaged that the principal functions of the Statutory Appointments Commission would be:

- To establish the characteristics as to suitability which members of the House of Lords should possess (and publish these criteria).
- To ensure that these characteristics deliver high calibre appointees who make a significant contribution to the work of the House of Lords.
- To select all non party-political members using an open and transparent selection procedure.

8.19 Under the current arrangements, the Appointments Commission has no responsibility for ministerial appointments, the Law Lords, representatives of the Church of England and ex-officio members. The Wakeham Commission, however, suggested that the Appointments Commission should be the only route into the reformed House although, in practice, their view was that this would be a formality in regard to the regionally elected members, the Law Lords and the Lords Spiritual.

8.20 The current proposals envisage following Wakeham's recommendations in this regard, with the exception of the Lords Spiritual and the elected members of the reformed House, who would enter the House without going through the Statutory Appointments Commission. It appears eccentric that those who have been elected to seats in the House should have to go through the Statutory Appointments Commission, even as a formality. However, the Government believes that where members of the legislature are not elected, it is important that the constitutional principle that the Prime Minister should pass names to the Monarch should be preserved. Therefore it is proposed that the Prime Minister will receive a list of names for appointment from the Statutory Appointments Commission, and pass this to the Monarch without alteration.

Non Party-Political Members

8.21 The principle that 20% of the reformed House should be non party-political members is discussed in Chapter 6. It is envisaged that the Statutory Appointments Commission would select these non party-political members to be recommended for appointment, with the exception of the Lords Spiritual. This would also include the retired Justices of the Supreme Court, although as the Wakeham Commission suggested, this will likely be a formality.

8.22 As with all public appointments, the Statutory Appointments Commission would be expected to consider nominations on the basis of merit and would follow strict criteria.

8.23 There would be a duty on the Statutory Appointments Commission to encourage nominations from a broad range of applicants and the Government will look at how appointments to the reformed House could better reflect the diverse makeup of the United Kingdom.

8.24 For example, the Government would want to urge the Statutory Appointments Commission to set up its procedures and methods of selection in a way that encourages the appointment of a widely representative House of Lords. In looking at diversity, the Statutory Appointments Commission could be expected to consider matters such as economic and professional background, as well as issues like gender, ethnicity and regional roots. The Government does not at this stage envisage any statutory provisions in this respect. Nor does it expect that those appointed by the Statutory Appointments Commission should feel that they have been appointed as 'representatives' of a particular group. Most people are likely to feel that they have multiple identities and interests, and appointed members in particular will be sitting as individuals with no mandate to act as representatives. The intention is that the House of Lords, taken as a whole and taking all the qualities that each member brings to it, should better reflect the diverse make-up of United Kingdom society.

8.25 It will clearly be important to assess this aspect of the Statutory Appointments Commission's work, and whether the requirement was being adhered to in an appropriate way, over a reasonably long timescale.

Political Party Members

8.26 Political party appointees would only form part of a reformed House in a hybrid model where the proportion of elected members was below 80%. In the event that the free vote resulted in support for an 80% elected chamber, there would then be no party political appointees. This is because of the principle that 20% of the reformed House would have to be non party-political members. The following paragraphs illustrate how this appointments procedure might work in practice.

8.27 It is envisaged that the Statutory Appointments Commission would have to take account of the balance of the parties at the last General Election and appoint party-political members in line with the proportion of votes cast.

8.28 So, for example, a party that polled 20% of the vote at the General Election would receive 20% of the party political seats. Based on the model of a House of 540 members, with a third of the appointed members put in place at each appointment round, this would mean they received 11 out of the 54 party political appointed seats available in that round.

8.29 This is of course a version of the secondary mandate proposal discussed above, but it does not make a direct link between the votes cast and the overall composition of the Lords, and therefore does not risk altering voter behaviour. It is designed to ensure that the party political appointments reflect the support of the parties in the country at that time. This, combined with the elected members, helps ensure that while the composition of the Lords would be different to the Commons, it would nevertheless have an element of similarity with it, and would help reduce the risk of a reformed Lords acting as a block to the decisions of the Commons.

8.30 As the Wakeham Commission proposed, the parties would put forward recommendations for suitable members to the Statutory Appointments Commission. In parallel to any diversity considerations used by the Statutory Appointments Commission, the political parties could be required to take account of diversity criteria in making their nominations. This would ensure that the Statutory Appointments Commission had an adequate pool of nominations from which to create the necessary balance of new nominations to the House.

8.31 It is proposed that the Statutory Appointments Commission would perform a more extensive role in relation to the party members than it does now, and assess the suitability of those put forward by the parties against its published criteria. The Statutory Appointments Commission would therefore have the power to refuse to recommend a person for appointment on more than simply grounds of propriety.

8.32 The Statutory Appointments Commission could ask the political parties for a list of candidates, perhaps ranked in preferential order, which would include more candidates than there were spaces. Should the Statutory Appointments Commission reject a candidate, it could refer to the next candidate on this list. It would be for the Statutory Appointments Commission to make the final selection in terms of its published criteria.

Prime Minister's Appointments

8.33 The Prime Minister is currently able to make a small number of appointments directly to the House, both of former public servants and individuals, to serve as Ministers. There is a question as to whether this practice should continue in a reformed House.

8.34 There is a case for retaining the current arrangements and allowing the Prime Minister to make Ministerial appointments and up to 10 appointments of former public servants per Parliament. The Statutory Appointments Commission would vet candidates for the House for suitability, and would be able to reject those they did not feel met the criteria for appointment.

8.35 However, some argue that, beyond the Prime Minister submitting the Statutory Appointments Commission's list of nominees to the Monarch, and his or her role in selecting party-political nominations as leader of their party, there should be no other role for the Prime Minister in appointments to the Lords. The Government agrees with this.

8.36 In this circumstance, Ministers could only be drawn from the already appointed and elected membership of the House. This is discussed further in Chapter 9. Distinguished former public servants and those that the Government felt would be suitable to be Ministers would be considered by the Statutory Appointments Commission as part of its usual appointment round (with potential Ministers being part of the governing party's allocation of appointed seats). Such former public servants would be likely to rate highly against the Statutory Appointments Commission's appointment criteria, as would individuals nominated to serve as Ministers, but the current situation, where the holders of certain offices are always offered a seat in the Lords on retirement, would end.

9. A Reformed Chamber: Membership

Size of the Chamber

9.1 Before the 1999 changes, the House of Lords had a membership of over 1000. The House of Lords currently has a membership consisting of around 740 Members, 92 of whom are hereditaries. This is larger than the House of Commons which has 646 MPs and is one of the largest Parliamentary chambers in the world. It is highly unusual for a second chamber to be larger than the first. However, not all members of the Lords attend on a regular basis. For instance, taking the 2005–2006 session, the average attendance was around 408, which better reflects the 'working' size of the House of Lords.

9.2 It would be practical and, in our view, desirable for the size of a reformed House to be reduced from its current membership, and it should be smaller than the House of Commons, to reflect its status as the second chamber. This in turn suggests that a form of remuneration might be needed to ensure that a higher proportion of members attend regularly than current attendance figures show.

9.3 There is no precise science for determining the exact size of the House but it must be large enough to allow for the right proportion of non party-political members for the House to be effective, but in its final form not larger than the House of Commons.

9.4 Suggestions for the size of a reformed House have ranged from 350 members in the PASC report and in *Breaking the Deadlock*, to the 550 mark suggested by the Wakeham Commission.

9.5 The Government believes that a House of 540 members, near Wakeham's suggestion, is a realistic target and an appropriate size. Given the lengthy transitional arrangements we are proposing (see Chapter 10) it is likely to be the middle of the century before the House reduces to the desired size. A House of 540 members on a 50/50 model would see 90 elected members being replaced at each election, and 84 appointed members being replaced in each round of appointments (36 non party-political, and 54 party-political appointments). Lords Spiritual would count towards the appointed total (which is why the number of appointed members at each election is lower than the number of elected members), but would be appointed on different terms to the remainder of the House.

9.6 Based on the percentages of votes cast at the last three General Elections, and assuming a House of 50% elected, 30% party-political appointments, and 20% non party-political appointments, Table 5 below shows the possible mak-eup of the House in numerical and percentage terms. Note that this is an estimate of the 'steady state' composition of the Lords under the proposed new arrangements, once any effects of the transition mechanism have dissipated.

Table 5. Possible make-up of the Lords in numerical and percentage terms

Group	Number of seats	Percentage share	Percentage share of all seats
Conservative	159	37	29
Labour	166	38	31
Liberal Democrat	78	18	15
Other	29	7	5
Non party-political	108	n/a	20

Minimum age limit

9.7 Traditionally membership of the House of Lords has consisted of individuals who have made a significant contribution to the role of their chosen profession and to society. Those individuals tend to be older, having worked for the majority of their career in their chosen field. It is important that in a reformed House of Lords the experience of fields other than politics is retained to achieve a broadly representative membership. Whether or not this would be achieved by introducing a minimum age limit is debatable.

9.8 The Wakeham Report highlighted that many overseas second chambers, including the USA, Canada, France and India, have a minimum age requirement higher than that set for the lower House. However the report did not suggest that a minimum age should be introduced for a reformed House of Lords, suggesting instead that the appointments commission should ensure that those nominated had the requisite experience and expertise to make an effective contribution to the work of the House. The Government agrees that this is the most sensible way forward, and that the minimum age to enter the House of Lords should be the same as for the House of Commons (currently 18).

Payment and Resourcing of Members

9.9 Currently the expenses of members attending the House are reimbursed up to certain maxima per sitting day as detailed in Table 6. [See below]

Allowance Provided to Members Attending the House

Overnight accommodation	£159.50
Day subsistence	£79.50
Office cost	£69.00

9.10 A new system of remuneration for members of a reformed House should be considered. The question of levels of remuneration is properly one that should be subject to consideration and recommendation by the Review Body on Senior Salaries (SSRB) once the final shape of the reforms has been decided.

9.11 However, recommendations 119–124 and recommendation 126 of the Wakeham Commission are likely to be the guiding principles for any changes to the remuneration of members of the Lords.

- *Recommendation 119: The financial arrangements which apply to members of the second chamber should make regular attendance economically viable for people who live outside the South East of England and who do not have a separate source of income. (Paragraph 17.7.)*
- *Recommendation 120: Payment should be made for the time members of the second chamber devote to their Parliamentary duties. (Paragraph 17.9.)*
- *Recommendation 121: Financial support for members of the reformed second chamber should be related to attendance in Parliament. (Paragraph 17.10.)*
- *Recommendation 122: Total payments made to members for time and lost income should be less than the basic salary of an MP over an average session. (Paragraph 17.11.)*
- *Recommendation 123: Chairmen of significant Committees of the second chamber should receive a salary in respect of their additional duties. (Paragraph 17.12.)*
- *Recommendation 124: The SSRB should consider the issue of severance payments and pension arrangements for members of the reformed second chamber. (Paragraph 17.13.)*
- *Recommendation 126: The SSRB should review the rules governing the payment of expenses incurred in respect of travel and overnight costs by members of the second chamber in the course of their Parliamentary duties with a view to ensuring that regular attendance is economically viable for people who live outside London. (Paragraph 17.17.)*

9.12 It will also be important that any new arrangements are flexible enough to allow members to attend the House on a full or part time basis.

9.13 The Wakeham Commission recommended that resources should be provided for additional office resources for Members of a reformed Lords. This is properly a matter for Parliament to consider. However, any future discussions on this particular aspect of resourcing will need to take into account the threat to complementarity which could result from a package which encouraged individuals to start working on a constituency basis, and which might distract members' attention from the work in the House and its Committees.

9.14 Consideration will have to be given to whether the existing members of the Lords could and should remain on the existing arrangements or be transferred onto any new ones. The Government will give careful consideration as to whether a retirement package could be provided for existing members who wish to leave the House of Lords.

9.15 The Government believes that there may be a case for additional remuneration for leaders of the opposition parties in the Lords, in addition to that already provided, and for the Convenor of the Cross-Bench peers, both in recognition of their hard work, and to make it easier for them to attend as often as possible. The Government will consider asking the Review Body on Senior Salaries to look at these posts in any review of remuneration in the Lords.

Ministers in the Lords

9.16 Two questions arise over the position of Ministers in the House of Lords. First, should there be any? Secondly, if so, how should they get there, and should they have special terms of membership?

9.17 It has been suggested that there should be no Government Ministers in a reformed House. This would further underline the distinction between the Commons, which gives a Government the authority and resources to govern, and the Lords, which scrutinises and revises legislation and policy proposals.

9.18 If there were no Ministers in the Lords, arrangements could be put in place to allow Commons Ministers to appear in the Lords to answer questions on Government policy and legislation, so that the role of the Lords in helping to hold Government to account is not diminished.

9.19 However, the Government proposes to maintain the current place of Ministers in the House of Lords, where they play a valuable role. As well as more easily allowing the Lords to hold the Government to account, and improving the Lords' understanding of the position of the Government, it also enhances the Lords' role in scrutinising legislation, because Ministers and Whips in the Lords help take legislation through. It also means that the Government has a better understanding of the concerns of the Lords because Ministers spend time there.

9.20 Ministers would be drawn from the elected and appointed members of the party of Government. In a House with a very high proportion of elected members, there is a possibility, albeit extremely slim, that the party of Government might not have enough members of the Lords from which to draw Ministers. The question of how Ministers enter the Lords may therefore need to be returned to if Parliament decides upon a very high proportion of elected members for a reformed House of Lords.

9.21 In making nominations for appointment, as noted by the Wakeham Report, it is likely that anyone nominated because they were felt suitable to serve as Ministers would easily meet the nomination criteria. It would be very unusual for a Statutory Appointments Commission to reject someone who was nominated to serve as a member of the Government.

Law Lords and Retired Justices of the Supreme Court

9.22 With the creation of the Supreme Court in 2009 to take over the appellate jurisdiction of the House of Lords, judges will no longer need to be members of the second chamber in order to be members of the United Kingdom's highest court. Indeed the Constitutional Reform Act 2005 will prevent any Justice of the Supreme Court and other holders of judicial office from sitting and voting in the House of Lords while they hold office.

9.23 There is, however, no doubt that retired Law Lords make a very valuable contribution to the work of the current House of Lords, and the non party-political peers have 19 retired Law Lords in their ranks.

9.24 Offering every retiring Justice of the Supreme Court a seat in the House of Lords would ensure the continuity of the kind of contribution brought by the current retired Law Lords. The value of the expertise brought to the work of the House by the retired Law Lords would justify the offer of a seat in the reformed House to retiring Justices. They would become part of the non party-political cohort of the reformed House, and would be appointed by the Statutory Appointments Commission at the next appointment round following their retirement.

9.25 It must also be remembered that the peerage, and a seat in the House of Lords, will be separate things in a reformed House. The question of whether all Justices of the Supreme Court should be offered an automatic peerage either on appointment or retirement is therefore separate from the question of a seat in the Lords, but will also be considered as part of the question of Lords reform.

Lords Spiritual

9.26 At present, the Church of England is represented in the House of Lords by the Archbishops of Canterbury and York, the Bishops of London, Durham and Winchester and the 21 Bishops next in seniority in order of appointment to a diocesan see (a Bishop who changes diocese keeps his seat in the Lords once he has entered it). This arrangement dates back to 1878, when it was agreed that the need to increase the number of Church of England dioceses should not lead automatically each time to an increase in their representation in the House of Lords. When the 1878 Act was passed, there were four qualifying Welsh Bishoprics. When the Church in Wales was disestablished, there were no changes in the number of seats allocated to the Lords Spiritual; instead, any seats then occupied by Welsh Bishops were re-allocated to the next qualifying English Bishops.

9.27 The Government has always recognised that the nature of diocesan Bishops' work means that it is very difficult for many of them to attend the House of Lords with regularity and therefore that their overall representation needs to be higher than would otherwise be appropriate. However, a smaller number than 26 would still deliver this. Much of the work in the House is already done by a smaller core team of Bishops. For example, of the Lords Spiritual between April 2005 and March 2006, 11 attended more than 25 times (out of a possible total of 134). 12 attended fewer than 20 times. 42% of the total number of attendances was accounted for by just 5 of the Bishops and the top 16 Bishops accounted for 89% of total attendances.

9.28 In the light of these figures, and taking into the account the reduction in the overall size of the House, the Government believes that the Church could continue to be well represented with fewer Bishops. It proposes reducing their number in discussion with the Church of England.

9.29 However, given that it would then be more important that those who were members of the House were those who were best able to contribute, the Government sees a strong case for the Church of England to have the legal flexibility to decide itself which Bishops should sit in the House, rather than this being determined on seniority.

Resignation

9.30 Members of the House of Lords should be able to relinquish their membership, should they wish to do so, irrespective of how they arrived in the House. This could be for a number of reasons, including ill health. It would also help address the current anomaly under which members cannot become MEPs, arising from the rules preventing an existing member of a domestic legislature from pursuing a career with the European Parliament at the same time.

9.31 No grounds should be required for a member to resign. It should be a formal but straightforward process.

Leave of Absence

9.32 The Government believes that if resignation provisions are introduced, together with a remuneration package based on attendance, then there is little case for continuing the present arrangements through which peers can seek leave of absence from the House, and that the system should be abolished.

Restriction on Former Members of the Lords Standing as MPs

9.33 To ensure that the complementary role of the House is enhanced, it is important that an individual should not use his or her membership of the Lords to build a political base for a career in the House of Commons. The intention would be that the House of Lords should attract those who have wider interests outside politics, including among the members representing political parties. To counteract the possibility of members using the House of Lords to build a political base, members who have held a seat in the House of Lords could be prevented from seeking election to the House of Commons for a certain period of time after their Lords' term expired.

9.34 It would remain open to former members of the Lords to seek election to other political bodies, or to serve in politics in another capacity, but a gap between service in the two Houses of Parliament is important in maintaining good relations between them, and in ensuring that members of the House of Lords are dedicated to the work of the House.

9.35 Both the Wakeham Commission and PASC proposed a waiting period of ten years. *Breaking the Deadlock* proposed a period of five years, and the Government is minded to agree with this, and that the period should be calculated from the moment when the member's term was due to expire, whether the member served the full term or resigned beforehand.

Breaking the Link with the Peerage

9.36 If, in a reformed House of Lords, members (whether appointed or elected) were to serve for a fixed number of years rather than for life, it would seem odd for those individuals to be given a lifetime honour simply to enable them to do a job for a fixed period of time. The automatic link between the peerage and membership of the House of Lords should therefore come to an end. The peerage would continue as an honour but unconnected with a seat in Parliament, though it is highly probable that many people of distinction holding a seat in the reformed Lords would receive this honour.

Franchise

9.37. Current rules prevent a member of the House of Lords (which includes all life peers) from voting in a General Election. This prohibition would no longer make sense if all peers did not automatically qualify for membership of the Lords. Therefore all members of the peerage and members of the reformed House of Lords (whether members of the peerage or not) should be allowed to vote in all elections, and members of either House would not be prohibited from voting in elections to the other House. Allowing members of the peerage outside the House to vote would also address the anomaly where the current Law Lords, who will eventually transfer to the Supreme Court, will not be able to vote in General Elections because of their peerages.

9.38 Hereditary peers outside the House can already vote.

Disqualification

9.39 MPs who are convicted of a criminal offence and sentenced to more than 12 months imprisonment are disqualified from the House of Commons, and their seat is automatically declared vacant (ex-MPs in these circumstances wishing to return to the House would need to seek re-election). Current rules however, allow a member of the House of Lords in the same circumstances to resume their seat immediately upon release from prison.

9.40 To address this anomaly, provisions could be brought in to bring the disqualification of members of the House of Lords into line with those of the House of Commons. Arrangements could be brought in as for the House of Commons in relation to members who are subject to a bankruptcy restriction order (BRO) or detained under the Mental Health Acts. Members currently cannot sit and vote in those circumstances but are free to return to the House immediately the condition is lifted. It would be more consistent to bring all these provisions in line with the Commons so that the member will lose his or her seat, rather than simply being disqualified for sitting and voting.

9.41 There may be an argument for having a minimum sitting requirement which members have to fulfil, and the Government will listen to suggestions, particularly from the House of Lords, on this issue.

Name of Reformed Chamber

9.42 For the time being, the future House of Lords will be referred to as the 'reformed chamber' but we will consult on the name in the lead up to legislation. Decisions on the name will partly depend on what final decisions Parliament reaches on composition. This was the approach adopted by the Wakeham Commission.

10. A Reformed Chamber: Transition

10.1 Although there is a range of different options for managing the transition to a reformed House, the Government believes that a long transitional period, where new members are introduced but none of the current members of the Lords are forced to leave, is the best way forward.

10.2 The current members have entered the House in the expectation that they will stay for life. Some will have given up careers and other roles to do so. It would be unfair to require them to leave in these circumstances.

10.3 A long transition period also helps ensure the continuity of the work of the Lords, blending the experience of the current membership with the qualities that new members would bring to the House.

10.4 The United Kingdom also has a history of gradual change, with institutions and practices adapting over time to changes in circumstances, and a long transition is in keeping with this tradition. It will allow the House of Lords, and Parliament as a whole, to adapt to the reform over time, moulding their procedures and traditions onto the new shape of the legislative process.

10.5 Critics will argue that the transitional period, which could last into the middle of the century, is too long. However, if the changes argued for in this paper are the right ones, then they are likely to last well beyond this relatively short period of change. As stated in the introduction, any change must be gradual or reform will not take place at all. We must learn from the lessons of previous efforts to reform the Lords. Of course, once reform has bedded down, it will be up to Parliament in the future to decide whether the proportion of the elected to appointed members, settled on after the free vote, continues to be the right one.

10.6 It is also important to remember that the transition period is not a period until reform starts and the first new members arrive; it is a period until the House is constituted only of members who have entered under the new arrangements.

10.7 Tables *7* and 8 below show what the House could look like. As can be seen, as new members are introduced, the size of the House starts to increase, and then fall away again in line with the decline in number of the current membership.

[...]

10.8 The modelling work for the transitional period is based on the eventual total size of the House being 540 (108 non-party, 432 party) with 50% elected, 30% party appointed, 20% non party-political appointed. Previous post-war General Election results have been used to generate estimates of the strength of the parties in the House.

10.9 The modelling is based on European election dates, where the first election date is 2014, the second 2019, the third 2024, and so on every five years. The decline in the size of the current House (including the hereditary peers) has been mapped onto these dates, and the appropriate number of elected and appointed party members added in. The modelling assumes that 36 non party-political members will be appointed when an election to the Lords takes place. It also assumes that 20% of the existing House will resign or retire.

10.10 It is important to remember that these figures represent all members eligible to sit. Attendance in the chamber may be lower. Under this model the maximum size of the House during the transition period is 751. Although this is still lower than the number of members eligible to sit before the 1999 reforms (which was well over a thousand) this could still create difficulties in terms of office space for that many active members. However, this will not arise as a question for some years, so there will be time for the House to decide what approach it wishes to take to this issue.

Removing the Hereditary Peers

10.11 The Government has been clear that in a modern democracy it is unacceptable that individuals still qualify for a seat in Parliament on the basis of their ancestry. The transitional arrangements made in 1999 should therefore come to an end by formally ending the right of the remaining hereditary members to membership of the second Chamber.

10.12 If Parliament indicates support for the further reform of the composition of the House of Lords (see Chapter 11 on Next Steps), then the Government intends formally to end the right of the hereditary peers to sit in the House of Lords, whatever the precise outcome of the Free Vote on the composition. This is an explicit commitment of its 2005 manifesto.

10.13 Removing the hereditary peers is technically straightforward. Legislation could be brought forward either (a) to remove their right to sit and vote (by cancelling the relevant provisions of the 1999 House of Lords Act), or (b) to cancel the provision for by-election of hereditary peers, effectively placing the existing 92 hereditary peers who sit in the Lords in the same position as the existing life peers.

10.14 The first alternative would be the most direct and obvious way of removing the remaining sitting hereditaries from membership of the Lords. This could be done with immediate effect as soon as the legislation came into force. Conversion of the existing sitting hereditaries into life peers would have the same formal effect – the removal of the hereditary peerage from the Lords, but it would mean that its full impact would take many years.

10.15 The first alternative is the one with the obvious advantage of fairness between the political parties – but for one important consideration. The Conservative group in the Lords relies disproportionately on sitting hereditary peers compared to the other parties, as table 9 below shows. So if the first alternative were chosen, it is the Government's view that in order to maintain the balance of the parties, the Leader of the Conservative Party would be entitled to nominate an equivalent number of life peers – some of whom of course might be existing hereditary peers (there could be much smaller rights of nomination to the Leaders of the other parties and a special invitation to the Appointments Commission to consider the claims of the outgoing non-party sitting hereditary peers to become life peers).

10.16 Currently, the membership of the three main parties breaks down as shown in Table 9. [See below]

Table 9. Current Membership of the Three Main Parties of the House

Group	Percentage of 3 main parties	Percentage of whole House
Conservative	159	37
Labour	166	38
Liberal Democrat	78	18

10.17 Removing the hereditary peers changes this picture to what is shown in Table 10. [See below]

Table 10. Forecast Membership of the Three Main Parties of the House

Group	Percentage of 3 main parties	Percentage of whole House
Conservative	36	25
Labour	47	32
Liberal Democrat	17	11

10.18 The removal of the hereditary peers will disadvantage the Conservatives much more than the other parties, not just because there are more Conservative hereditary peers but because the average age of Conservative life peers is higher than that of the other parties – 74 compared to 67 for Labour and 65 for the Liberal Democrats. Given a long overall transitional period this will not correct itself until around 2050.

10.19 Converting the existing hereditary peers into life peers goes some way to dealing with the imbalance in average ages. This is because the average age of Conservative hereditary peers is 62, which brings the overall average age of Conservatives down to 70.

10.20 Of course, if the hereditary peers were to be removed immediately, and new members appointed in their place, the Leader of the Conservative Party could chose to appoint younger members in order to bring down the party's average age.

10.21 Currently the non party-political peers, excluding the minor parties but including the Lords Spiritual, make up 28% of the whole House. Discussions thus far have indicated that at least 20% of a reformed House should be non party-political. If the hereditary peers were removed, the number of non party-political members would decline to 23% of the total House.

10.22 In terms of the percentage of non party-political peers in the House, there is no requirement to replace any hereditaries who leave. Nor does the removal of the hereditary peers bring the percentage fully down towards the 20% mark.

10.23 In a reformed House, the Statutory Appointments Commission would make enough non party-political appointments to ensure that the proportion of non party-political members was maintained at least at the 20% mark. Initially, it might therefore make relatively few appointments to the non party-political peers.

10.24 The question of what to do about the non party-political hereditary peers is therefore a fairly open one. However, it might be thought invidious if the non party-political hereditary peers were treated in a different way to the party-political hereditary peers. The arrangements should therefore be the same, party affiliation or not.

10.25 The Government believes that both options for removing the hereditary peers have their benefits and their disadvantages, and will discuss further the best way to proceed.

Titles

10.26 Existing hereditary titles, and the inheritance of such titles, will continue unchanged. The power vested in the Crown to create new hereditary peerages is little used (save for members of the Royal Family). Since the power when exercised confers no right to sit in the Lords, we make no proposals in the White Paper in relation to the continuance of this process. That could properly be considered alongside any wider review of the honours system.

Royal Office Holders

10.27 It would not be necessary for the Earl Marshal or Lord Great Chamberlain to be members of the House of Lords in order to perform their duties. There is a question as to whether or not these two posts should continue to be linked to a seat in a reformed House of Lords. We are consulting further on this point.

Costs

10.28 It is difficult to assess the overall cost of any reform to the House of Lords until the final shape of reform is known. Therefore the estimates provided are based on some of the aspects of reform, where this has been possible.

Statutory Appointments Commission

10.29 Assuming there is an appointed element in a reformed House, one-off costs will be incurred in establishing the new independent Statutory Appointments Commission. The expenditure for the current Appointments Commission in its first year of operation in 2000–2001 was £248,000. In addition the Cabinet

Office incurred further costs in recruiting the Commissioners – approximately £100,000 on top of the running costs for the first year.

10.30 The initial start-up costs for the new United Kingdom body will be higher than the current non-statutory Appointments Commission. This reflects the new body having a much broader remit, with powers over both non-party and party-political appointments and the overall size of the new body.

10.31 The annual expenditure for the current Appointments Commission for 2005/2006 was £103,000, which includes staff costs, and other administration costs including the Commission members' fees, travel and subsistence, communication advice, staff training and IT equipment. Annual expenditure on the new body will also be higher than the existing Appointments Commission.

10.32 It is difficult to estimate the one-off establishment, the first year running costs and the on-going running costs of the new body at this stage until it is clear what proportion of the House will be appointed. The proportion of appointed members will have cost implications on a number of other factors including the number of staff to recruit and accommodation.

Elections

10.33 Assuming there is an elected element in a reformed House, any likely costs incurred will depend mainly on the election system chosen. An advantage of holding the House of Lords elections alongside the European Parliament elections, as set out in Chapter 6 of the paper, is the efficiency saving it produces. Costs could be reduced in relation to polling staff, buildings and promotion, although the number of ballot boxes would increase significantly. We estimate the additional cost for House of Lords elections held alongside another national election to be in the region of £30m, and there are likely to be additional consequential calls on the public purse – for example the provision of free postage for campaign leaflets.

Members' Expenses

10.34 Members' expenses of £15.6m accounted for 15% of the total budget of £106.4m for the House of Lords in 2005–2006. It is difficult to estimate members' remuneration under any system of reform to the House of Lords at this stage. The levels of remuneration are likely to be affected by a change in the size of the House, and will of course be affected by changes to the way that members of the Lords are paid. There may be a requirement for additional staff in Parliament to support a reformed chamber. A reformed House will certainly cost more than the current House.

10.35 Once there are firmer decisions on composition, and whether members of a reformed House should be salaried rather than receive expenses, the Government would discuss proposals with the other parties, and then invite the SSRB to consider the matter in detail and make recommendations.

11. Next Steps

11.1 This paper is designed to inform the free votes in the House of Commons and the House of Lords on the composition of a reformed House.

11.2 As discussed, the Government believes that it is important that Parliament is able to express its preference on the composition of a reformed House. To enable a clear outcome, it is proposing that this be done using an alternative vote (AV) process. The detailed proposed arrangements for the vote itself are outlined at Annex B. But the process used for the free vote would ultimately be a matter for each House to decide.

How would the process work?

Commons

11.3 The Government proposes two stages separated by at least a week.

Stage 1: 'Paving' Motion

11.4 The Government would move a Motion setting out the procedure for the ballot on options for composition at Stage 2.

This paving motion would include reference to three Motions for debate at Stage 2: to take note of the White Paper; for the retention of a bicameral Parliament; and for further reform to the composition of the House of Lords (including the establishment of the Statutory Appointments Commission for any appointed members and the removal of the remaining retained places for hereditary peers). It would then make provision for the House to use the alternative vote procedure for the options for composition of a reformed House. The Motion would set out (by reference to Annex B of this White Paper) the rules for the ballot and the ballot paper. Members would have the opportunity at this discussion on the paving motion at Stage 1 to move amendments to the pattern outlined and to the ballot paper. No substantive votes would take place at this stage on the White Paper or on any potential final outcome for a reformed House of Lords.

Stage 2: Main Debate and Free Vote

11.5 There would be 4 motions preceding the alternative vote ballot itself – a 'take note' Motion for the White Paper; a Motion to seek approval for retention of a bicameral parliament; a Motion to approve further reform to the composition of the House of Lords (including the establishment of the Statutory Appointments Commission for any appointed members and the removal of the remaining retained places for hereditary peers); and a Motion to proceed to the AV ballot. Only if the House agreed to the retention of a bicameral Parliament would it move to a vote on the call for further reform (including the establishment of the Statutory Appointments Commission for any appointed members and the removal of the remaining retained places for hereditary peers). If the House agreed to the Motion for further reform, it would then proceed to agree to move to the AV procedure, using the ballot paper and the process agreed to in the earlier resolution.

11.6 Explanatory memoranda will set out, in more detail, the distribution of the ballot papers, the duration of the ballot, the arrangements for counting the votes, the announcement of the results the next day and placing the ballot papers in the public domain after the vote has been counted and the result announced. The detailed arrangements for the ballot would be under the direction of the Speaker.

Lords

Stage 1: 'Paving' procedure

11.7 The House will be invited to consider whether it wishes to adopt a procedure for the free vote which is similar to that being proposed for the Commons. No recommendations for any procedural change would be made without first being considered by the Procedure Committee. Any recommendations made by the Procedure Committee would be embodied in a report, and submitted for consideration by the House as a whole.

Stage 2: Main debate and Free Vote

11.8 There would be a full debate to take note of the White Paper, followed by the free vote using the process agreed by the House.

12. Conclusion

12.1 Reform of the House of Lords is an issue which has been on the political agenda for many years. The Government believes that, with the three main parties now committed to reform, there is currently an unusual opportunity to find a lasting solution to this question.

12.2 The Government believes that the centre of gravity on opinions for a reformed House lies around the hybrid option, with elections run on a partially-open list system in European constituencies at the same time as European elections. A hybrid House can deliver a second chamber which is a complement to the House of Commons, and delivers the important principles of representation which are essential for an effective House of Lords.

12.3 The benefits that would accrue from combining the two methods of entry to the Lords far outweigh the losses that, as with any compromise, come with a hybrid House. Such a House can deliver a chamber which properly represents the regions of the United Kingdom, and its gender, religious and ethnic balance. This system would ensure that the balance of support for the parties in the country is properly reflected in the membership of the Lords. And a hybrid House would be more democratically legitimate, while ensuring that the membership of the House is not overly political in the relatively partisan way of the House of Commons. It is the best compromise, and a sensible system for reform of the House of Lords.

Annex B – Arrangements for the Free Vote Using an Alternative Vote Ballot

1. The aim of the free vote proposal is to seek a clear final preference on the options put before the two Houses. The alternative vote procedure should encourage Members to vote 'for' a particular option, rather than against, as MPs did in 2003. Although it is an unusual method of voting, both Houses have decided to use a similar approach to choosing their Speakers (through a single ballot in the Lords and sequential votes in the Commons). The House of Lords used its adopted system in its Speakership election in 2006. A difference between those processes and that proposed here is that, whereas the votes in Speakership elections are anonymous, the votes for the proposed free vote on reform of composition of the House of Lords, as with normal Parliamentary votes, would be put into the public domain after the vote has been counted and the result has been announced.

Ballot by Alternative Vote for Options on Composition of a Future House of Lords

2. Members would, under this process, be invited to express their preferences on seven options, as set out on the ballot paper below. Members would indicate on the ballot paper their preferred option, or options, in order of preference, marking their first choice with a 1, their second choice with a 2 and so on, down to their lowest preference. Members would not have to allocate a

preference to all the options. They could vote for a single option only or for a number of the 7.

3. In the initial count, any option that obtained more than 50% of the first preference votes cast would become the endorsed option. If this was not achieved in the first round there would be a series of counts, with the lowest scoring option eliminated at each count and the votes redistributed to the next preference. All low scoring options which did not jointly reach the next highest option in total would be eliminated. If there was a tie for the option with the lowest number of votes in any round, then all tied options would be eliminated. This process of elimination and redistribution of the votes would continue until one option obtained more than 50% of the votes in that round.

4. It is proposed that the ballot papers in both Houses would take the form shown in Table 12 below.

5. The options reflect the analysis described in this White Paper. Accordingly, where the options on the ballot include appointed members, this includes the 20% of the House who would be the non party-political members. So for example, under the 80% elected 20% appointed option, none of the appointed members would come from the parties – they would all be non party-political.

6. The options on the ballot take account of the Bishops and the retired Justices of the Supreme Court, who would enter the House as part of the appointed element. The exception is the 100% elected option, which would contain no places for the Bishops or the retired Supreme Court Justices.

Table 12: Proposed Format of Ballot Paper:

BALLOT ON COMPOSITION
OF A FUTURE HOUSE OF LORDS
Proposed Format of Ballot Papers

Ballot on Composition of a Future House of Lords	
Option	Order of Preference
Fully appointed	
80% appointed and 20% elected	

60% appointed and 40% elected	
50% appointed and 50% elected	
40% appointed and 60% elected	
20% appointed and 80% elected	
Fully elected	
80% appointed and 20% elected	
Members may indicate on the ballot paper their preferred option or options in order of preference, marking their leading preference with a 1 and so on down to their lowest preference. Members need not allot a preference to all options.	

The White Paper in Parliament

The White Paper was debated in both Houses of Parliament. The House of Commons debated it on 6 and 7 March 2007.

Debate in the House of Commons

The leader of the House, Jack Straw, begged to move that 'this House supports the principle of a bicameral Parliament'.[4] The Speaker then read out the motions, 'Options for Reform of Composition':

> No. 1: That this House is of the opinion that a reformed House of Lords should be fully appointed.
> No. 2: That this House is of the opinion that a reformed House of Lords should be composed of 20 per cent elected members and 80 per cent appointed members.

---

4 *Parliamentary Debates*, House of Commons, vol. 457 (I), 6 March 2007, cols 1390–1488.

No. 3: That this House is of the Opinion that a reformed House of Lords should be composed of 40 per cent elected members and 60 per cent appointed members.

No. 4: That this House is of the opinion that a reformed House of Lords should be composed of 50 per cent elected members and 50 per cent appointed members.

No. 5: That this House is of the opinion that a reformed House of Lords should be composed of 60 per cent elected members and 40 per cent appointed members.

No. 6: That this House is of the opinion that a reformed House of Lords should be composed of 80 per cent elected members and 20 per cent appointed members.

No. 7 That this House is of the opinion that a reformed House of Lords should be fully elected.

Hereditary Places: That this House is of the opinion that the remaining retained places for peers whose membership is based on the hereditary principle should be removed.

The debate was both vigorous and controversial. It lasted for two days, and 46 MPs spoke. On 7 March the House voted on each motion separately.[5] The voting was free and it yielded the following results:

On the motion that 'this House supports the principle of a bicameral Parliament', the House divided: 'Ayes, 416; Noes 163. Question accordingly agreed to.'

On option 1, the House divided: 'Ayes, 196; Noes, 375. Question accordingly negatived.'

On option 2, 'Question put and negatived.'

On option 3, 'Question put and negatived.'

On option 4, the House divided: 'Ayes, 155; Noes: 418. Question accordingly negatived.'

On option 5, the House divided: 'Ayes, 178; Noes, 392. Question accordingly negatived.'

5   *Ibid.*, 7 March 2007, cols 1524–1639.

But then, on option 6, the House divided: 'Ayes, 305; Noes, 261. Question accordingly agreed to.'

And on option 7, the House divided: 'Ayes 337; Noes, 224. Question accordingly agreed to.'

Mrs Theresa May, shadow leader of the House, had proposed an amendment to the motion on 'Hereditary Places': 'at end add: "once elected members have taken their places in a reformed House of Lords"'. The question was put, should this amendment be made? 'The House divided: Ayes, 241: Noes, 329. Question accordingly negatived.'

Finally the main question on 'Hereditary Places' was put. 'The House divided: Ayes, 391; Noes, 111. It was resolved that 'this House is of the opinion that the remaining retained places for peers whose membership is based on the hereditary principle should be removed'.

Debate in the House of Lords

On 12 March 2007, the secretary of state for Constitutional Affairs and lord chancellor, Lord Falconer of Thoroton, moved in the Lords that 'this House takes note of the White Paper, *The House of Lords: Reform* (Cm 7072).[6] During the debate, on this day and the next, 130 Lords spoke.[7] On 14 March the House voted.[8] Again voting was free.

On 'fully appointed House', their Lordships divided: 'Contents, 361; Not-Contents, 121.'

On '20 per cent elected Members and 80 per cent appointed Members', the question was negatived.

On '40 per cent elected Members and 60 per cent appointed Members', the question was negatived again.

On '50 per cent elected Members and 50 per cent appointed Members', the House divided: 'Contents, 46; Not-Contents, 409.'

---

6   *Parliamentary Debates*, House of Lords, vol. DCXC, 12 March 2007, col. 451.
7   *Ibid.*, 12 March 2007, cols 451–66, 475–570; 13 March 2007, cols 571–729.
8   *Ibid.*, 14 March 2007, cols 742–59.

On '60 per cent elected Members and 40 per cent appointed Members', the House divided: 'Contents, 45; Not-Contents, 392.'

On '80 per cent elected Members and 20 per cent appointed Members', the House divided: 'Contents, 114; Not-Contents, 336.'

On 'fully elected Members', the House divided: 'Contents, 122; Not-Contents, 326.'

Their lordships' votes were diametrically opposed to those registered in the Commons. What would be the result? Lord Trefgarne had given notice of his intention to move that 'this House is of the opinion that there should be no change to the composition of the House of Lords', but after the lords' votes, he decided not to move the motion.

After the debate and the voting were over, Lord Steel of Aikwood tried to save the day. He begged to 'introduce a Bill to make a provision for the appointment of a commission to make recommendation to the Crown for the creation of life peerages; to restrict the membership of the House of Lords by virtue of hereditary peerage; to make a provision for permanent leave of absence from the House of Lords; to make a provision for the expulsion of Members of the House of Lords in specified circumstances and for connected purposes'.[9] He moved that this bill be read a first time be ordered to be printed. The bill did not move further, and was not re-considered until the year 2014.

9   *Ibid.*, 14 March 2007, col. 741.

CHAPTER FIFTEEN

2008. An Elected Second Chamber: The Cross-Party Group

On 27 June 2007 Tony Blair resigned as prime minister. Blair's continued support of the US president, George W. Bush during the Iraq War of 2003 and his reluctance to criticize Israel during the Israel-Lebanon conflict in 2006 had caused much unrest within the Labour Party. The Labour back-bench members were threatening an open revolt. Blair felt compelled to leave his office and cede it to Gordon Brown. Brown was himself a keen supporter of Lords reform. As new prime minister, he asked Jack Straw, now the lord chancellor and secretary of state for Justice, to continue further with reform of the Upper House. Jack Straw was eager to proceed with reform, but he was not prepared to do it alone. He invited a Cross-Party Group to face the challenge. The Group included the following members:

The Rt Hon. Jack Straw, MP (Chair)
Rt Hon the Baroness Ashton of Upholland (Labour)
 leader of the House of Lords and lord president of the Council
Rt Rev. John Gladwin, Bishop of Chelmsford
The Baroness D'Souza,
 convenor of the Crossbench
Rt Hon. the Lord Falconer of Thoroton (Labour)
Oliver Heald MP (Conservative)
David Heath MP (Liberal Democrat)
Nick Herbert MP (Conservative)
Simon Hughes MP (Liberal Democrat)
Lord Hunt of Kings Heath (Labour)
Rt Hon. Theresa May MP (Conservative)
Rt Hon the Lord McNally (Liberal Democrat)
Rt Hon the Lord Strathclyde (Conservative)

Lord Tyler (Liberal Democrat)

Rt Hon. the Lord Williamson of Horton (Cross-Bench)

The Group worked on Lords reform for nearly a year and prepared a draft of unusual length. This formed the basis of a White Paper presented to Parliament by the lord chancellor and secretary of state for Justice, Jack Straw in July 2008.[1] It was another bold attempt to reform the House of Lords.

The Text of the White Paper

[Fragments]

Foreword

The strength of our democracy is fundamental to our strength as a nation. A strong democracy needs effective, credible institutions, which command the support and engagement of citizens. A key part of the Government's *Governance of Britain* programme is to reinvigorate our democracy by strengthening Parliament itself, and renewing its accountability. We have set out elsewhere our plans for the House of Commons. The House of Lords – the second chamber of our legislature, and a vital part of our constitutional arrangements – plays a key role in scrutinising legislation, and holding the Government of the day to account. The creative tension between the Government, based primarily in the House of Commons, and the House of Lords, is essential for the making of good laws. But an unelected second chamber raises the question of legitimacy for this body which plays such a decisive role in the making of legislation: from whom does the authority of its

---

1   White Paper, *An Elected Second Chamber: Further Reform of the House of Lords* (14 July 2008). Cm 7438.

members derive, and to whom are they accountable? Arguments that an unelected House lacks sufficient legitimacy have been vigorous for at least 150 years, and gathered pace as the legitimacy of the Commons was gradually extended by a progressive widening of the franchise during the nineteenth century. An impasse between the Liberal government with a large Commons majority, and the House of Lords with an overwhelming Conservative majority and virtually equal powers came to a head in 1909 when the Lords sought to veto Lloyd-George's 'People's Budget'. Two General Elections followed in 1910. Then in 1911 the first legislative step on the road of reform was taken with the Parliament Act 1911. This established the absolute primacy of the House of Commons in matters financial, and reined in the decisive power of veto on all other legislation, held until then by the House of Lords, to a delaying power of three sessions. This was further reduced to two sessions by the Parliament Act 1949. These provisions, along with the Salisbury-Addison convention, which inhibits the second chamber from voting down legislation on a manifesto commitment and other key conventions, represent the overarching framework within which the two Houses operate and co-operate to this day.

Over time, the principles of further reform of the House of Lords have taken shape. The Life Peerages Act 1958 created life peerages and provided for women with life peerages to sit in the second chamber for the first time. Following Tony Benn's forced removal from the House of Commons following the death of his father Viscount Stansgate, the 1963 Peerage Act was passed allowing hereditary peerages to be disclaimed for life. The Act also allowed female hereditary peers and all members of the Scottish peerage to sit in the Lords. Building on a manifesto commitment, Harold Wilson's Government made a concerted attempt at reform after the 1966 General Election. Cross-party discussions were convened and a Bill introduced in 1968 but the Bill ran into such backbench opposition on both sides that it was aborted. More recently, this Government secured the House of Lords Act 1999,

which removed all but 92 of the hereditary peers, and appointed
a Royal Commission chaired by Lord Wakeham to examine and
make recommendations of the role, function and composition of
the second chamber. This proposed a House of around 550 peers
serving a fixed term, with a minority (with options from 65–195)
elected from the nations and regions of the UK. The Wakeham
Commission conducted much detailed research, and this and
its conclusions have proved invaluable in informing the discussion within the cross-party group and within the Government. A
non-statutory appointments commission for the Lords was established in May 2000. A Government White Paper on the Lords
was issued in November 2001 with the Government's response
to the Wakeham Commission. A debate with free votes on seven
options on composition was held in February 2003. In the event
the debate was wholly inconclusive. None of the options commanded support. An all-appointed House was defeated by the
largest margin (323 to 245) and an 80% elected House by the
smallest (284 to 281). All three main parties included pledges in
their 2005 manifestos in favour of further reform of the Lords. A
cross-party group (with representatives of Crossbenchers and the
Bishops) was established in June 2006, and met regularly over the
following eight months. In February 2007 the Government published its White Paper 'The House of Lords: Reform' which took
full account of the discussions in the cross-party group, which
informed the two-day debate which took place in the Commons
and the Lords in March 2007. On this occasion the Commons
voted in favour of a wholly elected second chamber (337 to 224)
and for an 80% elected chamber (305 to 267) and against all other
options. The cross-party group reconvened following these votes,
and I made an oral statement on progress on 19 July 2007. This
White Paper is a government document, but the text seeks to
inform readers where there was a broad consensus, and to record
where there were differences of view, as inevitably there will be
on such a fundamental issue. Parliament as a whole will not be an
effective and credible institution without further reform of the

House of Lords. The proposals and options in this White Paper are intended to generate discussion and inform debate, rather than representing a final blueprint for reform. The Government has long held that final proposals for reform would have to be included in a general election manifesto, to ensure that the electorate ultimately decide the form and role of the second chamber. Finally, I pay tribute to the constructive way in which members of the cross-party group have engaged in this process. This White Paper marks a key stage in the reform process, and I encourage everyone to contribute to the ensuing debate.

Rt Hon. Jack Straw MP
Lord Chancellor and Secretary of State for Justice

Executive summary

In March 2007, there were free votes in both Houses of Parliament on House of Lords reform. The House of Lords voted for a wholly appointed House and the House of Commons for a wholly or mainly elected second chamber. This White Paper sets out what giving effect to the votes of the House of Commons, which is the primary chamber in the UK legislature, might mean in practice. The proposals, which are Government proposals, follow cross-party talks. The cross-party talks reached consensus on a number of issues. The detailed text of this White Paper indicates where other members of the Cross-Party Group on House of Lords reform dissented from the Government's proposals. There is already widespread consensus over the role of the second chamber and its relationship to the House of Commons. The primacy of the Commons and the right of the Government to get its business through Parliament is acknowledged as beyond debate. But the second chamber has a crucial role to play. In its three main functions of scrutinising legislation, conducting investigations and holding Government to account, the second chamber should complement the work of the Commons. Irrespective of its membership, this should continue to be the case in a reformed second chamber. There are four key principles underpinning the reform

proposals to maintain the difference between the membership
of each House after members are elected to the second chamber:

– members of the second chamber should be elected on a different
  representative basis from members of the House of Commons;
– members of the second chamber should be able to bring independence of judgement to their work;
– members should serve a long term of office; and
– the second chamber should take account of the prevailing
  political view amongst the electorate, but also provide opportunities for independent and minority views to be represented.

The Government welcomes a confident and assertive second
chamber. It sees this as further enhancing our democracy and
something that is entirely consistent with the primacy of the
House of Commons. That primacy rests in the fact that the
Government of the day is formed from the party or parties that
can command a majority in the House of Commons. It also rests
in the Parliament Acts and in the financial privilege of the House
of Commons. The Prime Minister and most senior ministers are
also drawn from the House of Commons. A more assertive second
chamber, operating within its current powers, would not threaten
primacy. One of the key reforms proposed in this White Paper
is the introduction of elections to the second chamber. It was a
recommendation of Lord Wakeham's Commission and has since
enjoyed widespread support, including within the Cross-Party
Group, that elected members would normally serve a single, non-
renewable term of 12–15 years. They would be elected directly in
thirds and with each member serving three electoral cycles. Large
constituencies, each returning more than one member over the
three electoral cycles, would be used. The elections in thirds would
take place at the same time as general elections for the House of
Commons. To mitigate the risk of members serving very short
terms, where a general election occurred less than three years
after the previous one, it would not be accompanied by elections to the second chamber. The Government would welcome

views on the appropriate size for a reformed second chamber. Further consideration should be given to the options of using a First Past The Post, Alternative Vote, Single Transferable Vote or open- or semi-open list system. The Government would welcome views on the voting system to be used for electing members to a reformed second chamber. The current powers of the House of Lords and the conventions that underpin them have worked well. The second chamber is likely to be more assertive, given its electoral mandate. The Government and members of the Cross-Party Group welcome this. Increased assertiveness is compatible with the continued primacy of the House of Commons, which does not rest solely or mainly in the fact that the House of Commons is an elected chamber whilst the House of Lords is not. Instead it rests in the mechanisms identified above.

There is therefore no persuasive case for reducing the powers of the second chamber. The key argument for any appointments to the second chamber is that it would preserve a significant Crossbench element. If there were an appointed element in a reformed second chamber, appointments would be made by an Appointments Commission, which would seek applications and nominations, against published criteria. Appointments would be made on merit, with the key focus being an individual's ability, willingness and commitment to take part in the full work of the second chamber. As with elected members, appointed members would serve for three electoral cycles without the possibility of re-appointment. One-third of appointed members would be replaced at each set of elections to the second chamber.

The Appointments Commission would operate on a statutory basis. Legislation would contain only broad parameters in relation to the role and operation of the Commission, to give it flexibility. The Commission would be accountable to the Prime Minister. There would be no reserved seats for Church of England Bishops in a wholly elected second chamber. If there were an appointed element in the second chamber, there would be a proportionate number of seats reserved for Church of England

Bishops. Retired Law Lords, or after 2009, Justices of the Supreme Court who were formerly Law Lords, would have the same status as other existing life Peers. Membership of a reformed second chamber would no longer carry with it a peerage, nor would it be associated with the award of any other honour. Eligibility requirements for membership of the reformed second chamber would be brought more into line with those for membership of the House of Commons. The minimum age for membership of the second chamber would be 18, and there would be no maximum limit. British, qualifying Commonwealth and Republic of Ireland citizens would be eligible for membership, as they are now. Those subject to a bankruptcy restriction order, those holding full-time judicial offices, those with certain criminal convictions, those detained for mental health reasons, those who had been convicted of electoral fraud and those who were not UK taxpayers would be ineligible. Those who had served as elected members would not be eligible to be appointed as members and vice versa.

There would be provision for members to resign, but not to take leave of absence except if they had a major illness. Members would be allowed to vote in elections to both the House of Commons and the second chamber at all times. The Government would welcome views on whether there should be provision, similar to that which applies for the House of Commons, disqualifying those in certain public professions and offices, or who are members of certain public bodies, from membership of a reformed second chamber. Further consideration would need to be given to the accountability arrangements for members of the reformed second chamber, particularly in light of proposals that they serve long, single terms. The Cross-Party Group discussed the possibility of introducing recall ballots, along the lines of those that exist in some states of the USA.

The Government would welcome views on the proposals for such ballots set out in this White Paper. Members of a reformed second chamber would receive taxable salaries. The Senior Salaries Review Body would advise on an appropriate level of salary and on the possibility and desirability of linking it to a member's contribution to the work of the second chamber. There would be a transitional phase of three electoral cycles during which the three tranches of new members took up their places. During this time, new practices both internally and in relations with the House of Commons would develop. Existing peers would have key roles in ensuring that the second chamber continued to work effectively with the House of Commons and in transmitting knowledge to new members. The sitting and voting rights of the remaining hereditary Peers would be removed, but the timing of this is for further consideration. This is linked to the need for further discussion about how far the rights of life Peers to sit and vote should continue during the transition and about whether they should continue after that phase is complete.

The White Paper sets out three options, on which the Government would welcome views. A common feature of almost all recent proposals is that the peerage itself, as an honour bestowed by the Crown, should be distinct from membership of a reformed second chamber. A peerage would therefore be neither a qualification nor a disqualification for membership. This would make it anomalous for the reformed chamber to be called the 'House of Lords', and a new name would be needed. Many, though by no means all, second chambers around the world are called 'Senates', and the title is no guide to their powers and functions. Such suggestions have been made for the reformed second chamber here. There may be others. The Government is open minded on this, though there was a strong consensus among members of the Cross-Party Group for the name 'Senate'. To avoid a preoccupation with name over function and composition in the debates about the future, we use the neutral term 'reformed second chamber' throughout this document.

1. Introduction

In 1999, the Government carried out substantial reform the House of Lords.

1.1 The House of Lords Act 1999 provided for the removal of the sitting and voting rights of the majority of hereditary Peers and established a mechanism for retaining 90 hereditary Peers through a process of election. In May 2006, the Government supported the establishment of a Joint Committee to examine the conventions governing the relationship between the two Houses of Parliament. The Government also set up cross-party talks on House of Lords reform. The consensus reached in these talks was reflected in the White Paper published in February 2007. That White Paper provided the foundation for a series of free votes in both Houses in March 2007.

1.2 The foreword to the February 2007 White Paper noted that although the 1999 changes were significant and overdue, reform of the House of Lords remained unfinished business. The Director of 'Unlock Democracy', Peter Facey, has said: 'The question is no longer whether the Government will complete reform, but when.'

1.3 Also, it can be argued that a modern state should seek to have in its legislature those who are best fitted to fulfil its roles. The main role of the second chamber in the UK is to revise and scrutinise legislation, providing a second opinion. It also helps hold government to account and carries out investigative work. However, members of the current House of Lords are not salaried. The award of a life Peerage continues to be both an honour and something that carries with it the right to sit and vote in the House of Lords. It is explicit that non party-political appointed members are not expected necessarily to make the same amount of time available to take part in the business of the House as 'working peers' and it is recognised that they may continue with their other interests. (It is, however, important to emphasise that many 'working peers' also have other occupations and interests.) These and other aspects of the composition of the second chamber need to be considered, to ensure not only that the chamber has the people it needs but also that its legitimacy and authority are not called into question.

1.4 A reformed second chamber will play a key role in the Government's programme to strengthen Parliament and renew its accountability to the electorate, as part of a programme of wider constitutional renewal.

1.5 Following on from the February 2007 White Paper, in the March 2007 free votes, the House of Commons voted by a margin of 113 for a wholly elected House of Lords. The Commons also backed, by a margin of 38, a mainly elected second chamber based on 80% elected and 20% appointed. It voted by a majority of 280 to remove the remaining hereditary Peers. The House of Lords voted by a majority of 240 for a fully appointed House. It rejected the options of a wholly or 80% elected second chamber (respectively by majorities of 204 and 222). Given the difference of view between the two chambers, the Government said that it would look at how best to deliver a mainly or wholly elected second chamber in accordance with the wishes of the House of Commons, which is the primary chamber in the UK legislature.

1.6 Since the free votes, the Justice Secretary and Lord Chancellor has continued to chair the cross-party talks that led to the February 2007 White Paper. The continuing talks have considered what giving effect to the votes of the House of Commons for a wholly or mainly elected second chamber might mean in practice. The Cross-Party Group has considered the respective roles of the two Houses, the powers that a reformed second chamber might have, electoral systems, how an appointed element might operate, and the transitional arrangements. The Cross-Party Group consists of members of the front benches of the political parties in both Houses, the Lords Spiritual and the Cross-benches. The Group's current and previous membership is set out at Annex 1. The Convenor of the Cross-bench Peers expressed concern in the talks that the basis on which they were proceeding ignored the outcome of the free votes in the House of Lords. The Convenor continues to believe that this is unacceptable and that therefore any use of the term 'consensus' in the White Paper is inappropriate.

1.7 This White Paper sets out the Government's proposals for a reformed second chamber. It stems from the constructive discussions in the Cross-Party Group. The Group reached consensus on a number of key issues. This White Paper states where the Group did not reach agreement.

1.8 This White Paper sets the context for decisions on House of Lords reform and goes on to consider issues around, and options for, electoral systems. The effect of different electoral systems is examined against two scenarios – that the House is either 100% or 80% elected. The White Paper then looks at the powers of the second chamber. It suggests possible arrangements for any appointed element, but at this stage, the Government is not making proposals about whether there should be one. Finally, the White Paper addresses other issues around the operation of a reformed second chamber and explores transitional arrangements.

Next steps

1.9 Details of how people can put forward their views on the proposals in this White Paper are presented in Chapter 10. Ministers will consider the responses to this White Paper and how it should be taken forward. The Government intends to formulate a comprehensive package of reform that can be put to the electorate as a manifesto commitment at the next general election. It hopes that other parties will be able to include similar commitments in their manifestos, so that the cross-party consensus on House of Lords reform is clear.

2. A reformed chamber: context for decisions

2.1 The most significant change in a reformed House of Lords will be its composition. The move to a wholly or mainly elected second chamber should increase the extent to which the membership of the second chamber represents the UK as a whole, with members drawn from England, Scotland, Wales and Northern Ireland. The change will also give the second chamber more legitimacy, making Parliament more accountable to the people it serves. In addition, consideration needs to be given to what powers a reformed second chamber should have, as well as to its ways of working. These issues will bear significantly on its ability to play a proper role in its key work of scrutinising legislation and so ensuring better law, as well as its role of holding the executive to account. The reformed second chamber will need the right level of resources to deliver these roles effectively and build on the work of the House of Lords.

2.2 One of the strengths of the British constitution is that it evolves to meet new situations and challenges. The Government's proposals for constitutional renewal envisage that after its reform, the second chamber will continue to develop and change as it enhances its role and performance. This will take place within the context of the primacy of the House of Commons.

2.3 The Hunt Report noted, 'the primacy of the elected House of Commons is the cornerstone of this country's parliamentary system. A second chamber has a valuable role to play as a constitutional back-stop and as a complement to the Commons.' There are a number of aspects to this primacy. The government of the day is formed from the party or parties that can command a majority in the House of Commons and most members of the Cabinet, including the Prime Minster, are members of the House of Commons. The Parliament Acts provide that the House of Commons can, eventually, secure legislation in the absence of the agreement of the House of Lords. Finally, the House of Commons has financial privilege. There are two elements to this. First, the 1911 Parliament Act provides for a Money Bill to be presented for Royal Assent without the consent of the House of Lords. This is only possible provided that the Commons passes the Bill and sends it to the Lords at least one month before the end of a session and that the Bill is not passed by the Lords, without amendment, within a month after it was received. The second element is that the House of Commons has the right to decide on Bills of Aids and Supplies, though in theory, the Lords is entitled to reject such Bills. The creation of a reformed second chamber should not mean changes to any of these aspects of the primacy of the House of Commons.

2.4 In addition to these underpinning elements, the conventions which currently inform the working relationship between the two Houses were set out in the report of the Joint Committee on Conventions in 2006 and endorsed by both Houses in 2007.

2.5 Since the passage of the House of Lords Act 1999, there has been a significant change in the way the House of Lords exercises its role. In recent years, the second chamber has become more assertive. The primacy of the House of Commons remains, but the House of Lords has challenged proposed legislation more often. In the 1997–98, 1998–99 and 1999–2000 sessions, the Government suffered 39, 31 and 36 defeats in the House of Lords respectively. (The 2000–2001 session was very short and has therefore been omitted.) From the 2001–02 to the 2006–07 session inclusive, the average number of such defeats in each session was almost 60. It is noted that where the House of Lords has serious concerns about proposed legislation, it gives voice to them.

2.6 The Government welcomes this change in the way in which the House of Lords behaves as part of the evolution of the British constitution. There is no reason why any further increase in the authority and effectiveness of the second chamber following elections should undermine the primacy of the House of Commons. As noted in paragraph 2.3, primacy does not lie in the way that the second chamber approaches its business.

2.7 This White Paper covers the various aspects of reform referred to in paragraph 2.1 and presents proposals for how the scenarios voted for by the House of Commons – i.e. that the House of Lords is either 100% or 80% elected – might be achieved.

3. A reformed chamber: role and composition

3.1 The reformed second chamber should be confident in challenging both the executive and the House of Commons. The second chamber should be able to make the government pause and reconsider. Ultimately, however, the government should be able to get its business through the legislature, through effective resolution of disagreements between the two Houses and, if necessary in the most exceptional cases, by using the Parliament Acts. This ensures the primacy of the House of Commons and means that, ultimately, any gridlock between the two Houses can be resolved.

3.2 In performing its roles of scrutinising legislation, holding the executive to account and investigative work, the second chamber should complement the House of Commons. This complementarity is partly about the organisation of the work of the two Houses. For example, the House of Lords Committee on the Merits of Statutory Instruments has a specific function and has added value to Parliamentary scrutiny in a unique way. The Committee reports to the House on whether secondary legislation is legally or politically important; may be inappropriate in view of changed circumstances since the passing of the parent Act; implements European Union legislation inappropriately; or may achieve its policy objectives imperfectly. The expectation of a reformed second chamber is that it would develop new and fresh approaches to scrutiny. It might, for example, want to consider some of the changes that have been made as part of the modernisation of the work of the House of Commons, such as taking evidence as part of the Committee stage when primary legislation is being considered. However the complementarity of the reformed second chamber will also be about its composition. There is a need for a different basis for membership from that of the House of Commons, bringing different perspectives to bear on relevant parliamentary processes. This can be achieved through implementing a number of key principles, within the context of the democratisation of the House.

3.3 The representative basis for elected members of the reformed second chamber should be different from that for members of the House of Commons. This is not necessarily to say that the voting system would be different but that the arrangements for elections taken as a whole, including the size of constituencies and the frequency and timing of elections, should not duplicate those for the House of Commons. Different voting arrangements should encourage diversity in the membership of the two chambers.

3.4 Members of the reformed second chamber should be able to bring independence of judgement to their work. Members who are elected will, for the most part, achieve membership on the basis that they represent a particular political party, although there will be scope for independent candidates. While most of the elected members will have party affiliations, the intention is that they should exercise their independent judgement in the second chamber. Some of this will be a matter for the parties, but Chapter 4 of this White Paper considers how electoral systems could help achieve this, including by providing that members of the reformed second chamber should serve a single term of around 12–15 years. If there is to be an appointed element in the reformed second chamber, appointments should be made on an independent basis, reflecting the merits of the particular individual. No party appointments are envisaged. Chapter 6 considers in detail how this might be achieved.

3.5 *Long tenure.* The work of any legislature is challenging. If all the members of the second chamber at a particular point in time were newly appointed or elected, it would take some time for them, individually and collectively, to understand their new roles and maximise their effectiveness in carrying them out. Significant continuity in the membership of the House of Commons is maintained by virtue of the fact that, even when there is a change of Government, many of those elected will have been Members of Parliament previously. There is a need to ensure similar continuity in the second chamber. Chapter 4 of this White Paper considers how this might be achieved in relation to elected members. If the reformed second chamber is to include appointees, suitable arrangements need to be in place to provide continuity amongst appointed members. Proposals about any appointed element are set out in Chapter 6.

3.6 The reformed second chamber should take account of the prevailing political view amongst the electorate, but also provide opportunities for independent and minority views to be represented. The Government wants the reformed second chamber to complement the House of Commons. The composition of the Commons will reflect the prevailing political view of the country and if the second chamber is to have increased legitimacy, it should do so too. However, it should also reflect a diversity of views. Chapter 6 of this White Paper considers further how this might be achieved through voting systems for the second chamber. Chapter 6 considers how any appointed element could be used to ensure that the reformed second chamber reflects a wide range of views.

4. A reformed chamber: increased legitimacy

Summary

4.1 A key recommendation of Lord Wakeham's Royal Commission, which has since enjoyed widespread consensus, is that elected members of the second chamber should normally serve a single, non-renewable term of 12–15 years. They should be elected in thirds, with each member serving three electoral cycles.

4.2 The Government proposes that staggered elections for the second chamber take place at the same time as general elections for the House of Commons. To mitigate the risk of members serving very short terms, where a general election occurred shortly after the previous one, it would not be accompanied by elections to the second chamber. The Government proposes that such provision would apply where a general election took place less than three years after the previous one. The Conservative Party proposes that such provision apply where there was less than two years between general elections.

4.3 The Liberal Democrats propose that second chamber elections should take place at the same time as those for the devolved legislature and assemblies, i.e. every four years. There are also significant English local authority elections on the same cycle.

4.4 The Government proposes that large constituencies, each returning more than one member over the three cycles, would be used to elect members to the second chamber.

4.5 The Government proposes that the size of the second chamber should over time reduce from the current membership of the House of Lords and that it should be smaller than the House of Commons. It would welcome views on the eventual size of the second chamber. The Conservative Party considers that there is a strong case for a second chamber of 250–300 members.

4.6 The Government proposes that members of the second chamber should be elected directly. There was no consensus about the system that should be used for such elections. The Conservative Party favours a First Past The Post system. The Liberal Democrats favour the use of an open list or Single Transferable Vote system. The Government believes that further consideration should be given to the options of using either a First Past The Post, Alternative Vote, Single Transferable Vote (STV), open or semi-open list system. The Government would welcome views on what system should be used for elections to a wholly or mainly elected second chamber.

4.7 The Government would also welcome views on whether arrangements should be put in place to fill seats for elected members that become vacant.

Introduction

4.8 Chapter 2 of this White Paper makes clear that the reformed second chamber will continue as the second chamber and there will be no change to the primacy of the House of Commons. Chapter 3 sets out a number of principles that would help ensure that the second chamber continued to be complementary to the House of Commons, without challenging its primacy. These include:

– members of the second chamber should be elected on a different representative basis from members of the House of Commons;

- members of the second chamber should be able to bring their independent judgement to their work;
- members should serve long terms of office; and
- members should take account of the prevailing political view amongst the electorate, but also provide opportunities for independent and minority views to be represented.

4.9 The voting system is only one aspect of the arrangements for electing members to the second chamber. Other aspects that will help determine the nature of the chamber and how it operates include:

- the length of term that members serve;
- whether they are eligible for re-election;
- the frequency and timing of elections;
- the size of constituencies and whether they return a single member or more than one; and
- the size of the reformed second chamber.

4.10 The Cross-Party Group considered extensively how different voting systems using these parameters would help:

- achieve a second chamber that was complementary to the Commons; and
- encourage the election of people with a range of views, including those from smaller political parties and independent candidates, whilst providing for the prevailing political view amongst the electorate to be reflected.

Length of term

4.11 Provision that members of the second chamber could serve only a single term would help enhance the independence of, and reinforce the distinct role for, members of the second chamber. However, if members could serve only one term, that term would need to be sufficiently long to attract able people. There is widespread consensus that elected members of the second chamber should serve a single, non-renewable term of 12–15 years.

4.12 Chapter 7 considers in more detail possible arrangements to ensure the accountability of members in the second chamber, e.g. possible provisions on disqualification, whether changes to the House of Lords Code of Conduct are needed and whether a system of recall ballots might be appropriate.

Electoral cycle

4.13 The Wakeham Commission recommended that regional members of the second chamber should be selected on a phased basis, in thirds and serve for the equivalent of three electoral cycles. Appointed members would serve for fixed terms of 15 years. These proposals have been generally supported since then. Elections for the second chamber that were staggered over a number of electoral cycles could help ensure continued primacy of the House of Commons, as the latter would always have a more recent mandate than the second chamber taken as a whole. Under 'staggered election' arrangements, each constituency would be represented by more than one member. Under elections staggered in thirds, three members, or a number of members that was a multiple of three, would represent each constituency. In a six-member constituency:

- Two members (A and B) would be elected at the first round.
- Two further members (C and D) would be elected at the second round. A and B would continue to be members.
- Two further members (E and F) would be elected at the third round. A, B, C and D would continue to be members. At this point, the constituency would have reached the point where it had its full quota of six members.
- At the fourth round, A and B's terms of office would end and two new members would be elected, so that the total would remain at six.
- At the fifth round, C and D's terms of office would end and two new members would be elected.
- At the sixth round, E and F's terms of office would end and two new members would be elected.

– At the next round, the members elected at the fourth round would retire and two new members would be elected. This process would continue, so that the constituency continued to be represented by six members, elected in 'rolling thirds'.

4.14 Staggered elections would create significant continuity of membership. It would reduce the scope for the membership of the second chamber to 'mirror' that of the House of Commons. In particular, they would damp the effect of substantial swings between the support for the main political parties and hence reduce the scope for one particular party to gain an overall majority in the second chamber. A party is likely to have to win the majority of seats at a succession of elections to be guaranteed a majority in the chamber overall under all four voting systems modelled, particularly under a list or STV system. However, if a particular party did command widespread support continuing over several electoral cycles, this would, in due course, be reflected fully in the membership of the second chamber. In the short term, staggered elections will in any event be necessary to ensure a smooth transition from a wholly appointed House to a mainly or wholly elected chamber. The Government proposes that elections to the second chamber should be staggered.

4.15 On the number of electoral cycles, there is a balance to be struck. A lower number of cycles would increase the extent to which the mandate of the second chamber as a whole would be as recent as that of the House of Commons. A higher number of cycles would mean that fewer members changed following each election, which could make for greater continuity and stability. The Government believes that staggering elections so members of the second chamber were elected in thirds would achieve the right balance.

Timing of elections

4.16 Combining elections to the second chamber with other elections is likely to increase voter turnout. Historically, the highest turnout in UK elections tends to be in general elections to the House of Commons, followed by those for the devolved legislature and assemblies and for local authorities. Elections to the European Parliament have so far generally achieved lower turnouts.

General elections

4.17 Combining staggered elections to the second chamber with general elections could help maximise turnout. Voters would vote for both chambers of the UK legislature at the same time and it would be clear what each election was for. No group of members of the second chamber would have a more recent mandate than Members of the House of Commons. Combining elections for the second chamber with general elections would avoid potential disruption to the legislative programme, as newly elected members would not be joining the second chamber partway through the consideration of legislation. However, combining elections to the second chamber with general elections under a system of single, non-renewable terms could mean that some members would serve very short terms. Where general elections were held very close together (as in 1950 and 1951, 1964 and 1966 and two general elections in 1974), a 'rider' provision could help mitigate this risk. Such provision would preclude elections to the second chamber accompanying a general election if the latter happened shortly after the previous general election.

Devolved legislature and assemblies and local authority elections

4.18 Combining elections with those to the devolved legislature and assemblies and the accompanying local authority elections would provide certainty. Members of the second chamber would know that they would serve for three electoral cycles, each of four years, and exactly when their terms would end. Typically, they would not be elected at a time when the electorate was voting for a choice of government and hence the election would be clearly about the role of members of the second chamber. Unless General Elections coincided with those of the devolved legislature and assemblies, new members would join the second chamber part way through a legislative session and in order to avoid disruption to parliamentary business, members would have to defer taking up their seats immediately upon election. They could do so at the start of the next parliamentary session in the autumn. It is likely that some members of the second chamber would have a more recent mandate than members of the House of Commons.

European Parliament elections

4.19 Combining elections with the European Parliament elections would provide certainly of terms (three cycles of five years each). It would have the same disadvantages as holding elections alongside those for the devolved legislature and assemblies and local authorities, and is least likely to result in a high turnout.

4.20 The Government proposes that the timing of elections take place at the same time as general elections. The Conservative Party agrees. The Liberal Democrats propose that second chamber elections should take place at the same time as those for the devolved legislature and assemblies. (There are also significant English local authority elections on the same cycle.) They argue that this would ensure clear, consistent terms of office, while avoiding confusion on the part of those electors who see General Election time as the opportunity to support or oppose a mandated Government.

4.21 Under the Government's proposal there would be the chance that members would serve relatively short terms of office if general elections were held in quick succession. A 'rider' provision would help ensure elected members served a minimum number of years in the second chamber and hence it would encourage people to stand for election. The Government proposes that a 'rider' would apply where a general election is held less than three years after the previous one. In these circumstances, the second general election would not count towards the three electoral terms to be served. Hence a 'rider' of three years would guarantee members of the second chamber a minimum term of nine years.

4.22 The Conservative Party supports the proposal for a 'rider', but for two years rather than the three proposed by the Government. The Conservative Party proposal would guarantee members of the second chamber a minimum term of office of six years.

Constituencies

4.23 If the membership of the second chamber is to be distinctive from that of the House of Commons, the Government believes members should be elected on a different representative basis. As far as possible, the constituencies used for elections to the second chamber should require alteration only infrequently, should reflect some sort of community or geographical area and should provide an equal level of representation for all voters. Relatively large geographical areas with constituencies that each returned more than one member would meet these criteria, and could also help reduce the risk of elected members competing with Members of Parliament over constituency work. They could also help ensure that the memberships of the two chambers were distinctive, although the degree of difference between them will vary with the voting system used. The Government proposes that large constituencies that return more than one member each over three electoral cycles should be used to elect members to the second chamber.

4.24 The Conservative Party agrees with the broad approach of multi-member constituencies and long terms; however, it believes that the constituencies should not be large and amorphous, but should reflect traditional city and county boundaries to which people have loyalty.

4.25 The number of members returned for each constituency at each round of elections would depend on the size of the second chamber and the voting system used. For some of the options considered by the Cross-Party Group, which are described later in this chapter, each constituency would return one member at each round of elections, giving a total of three members for the constituency as a whole. For other options, more than one member would be returned at each round of elections. The views of the different participants in the cross-party talks about whether more than one member should be returned for each constituency at each round of elections varies according to their view on the desirable size of the second chamber and on which voting system should be used.

Size of the second chamber

4.26 An important distinguishing feature of second chambers around the world is that they tend to be smaller than the first chamber. The current membership of the House of Lords is 746. This exceeds the House of Commons, which consists of 644 members. Italy has just over 300 members and Spain, India and Japan have more than 200 members in their second chambers. In Australia, the Senate is just over half the size of the lower chamber with just over 70 Senators. Similarly, in France, the Sénat is composed of 331 members, while the lower house has a membership of 577. In the USA, the Senate is a quarter of the size of the House of Representatives with 100 Senators.

4.27 However, not all members of the House of Lords attend regularly. The average daily attendance for the 2006–07 session was 415 members. The UK second chamber would be a working chamber and should be large enough to carry out its roles and functions adequately, but represent value for money in terms of its costs.

4.28 If members would normally be expected to attend when the second chamber was sitting, a membership of 400–450 would provide broadly the same number of people to undertake the work of the second chamber as at present. A membership of 400–450 members would also be commensurate with international comparisons in terms of its size relative to the House of Commons.

4.29 Some have argued for smaller numbers in the second chamber. A significantly smaller second chamber of around 150–200 would require a complete overhaul of the current working practices and arrangements to enable the reformed second chamber to play an effective role in the parliamentary system. The overriding objective is to ensure that, whatever its size, the second chamber can carry out its work effectively and cover the extensive scrutiny and select committee business that the House of Lords does so effectively at the moment.

4.30 The Government proposes that the size of the second chamber should be significantly reduced from the current membership of the House of Lords and that it should be smaller than the House of Commons. The Government would welcome views on the size of the second chamber. The Conservative Party considers that there is a strong case for a second chamber of no more than 250–300 members as part of a policy of reducing the overall number of elected politicians in the country.

Which voting system?

4.31 The Cross-Party Group considered the effect of different voting systems on a second chamber:

- with between 400 and 450 members, whether all or most of them are elected; and
- which comprised or included elected members who represent large constituencies each represented by more than one member and who are elected in thirds at elections whose timing coincides with that for general elections. A 'rider' provision would mean that where a general election occurred soon after the previous one, it would not be accompanied by elections to the second chamber.

4.32 These provisions would help achieve a non-renewable term of 12–15 years for members of the second chamber.

4.33 The figure of between 400 and 450 members used for the modelling reflects the current average daily attendance in the House of Lords.

4.34 The Government believes that the voting system for the second chamber should be straightforward and easy for voters to understand as well as giving them as much choice as possible. This will help maximise voters' participation in elections and hence their degree of engagement with the democratic processes of the UK.

Direct or indirect elections?

Indirect elections

4.35 There are two broad options for a system of indirect election: an electoral college or representation of vocational and interest groups or the secondary mandate, where the second chamber would be composed from a regional list system according to votes cast at the General Election. Indirect election could offer some degree of democratic legitimacy to the reformed second chamber. However, as the electorate does not cast a specific vote for the second chamber it is difficult to see any direct link. The practical difficulties in reaching agreement on which institutions should be represented is also a hindrance to the system and some could argue that there is very little difference between indirect electoral systems and an appointed House.

4.36 Proposals for indirect electoral systems for the second chamber have been put forward on a number of occasions but have never gathered a great deal of support. The Wakeham Commission Report was concerned that indirect election from the devolved institutions or from UK members of the European Parliament would create 'a total mismatch between the responsibilities which the people concerned were elected to discharge and their role in the second chamber, which would open up a significant gap in accountability and there would be a risk that members chosen in this way would act as delegates from those who appointed them to the second chamber rather than as representatives in the wider sense'.

4.37 'These difficulties would arise in an even more acute form if members of the second chamber were elected or appointed by, rather than being drawn from, the institutions concerned.'

The Commission was also opposed to members of the second chamber being indirectly elected by local government electoral colleges. They also said: 'Additionally, we see no reason to believe that indirectly elected members of the second chamber would be broadly representative of British society, be likely to have the requisite range of expertise and experience or possess the other specific characteristics which members of the second chamber should have.'

4.38 A separate system of indirect election that has been proposed is the Secondary Mandate. This would involve composing the second chamber from votes cast for candidates to the House of Commons at the General Election. Parties would use a regional list system and individuals would be elected according to the share of the vote in each region at the General Election.

4.39 Proponents of this system argue that it enshrines the primacy of the House of Commons because the second chamber is drawn from votes for the first. By ensuring that all votes cast at a General Election were counted in the composition of Parliament as a whole, it is claimed that it would enhance the democratic process and give people more reason to use their vote even in constituencies perceived to be 'safe seats' for one of the main parties. Such a system would produce a second chamber that reflected the broad pattern of political opinion across the country and, by using regional lists, was fully representative of all parts of the country. It has also been claimed that it might offer some of the advantages of appointment and is more administratively efficient and cost-effective than direct elections.

4.40 On the other hand, it has been argued that a Secondary Mandate system would not be successful in bringing the necessary degree of independence of judgement to the second chamber. Further, such a system would not sit easily with the aim of members serving long terms.

4.41 The Government's February 2007 White Paper concluded that: 'Direct election of individuals plainly would confer more legitimacy than an indirect system. Many other second chambers around the world use direct election as the method for selecting the whole or part of their membership, and it allows every voter in the country to have a say in who sits in the House of Lords.' There was strong consensus in the Cross-Party Group for, and the Government proposes that there should be, direct elections to the second chamber.

Direct elections

4.42 The Cross-Party Group considered possible systems of direct elections that could be used for the second chamber. All these systems have been modelled on the parameters set out in paragraph 6.10. The modelling has formed part of the process of assessing how each voting system would contribute to the aims set out in paragraphs 6.8 and 6.9.

4.43 Four voting systems options were modelled for elections to the second chamber:

- Model A – First Past The Post (FPTP), i.e. a plurality system;
- Model B – Alternative Vote (AV), i.e. a majority system;
- Model C – Single Transferable Vote (STV), i.e. a proportional-based system; and
- Model D – list, i.e. a proportional-based system.

4.44 These models give only a general illustration of the distribution of seats in a reformed second chamber between the parties over time under each electoral system. Annex 2 provides a detailed description of the modelling and its limitations.

4.45 In the absence of any historical data on elections to the second chamber, some very broad assumptions have had to be made. For instance, ten previous general election results were aggregated to derive votes for each party over a certain period. Independent candidates were excluded from the analysis due to the difficulties in assessing their popularity in any constituency and election other than that in which they actually stood. Hence the closed list system was modelled showing the effect only on the parties, rather than on individual candidates. Some general assumptions were made about the allocation of preference votes under the STV system and a simple counting process was used to determine the allocation of seats to parties.

4.46 Large constituencies were created broadly based on the Jenkins Report's Top-up areas for FPTP system and an AV system. The constituencies created are purely for the purposes of modelling and do not reflect the actual constituencies that would be used for elections to the second chamber. The Government proposes that the Parliamentary Boundary Commissions should be asked to draw up any new electoral boundaries that might be needed.

4.47 Notwithstanding the accepted limitations of the modelling, the Cross Party Group found its outcomes very helpful in informing its discussion of the potential outcomes of different electoral systems.

Modelling the voting systems

Breakdown of the total number of members that could be elected in the second chamber over three elections under each voting system modelled:

(a) First Past The Post system.
(b) Alternative Vote system.
(c) Single Transferable Vote system.
(d) List system.

[...]

Model A: First Past The Post (FPTP) system with sub-regional constituencies

4.48 Under an FPTP system voters indicate a single candidate of their choice. The winner in each constituency is the person who secures the most votes. Annex 3 includes a sample ballot paper for an FPTP system. An FPTP system is used in the UK for elections to the House of Commons. Although the period of office is much shorter than that proposed in relation to the second chamber, the arrangement of FPTP elections in thirds in three-member wards is common in local elections, being used in English metropolitan district councils and in many English non-metropolitan district councils.

Summary of modelling of the FPTP system

4.49 Model A(1) provides for an FPTP system creating a wholly elected second chamber of 420 members. A total of 140 constituencies were created for modelling purposes, based on the 80 Top-up areas recommended by the Independent Commission on the Voting System (the Jenkins Commission). The 60 Jenkins Top-up areas with the largest number of votes cast in the 2005 general election were split in two, to create more constituencies. Under the modelling assumptions, at each of the three rounds of staggered elections, one member would be elected for each of the 140 constituencies.

4.50 Model A(2) provides for an FPTP system creating an 80% elected second chamber of 420 members. This consists of 336 elected members and 84 appointed members. In this case, the 32 Jenkins Top-up areas with the largest number of votes cast in the general election were split to create additional constituencies. Under the modelling assumptions, at each of the three rounds of staggered elections, one member would be elected for each of the 112 constituencies.

Model B: Alternative Vote (AV) system with sub-regional constituencies

4.51 Under an AV system, voters rank all the candidates in their order of preference. Annex 3 includes a sample ballot paper for an Alternative Vote system. Under an AV system, only one candidate can be elected and the winning candidate must gain more than 50% of the votes cast. If this is not secured on the basis of first preferences, the candidate with the lowest number of votes is eliminated and their votes are reallocated on the basis of second preferences. The process continues until one candidate has more than 50% of the votes, after the second preferences of the least popular candidates are redistributed.

Summary of modelling of the AV system

4.52 Model B(1) provides for an Alternative Vote system creating a wholly elected second chamber of 420 members. The 140 constituencies used for Model A(1) were also used here. Under the modelling assumptions, at each of the three rounds of staggered elections, one member would be elected for each of the 140 constituencies.

4.53 Model B(2) provides for an Alternative Vote system creating an 80% elected second chamber of 420 members. This consists of 336 elected members and 84 appointed members. Under the modelling assumptions, at each of the three rounds of staggered elections, one member would be elected for each of the 112 constituencies.

Model C: Single Transferable Vote (STV) system with sub-regional constituencies

4.54 The STV system is a broadly proportional system in terms of allocating seats to the parties in multi-member constituencies. It is a preferential voting system where the voter can rank all or some of the candidates according to their preferences across as well as between parties on the ballot paper. Annex 3 illustrates how the ballot paper might look under an STV system. An electoral formula is used to allocate seats and an agreed quota or threshold of votes is required for a candidate to win a seat in a constituency.

Summary of modelling of the STV system

4.55 Model C (1) assumes that the members of the second chamber are elected on an STV system using 24 sub-regional boundaries. These were constructed for modelling purposes by combining two or more adjacent Jenkins Top-up areas, to create new constituencies with approximately 1.5 million to 2 million electors in each. The model assumes the total membership in a wholly elected second chamber is 432 with 144 members elected at each of three election cycles. The number of seats allocated per region for each multi-member constituency is the same throughout the country at 18 seats, with six seats available at each round of election per region. The commonly used Droop quota is used to allocate seats to the parties. To win a seat in a constituency a candidate is required to obtain nearly 15% of the total votes cast in that region.

4.56 Model C(2) assumes the total membership in a mainly elected second chamber is 450 members. This consists of 360 elected members and 90 appointed members. The new intake at each of three rounds of election would be 120 elected members and 30 appointed members. The number of seats allocated per region for each multi-member constituency is the same throughout the country at 15 seats, with five seats available at each round of election. To win a seat in a constituency a candidate is required to obtain nearly 17% of the total votes cast in that region.

Model D: List system with sub-regional boundaries

4.57 The list system is a broadly proportional system in terms of allocating seats to the parties. The proportion of votes cast determines the total number of seats that each party receives. Parties publish a list of candidates for each constituency and the size of the ballot paper is determined by the number of seats to be filled in a particular region. The number of members elected from each party list in a region will broadly reflect the share of the votes cast for the party or individual candidate in that region. An electoral formula is used to allocate seats to the parties. The type of list used will determine the level of choice the voter has and the allocation of seats between the party candidates on the party list.

A closed-list system

4.58 The closed-list system is used in European Parliamentary elections in England, Scotland and Wales. It allows the voter one vote. Annex 3 illustrates how the ballot paper might look under a closed list system. The political parties publish lists of candidates and the voter votes for one such list. The voter has no influence on the position of a candidate on the party list. Members are elected on the basis of where their parties have placed them on their lists. The list ranking therefore determines whether or not a candidate is chosen, with those near the top of the list more likely to be elected. Voters are not required to make decisions about particular candidates and the system involves a high degree of party control.

An open-list system

4.59 The open-list system allows the voter one vote, for the candidate of their choice. Voters are required to make a choice of a candidate from various party lists on the ballot paper. The total votes cast for candidates of a particular party are used to calculate how many seats that party will have. Once the shares of the seats have been allocated to the parties, an agreed formula, quota or threshold is then used to determine which candidates from that party's list are chosen. One variant is to determine the candidates on the basis of the absolute number of votes cast. If a party won four seats in a region, the candidates from that party would be ranked according to the number of votes that had been cast for them and the top four would be elected. Alternatively, an electoral formula could be used to determine the threshold required for a candidate to secure a seat, e.g. the commonly used Droop quota. This would have the effect that if a party was allocated four seats in a region, any candidate with more than one fifth of the party's share of the vote would be guaranteed a seat. The option of reverting back to the list ranking is possible where insufficient candidates reach the threshold to allocate any remaining seats.

Semi-open list system

4.60 A semi-open list system allows the voter one vote but two choices. They can either place an 'X' next to the preferred candidate on the ballot paper or place an 'X' next to the preferred party list as published. A vote either for the party list or an individual candidate on that party list would count towards the party's allocation of seats in that region. A semi-open list system would require an individual candidate to reach an agreed threshold of personal votes to override the list ranking. This system offers a certain degree of flexibility to the voter, who does not have to choose a specific candidate, but can opt for the party list if they do not have a preference for a specific candidate. Under a semi-open list system a vote for the party list or for an individual candidate on the party list both count towards the total votes cast when allocating the share of the seats to the parties. Each candidate's position on the party list will have a bearing on allocating seats within the party, i.e. candidates who appear at the top of the list are more likely to be allocated a seat within the party's total. An individual candidate on the party list would have to secure a certain percentage of the party's vote to enable their personal votes to override the party list. For instance in Sweden, in elections to the national parliament, the Riksdag, an individual candidate must gain 8% of their party's votes in a constituency in order for him or her to override the order of the party list. The worked example below shows how a party's seat would be allocated to its candidates under a semi-open list system where an 8% threshold is applied. In Constituency Z, a total of 800 votes have been cast for Party X in elections to the second chamber. Party X is therefore allocated four seats in that constituency. A total of 500 votes were cast for the party list and a further 300 votes were cast for individual candidates on the party list. The order in which the candidates appear on the ballot paper (i.e. the party's ranking) is as follows:

[...]

Summary of modelling of the list system

4.61 In the absence of any historical data on elections to the second chamber some very broad assumptions have had to be made. These are outlined at paragraph 4.45. As a result, the closed list system was modelled showing the effect only on the parties, rather than on individual candidates.

4.62 Model D(1) assumes that all members of the second chamber are elected on a list system using twelve regional boundaries broadly based on the European Parliament constituencies, i.e. the nine Government Office Regions of England, plus Scotland, Wales and Northern Ireland. The model assumes the total membership in a wholly elected second chamber is 438, with 146 members elected over three election cycles. The number of seats allocated per region differs according to the size of the region. A region with a higher concentration of the population, such as the south-east, attracts a greater number of seats.

4.63 Model D(2) assumes the total membership in a mainly elected second chamber is 435 members. This consists of 348 elected members and 87 appointed members. The new intake at each of the three rounds of election would be 116 elected members and 29 appointed members.

Outcomes of the modelling of the voting systems

4.64 Annex 2 gives details of the modelling that has been done to illustrate the possible outcomes of different voting systems using the parameters described in paragraphs 6.10. The annex considers how many seats the various parties might have secured in the second chamber if electors had voted as they did in general elections between 1966 and 2005. The constituencies modelled do not reflect the actual size of the constituencies that would be used for elections to the second chamber. The Government proposes that the Parliamentary Boundary Commissions should be asked to draw up any new electoral boundaries that might be needed.

4.65 The outcomes of the modelling show that:

– Under a First Past The Post system or Alternative Vote system there would be a significant possibility that the party forming the government of the day would also secure a majority in the second chamber, if they won a number of successive elections, even with elections staggered over three cycles. However, if there were repeated changes of government at general elections, the government of the day would be unlikely to have a majority in the second chamber under either system. Similarly, if there was a change of government after a long period, the new government might not have a majority in the second chamber after the first election when the change occurred.

- Under an STV or list system with staggered elections over three cycles, it would be hard for a single party to achieve an overall majority in the second chamber. A party would need to gain a large proportion of the votes in each successive election to do so.
- Parties other than the main two and independent candidates would stand a better chance of gaining seats under STV and list systems than FPTP and AV. Under FPTP, a successful candidate must win a constituency outright, beating all other candidates. Under AV, a candidate would need to obtain 50% plus one of votes, once preference transfers are counted. In a six-seat constituency under STV, a candidate would need just under 15% of the vote (including preference transfers from successful or eliminated candidates) to be guaranteed a seat. In a ten-seat constituency under a list system, obtaining about 10% of the vote would be sufficient for a party to secure representation.

A number of reports on Lords reform have considered the merits of various electoral systems. In 2000, the Wakeham Commission recommended 'an arrangement which would give the regional electorate a voice in the selection of regional members'. Options for realising this principle were (a) indirect election using votes cast at general elections and party lists and (b) two proportional systems using European election constituencies with different numbers of members in the constituencies and with different timings for their election. In 2001, the White Paper *House of Lords: Completing the Reform* endorsed a version of one of the Wakeham Commission options, which was a proportional system using European election constituencies with all constituencies returning members at each election. In 2002, the Public Administration Select Committee set out a number of principles which 'would be best realised using multi-member constituencies and a proportional voting system. This could be either STV or regional lists, so long as the lists are fully open, which maximises voter choice'. The Joint Committee on House of Lords Reform noted the advantages of both these systems: 'they provide for much larger constituencies than for MPs, minimising the risk of overlap.' The Committee added that a FPTP system ruled out the election of independents and small parties. The Committee's second report (April 2003) recorded some MPs' desire for indirect election either through regional structures or a secondary use of votes cast at general elections using regional lists. In 2005, the cross-party authors of the *Breaking the Deadlock* report recommended that 'elections should be carried out using either open lists or STV. On balance we believe that STV is more in keeping with the needs of the second chamber.' In 2007, the White Paper *House of Lords: Reform* recommended a partially open regional list system.

In addition, the Jenkins Report considered electoral systems for the House of Commons as a whole. It recommended a two-vote mixed system ('AV Top-up') with the majority of MPs being elected on an individual constituency basis. The remainder would be elected on a Top-up basis to address 'the dis-proportionality and the geographical divisiveness which are inherent in FPTP'. One member of the Commission, Lord Alexander, supported the idea of an additional member system while keeping FPTP in the constituency elections. He expressed reservations that AV received little, if any, support in the submissions received by the Commission and highlighted a potential unfairness that the only second preferences to be counted were those of the most unsuccessful candidates.

Pros and cons of different voting systems

4.66 These outcomes have been considered in relation to the potential extent to which each voting system could contribute to the aims set out in paragraphs 6.8 and 6.9 of achieving a second chamber that was complementary to the Commons; and encouraging the election of people with a range of views, including those from smaller political parties and independent candidates, whilst providing for the prevailing political view amongst the electorate to be reflected. In addition, consideration has been given to the degree of choice and ease of operation that different electoral systems provide for voters and how easy it is to understand how the final results are reached.

4.67 As paragraph 4.45 makes clear, the modelling presented in this White Paper is based on historical results for the House of Commons. These are the most relevant data available. It is possible that voting patterns for the second chamber could differ from the House of Commons even if elections for both took place on the same day.

4.68 A FPTP system would make it more difficult for representatives of smaller parties and independent candidates to be elected. It would ensure that the prevailing political view amongst the electorate was reflected in the second chamber. However, this carries with it an increased risk of the membership of the second chamber 'mirroring' that of the House of Commons. FPTP systems are widely understood and easy to operate. The FPTP system presented in this White Paper would provide for 140 constituencies if there were a fully elected second chamber and if it were 80% elected. By contrast, the STV system would use 24 constituencies and the list system the twelve European Parliament ones. The smaller constituencies that are a feature of the FPTP system and the AV system modelled would cover cities and counties, which are naturally understood areas. They contrast with the much larger and in the case of the STV system, artificially-created, constituencies that would be used for the STV and list systems.

4.69 The AV system modelled in this White Paper would use the same constituencies as the FPTP system. It is very difficult to assess the outcomes from an AV system because there is no direct evidence from the general election results about how people would have allocated subsequent preferences between parties. (In modelling STV systems, various assumptions have been made, including the simplifying one that people would allocate their preferences to candidates of the same party only. This assumption would not be relevant to modelling the AV system proposed here, as there would almost certainly only be one candidate from each party standing in each constituency.) Insofar as there is evidence, this might not hold for elections to the second chamber. It also seems likely that people would allocate subsequent preferences differently in elections at different times, depending on the political and other circumstances prevailing.

4.70 However, it can be argued that an AV system would be more preferential than FPTP for the second chamber, in the sense that all those elected would have to receive more than half the votes cast, including redistributed votes. This aspect is particularly important now that the UK is in an era where almost all contested elections occur between more than just the two main parties and where many elections, which would probably include any to the second chamber, also involve smaller parties. The Conservative Party disagrees that AV would be more preferential than FPTP because promoting second choice votes weakens a mandate and gives weight to tactical rather than preferential voting.

4.71 An AV system could encourage the election of well-known independent candidates, insofar as they picked up voters' alternative preferences. The operation of an AV system would be more complex than that of a FPTP one and the calculation of the results would have to be explained to voters. For example, it is only a losing candidate's second preferences that are reallocated to enable another candidate to gain a majority of votes.

4.72 The two proportional systems that have been modelled – STV and a list system – would both provide enhanced opportunities for candidates from parties other than the main two and for independent candidates to be elected, and would help produce a balance between parties in the second chamber.

4.73 In the large constituencies each returning more than one member, which the Government envisages for elections to the second chamber, it could be argued that a list system would be much easier for voters to operate than an STV system. Both systems could result in long ballot papers, because a large number of candidates can be expected to stand in large, multi-member constituencies. However, under a list system, electors would have only one vote and they would use an 'X', rather than having to rank candidates. The former is straightforward and more consistent with other voting systems used in the UK.

4.74 Under an STV system, voters would be asked to rank candidates. An STV system in large constituencies, each returning more than one member, would be complicated for voters. Although it should be noted that this system has been used successfully in Northern Ireland for many years in local, Assembly and European elections, it is more complex to count the votes under an STV system and to explain how the results were arrived at. Election results under STV typically take longer to be determined, sometimes up to two days.

4.75 A closed list is not favoured for elections to the second chamber because this would restrict voters' choices about individual candidates. However, the modelling assumes a closed list system (where voters express a preference for a party and not an individual candidate) and no assumption has been made to try to reflect the popularity of individual candidates which is required under a semi-open and open list system. An open list on the other hand would require voters to make a well-informed decision about candidates on party lists and is more likely to lead to greater competitiveness within the parties. A semi-open list would be more flexible. Voters are familiar with voting for a party as a whole in some other UK elections but a semi-open list system also offers the voter a choice to vote for a particular candidate on the party list should they wish to do so.

4.76 There was no consensus in the Cross-Party Group about which electoral system would be the most appropriate for elections to the second chamber.

4.77 The Conservative Party favours a First Past The Post system for elections to the second chamber. In particular, they favour using the 80 constituencies proposed by Jenkins, leading to a total membership of 300 (of which 60 who would be appointed), plus the Bishops.

4.78 The Liberal Democrats consider that an Alternative Vote system would have the disadvantages of a First Past The Post system. They also think that it would have the additional disadvantage that members of the second chamber elected on an Alternative Vote system could claim to have more substantial public support and therefore a more substantial mandate than members of the House of Commons. The Liberal Democrats favour the use of the Single Transferable Vote system for elections to the second chamber to give the widest possible choice to the elector – including support for independents – rather than perpetuating party patronage. The Liberal Democrats are strongly opposed to a closed or semi-open list in all circumstances.

4.79 The Convenor of the Cross-bench Peers favours the use of a Single Transferable Vote or Alternative Vote system and is opposed to the use of any form of list system for elections to the second chamber.

4.80 The Government believes that further consideration should be given to the following voting systems options for elections to the second chamber:

– a First Past The Post system;
– an Alternative Vote system;
– a Single Transferable Vote system; or
– an open or semi-open list system.

4.81 The choice of a voting system for elections to the second chamber is the subject of much discussion. It is a key decision about the way forward for a reformed second chamber and hence about the institutions of our democracy. The Government is therefore keen to facilitate an extensive and wide-ranging debate on this issue. Hence it would welcome views from all quarters.

Filling vacancies for elected members

4.82 The long terms of office that the Government proposes for elected members of the second chamber mean that inevitably, some seats will become vacant. If elected members were not replaced soon after a seat became vacant, it could be argued that, even with constituencies each returning more than one member, the electorate for that seat was not being fully represented.

4.83 Any detailed arrangements for filling vacancies would depend on which voting system was used for the second chamber. In general, where FPTP, AV and STV systems operate, a by-election is held to fill vacancies. It is worth noting that vacancies in the Northern Ireland Assembly, which is elected under an STV system, are currently filled through a system of substitutes. Under a list system, it might be possible to fill the vacancy on the basis of the votes cast at the original election. The seat could be offered to the person who would have been elected next at the most recent election, with the process continuing until someone was found who was willing and able to fill the seat. It might, of course, be some time since the original election, and consideration could be given to the necessary arrangements that would need to be in place where there is a difficulty in filling a vacant seat. In these circumstances, one option might be to offer the vacancy to someone from the relevant party who had stood unsuccessfully at a more recent election to chose members to represent that constituency in the second chamber.

4.84 Any proposal to fill vacant seats could result in some members of the second chamber serving terms that were much shorter than usual ones, if they were elected to fill vacancies that had been filled by someone else for most of a 12–15 year period of office. The situation would occur where a seat that was due to be filled at the time of the next general election became vacant and that a general election followed shortly afterwards.

4.85 The Cross-Party Group considered this issue at some length. The group could see merit in arrangements by which an elected member would be eligible to stand for re-election, if they replaced someone who left before their term was exhausted and there was less than a certain period to run on that term. The period could be, say, three years. Under this proposal, the provision would apply only in relation to the next election for that seat (or its equivalent following boundary changes) and not to any other election, for that seat or any other. This would be the only circumstance in which someone who had previously been an elected member of the reformed second chamber would be eligible for re-election.

4.86 However, it might prove difficult to find people to stand for election where a vacancy had only a short period to run. An alternative would be to extend the period, possibly by saying that re-election would be allowed if the vacancy occurred at any stage during the second or third electoral cycle which applied to the vacancy. This would mean that a vacancy would be likely to have up to eight years to run. There are concerns that allowing someone to stand for re-election for 15 years after they had served an initial term of up to eight years would provide for a long period of office.

4.87 The Government believes that there should be a process to fill vacancies and would welcome views on what those arrangements should be.

5. A reformed chamber: powers

Summary

5.1 The current powers of the second chamber, the Parliament Acts and the conventions that underpin them have worked well. Given its electoral mandate, a reformed chamber is likely to be more assertive. The Government welcomes this. Increased assertiveness on the part of the second chamber is compatible with the continued primacy of the House of Commons, which does not rest solely or mainly on the fact that the House of Commons is an elected chamber whilst the House of Lords is not. (One aspect of the primacy of the House of Commons is the operation of the 1911 and 1949 Parliament Acts, which the Government does not intend to change.) There is no persuasive case for reducing the powers of a reformed second chamber.

Primary legislation

5.2 There are a number of constraints on the way in which the current House of Lords exercises its legislative functions and powers in relation to primary legislation (Bills). The 1911 Parliament Act provided that Money Bills could receive Royal Assent without the approval of the House of Lords, if not passed by the Lords without amendment within one month. It also provided that any other public bill first introduced in the Commons, other than one extending the life of a Parliament, would receive Royal Assent without the consent of the House of Lords, if it had been passed by the House of Commons in three successive sessions and as long as two years had elapsed between its Commons second reading in the first session and its final passing by the Commons. Subsequently, the 1949 Parliament Act decreased the number of sessions in which the Commons must pass a Bill from three to two and reduced the period between the first Commons second reading and final passage in the Commons to one year.

5.3 Following the 1945 general election, which resulted in strains between a Labour Government with a majority of 156 in the House of Commons and a House of Lords with only 16 Labour peers out of a total of 831, the so-called 'Salisbury-Addison Convention' evolved. This came to imply that the House of Lords should not reject at second or third reading an intention to legislate mentioned in the Government's election manifesto. The 2006 report of the Joint Committee on Conventions noted that the Salisbury-Addison Convention had changed, particularly since 1999. The report set out the key conventions that now governed the relationship between the two Houses of Parliament. The Government accepted the Joint Committee's recommendations and conclusions and the Committee's report was debated by both Houses, which passed resolutions in identical terms approving it. While the Joint Committee was clear that the conventions it set out would be called into question in the event of reform, it is equally clear that the two Houses must continue to maintain effective working relationships in the context of the primacy of the Commons. The Joint Committee concluded that the key conventions that now governed the relationship between the two Houses were:

Salisbury-Addison Convention: that in the House of Lords, a manifesto Bill is accorded a second reading; is not subject to 'wrecking amendments' which change the Government's manifesto intention as proposed in the Bill; and is passed and sent (or returned) to the House of Commons, so that it has the opportunity, in reasonable time, to consider the Bill or any amendments the Lords may wish to propose.

Reasonable time: the House of Lords considers Government business in reasonable time.

Secondary legislation: neither House of Parliament regularly rejects secondary legislation, but in exceptional circumstances it may be appropriate for either House to do so. There are situations in which it is consistent with both the Lords' role in Parliament as a revising chamber, and with Parliament's role in relation to delegated legislation, for the Lords to threaten to defeat a statutory instrument.

Financial privilege: If the Commons have disagreed to Lords amendments on grounds of financial privilege, it is contrary to convention for the House of Lords to send back amendments in lieu which clearly invite the same response. In addition, the Committee concluded that the evidence they had heard pointed to the emergence in recent years of a practice that the House of Lords will usually give a Second Reading to any government Bill, whether based on the manifesto or not.

Secondary legislation

5.4 In addition to Bills, both Houses of Parliament also consider proposals for delegated or secondary legislation. This arises where the original Act of Parliament includes provision enabling the law to be changed or fleshed out through statutory instruments, rules or codes of practice. The sort of changes and provisions provided for include technical changes, detailed rules and procedures and changes or details that need to be made or set out regularly (for example because levels of payment are to increase over time). Typically, Parliament considers about 3,000 statutory instruments each year.

5.5 Like the House of Commons, the House of Lords can currently only accept or reject a proposed statutory instrument – it has no power to amend it. The Lords has developed the practice of expressing its concerns about a statutory instrument through the use of non-fatal amendments to motions approving statutory instruments, sometimes giving explanations or reasons. The existence of such amendments may cause the Government to reconsider its proposals. The House of Lords very rarely rejects a statutory instrument and it has done so on only three previous occasions.

A reformed second chamber

5.6 A reformed second chamber will almost certainly be more assertive than the current House of Lords, because it will be wholly or mainly elected. As noted in paragraphs 2.5–2.6, the Government welcomes the fact that where the House of Lords has serious concerns about proposed legislation, it gives voice to them. The Cross-Party Group on House of Lords reform considered that such assertiveness is unlikely to pose a risk to the primacy of the House of Commons. This primacy is currently based on the fact that the Government of the day is formed from the party or parties that can command a majority in the House of Commons. It is also based on the Parliament Acts and the financial privilege of the House of Commons. The Prime Minister and most senior ministers are also drawn from the House of Commons. A second chamber that is more assertive than the current House of Lords, operating against the background of the current arrangements for its powers, would not threaten primacy.

5.7 Given this, the Cross-Party Group saw no reason to change the current arrangements for the powers of the second chamber once it became wholly or mainly elected. Moreover, the group concluded that it would also be difficult to justify making changes on a contingency basis, and before there was any evidence of the likelihood of inappropriate challenges to the primacy of the House of Commons arising. The Government proposes that there should be no change to the powers of a reformed second chamber.

Parliament Acts

5.8 Although the Government considers that there is no case for changing the powers of the second chamber, the cross-party discussions did consider options for changes in some detail. One would be to extend the scope of the 1911 and 1949 Parliament Acts, so that they covered Bills that began in the second chamber. The group noted that in practice non-applicability of the Acts to Bills that begin in the second chamber has not given rise to recent problems or issues. Hence it would be difficult to argue that the scope of the Acts should be extended.

Exchange of amendments

5.9 The group also noted that any arrangements in relation to exchange of amendments to primary legislation would have to ensure that ultimately the views of the House of Commons would prevail, so as to safeguard the primacy of the Commons. Current practices allow the exchanges between the two Houses to complete the parliamentary passage of a Bill (except for Money Bills or Bills of Aids and Supplies, or other Bills covered by the Parliament Acts) to continue until a final agreement is reached. Hence resolution is almost invariably reached without the Commons insisting on its primacy.

Time limits

5.10 An alternative to changing the scope of the Parliament Acts or putting new arrangements in place in relation to exchange of amendments would be to specify how long any Bill should spend in the second chamber, including Bills that start there, in line with the 'reasonable time' convention. The Cross-Party Group noted the 2006 Joint Committee view that 'there is no problem which would be solved' by defining 'reasonable' or setting a time limit; and the reasons the Committee gave to support this statement. The group also noted that there could be difficulties of definition and the possible risk of bringing the Speaker of the House of Commons into areas of political controversy if they had to decide on such issues.

Codifying conventions

5.11 The option of codifying the Salisbury-Addison Convention would create more difficulties of definition, as not only 'reasonable time', but also terms like 'manifesto Bill' and 'wrecking amendments' (or the type of amendments that would be prohibited) would have to be set out in writing. Any codification of the Convention could in principle be through statute or through some form of resolution of both Houses of Parliament. The former route in particular could open up a role for the courts in deciding matters relating to the business of Parliament, such as whether a particular Bill met a statutory definition for a 'manifesto Bill'. This could place a strain on the principle of exclusive cognisance, where each House has the power to control its own affairs. Alternatively, the option could run the risk of bringing the Speaker of the House of Commons into areas of political controversy.

5.12 The Cross-Party Group agrees with the conclusion of the Joint Committee on Conventions, which looked at the practicality of codifying the key conventions on the relationship between the two Houses of Parliament. The Government agreed with the Joint Committee's views that legislation, or any other form of codification that would turn conventions into rules, was not the way forward. Codification would remove flexibility, exclude exceptions and inhibit evolution in response to political circumstances.

Secondary legislation

5.13 The cross-party discussions raised a number of issues in relation to the arrangements for secondary legislation that the

group considered could be taken forward as part of the process
of Parliamentary reform more generally.

6. A reformed chamber: an appointed element?

Summary

6.1 This White Paper considers what the arrangements for a
reformed second chamber on either a wholly or mainly elected
basis might be. The Government considers that the key argument for any appointments in the second chamber is that they
would preserve a significant independent element. Given this,
the Government proposes that there should be no party-political
appointments to a reformed second chamber. However, there
should not be a bar on those who have or who have had party-
political affiliations or connections being considered.

6.2 There was a difference of views in the cross-party talks
on whether individuals who have held certain offices as public
servants (for instance the Cabinet Secretary) should continue to
be considered for membership of the reformed second chamber
in the same way that they are now. The Government proposes
that this practice should cease as part of reform, although the
characteristics of distinguished former public servants are typically such that they would be extremely credible candidates for
appointment to a reformed second chamber if it were mainly,
rather than wholly, elected.

6.3 The Government will give further consideration to and
would welcome views on whether there should be provision for
appointments to a reformed second chamber specifically for
the purposes of enabling a particular individual to become a
Government Minister.

6.4 The Government proposes that if there is an appointed
element in a reformed second chamber, there should continue
to be an Appointments Commission, which would seek applications and nominations, against published criteria. Appointments
would be made on merit, with the key focus being an individual's

ability, willingness and commitment to take part in the full work of the second chamber. The Government also proposes that any appointed members of a reformed second chamber should take part fully in its work, in general terms devoting the same amount of time to that work as elected members.

6.5 The Government proposes that, as for elected members, appointed members of a reformed second chamber should serve for three electoral cycles without the possibility of reappointment. One-third of appointed members would be replaced at each set of elections to the second chamber. The Government proposes that the Commission replace members who leave the second chamber before their term of office ends.

6.6 The Government proposes that if there is to be an appointed element in a reformed second chamber, with an Appointments Commission as a permanent part of those arrangements, that Commission should be on a statutory basis. Legislation should contain only broad parameters in relation to the role and operation of the Appointments Commission, to give it flexibility to respond effectively to changing needs and circumstances.

6.7 The Government proposes that any appointments commission should be accountable to the Prime Minister.

6.8 The Government proposes that there should be no reserved seats for Church of England Bishops in a wholly elected second chamber. It also proposes that if there is an appointed element in a reformed second chamber, there should be a proportionate number of seats reserved for Church of England Bishops. These seats would not count towards the proportion to be filled following nomination or application to the Appointments Commission. The Church of England would be invited to consider how it would in future select Bishops for membership of the second chamber.

6.9 After careful consideration, the Government proposes to endorse the recommendations of the Wakeham Commission that providing reserved places for churches and faith communities other than the Church of England in a reformed second chamber would be problematic. Any appointments to represent other churches and faith groups should be made through the Appointments Commission in the usual way. The Government would welcome views on whether the Appointments Commission should be given a specific remit to provide for representation of other churches and faith groups in making its appointments.

6.10 On the Government's proposals, the Convenor of the Cross-bench Peers considers that there should be a bar on those who have or have had recent party-political affiliations or connections from being considered for any appointed element. The Conservative Party considers that some individuals should be considered automatically for membership of an appointed element and that any future Appointments Commission should continue to be non-statutory to maximise its flexibility. The Liberal Democrats propose that there should be no reserved seats for Church of England Bishops in a reformed second chamber if it includes an appointed element. However, Bishops or other representatives of the Church of England could be nominated or apply to the Appointments Commission in the usual way.

Introduction

6.11 The basis for the further work of the Cross-Party Group was to illustrate how a reformed second chamber constituted on the basis voted for by the House of Commons in March 2007 (i.e. either wholly or mainly elected) might be achieved. This chapter therefore explores the arguments for an appointed element. It goes on to set out views on the possible composition of any appointed element and on how members might be appointed. Views would be welcomed on whether the reformed second chamber should include appointees and if so, on the detailed proposals presented here.

The case for an appointed element

6.12 A number of reports have recommended that elections to a reformed second chamber should be complemented by an appointed element. In February 2002, the House of Commons Public Administration Select Committee recommended that 60% of the members of a reformed chamber be elected, 20% be nominated by the political parties and 20% be independent, non-aligned members. It noted that a wholly elected chamber would leave little or no room for non-aligned people who were independent of party affiliations. It could also jeopardise the principles that no party should have an outright majority, that the House should be more diverse, and that the second chamber should include expertise and experience from people whose careers have lain outside politics. The first report of the Joint Committee on House of Lords Reform and the report *Reforming the House of Lords: Breaking the Deadlock* set out a number of options, noting that a wholly elected chamber would be likely to have few if any independent members.

6.13 The view that a reformed second chamber should have both an elected and an appointed element was echoed in the manifestos of the Conservative Party and Liberal Democrats for the May 2005 elections.

6.14 The Government believes that the key argument for any appointments in a reformed second chamber is that it would preserve a significant independent element. The Cross-benchers have played a valuable role in the House of Lords, bringing a non-party perspective to the work of the chamber. The introduction of an elected element into a reformed second chamber would mean that in future, most members will have been elected as representatives of one of the political parties. Without an appointed element, the advantages of a significant independent element would be lost.

6.15 The Government considers that any appointed element in a reformed second chamber would be an effective way of securing the continuation of a number of independent members. The presence of a significant minority of independent members would both distinguish the second chamber clearly from the House of Commons and complement the work of the Commons by providing non-partisan viewpoints in the legislative revision process.

The size of any appointed element should be at the level of the 20% voted for by the House of Commons in March 2007.

Composition of any appointed element

6.16 Currently, appointments to the House of Lords come from a number of sources. If someone is independent of any political party, they can apply or be nominated for a life Peerage. The House of Lords Appointments Commission was established in May 2000 on a non-statutory basis to assist with the transitional phase in reforming the House of Lords. It is an independent non-departmental public body supported and funded by the Cabinet Office. The Commission considers applications and nominations, within provisions set by the Prime Minister about the timing of appointments and the number of such peers that can be created. It makes recommendations for non-party political appointments to the Prime Minister, who then makes nominations to the Monarch. The current Prime Minister has followed the precedent set by his predecessor and undertaken to pass recommendations from the Commission for non-party political appointments to the Monarch without alteration.

6.17 The Prime Minister also makes a number of nominations from across a range of political parties to the Monarch other than on the advice of the Commission. The Commission vets these proposed nominations for propriety. These are referred to as 'party-political nominations'. The Prime Minister also nominates a small number of former public servants (up to ten per Parliament). In addition, although many Government Ministers in the Lords have been chosen from among existing peers, Prime Ministers also nominate individuals for membership of the Lords specifically so that these people can serve as Ministers. The two most significant roles of the second chamber will continue to be considering legislation and scrutinising the work of the executive. This creates a need for sufficient members of the Government in a reformed chamber to carry out work there in relation to each Government Department.

6.18 Given the Government's view that the primary purpose of any appointed element in a reformed second chamber should be to secure the continuation of a number of independent members, it believes that, subject to paragraph 6.23, there should be no party-political appointments to that chamber. The existence of a substantial number of elected members in a reformed second chamber will ensure proper representation for political parties, which are the cornerstone of democracy in this country.

6.19 However, if there is an appointed element in a reformed second chamber, the Government proposes that, as is the case now, there should not be a bar on those who have or who have had party-political affiliations or connections being considered. Those appointed to a reformed chamber should be, individually and collectively, those able to make the best contribution to its work. Any political affiliations should be disregarded when considering whether someone is suitable to serve and should not be the basis for either preferential or detrimental consideration. However, as the basis for appointment would be to provide an independent element, appointed members of a reformed second chamber would be expected to act independently from any political party.

6.20 The Cross-Party Group considered whether the Prime Minister should continue to be able to nominate a limited number of former public servants to the second chamber. It can be argued that nomination by the Prime Minister should be automatic for people who had held roles such as Archbishop of Canterbury, Cabinet Secretary and Chief of the Defence Staff, who could be unlikely to put themselves forward for appointment to the second chamber but who would bring valuable perspectives to its work.

6.21 The Cross-Party Group expressed a variety of views on the idea of 'automatic' nomination to a reformed second chamber. The Government considers it would be difficult to justify 'automatic' consideration for membership for any one group above others, with the exception of serving Church of England Bishops (see paragraphs 6.45–6.52). If there were an appointed element in a reformed second chamber, former public servants could be appointed through the general arrangements for appointments. Their suitability could be considered alongside that of other applicants and nominees. Therefore, although there would be no certainty of a place, the characteristics of distinguished former public servants would mean that they would be extremely credible candidates. The Government proposes that there should be no expectation of membership of the reformed second chamber in the case of distinguished former public servants: each application would be considered on an individual basis.

6.22 The Conservative Party considered that there was a case for an element of automaticity in the case of distinguished former public servants.

6.23 The Government would welcome views on whether there should be provision for appointments to a reformed second chamber specifically for the purposes of enabling a particular individual to become a Government Minister.

Identification of potential appointees

6.24 The current House of Lords Appointments Commission invites applications and nominations. The Commission considers applications against published criteria and makes recommendations on merit. These principles have worked well and commanded general support. The Government proposes that if there is to be an appointed element in a reformed second chamber, there should continue to be an Appointments Commission and that it should seek applications and nominations. These should be considered on merit, against published criteria.

Principles for appointment

6.25 The criteria used currently by the House of Lords Appointments Commission for non-party political appointments are attached at Annex 6. They include that applicants and nominees should:

- have a record of significance that demonstrates a range of experience, skills and competencies;
- be able to make an effective and significant contribution to the work of the House across a wide range of issues;
- have some understanding of the constitutional framework and the skills and qualities needed to be an effective member of the House;
- have the time available to make an effective contribution within the procedures of working practices of the House; and
- be able to demonstrate outstanding personal qualities, in particular integrity and independence.

6.26 If there is to be an appointed element in a reformed second chamber, the Government proposes that the key focus in assessing potential appointees should be their ability, willingness and commitment to take part in the full range of the work of the chamber. Both elected and any appointed members will bring these qualities. While account should be taken of achievement or expertise, those appointed to a reformed second chamber should hold their membership because they are the best people for the job and will make an effective contribution to the work of the chamber, rather than because they are the most successful in their chosen field.

6.27 The Government proposes that an Appointments Commission for a reformed second chamber should not have a general remit to ensure that aspects of society such as sport or the arts were represented, with the possible exception of faith (see paragraphs 6.53 and 6.54). The role of all members of the second chamber, including any appointed element, will be to take part in debates and scrutiny across a wide range of areas. As with the current House of Lords, a reformed second chamber would be able to get access to specific expertise and experience through, for example, committees taking written and oral evidence, rather than through the appointment of members with particular expertise and experience.

6.28 The Government proposes that any appointed members of a reformed second chamber should take part fully in the work of the chamber, in general terms devoting the same amount of time to this work as elected members. This is consistent with the principle that the status of any appointed members should be on a par with those who are elected.

Status of any Appointments Commission

6.29 The current House of Lords Appointments Commission is a non-statutory body. Generally, non-statutory status provides bodies of this sort the flexibility to respond to changing needs and circumstances.

6.30 However, a number of reports have argued that any Appointments Commission for a reformed second chamber should be statutory. The Wakeham Commission recommended that an Appointments Commission be established by primary legislation. It noted that the option of a non-departmental public body would not offer the level of independence and entrenchment required. As noted above, the current Prime Minister follows the precedent of his predecessor in passing recommendations from the House of Lords Appointments Commission for non-party political peers to the Monarch without alteration. However, these 'self-denying ordinances' do not provide the sort of guarantee about the future behaviour of Governments that some people are seeking.

6.31 The House of Lords and House of Commons Joint Committee on House of Lords Reform and the February 2005 report *Reforming the House of Lords: Breaking the Deadlock* by a cross-party group of parliamentarians both recommended that a new Appointments Commission be established on a statutory basis.

6.32 In 2006–07, the House of Commons Public Administration Select Committee considered the possible future status, role and operation of the House of Lords Appointments Commission, in the context of considering the policy and regulatory issues arising from matters investigated by the police in response to allegations concerning the possible offer of peerages in exchange for financial assistance to political parties. The Committee reported in December 2007. It recommended, in advance of the introduction of any elected element, that the current Appointments Commission should be put onto a statutory footing, to clarify its remit and remove the Prime Minister from decisions on the size and composition of the House of Lords.

6.33 In its February 2007 White Paper *The House of Lords: Reform*, the Government set out its view that: 'Whilst it would be acceptable for the Appointments Commission to remain on a non-statutory basis if its current role were to continue, it would not be appropriate if its role were to increase significantly.' It remains the Government's view that if there is to be an appointed element in a reformed second chamber, with an appointments commission as a permanent part of the arrangements, that commission should be on a statutory basis. However, any legislation providing for an appointments commission should contain only broad parameters in relation to its role and operation, to give the Commission flexibility to respond effectively to changing needs and circumstances.

6.34 The Conservative Party considers that any future appointments commission should continue to be non-statutory, to maximise flexibility.

Accountability

6.35 Whether a statutory or non-statutory body, any appointments commission would have the power to appoint a small but significant part of the UK Parliament. Considerable power is therefore invested in it. The Government considers that confidence in any appointments commission and its decisions would be improved by a clear system of accountability. This would enhance the authority of those appointed, and so enable them to carry out their duties more effectively.

6.36 Public bodies are usually accountable to Government or directly to Parliament. The Government proposes that the Appointments Commission should be accountable to the Prime Minister.

Making appointments to a reformed second chamber

Criteria for appointment

6.37 The Government proposes that the published criteria for appointments would need to be devised by the Commission itself and approved by Parliament. The criteria would need to reflect the broad principles (see paragraphs 6.25–6.28) that appointments should be based on ability, willingness and commitment to take part and a recognition that appointed and elected members should be on a par, including in relation to the contribution they are expected to make. Leaving any more detailed criteria to the Commission itself would enable the Commissioners to take into account past experience, and would provide the flexibility needed to appoint the best candidates over time.

Terms of appointment

6.38 The arrangements for any appointed members of a reformed second chamber should equate as far as possible to those for elected members. Therefore, the Government proposes that, as for elected members, those appointed would serve for three electoral cycles without the possibility of reappointment. One-third of appointed members would be replaced at each election.

6.39 Options for replacing elected members mid-term are considered in paragraphs 4.82–4.87. The Government proposes that there should be arrangements to replace appointed members who leave before their term of office is due to end, analogous to whatever arrangements are made for elected members.

The process of appointing members

6.40 The detailed process for assessing and selecting individuals to become members of the second chamber would be a matter for any appointments commission itself to devise. The Government therefore proposes that the process should be underpinned by two broad criteria:

- The selection process should be straightforward and clearly understandable, with published guidelines to help those undergoing the selection process.
- Selection would be based on candidates providing evidence, which the Commission could verify and assess against its published criteria.

Formal approval of appointments

6.41 Any Appointments Commission would recommend candidates for appointment to the reformed second chamber. The Monarch would make the appointment, on the advice of Ministers. It is constitutionally impossible for the Monarch to approve these decisions on the advice of anyone else. Government advice to the Monarch is therefore a constitutional necessity.

6.42 The only circumstance under which the Prime Minister would alter the Commission's advice to appoint a particular individual would be if there were information about a candidate relevant to their suitability that was not available to the Commission, for example because it concerned national security. In such circumstances alone, the Prime Minister might decide not to pass on a nomination.

6.43 These arrangements would provide the appointee with the appropriate level of authority to contribute to making laws that affect the whole country.

6.44 The Liberal Democrats think that the Government of the day should have no role, either actual or formal, in appointments to a reformed second chamber and that consideration should be given to appointments being made other than through the Monarch.

Church of England Bishops

6.45 The Church of England's unique place in society and the valuable role it plays in English national life, both religious and secular, is widely recognised. Within England, the position of the Church of England is that of the Church by law established, with the Sovereign as its supreme Governor. The relationship between the Church and State is a core part of our constitutional framework that has evolved over centuries. The presence of Bishops in the House of Lords signals successive Governments' commitment to this fundamental constitutional principle and to an expression of the relationship between the Crown, Parliament and the Church that underpins the fabric of our nation.

6.46 However the Church of England's role stretches further than constitutional principles. The Church takes a leading part in a range of spheres, both religious and secular. In partnership with many of the UK's other religious communities, the Church offers spiritual support to everyone, regardless of their beliefs. The fact that the Church's staff and volunteers often live in the heart of the community they serve adds to the effectiveness of this support. The Church of England Bishops' position in Parliament reflects this culture of promoting tolerance and inclusiveness.

6.47 The Wakeham Commission highlighted the valuable parliamentary role that the Church plays and its wider implications: 'The Church of England Bishops' position as Lords of Parliament reflects the British history and culture of seeking to heal religious conflict and promoting ever greater religious tolerance and inclusiveness.'

6.48 The Government is clear that if a reformed second chamber is wholly elected, there should be no seats for Church of England Bishops or any other group.

6.49 If the number of seats available in a mainly elected second chamber was reduced compared with the current House of Lords, it would be logical to reduce proportionally the number of seats available for Bishops. However, the practice is that the Bishops attend the House of Lords on a rota basis, reflecting their other commitments. Reducing the number would make it harder for the Bishops collectively to carry out their functions in the second chamber and to continue to make their current level of contribution. The Government therefore proposes that if there is an appointed element in a reformed second chamber, there should be a number of seats reserved for Church of England Bishops. As the number of seats generally available in the second chamber will be reduced in comparison with the current House of Lords, it would also be logical to reduce proportionally the number seats available for Bishops. These would not count towards the 20% of members appointed by an appointments commission.

6.50 The Church of England would be invited to consider how it would in future select Bishops for membership of the second chamber.

6.51 The Liberal Democrats do not think there should be reserved seats for Church of England Bishops in a reformed second chamber. Their view is that if there were to be an appointed element, there would be opportunities for Bishops or other representatives of the Church of England, as well as from other faiths, to be put forward to the Appointments Commission as candidates for membership.

6.52 Before any firm decisions can be made, consultation with the Church of England authorities would be necessary on the details of any proposals affecting Bishops' membership of the second chamber.

Other churches and faiths

6.53 The Wakeham Commission considered providing for similar representation from other faith communities. The Commission concluded that providing reserved places for other faith communities would be problematic because of the small number of seats available and the large number of faiths represented in the UK. In addition, the Commission noted that 'none of them has a suitable representative body'. It went on to recommend that the Commission should make clear to the various faith communities that it is open to receive nominations from them.

6.54 After careful consideration, the Government proposes that these recommendations be endorsed. However, it is likely that many church and faith leaders would be strong candidates for appointment by the Appointments Commission. The Appointments Commission should make this clear to leaders of all churches and faith communities and encourage applications from them. Views would be welcomed on whether the Appointments Commission should be given a specific remit to provide for representation of other churches and faith communities in making its appointments.

Law Lords

6.55 Law Lords are life Peers and the Government proposes that they should be treated on a par with other life Peers. Currently, serving Law Lords do not take an active part in considering legislation in the House of Lords. This effectively rules out active participation in legislative work when serving as a member of the judiciary. However, some Law Lords take an active part in the proceedings of the House on retirement.

6.56 In 2009, the Supreme Court will begin its work. Law Lords sitting at the time of the change will become Justices of the Supreme Court. The Constitutional Reform Act 2005 will prevent these judges from sitting and voting in the House of Lords for as long as they remain full-time judges. However, the Act allows former Law Lords to take up their place in the House of Lords on retirement from the Supreme Court.

6.57 The terms of appointment for Law Lords and life Peers are effectively the same once the judicial functions taken on by the Supreme Court have been excluded. Proposals about the role of existing life Peers in a reformed second chamber (see paragraphs 8.15–8.17) would therefore apply to those retired Justices of the Supreme Court who were formerly Law Lords and to retired Law Lords who will not become Justices of the Supreme Court. This will be irrespective of whether there is an appointed element in a reformed second chamber. If there were an appointed element, none of the existing life Peers, including Law Lords, would count towards the total for that element.

6.58 Any Justice of the Supreme Court appointed after the Supreme Court begins work will not be a member of the second chamber in Parliament. Therefore, the question of some form of automatic membership of the second chamber would not arise. However, the Appointments Commission could consider retired Justices of the Supreme Court for appointment in the normal way.

6.59 The Government proposes that the arrangements for membership of a reformed second chamber for those retired Justices of the Supreme Court who were formerly Law Lords should be the same as the arrangements for other life Peers. Justices of the Supreme Court who are not former Law Lords would not be members of a reformed second chamber.

Appointing the Appointments Commission

Current Commissioners

6.60 The House of Lords Appointments Commission is a non-departmental public body with two core functions: to recommend individuals for appointment as non-party political life peers; and, to vet most nominations for life peers, including those nominated by the UK political parties, to ensure the highest standards of propriety. The current terms of appointment of the Chairman and Members of the House of Lords Appointments Commission ended on 30 June 2008. A recruitment exercise is underway to recruit a new Chairman and Independent Members, which is being run in accordance with the independent Commissioner for Public Appointments' Code of Practice. To ensure continuity, and with the approval of the Commissioner for Public Appointments, the Chairman has agreed to remain in post until the Autumn.

Proposed membership of any appointments commission

6.61 In order to ensure the appointments process does not become unwieldy or protracted, the Government proposes that any commission would comprise seven Commissioners. An odd number of Commissioners would help reduce the possibility of stalemate in any decisions where opinions were divided.

Eligibility for the role of Commissioner

6.62 The Government proposes that serving members of the House of Commons would be barred from serving as Commissioners. This would be consistent with the long-held principle that it is not right for members of one House of Parliament to be involved in the business of the other (exclusive cognisance), which was endorsed by the Wakeham Commission.

6.63 The Government thinks that not all Commissioners need to be members of the second chamber. However, in order to ensure familiarity with the chamber and its procedures, it would be helpful for a number of the Commissioners to have experience of working there.

6.64 The Government proposes that in order to ensure impartiality, a Commissioner would be ineligible for appointment to a reformed second chamber for five years after ceasing to serve on the Commission.

Appointment of Commissioners

6.65 The Government proposes that the Monarch appoint Commissioners to a statutory Appointments Commission, on the advice of Ministers. The appointment of any Commissioners would be made through open competition in accordance with the Nolan principles. Parliament would agree detailed criteria for the role of Commissioner. The appointment of Commissioners themselves would be based on the individuals' abilities.

6.66 The Government proposes that any Commissioners would be recruited on a non-party political basis. This would not mean that candidates should have no political affiliations, but simply that political parties would have no role in nominating or supporting candidates: candidates would apply as individuals. Indeed, just as political affiliation should neither qualify nor debar an individual from being considered for appointment to a reformed second chamber, so the same principle should apply to Commissioners themselves. A total ban on those with party connections might exclude a large number of able candidates, as experience of a political environment may well be of benefit to those appointing members of an upper House.

6.67 Whether involved in politics or not, candidates would be required to demonstrate sufficient independence of mind to be able to make non-partisan decisions in the appointment process.

6.68 The Government's view is that there should be a balance of political views among the Commissioners. This could involve applicants declaring any political interests in order for the final Commission to be perceived as balanced and fair in its decisions.

Terms of appointment

6.69 The Government proposes that there should be fixed, non-renewable terms for the Commissioners serving on any appointments commission. There should be provision for replacement of Commissioners who leave mid-term.

6.70 The Wakeham Commission proposed that Commissioners hold office for no longer than ten years, in accordance with the *Code of Practice* of the independent Commissioner for Public Appointments. The Office of the Commissioner for Public Appointments (OCPA) requires that public appointments be no longer than ten years.

6.71 The Government proposes that Appointments Commissioners serve for one ten-year non-renewable term. This would be in line with OCPA guidelines. A ten-year term would address the fact that if appointments were made to coincide with each general election, significant numbers of appointments would be required only every four to five years. Also, a longer term, but one with no prospect of renewal, would enable a high degree of perceived and actual independence in Commissioners' decision-making.

6.72 The Government proposes that, on the establishment of the Commission, three of the seven Commissioners would be recruited initially for five years only, and the remaining four would be recruited for ten years. After five years, three new Commissioners would replace the first three, each of the new Commissioners then being appointed for the normal term of ten years. With half the Commission being replaced every five years, this staggered recruitment programme would provide for continuity and the retention of experience within the Commission.

Remuneration and running costs

6.73 The work of the current House of Lords Appointments Commissioners is undertaken on a part-time basis. If a reformed second chamber were around 400 strong, then the number of appointments needed at each round of appointments would be similar to the number currently required over the lifetime of a Parliament. The Government proposes that the remuneration arrangements for any Commissioners should be broadly the same as those for the current House of Lords Appointments Commissioners, taking account of any reduction in the size of the second chamber and subject to the advice of the Senior Salaries Review Body.

7. A reformed chamber: other issues

Summary

7.1 This chapter considers issues regarding the arrangements for a reformed second chamber that have not been considered elsewhere. It confirms the Government's view that membership of a reformed second chamber should no longer carry with it a peerage, nor should it be associated with the award of any other honour.

7.2 The Government proposes a range of provision on eligibility for a reformed second chamber. The minimum age for membership would be 18 and there would be no maximum limit. As now, British, Commonwealth and Republic of Ireland citizens would be eligible. Those subject to a bankruptcy restriction order, those holding full-time judicial offices, those with certain criminal convictions, those detained for mental health reasons, those who have been convicted of electoral fraud and those who are not UK taxpayers would be ineligible. Views would be welcomed on whether there should be provision similar to that which applies for the House of Commons, disqualifying those in certain public professions and offices or who are members of certain public bodies.

7.3 The Government proposes that those who had served as elected members of a reformed second chamber would not be eligible to be appointed as members and vice versa. There would be provision for members to resign. There would be provision for them to take leave of absence only where they had a major illness.

7.4 Further consideration would need to be given to the accountability arrangements for members of a reformed second chamber, particularly in light of proposals that they serve long, single, fixed terms. The Cross-Party Group discussed the possibility of introducing recall ballots for elected members of a reformed second chamber, along the lines of those that exist in some states of the USA. These ask electors to consider whether a person should continue in public office. It is envisaged that any system of recall ballots would apply to concerns that a member was incompetent, had neglected their duties as a member of the second chamber, was corrupt (other than in relation to electoral fraud) or had committed misconduct. It is proposed that if there were a system of recall ballots for elected members of a reformed second chamber, there should be analogous arrangements for any appointed members. Proposals for recall ballots are set out in paragraph 7.23–7.34. Views are invited on whether there should be a system of such ballots for a reformed second chamber and if so, what the detailed arrangements for these ballots should be.

7.5 The Government proposes that members of a reformed second chamber should receive taxable salaries and that the Senior Salaries Review Body should be asked to advise on the level of salary that would be appropriate. It also proposes to ask the Review Body whether any salary could be linked to members' contributions to the work of the second chamber.

7.6 The Government proposes that members of a reformed second chamber should be allowed to vote in elections to both the House of Commons and the second chamber. A cooling off period of five years between someone ceasing their membership of the second chamber and being eligible for election to the House of Commons is proposed. This would prevent membership of the second chamber being used as an immediate launch pad for a career in the House of Commons. Comments would be welcomed on whether there should be a cooling off period between someone ceasing to be a member of the House of Commons and being eligible for election or appointment to the second chamber.

Link between the award of a peerage and membership of the second chamber

7.7 As set out in its February 2007 White Paper, the Government proposes that the link between the award of a peerage and membership of the second chamber should cease as part of the process of further reform of the House of Lords. Membership of the second chamber should also be dissociated from the award of any other honour.

Eligibility for membership of a reformed second chamber

7.8 Under current arrangements, eligibility for membership of the House of Lords is restricted to British and qualifying Commonwealth citizens (who include citizens of British Overseas Territories) and citizens of the Republic of Ireland. This provision is the same as that for membership of the House of Commons. The following groups are not eligible to sit and vote in the House of Lords:

- those under the age of 21;
- those subject to a bankruptcy restriction order; and
- when relevant legislation comes into force, full-time judicial office holders.

Age limits

7.9 The Cross-Party Group considered whether this provision should apply to a reformed second chamber. On the minimum age limit, it was noted that the minimum age limit for membership of the House of Commons is 18. It was also noted that some other countries set a much higher limit for their second than their primary chamber, in order to encourage the entry of more experienced people. For example, Italy has a minimum age limit of 40, and France, 30. It is proposed that for a wholly or mainly elected second chamber in the UK it would not be appropriate to constrain electoral choice unduly by imposing an unnecessarily high minimum age limit for membership. The Government proposes that the minimum age limit for membership of a reformed second chamber would be 18 and that there be no maximum age limit.

7.10 The Convenor of the Cross-bench Peers considers that the minimum age limit should be 30 and that there should be a maximum age limit of 70 for standing for election or being considered for appointment to a reformed second chamber. This minimum age limit would be the same as that for Senators in the USA.

Nationality requirements

7.11 The Government's view is that there is no case for changing current nationality and citizenship requirements for membership of the second chamber, in advance of any wider changes in this area. The Government proposes that in the absence of any other changes to nationality requirements for membership of the legislature, British citizens and qualifying citizens of the Commonwealth (including citizens of British Overseas Territories) and citizens of the Republic of Ireland would be eligible for membership of a reformed second chamber.

Those subject to a bankruptcy restriction order

7.12 The Government proposes provision excluding those subject to a bankruptcy restriction order from membership of the reformed second chamber.

Other office holders and members of particular public professions and public bodies

7.13 As noted in paragraph 6.56, provision is due to come into force barring fulltime judicial office holders from membership of the House of Lords. There is already wider provision barring the holders of certain offices or members of certain professions from sitting in the House of Commons. The House of Commons Disqualification Act 1975 bars not only certain judicial office holders, but also members of the armed forces or the police, civil servants, those who hold offices listed in a schedule to the Act and members of certain public bodies that are also listed. The Cross-Party Group has considered whether there should be similar provision in relation to members of a reformed second chamber. Such provision would reduce the scope for conflict of interest on the part of members. However, it could restrict membership of the second chamber unnecessarily. It could be argued that the work of the chamber could benefit from having as members some of those whose public office would disqualify them from the House of Commons, provided that their position and interests were declared and public. The Government's view is that further consideration should be given as to whether people in particular public professions, holding certain public offices or who are members of specific public bodies would be excluded from a reformed second chamber. Views would be welcomed on this issue, including on which professions, offices and bodies it might be appropriate to include in any disqualification provision.

Those convicted of criminal offences or subject to certain mental health detention orders

7.14 Unlike the House of Commons, there is no provision barring from the House of Lords those who have been convicted of criminal offences and sentenced to a prison term of more than twelve months, nor those subject to certain mental health detention orders. The Government's February 2007 White Paper on House of Lords reform proposed that provision similar to that which operates for the House of Commons in relation to criminal convictions and detentions for reason of mental health should apply to a reformed second chamber. The Government proposes that provision along these lines should be introduced.

Those found guilty of electoral fraud

7.15 The House of Commons also disqualifies from membership certain people found guilty of electoral fraud. Broadly, someone is disqualified from being a Member of Parliament for three years if they have been found guilty of illegal practices and for five years if they have been found guilty of corrupt practices. With the introduction of elected members, the Government proposes that provision on electoral fraud along the lines of that for the House of Commons should apply to a reformed second chamber. However, members of the House of Commons who have been disqualified for electoral fraud can stand again, once the period of their disqualification has expired. It was proposed earlier (see paragraph 4.11) that elected members of a reformed second chamber should be able to stand for only one term. The Government proposes that anyone who is disqualified from being a member of a reformed second chamber for electoral fraud would not be able to stand again.

Tax status

7.16 Over the past year, a number of members of both Houses of Parliament have proposed that members of the UK Parliament should be resident in the UK for tax purposes. It is an important way in which they demonstrate their connection with and commitment to the UK. The Government has said that it agrees with this principle, in relation to both Houses. The Government therefore proposes that the creation of a reformed second chamber would include provision disqualifying from membership anyone who is not resident in the UK for tax purposes.

Accountability of members of the second chamber

Members to serve one term only

7.17 It has been proposed (see paragraph 4.11 that elected members of a reformed second chamber should serve long terms and that they should not be eligible for re-election. Similar provision is also proposed for any appointed members (see paragraph 6.38). The Government proposes that those who have served as elected members of the second chamber would not be eligible to be appointed to the chamber; and that those who have served as appointed members would not be eligible to stand for election. Such provision would ensure that, in taking part in the work of the second chamber and putting forward their views, members would not be influenced by the prospect of continued membership.

Provision for members to resign

7.18 The proposals for long fixed terms for members of a reformed second chamber, without the prospect of a second term, create a need to consider what arrangements would be appropriate to ensure the accountability of members. One particular point of concern in relation to the current House of Lords is that there is no provision for members to resign, although they can apply for leave of absence. It is proposed that these arrangements be changed. If a member were to feel unable to continue working as such or wanted to cease to be a member for any other reason, they should be able to do so. If this were, as now, through application for leave of absence, the electorate in a particular constituency would not be represented fully in the second chamber while the member was away. (Paragraphs 7.36–7.37 considers further what arrangements might be made in relation to any member whose attendance were to fall below a prescribed level.) The Government proposes that there would be provision for members of the second chamber to resign and for any vacancy created by such a resignation to be filled. Provision allowing existing members of the House of Lords to resign from the second chamber would come into force well ahead of the first set of elections to the second chamber. This would enable existing peers to resign before the start of the transition, should they want to do so.

7.19 The Government believes that in most circumstances where members may want to absent themselves from a reformed second chamber, it would be appropriate for them to resign.

However, where the reason for the absence is a major illness, resignation might be inappropriate, but the member might wish to indicate that they would be absent from the chamber for some time. The Government therefore proposes that members would be able to seek leave of absence from a reformed second chamber, but only in the case of major illness.

Misconduct

7.20 The House of Lords Code of Conduct sets standards for the personal conduct of members of the House. It goes on to reproduce the seven general principles of conduct identified by the Committee on Standards in Public Life and states that members should observe these. It also describes the primacy of the public interest and covers financial and relevant non-financial interests of members. The Code provides for ways in which complaints for alleged breaches of the Code can be made and investigations undertaken. There are no specific sanctions for breach of the Code and no precedents for the House securing a time-limited disqualification of a member. These arrangements reflect the fact that members of the House of Lords do not receive salaries and that many of them continue with their professional and other working interests, which can help maintain expertise and experience.

7.21 The House of Commons Code of Conduct is more extensive than the House of Lords Code of Conduct. Where there are alleged breaches of the House of Commons Code of Conduct, any member of the House of Commons or a member of the public can complain in writing to the Parliamentary Commissioner for Standards. There are procedures for a preliminary and if necessary a full investigation by the Commissioner. In the most difficult cases, an Investigatory Panel, comprising the Commissioner, a legal adviser and a senior member of the House of Commons, can sit. In minor cases or inadvertent cases, the Commissioner has discretion to allow the Member to rectify the matter. The Commissioner reports all investigations to the Committee on Standards and Privileges which, if it agrees with the Commissioner's findings, considers what if any penalty is appropriate. The Committee reports to the House. Possible penalties for breaches of the Code include requiring an apology, suspension and/ or withdrawal of salary. The latter two sanctions require the approval of the House through a specific Motion.

7.22 The Government proposes that in the run-up to the creation of a reformed second chamber, the House of Lords should give further consideration to the accountability arrangements that would apply to the new chamber. In particular, the House could consider:

– whether any changes to the House of Lords Code of Conduct might be appropriate;
– whether it might be appropriate to establish a Commissioner for Standards, similar to the post established in the Commons, who could carry out investigations in relation to alleged breaches of the House of Lords Code of Conduct; and
– whether it might be appropriate for a reformed second chamber to have provision whereby it could require an apology from a member and/or suspend them and/or withdraw their salary.

Alleged incompetence, neglect of duties, corruption (other than electoral fraud) and/or misconduct

7.23 With the long, non-renewable terms of office suggested for members of a reformed second chamber, concerns about the accountability of elected members to the electorate could arise. It is possible to envisage circumstances in which the voters in a particular constituency might feel that a particular member should no longer represent them. Such circumstances might include where there were allegations that a member:

– was incompetent;
– had neglected their duties as a member of the second chamber;
– was corrupt (other than in relation to electoral fraud; proposals addressing electoral fraud are described in paragraph 7.15); and/or

– had committed misconduct. (Any definition of misconduct could refer back to the House of Lords Code of Conduct.)

7.24 The Cross-Party Group therefore discussed the possibility of introducing arrangements for recall ballots, similar to those that exist in some states of the USA, for elected members of a reformed second chamber. Recall ballots ask electors to consider whether a particular person should continue in public office. If the ballot is successful, the individual ceases to serve in that office. In the USA, ballots can be held only in a specified range of circumstances, including that a certain proportion of relevant voters have petitioned for the ballot to be held.

7.25 It would be possible for a system of recall ballots to apply throughout a member's term of office. Given that the rationale for such ballots would be the need for additional accountability mechanisms during the later part of what would be long, non-renewable terms of office, it might be appropriate for the provision to apply only after a member had served five years. The Government would welcome views on the idea that any system of recall ballots for elected members of a reformed second chamber in the UK should apply only after they had served for five years.

7.26 The proposals discussed by the Cross-Party Group included that any system of recall ballots for members of a reformed second chamber in the United Kingdom should apply only where a voter or voters in the constituency of a member consider that the member: [...]

7.27 Under a recall ballot system, the voter or voters would be required to set out the reasons why they considered the member fulfilled these criteria. It would be explicit that the criteria would not be fulfilled simply because the member had spoken or voted or failed to speak or vote in a particular way in the second chamber or more widely. Any system of recall ballots would have to be such that there was no danger of it being used as a plebiscite on a particular issue. It would be important that members were able to exercise their judgement as they saw fit, without fear of being removed as a result of their views.

7.28 Depending on the outcome of the consultation, further consideration will be needed on how far it might be appropriate to include the detailed criteria in primary legislation. To the extent it would not, consideration on how workable definitions of misconduct might be devised will also be necessary.

7.29 The Government has concluded that any system of recall ballots should include the following provision, which is based on practice in the USA.

7.30 A ballot could occur only if sufficient electors in the relevant constituency called for one. This would be done through the circulation of a petition, which would have to gather a certain number of signatures within a certain time for the ballot to take place. It is proposed that the requirement about the number of signatures and the time allowed for the petition should be stringent, to deter malicious or frivolous ballots. It is considered that the requirement for support could be set at 40% of the number who voted in the election at which the member was elected. It is considered that 90 days might strike an appropriate balance between the time needed to organise a petition and the need to minimise the period during which there was uncertainty about the member continuing in office.

7.31 If the requirements for the petition were met, a ballot would take place within a short, specified period of time. The ballot would ask voters whether the member should continue in office. It is considered that it may be appropriate to set a minimum threshold that would have to be met for a member not to continue in office. This could be a proportion of the total registered electorate in the constituency (i.e. not just those voting in the recall ballot). It would not be appropriate to have a threshold higher than half the total electorate. A higher threshold could result in a situation where the majority of voters in the constituency considered that the person should leave office but they remained nonetheless.

7.32 If the recall ballot were unsuccessful (i.e. more than the required number of people voted for the member to continue in office), the member would continue automatically as such for the remainder of their term.

7.33 If the recall ballot were successful (i.e. less than the required number of people voted for the member to continue in office), a by-election would be held. The previous office holder would not be allowed to stand in that by-election (or to stand for election again, or to be appointed as a member of the second chamber). The person who was successful at the by-election would be elected for the remainder of the term of the person who had been removed as a result of the outcome of the recall ballot. The Government's view is that there should be provision to cover instances where the remaining term of office of the person who was successful at the by-election is relatively short. These arrangements should reflect whatever is decided on in relation to filling vacancies for elected members mid-term. (See paragraphs 4.82–4.87.)

7.34 If a system of recall ballots were adopted in relation to elected members, there would be analogous provision in relation to any appointed members. This could take the form of arrangements by which the Appointments Commission could consider adverse reports about the standard of behaviour of appointed members. This would be only in relation to the grounds that applied for recall ballots. If the Appointments Commission were to consider that the member had not behaved in an appropriate way, it would be able to recommend ending their membership of the second chamber, and there would be a process for cessation of membership in such cases.

7.35 Views and comments would be welcomed on whether there should be arrangements for recall ballots for elected members of a reformed second chamber, and on analogous arrangements in relation to any appointed members and if so, on the detail of those arrangements.

Attendance

7.36 The Government is clear that members of a reformed second chamber should be held to account if they do not attend regularly.

The Local Government Act 1972 provides that if a member of a local authority fails to attend meetings of the authority (or relevant committees of that authority) for a period of six months, they will be disqualified. There is provision whereby this provision is disregarded, if the authority approves the reason for absence before the end of the six-month period. It is proposed that there be similar provision in relation to members of a reformed second chamber. The Government proposes that those who do not attend for any period of six months should be disqualified as members, unless they have put their reasons for nonattendance to a committee of the second chamber, which has approved those reasons before the expiry of the period.

7.37 It is also proposed that consideration be given to including nonattendance in any system of recall ballots for elected members. The arrangements could be triggered in circumstances where voters were dissatisfied with the level of the member's attendance in the second chamber, but where the non-attendance was not sufficient to invoke any disqualification provision. There would be analogous arrangements in relation to appointed members. Views on this proposal would be welcomed.

Remuneration for members of a reformed second chamber

7.38 Currently, members of the House of Lords are unpaid, with the exception of certain office holders, Ministers and the Law Lords. They do, however, receive non-taxable allowances to cover expenses incurred in relation to their parliamentary duties. The members of virtually all the second chambers in other countries are paid. The Government proposes that members of a reformed second chamber in the UK should receive taxable salaries.

7.39 On the level of salary to be paid, the Government considers that the advice of the Senior Salaries Review Body should be sought. In seeking the advice of the Review Body, it is proposed to set out particular factors for the Review Body to consider in formulating its advice. The following factors might be considered:

- the particular roles of the second chamber as set out in Chapter 5;
- either all or the majority of the members would be elected;
- the eligibility criteria of any appointees, as set out in Chapter 8;
- the expectations for the levels of skills (eg the ability to speak authoritatively), as set out in Chapter 6;
- the expectation of the highest levels of personal integrity;
- the expectation of high levels of attendance and various eligibility and disqualification criteria, as set out earlier in this chapter.
- that members would be allowed to undertake other work part-time;
- that members would not have constituency responsibilities to the extent that members of the House of Commons do; and
- the length of members' terms of office (12–15 years).

7.40 The Review Body would also be asked to set the level of salary for members of a reformed second chamber by reference to the comparative responsibilities of associated members of other UK legislatures. The current salary for a Member of Parliament is £61,820; for a Member of the Scottish Parliament, £53,091; for a Member of the Welsh Assembly, £50,692; and for a Member of the Northern Ireland Assembly, £43,101. As indicated above, the Government considers that the responsibilities of members of a reformed second chamber would be less than for members of the House of Commons. The Government considers that as members would be members of the UK legislature, their salaries should be more than those of members of the devolved legislature and assemblies.

7.41 The Cross-Party Group discussed the idea of linking any salary for members of a reformed second chamber to the extent to which they participate in the work of the chamber. The Government proposes that the Senior Salaries Review Body be asked to advise on the feasibility of linking a salary to a member's contribution. This could be done through either linking the salary to a member's attendance or through deductions if attendance were to fall below a certain level (other than where there was a valid reason for absence, e.g. sickness). There are currently a number of salaried posts in the House of Lords. The Senior Salaries Review Body has previously made recommendations on what salaries should be paid to the holders of these offices. It is proposed that the Review Body be asked to consider what, if any, changes to these salaries should be made alongside any introduction of salaries for all members of the reformed second chamber. The Review Body has also made recommendations about the entitlements payable to Government Ministers in the House of Lords. Again, it is proposed that the Review Body be asked to consider what, if any, changes would be appropriate to these entitlements, if there were a general system of salaries.

Implications of membership and past membership of a reformed second chamber

7.43 The Government proposes that someone should not be a member of the second chamber and a Member of the House of Commons simultaneously. These are both demanding roles and it would not be practical for someone to fulfil them both effectively at the same time.

7.44 Current rules prevent members of the House of Lords from voting in a general election. The Government proposes, in line with its view set out in its February 2007 White Paper, that members of a reformed second chamber should be allowed to vote in elections to both the House of Commons and the second chamber.

7.45 The Government also set out in the February 2007 White Paper its intention that a reformed second chamber should attract into the UK legislature those who have wider interests outside politics, including among the members representing political parties. The White Paper set out the Government's view that membership of a reformed second chamber should not be used to build a political base for a career in the House of Commons. The Government proposes that a cooling off period of five years be required between someone ceasing their membership of the second chamber and being eligible for election to the House of Commons.

7.46 The Conservative Party considers that rather than any cooling off period, former members of a reformed second chamber should be ineligible to stand as Members of Parliament.

7.47 The Government's proposal for a cooling off period raises the question of whether there should be a similar cooling off period for former MPs. During such a period, they would not be eligible for election or appointment to the second chamber. The Government would welcome views on whether there should be a cooling off period.

8. A reformed chamber: making the transition

Summary

8.1 Decisions will have to be made about how quickly proposals for moving to a fully reformed second chamber are implemented, in particular about the future arrangements for existing members of the House of Lords.

8.2 The transitional phase will be critical to the effective operation of a reformed second chamber, both during the transition itself and in the longer term. Peers, as members of the second chamber, will have a crucial role during the transitional phase, ensuring the chamber works effectively with the House of Commons and transmitting knowledge to new members.

8.3 The Government proposes that during the transition to a fully reformed second chamber, there should be no further by-elections for hereditary Peers to become members of the chamber. The sitting and voting rights of the remaining hereditary Peers would be removed, but the timing of this requires further consideration. This is linked to the need for further discussion about how far the rights of life Peers to sit and vote should continue during the transition, and whether they should continue after that phase is complete.

8.4 This White Paper sets out three options in relation to the transition to a fully reformed second chamber. One is to allow all life Peers to continue to be members of the second chamber for life, but for hereditary Peers to leave when the third group of elected members arrives in the reformed second chamber. Another is for all existing peers to leave when the third group of elected members (and any appointed members) arrives. This would be the first point at which there would be a full complement of new members. The third option provides for existing peers to leave in three groups, each coinciding with the arrival of a group of new members.

8.5 The Government would welcome views on these options.

Introduction

8.6 Earlier chapters of this White Paper have made proposals for how and when groups of elected (and possibly some appointed) members might take up their places in a reformed second chamber. The Government proposes that the entry date for each group would coincide with the start of a new parliamentary session following a general election to the House of Commons. Members of a reformed second chamber would serve for three terms. Under the Government's proposals, the length of each term would be determined by the timing of general elections. Terms would run from the start of a new session following a general election to the date Parliament was next dissolved for a general election. Very broadly, members might expect to serve for around 12–15 years (see paragraphs 4.11 and 6.38).

8.7 Under the proposals put forward by the Liberal Democrats, the entry date for each group of new members would coincide with elections to the devolved legislature and assemblies and to local authorities. Members would therefore serve fixed terms of twelve years.

8.8 Under either of these proposals, decisions will have to be made about how quickly they are implemented. In particular, decisions will have to be made about the future arrangements for existing members of the House of Lords.

The transitional phase

8.9 During the build up of the reformed second chamber there would be a transitional phase, when initially only one group and then two groups of new members had joined. With the entry of the third group, the new membership of the second chamber would be complete.

8.10 The transitional phase will be critical to the effective operation of a reformed second chamber, not just during the transition itself, but also in the longer term. In particular, it will be during the transitional phase that the working relationship between the reformed second chamber and the House of Commons is forged. As noted in paragraph 2.2, the Government is clear that a reformed second chamber should continue as the second chamber and that there will be no change to the primacy of the House of Commons.

8.11 During this transitional phase, new internal practices and relationships with the House of Commons will develop. The Government welcomes this. As with many aspects of the British constitution, the process of development will most likely be a gradual one, combining valuable aspects of the working of the current House of Lords with the evolution of new conventions, which may better suit new circumstances. A sudden, radical change in the way the second chamber operates, coinciding with the start of the next phase of reform, would be unhelpful and potentially destabilising.

8.12 That is why the Government believes that there would be a crucial role for peers as members of the second chamber during the transitional phase. Peers would have key roles in ensuring that the second chamber continues to work effectively with the House of Commons and in transmitting knowledge to new members.

8.13 Consideration needs to be given to how many peers should remain during the transition and for how long. Decisions also have to be made about whether any existing peers should remain in the second chamber beyond the point at which the third group of new members arrives and at which the chamber would, in the absence of any peers, be constituted fully on its new basis.

The position of existing hereditary Peers

8.14 The right of most hereditary Peers to sit and vote in the House of Lords was removed by the House of Lords Act 1999. Ninety hereditary Peers (plus the holders of the offices of Earl Marshal and Lord Great Chamberlain) remain as members of the House of Lords pending the next stage of reform. When a hereditary Peer dies, there is a by-election to fill the vacant place. During the passage of the 1999 Act the intention was made clear that the next phase of House of Lords reform would include the removal of the sitting and voting rights of the remaining hereditary Peers in the second chamber. Under the provisions of the House of Lords Act 1999, two hereditary Peers who are Royal Office holders – the Earl Marshal and the Lord Great Chamberlain – retained their seats in the House. The office holders do not need to sit in the second chamber to fulfil their duties as members of the Royal Household. The Government proposes that there should be no further by-elections to select hereditary Peers to sit in the House of Lords during the transition to a reformed second chamber.

The position of existing life Peers

8.15 The Government noted in its February 2007 White Paper that: 'The current members have entered the House in the expectation that they will stay for life. Some will have given up careers and other roles to do so. It would be unfair to require them to leave in these circumstances.' The Government remains very conscious that this is the formal basis on which existing life Peers entered the House of Lords.

8.16 The context for the February 2007 White Paper was that it considered the range of options for the composition of a reformed second chamber. It looked at an all-appointed membership, an all-elected membership and hybrid options. It presented a model of how a hybrid House might work, based on the assumption that half its membership was elected. Options for a second chamber which include a substantial appointed element provide a different context for consideration of the position of existing life Peers than that provided for by the outcome of the free votes in the House of Commons in March 2007. The model in the February 2007 White Paper showed 540 members, of whom half (270) would be appointed. This White Paper considers a reformed second chamber with a maximum size of 450 members. Based on the outcome of the free votes in the House of Commons, the membership of the reformed second chamber would be either wholly elected or 20% appointed. On a chamber of 450 members, the appointed element would be 90. If the size of the reformed chamber were smaller, any appointed element would be reduced proportionately.

8.17 It is for further consideration and discussion how far the rights of life Peers to sit and vote should continue during the transition to a wholly or mainly elected second chamber and whether they should continue after that phase is complete. This White Paper looks at a number of options which were discussed by the Cross-Party Group. The Government would welcome comment and debate on these options.

Option one: Allowing all life Peers to continue to be members of the second chamber for life

8.18 Chart 8.1 illustrates the possible composition of the second chamber over time on the basis of the Government's proposals in this White Paper. It assumes the final size of the second chamber, once all existing peers have departed, would be 435, of whom 80% would be elected. This chart excludes any seats reserved for Church of England Bishops in an 80% elected chamber. The final total of 435 new members is reached through the arrival of three groups, each of 145 members. This reflects the proposals in this White Paper that new members be elected (and any appointed members appointed) in thirds, with elections taking place at the same time as general elections. Each new member would serve for three electoral cycles. In the illustration in Chart 8.1, 2013,

2017 and 2021 are hypothetical general election dates. After the third group of new members arrives in 2021, the total of members elected or appointed under the new arrangements would remain at 435. At each subsequent election, one group of 145 members would end their term of service, but a new group would arrive. Chart 8.1 assumes that the remaining sitting and voting rights for hereditary Peers are removed at the point at which the third group of new members is elected (or appointed) to the second chamber and the total of 435 new members is reached.

[...]

8.19 Chart 8.1 shows that if existing life Peers were to remain in the second chamber for life, it is likely to be at least 2040 before the chamber is constituted fully on a new basis.

8.20 The Cross-Party Group has also considered two alternative approaches which would ensure that the reformed chamber would be constituted fully on a new basis by the time the third group of new members were elected (and possibly appointed). These options reflect the view that existing peers should contribute during and to the transition to a reformed second chamber. The Government is also concerned to ensure that any arrangements that do not provide for life Peers to remain in the second chamber for life while hereditary Peers left at the third election would not have an adverse effect on the balance between the parties that currently exists across peers in the House of Lords.

The Government's February 2007 White Paper noted that: 'The removal of the hereditary Peers will disadvantage the Conservatives much more than the other parties, not just because there are more Conservative hereditary Peers but also because the average age of Conservative life Peers is higher than that of the other parties.' The Government noted that the cross-party talks would consider 'the need for action to avoid gratuitously cutting Conservative Party representation in the Lords when and if the remaining hereditary Peers are removed'. The average age of those on the Cross benches is also higher than that of members of the Labour Party and the Liberal Democrats in the House of Lords.

The alternatives to allowing life Peers to remain in the second chamber for life that have been considered therefore provide for hereditary Peers to depart at the same time as life Peers, in order to maintain the current party balance.

Option two: Existing peers depart when the third group of new members arrives

8.21 Chart 8.2 makes the same assumptions as Chart 8.1 in terms of the final size of the second chamber and the timing of the arrival of new members. This example also uses the same assumptions about the creation of new life Peers between 2007 and 2013 and about the deaths of hereditary Peers between 2007 and 2013, and 2013 and 2017. However, in this example, it assumes that those hereditary and life Peers who are members of the House of Lords at the time of the first elections (and possibly appointments) to a reformed second chamber (assumed as 2013 for modelling purposes) will leave at the time of the third elections (assumed as 2021 for modelling purposes). This option means that at the first point at which there would be a full complement of new members, the fully reformed chamber would also come into existence (because those peers remaining in the chamber at that point would all leave).

[...]

8.22 This option minimises the extent to which life Peers would be compelled to leave, commensurate with putting the second chamber fully onto its new basis at the time at which the third group of new members arrived. The modelling suggests that under this option, around 340 of the current total of 615 life Peers (excluding those on leave of absence) would need to leave at the time of the third election.

Option three: Existing peers depart in three groups, each coinciding with the arrival of a group of new members

8.23 Broadly, this option provides for around one-third of existing peers to leave at the time of the first elections to a reformed second chamber, around half the remainder to leave at the time of the second elections and the rest to leave at the time of the third elections. This final date is when the fully reformed chamber would otherwise come into existence.

8.24 Chart 8.3 reflects the same assumptions about the deaths of existing peers as Charts 8.1 and 8.2. These are reflected in the falls in the number of existing peers shown between the first and second and second and third elections to the second chamber. However, under this option some peers would have to leave at the times of the first, second and third elections. There would be a need to decide which individual peers would depart and which remain at each of these times. It is possible that some peers, particularly those who were older and/or who do not attend the House of Lords frequently, might choose to resign, mitigating the need for compulsory departures. However there would need to be 'long stop' provision to manage departures.

8.25 One option would be to leave it to the parties and groups to decide which peers should remain at which stage, using whatever basis they considered appropriate. Alternatives would be provision for elections organised by the House authorities, along the lines of those held for hereditary Peers following the passage of the House of Lords Act 1999 or managing departures by age.

General

8.26 Any life Peers who resigned from or were compelled to leave the second chamber would continue to hold their titles.

8.27 The Government would welcome comments on the three options for the position of existing peers presented here.

Financial arrangements for life Peers remaining during the transition

8.28 Chapter 7 includes proposals for remuneration of members of the reformed second chamber. The Government proposes that the arrangements for elected members (and any members appointed under new arrangements) should be on a different basis from that of existing peers.

8.29 It could be argued that all those serving as members of the second chamber during the transition to a fully reformed chamber should receive the same remuneration. The Government proposes that this be the case if there is an appointed element in the reformed chamber. If, however, a reformed second chamber is wholly elected, then it could be argued that elected members should receive different remuneration from life Peers remaining for some or all of the period of the transition. Different remuneration would reflect the fact that the Government proposes that new members of the reformed second chamber should make themselves available when the chamber is sitting and take a full part in its work. This is a different basis to that on which existing life Peers were appointed. It is proposed that, if it is decided that the reformed second chamber will be wholly elected, further consideration should be given to whether, during the transition, existing peers continue to be remunerated on the current basis or in the same way as new members.

9. Costs

Costs of a reformed second chamber

9.1 There are a number of variables to consider before making any assumptions about the overall cost of a reformed second chamber. The Government will work up a more detailed analysis once there are firmer proposals in particular areas, for instance the trajectory for reducing the size of the second chamber. The steady state of the cost of the reformed second chamber will depend on the remuneration of new members, which the Government proposes be the subject of consideration by the Senior Salaries Review Body (see Chapter 7). It is important to bear in mind that newly elected members of a reformed second chamber would not be performing a constituency role to the same extent that Members of Parliament do and would therefore not have the same needs for accommodation and staff.

9.2 The net operating cost of the current House of Lords over the past three financial years is set out in the table below. The

Government's intention is to ensure that the costs of a reformed second chamber are maintained at current levels or lower.

[...]

Cost of elections

9.3 Combining elections to the second chamber with other elections could generate efficiency savings. There would be separate costs for printing and counting ballot papers, but the cost of polling stations (both staff and accommodation) could be shared. There would also be opportunities to combine postal voting and to share equipment. The additional cost of elections to the second chamber alongside general elections could be in the region of £43m. This takes into account approximately £13m for election mailings, such as the provision of free postage and campaign leaflets, as elections to the second chamber are likely to generate more candidates than there are seats compared to general elections.

Costs of a statutory Appointments Commission

9.4 Chapter 6 discusses setting up a statutory Appointments Commission and the need for further consideration of the Senior Salaries Review Body about the remuneration of Commissioners. The cost of creating a new body is likely to be in the region of £1.5m, including the set-up and initial running costs of the Commission.

10. A reformed chamber: next steps

10.1 Comments and views are sought from as wide a range of people as possible on the proposals contained in this White Paper. Arrangements will be made for discussions with parliamentarians, including non-party independent members. Views from interest groups and members of the public are also very welcome. Views can be put forward by:

10.2 Writing to:

House of Lords Reform Team
Ministry of Justice

Selborne House
54 Victoria Street
LONDON
SW1E 6QW

10.3 E-mailing: lords.reform@justice.gsi.gov.uk

11. Conclusions

11.1 Reform of the House of Lords, to bring it into line with our modern society and thinking, is a key part of the Governance of Britain programme. This White Paper sets out specific proposals, aimed at achieving reform through cross-party consensus, on how a reformed second chamber that is wholly or mainly elected might be achieved.

11.2 Although differences between the parties exist on some of the detail of reform, there is broad consensus that current arrangements do not reflect as well as they could the needs of a twenty-first century democracy. All, or at least the majority, of those people who sit in the second chamber of the country's legislature should be there because the citizens of the country have elected them. This White Paper proposes how such change might be realised and implemented.

11.3 The White Paper is set against the backdrop of this Government's commitment to thorough and ongoing constitutional reform across a range of issues. The Government believes it is vital that our democratic institutions enjoy increased legitimacy, are more trusted and are more responsive to the people they serve.

11.4 As Parliament is the supreme legislative body of the UK, reform of its upper chamber is a major element of this wider constitutional renewal. It is hoped the proposals in this White Paper will be the launch pad from which a reformed second chamber will be able to continue the process of adapting to new times and circumstances. They follow on from the votes in the House of Commons and set out what the House could look like as a result of the views expressed by the Commons. The Government's vision is of a renewed second chamber, with clear legitimacy, playing its full part in scrutinising the proposed laws, policies and work of the government of the day. Creating such a chamber is a key part of this Government's plans to reinvigorate our democracy.

[...]

Annex 6: House of Lords Appointments Commission appointment criteria

The following are the criteria used by the House of Lords Appointments Commission, which guide the assessment of nominations for non-party political life Peers.

Criteria Guiding the Assessment of Nominations for Non-Party Political Life Peers

Any British, Irish or Commonwealth citizen over the age of 21 may be nominated for membership of the House of Lords. To be able to devote the time necessary to make an active and effective contribution to the work of the House, the Commission considers that you must have your main home in the United Kingdom. It will decline to consider any nominee who is not resident in the United Kingdom for tax purposes. The Commission will assess nominations against its stated criteria. It is committed to independent and fair assessment of nominations. Its recommendations will be made on individual merit and not on any other basis. The Commission recognises the role it can play through an open, meritocratic process in ensuring that the composition and balance of the House better reflects the different experience and backgrounds of those living in the United Kingdom. It wishes to attract as wide a range of nominees as possible from all parts of the United Kingdom. The Commission recognises that it may recommend some individuals in the full knowledge that the demands of working life may limit his or her involvement in the House. This will only be on the basis of a judgement that the House of Lords will benefit immediately from their expertise and at a later stage in his or her career they will spend more time in the House.

The criteria:

The Commission will be seeking to recommend nominees:

- with a record of significant achievement within their chosen way of life that demonstrates a range of experience, skills and competencies;
- who are able to make an effective and significant contribution to the work of the House of Lords, not only in their areas of particular interest and special expertise but the wide range of other issues coming before the House;
- with some understanding of the constitutional framework, including the place of the House of Lords, and the skills and qualities needed to be an effective member of the House – for example, nominees should be able to speak with independence and authority;
- with the time available to ensure they can make an effective contribution within the procedures and working practices of the House of Lords. This does not necessarily mean the same amount of time expected of 'working peers'. The Commission recognises that many active members continue with their professional and other working interests and this can help maintain expertise and experience;
- who are able to demonstrate outstanding personal qualities, in particular integrity and independence;
- with a strong and personal commitment to the principles and highest standards of public life. Details of the resolutions adopted by the House on the declaration and registration of Lords' interests can be found on Parliament's website at www. parliament.uk.
- who are independent of any political party. Nominees and the Commission will need to feel confident of their ability to be independent of party political considerations whatever their past party-political involvement. For this reason, all nominees are asked to respond to the questions on political involvement and activities which are similar to those used for most public appointments.

[...]

[In Charts 8.1–8.3, House of Lords membership for 2008 is as at June 2008. The starting figure of 707 peers does not include Lords Spiritual and peers on Leave of Absence. Law Lords are included in the model in the same way as life Peers. It is assumed that between June 2008 and 2013, 28 new life Peers are appointed. Broadly, this figure reflects the current rate of appointments by the House of Lords Appointments Commission. During the same period, 130 life and hereditary Peers are assumed to die. This figure reflects survival probabilities (based on the gender and age of existing life and hereditary Peers) published by the Government Actuary's Department. In Charts 8.1 and 8.2, between 2013 and 2017, a further 108 life and hereditary Peers are assumed to die, again based on actuarial rates. The number of assumed deaths between 2017 and 2021 is also 103. No other departures are assumed. The rate of deaths beyond 2021 also reflects survival probabilities published by the Government Actuary's Department.]

Response to the White Paper

The White Paper was the product of intensive discussion of reasons for and against reform of the House of Lords. It made perfectly plausible reading, but did not move anything further forward. One wonders whether it had been sensible to appoint yet another joint committee, with members spending so much time and energy drafting proposals that might perhaps prove useful later, but for the present would be more or less cast aside.

Since the White Paper had invited comments, we should at least quote the views of two Conservative MPs, Andrew Tyrie and Sir George Young, who, as they stated, had 'contributed to debate on parliamentary and constitutional issues over many years'. In July 2009 they published their views with the hope of influencing their own party, 'as it draws up its manifesto for the next election'. We print below the 'Executive Summary' of their views:[2]

> (i) We believe strongly in the role of a second chamber as a check on the concentration of power in the executive. In this we follow a strong Conservative tradition of bicameralism, and of support for reform to entrench the role of the second chamber. We see it as a partner with the Commons in holding the government to account, not as a rival for power.
>
> (ii) We support a predominantly elected second chamber, but believe that there is a strong case for a 20% appointed element, following one of the two options favoured in the Commons vote of March 2007.
>
> (iii) We favour a system of Proportional Representation for elections to the chamber. We believe that the First past the post system with its ability to deliver clear party majorities, works well for the Commons and entrenches its role as the source of legitimacy for a government; however, the second chamber requires a demonstrably different system.
>
> (iv) Elections for the chamber should be on the basis of the regions that are used for European elections, although the electoral system should favour greater vote choice than a pure party list approach. Large electoral areas, coupled with the use of a long, non-renewable term, will reduce the danger of members of the second chamber encroaching on MPs' constituency work and thereby diluting their own revision and scrutiny role.
>
> (v) We believe that the initial aim should be for a reformed chamber with 400–450 members, although this will in any case be accomplished only gradually because of the continuing presence of existing life peers. Longer-term, there should be a review to examine the possibility of further reductions in numbers.

2 See Andrew Tyrie, George Young and Roger Gough, *An Elected Second Chamber: A Conservative View* (London: The Constitution Unit, July 2009), pp. 5–6.

(vi) We believe that, until reform is accomplished, the Appointments Commission should undertake the appointment of all peers, not only 'non-political' appointees; the current system retains far too much patronage for the parties and thus fails to break the potential link to financial contributions.

(vii) We support David Cameron's proposal for a wholly independent Appointments Commission, put on a statutory basis, to be implemented immediately.

(viii) We agree with the White Paper's proposal that, so long as there is an appointed element in the chamber, Church of England Bishops should retain their presence, albeit with their numbers reduced in line with the overall size of the chamber. The issue of faith representation should periodically be reviewed by the Appointments Commission.

(ix) We believe that existing proposals for filling vacancies are inadequate. The new member should serve out the remainder of parliament in which the vacancy arose, and the two subsequent parliaments.

(x) We are not persuaded of the arguments for recall ballot provisions. We believe that adoption of an independently supervised register of interests, as applied in the Commons, and of appropriate disciplinary sanctions, would be a more effective safeguard against misconduct or neglect of duties by a member of the second chamber. These measures should be put in place as soon as possible.

(xi) With respect to the transition arrangements, we believe that existing life peers should remain members of the chamber for life if they so wish, and that the remaining hereditary peers should be able to take life peer status for this purpose. Existing peers should be offered one-off payments for voluntary retirement. We believe that this approach would be just to existing peers who wish to continue to contribute; does not work against the interests of any political party; and nonetheless will encourage a reasonably rapid transition to the new, smaller chamber.

(xii) We believe that 'Upper House' is an appropriate name for the reformed second chamber; however, the issue of the chamber's name should not be a distraction from substantive reform.

(xiii) While most of our recommendations reflect the aim of moving to a predominantly elected chamber, we also set out interim measures that could be beneficial while avoiding the full-scale confrontation with the Lords that a shift to election is likely to trigger. This embraces not only the standards and sanctions regime, as well as changes to the appointments process, but also a move to 'term peerages' as the basis for new creations. Term peers would serve for the single, three-parliament term envisaged for the reformed chamber.

The views had substance in them. They were short and precise, well suited for a bill, that might perhaps have been more welcome to parliamentarians than the proposals contained in the White Paper (2008). But it was now too late for any consideration.[3] In 2010, the parties were preparing for an imminent general election.

3   In its final term in office the Labour government made one last effort to effect some reform of the Lords by publishing The Constitution Reform and Governance Bill. This was on 20 July 2009. The bill contained three clauses relating to Lords reform: clause 53: 'ending of by-elections for hereditary peers'; and clauses 54–55: 'exclusion and suspension of members of the House of Lords'. These clauses were thrown out by the Lords on 7 April 2010 (division on clause 53: 'Contents 42; Not-Contents 98'; division on clauses 54–55: 'Contents 45; Not-Contents 94'). See *Parliamentary Debates*, House of Lords, vol. DCCXVIII, 7 April 2010, cols 1632–34. The bill then proceeded further without these clauses.

The Rt Hon. the Lord Lloyd of Berwick *by Photoshot.com.*
Reproduced by permission of Photoshot.com.

The Rt Hon. Dan Byles MP *by Danielle King.*
Reproduced by permission of the Rt Hon. Dan Byles.

The Baroness D'Souza *by Chris Moyse.*
Reproduced by permission of the House of Lords, 2014.

Rt Hon. the Lord Falconer of Thoroton *by Michael Tylor. Reproduced by permission of the Palace of Westminster Collection, WOA 6560 www.parliament. uk/art.*

The Rt Hon. the Baroness Hayman *by Anita Corbin. Reproduced by permission of the Baroness Hayman.*

Rt Hon. the Earl Ferrers *by an unknown artist.*
Reproduced by permission of Annabel, Countess of Ferrers.

Rt Hon. the Lord Richard QC *by an unknown artist.*
Reproduced by permission of the Lord Richard.

David Martin Scott Steel, Baron Steel of Aikwood *by Bassano & Vandyk Studios.*
Reproduced by permission of the National Portrait Gallery, London.

The Rt Hon. Jack Straw MP *by an unknown artist.*
Reproduced by permission of the Ministry of Justice/Open Government Licence v.1.0.

CHAPTER SIXTEEN

2011. A Draft Reform Bill

Run-up to the Bill

The general election was due to be held on 6 May 2010. In their election manifestos, all the major parties had pledged to reform the House of Lords.[1]

The Labour Party manifesto declared that it would 'ensure that the hereditary principle is removed from the House of Lords', and that then further democratic reform would be 'achieved in stages' to create a fully elected second chamber. The proposals would be put to the people in a referendum.

The Conservatives promised that they would 'work to build a consensus for a mainly-elected second Chamber to replace the current House of Lords, recognising that an efficient and effective second Chamber should play an important role in our democracy and requires both legitimacy and public confidence'.

The Liberals gave assurance that they intended to 'replace the House of Lords with a fully-elected second Chamber with considerably fewer members than the current House'.

---

[1] See the Labour Party Manifesto 2010: 'A Future Fair for All' (2010); Conservative Party, 'An Invitation to join the Government of Britain' (2010); and the Liberal Democrat Manifesto 2010 (2010).

A Range of Opinions

The prospects of eventual reform of the House of Lords animated debate within various academic schools of thought.[2]

The Bishop of Bradford (Church of England) thought that a fully elected House of Lords was a 'naive attempt at improving democracy'. It was important to draw upon the 'expertise of people from beyond the political sphere'.[3]

The British Humanist Association argued that no member of the House of Lords 'should be elected or appointed on religious grounds alone'.[4]

Meg Russell and Meghan Benton (the Constitution Unit) identified that a number of areas of expertise – such as architecture, engineering, environmental protection, public health, and non-higher education – were 'less well represented' in the House of Lords.[5]

Iain McLean (Nuffield College, Oxford) argued for an elected house of Lords and Vernon Bogdanor (Brasenose College, Oxford) opposed this idea.[6]

Tim Bale (London School of Economics) suggested that the Government might be better 'served trying to implement less fundamental changes that could improve the efficiency of the House, rather than trying to find a solution to a problem that has not actually been identified'.[7]

2   A helpful source is Russell Taylor, *Bibliography on Lords Reform*, House of Lords, 26 April 2012. LLN 2012/014.

3   Bishop of Bradford, 'Against the grain' (Nick Baines' Blog, 14 March 2010).

4   British Humanist Association, *Religious Representation in the House of Lords*, March 2010.

5   Meg Russell and Meghan Benton, *Analysis of existing data on the breadth of expertise and experience in the House of Lords* (London: The Constitution Unit, March 2010).

6   Iain McLean and Vernon Bogdanor, 'Debate: Shifting Sovereignties: Should the United Kingdom have an elected upper house and elected head of state?', *Political Insight*, April 2010.

7   Tim Bale, 'Nick Clegg's proposed reforms to the House of Lords is a solution seeking a problem' (LSE Blog, 6 June 2010).

Meg Russell (the Constitution Unit) presumed that the 'most likely outcome for reform would see a move to a proportionally elected second chamber, increasing the power of the House of Lords further still.[8]

Rafel Heydel-Mankoo (Res Publica) argued that the introduction of elected members 'will negatively impact upon the work of the two Houses'.[9]

Establishment of an Official Committee. Lord Steel's Motion

The results of the general election of 6 May 2010 were inconclusive: the Tories won with 307 seats in the Commons, but Labour had 258 seats, the Liberal Democrats 57, and other parties 28. Thus no single party could claim a majority to form a government. The Conservatives and the Liberal Democrats agreed to form a coalition government, with David Cameron as prime minister and Nick Clegg as his deputy. In its Coalition Agreement, published on 20 May 2010, the new government promised to

> establish a committee to bring forward proposals for a wholly or mainly elected upper chamber on the basis of proportional representation. The committee will come forward with a draft motion by December 2010. It is likely that this will advocate single terms of office. It is also likely that there will be a grandfathering system for current Peers. In the interim, Lords appointments will be made with the objective of creating a second chamber that is reflective of the share of the vote secured by the political parties in the last general election.

On 26 May, while the Coalition government was still busy establishing this committee, Lord Steel of Aikwood tabled a motion in the Lords to be read

---

8   Meg Russell, 'A Stronger Second Chamber? Assessing the Impact of House of Lords Reform in 1999 and the Lessons for Bicameralism', *Political Studies*, 4 November 2010.

9   Rafel Heydel-Mankoo, *Lords reform: A century in the making*, Part 2 (Res Publica Blog, 9 December 2010).

a first time: that the House pass a bill to 'make provision for appointment of a commission to make recommendations to the Crown for the creation of life peerages; to restrict membership of the House of Lords by virtue of hereditary peerage; to make provision for permanent leave of absence form the House of Lords; to provide for the expulsion of Members of the House of Lords in specified circumstances; and for connected purposes'.[10] A second reading of the motion took place about a month later.

The new government moved swiftly. The membership of what we may call the Coalition Government Committee was announced on 7 June. It included representatives of all the main parties, from both Houses of Parliament. Nick Clegg would take the chair. Other members of the Committee were:

> Mark Harper MP (minister for Political and Constitutional Reform)
> George Young MP (leader of the House of Commons)
> David Heath MP (deputy leader of the House of Commons)
> Hilary Benn MP (shadow leader of the House of Commons)
> Sadiq Khan MP (shadow secretary of State for Justice)
> Lord Strathclyde (leader of the House of Lords)
> Lord McNally (deputy leader of the House of Lords)
> Baroness Royall of Blaisdon (shadow leader of the House of Lords)

Voices in the House of Lords

On 29 June, before the Committee had begun its deliberations, the chancellor of the Duchy of Lancaster, Lord Strathclyde, rose in the House of Lords to move that 'this House takes note of the case for reform of the House of Lords'.[11] The government, he said, was giving priority to the reform of the Lords. The government had decided to set up a committee charged with producing a draft bill by the end of the year. His motion would enable the

---

10   *Parliamentary Debates*, House of Lords, vol. DCCXIX, 26 May 2010, col. 26.
11   *Ibid.*, 29 June 2010, col. 1661.

Lords to express their views. A very long debate followed, which lasted from 3 p.m. until 11 p.m. The government's intentions were criticized.

Some speakers (Lord Barnett and Lord Hanny of Chiswick) complained that there were no back-benchers represented on the Committee.[12] Lord Strathclyde guaranteed their full presence once a Joint Committee of both Houses was set up.

Baroness D'Souza believed that there was no need to have an elected House of Lords since the House itself was about to have such reform measures as would 'encompass greater pre- and post-legislative scrutiny of primary legislation; better legislative standards; public evidence hearings for government bills; improving lines of accountability and transparency in all our work; and measures to make the planning and execution of business more efficient'.[13]

The Archbishop of York said he was uncertain whether a 'wholly elected House' that looked 'very much like the House of Commons will do its [the second chamber's] job', which was to revise legislation and 'seek answers to questions'.[14]

Many speakers agreed with Lord Howe of Aberavon when he expressed his fear that 'making us elected would to be to provoke much more savage and regular conflicts between the two Houses'.[15]

At the end of the debate the motion was agreed to. Then at past 11 p.m. Lord Steel of Aikwood rose to move a second reading of his motion:[16]

> That this House calls on Her Majesty's Government, notwithstanding their proposals for Lords reform whose legislative timetable is unclear, to table Motions before the Summer Recess enabling the House to approve or disapprove:
>   (i)   a scheme to enable Members of the House to retire,
>   (ii) the abolition of by-elections for hereditary Peers,

12   *Ibid.*, cols 1663–4.
13   *Ibid.*, col. 1673.
14   *Ibid.*, col. 1676.
15   *Ibid.*, col. 1678.
16   *Ibid.* cols 1785–8.

(iii) the removal of Members convicted of serious criminal office,

(iv) the creation of a statuary appointments commission.

Defending his motion, Lord Steel said that this simple legislation could go through 'this Session and we could achieve the running repairs which this House badly needs'. He begged to move.

The chancellor of the Duchy of Lancaster, Lord Strathclyde, opposed the motion. It was 'unusual', he argued – 'unusual because it is unclear what its intended effect is'. A very short debate followed. Lord Lea of Crondall supported the motion. The House divided: 'Contents, 44; Not-Contents, 29. Motion agreed to.' The House adjourned at 11.45 p.m. The motion did not proceed further.

The Government's Draft Bill

The Coalition government's Committee met seven times between July and December 2010. On the basis of its recommendations, a 'House of Lords Draft Bill' was issued in May 2011.[17] Attached to the draft were lengthy 'Explanatory Notes'. Thus another White Paper appeared, this time in the name of the Coalition government. It was presented to Parliament by the deputy prime minister on 17 May 2011. In the Foreword to the draft, the prime minister, David Cameron and the deputy prime minister, Nick Clegg, stated that the Cross-Party Committee had 'considered all the issues related to reform of the House of Lords and reached agreement on a large number of issues, but differences in opinion remain on the size of the elected elements and the type of electoral system'. The draft bill, they wrote, was being published for pre-legislative scrutiny, and the government

---

17   *House of Lords Reform: Draft Bill.* Presented to Parliament by the Deputy Prime Minister by Command of Her Majesty, May 2011. Cm 8077.

hoped that the two Houses would 'quickly establish a Joint Committee to consider and report on the draft Bill well before the end of the session'. Although the Joint Committee would ultimately be responsible for the 'next steps', the government would welcome 'everyone's comments' on the draft. These could be sent either to the Cabinet Office or be given in evidence to the Joint Committee.

Space does not permit us to print the full text of the White Paper. We will quote only 'The Proposals' printed at the beginning of the draft.[18] These give a sufficient overview of the project. However, the full text of the final bill can be found in our next chapter.

The Bill's Proposals

Name

1. The Government proposes to retain the name of the House of Lords, at least for the purposes of pre-legislative scrutiny. The cross-party Committee considered a wide range of names, including the Senate. However, the package of proposals in the White Paper represents incremental reform and, therefore, there is a logical argument for retaining the name of the House of Lords for the time being. The Government does not want discussion of the name to be a distraction from the more fundamental issues of the composition of the second chamber.

Functions

2. The House of Lords plays an important role in our legislature and, as a second chamber, is a vital part of our constitutional arrangements.

3. The House of Lords shares responsibility for legislating with the House of Commons. Bills are debated and scrutinised in both Houses. The House of Lords has a reputation for the careful

18   *Ibid.*

consideration of legislation and has the ability to delay and ask the Government and House of Commons to think again and, in some cases, offer alternative amendments for further consideration.

4. The House of Lords also plays a vital role in scrutinising the work of the Government and holding it to account for its decisions and activities. It does this by members asking oral and written questions, responding to Government statements and debating key issues.

5. Select Committees of the House of Lords conduct inquiries into matters of public policy and publish their findings to Parliament.

6. The Government believes that these functions should remain unchanged when the House of Lords is reformed and that it should continue this valuable work.

Powers

7. The Government believes that the change in composition of the second chamber ought not to change the status of that chamber as a House of Parliament or the existing constitutional relationship between the two Houses of Parliament.

8. The relationship between the two Houses of Parliament is governed by statute and convention. The Parliament Acts of 1911 and 1949 provide the basic underpinning of that relationship and set out that the House of Lords is, ultimately, subordinate to the House of Commons. They provide that, in certain circumstances, legislation may be passed without the agreement of the House of Lords. The Government does not intend to amend the Parliament Acts or to alter the balance of power between the Houses of Parliament. The Parliament Acts are, however, a long-stop which are rarely resorted to: the relationship between the Houses is governed on a day to day basis by a series of conventions which have grown up over time. These include that the House of Lords should pass the legislative programme of the Government which commands the confidence of the House of Commons; the principle that the Government of the day can continue in office

only if it retains the confidence of the House of Commons and the consequence that, whether or not a Bill has been included in a Manifesto, the House of Lords should think very carefully about rejecting a Bill which the Commons has approved; and the principle that the House of Lords will consider Government Bills in reasonable time. Most important, though, are the conventions which support the financial privileges of the House of Commons.

9. The Government's position is that these conventions have served the relationship between the Houses well and that they represent a delicate balance which has evolved over the years.

10. The Government believes that the powers of the second chamber and, in particular, the way in which they are exercised should not be extended and the primacy of the House of Commons should be preserved. The present balance between the two Houses as expressed by the principles set out above serves the legislative process well, and gives the second chamber the opportunity to make a substantive contribution while not at the same time undermining the relationship between the Government and the House of Commons.

11. The Government believes that clause 2 of the draft Bill is the best way of achieving this because it does not attempt to codify the existing powers of the Houses in legislation but rather, as now, accepts that the position is a matter of convention.

Size and Composition

12. There are 789 members of the House of Lords, but the average daily attendance in the 2009–2010 session was only 388 members. Whilst the total membership of the House of Lords is thus more than the House of Commons, the size of the 'working house' is significantly smaller. In most other countries the second chamber is substantially smaller than the first chamber. The Government proposes that the reformed House of Lords would comprise 300 members. The Government expects members of the reformed House to be full-time Parliamentarians. 300 full-time members would therefore be well able to fulfil the same range of duties

as the current average daily attendance of 388, given that the expectation at present is that many of the current members of the House, including those who do attend regularly, will have outside commitments.

13. The Coalition Agreement said that we would develop proposals for a wholly or mainly elected second chamber. This is the fundamental democratic principle.

14. Many people, however, value the contribution to Parliament from independent, non party-political voices. The wisdom and experience of people who are pre-eminent in their field and have done great things can be of benefit to Parliament's consideration of legislation. These people would not consider seeking elected office and would not see themselves as politicians.

15. The draft Bill sets out our proposal for an 80% elected House. This enables the draft Bill to demonstrate how a partly appointed House would work but it is a draft and we will consider options including a wholly elected House.

16. It, therefore, provides that the reformed House would have 240 elected members and 60 appointed members. The Government also proposes that a maximum of 12 Church of England Bishops would sit as *ex-officio* members.

17. Adapting the provisions for a wholly elected reformed House of Lords, would mean amending the draft Bill in the following ways:-

18. Clause 1 would be amended to provide that the composition in the first transitional period would be:

- 100 elected members
- ministerial members;
- Bishops and
- the transitional members for that period.

19. In the second transitional period the composition would be:

- 200 elected members;
- ministerial members;

- Bishops and
- the transitional members for that period.

20. During each subsequent electoral period the reformed House of Lords would consist of 300 elected members and ministerial members. Clause 5 would be amended to provide for 100 members to be elected at each House of Lords election.

21. The provisions on the Appointments Commission (Part 3, and Schedules 4 and 5) would be removed. Clauses 38 and 39 on disqualification of appointed members would be removed and other minor amendments would be made to the disqualification provisions in Part 7 to remove references to appointed members. Some similar consequential amendments would be needed to other provisions in the draft Bill.

22. The Government is interested to hear people's views on this choice between a wholly or mainly elected House of Lords.

23. The Government proposes that the link with the peerage would be broken. Membership of the second chamber would no longer be dependent on the award of a peerage nor would membership confer a right to a peerage. The peerage would revert to being an honour.

Term

24. The Government considers that serving a single term, with no prospect of re-election would enhance the independence of members of the reformed House of Lords. It would also reinforce the distinct role for members of the House of Lords, which is different from that of MPs. In order to attract able people, the Government recognises that the term would need to be sufficiently long. The Government therefore proposes that members should normally serve a single, non-renewable term of three normal Parliaments.

25. Elections would be for a third of the House at a time, with 80 elected members and 20 appointed members (if the House were 80% elected) entering the House after each election. This would ensure that members of the reformed House of Lords would never collectively have a more recent mandate than MPs.

Staggered elections would also make it less likely that one particular party would gain an overall majority. It would also mean that the Government of the day would be unlikely to have a majority in both Houses.

Timing of elections

26. The Government considers that elections to the reformed House of Lords should take place at the same time as elections to the House of Commons in order to maximise voter turnout and provide the least disruption to the work of Parliament and on grounds of efficiency. The Government considered holding elections to the reformed House of Lords at the same time as elections to the devolved legislatures, local authorities or to the European Parliament. However, historically the highest turnout tends to be at general elections, so holding elections to the House of Lords at the same time as elections to the House of Commons would maximise voter turnout. It would also mean that elections to the House of Lords would not disrupt the legislative programme with new members joining the reformed House partway through the consideration of legislation.

27. However, if there is an election to the House of Commons within two years of the previous election to the House of Lords, then there would be no House of Lords election at that time. As members' terms would be non-renewable, the Government considers it would be unfair to cut them unexpectedly short.

Electoral System

28. The Coalition Agreement set out our commitment to a system of proportional representation for the reformed House of Lords. Proportional representation systems are designed to ensure the proportion of the available seats won by a given party corresponds closely to the proportion of votes cast for that party at the election. For example, under a proportional system, a party with 30% of the votes cast at an election should win as close as possible to 30% of the seats available.

29. Proportional representation systems deliver this relationship between the proportion of the vote and the proportion of seats won because they are based on 'multi-member constituencies' – that is, voters in each constituency return more than one representative.

30. The Government believes that a proportional representation (PR) system will help achieve its aspirations for a reformed second chamber – that it should perform the same role as at present, but have a clear democratic mandate. The Government wishes to protect the important link between constituents and their Member of Parliament in the Commons, and we believe that establishing larger, multi-member constituencies as the basis of representation in the reformed House of Lords will provide a role and mandate for members of the reformed second chamber that is complementary to the important work undertaken by MPs. A PR system is likely to result in no party having an overall majority which, in addition, should assist in ensuring that the reformed House of Lords as a whole considers issues from a different perspective to that of the House of Commons.

31. There are a number of PR systems that could be used for elections to the reformed House of Lords. The draft Bill sets out how a Single Transferable Vote (STV) system would operate for elections to the reformed House of Lords. STV elections are currently used in the UK in all Northern Ireland elections (except elections to the House of Commons) and for local elections in Scotland.

32. The individuals elected to the reformed House of Lords will serve a long term, and will inherit the important scrutiny role presently exercised by the House of Lords. Their role, and that of the reformed chamber, will be different from that of the House of Commons. For these reasons, it is important that the individuals are elected with a personal mandate from the electorate, distinct from that of their party.

33. STV has a number of advantages compared with other PR systems that suggest it could be the most effective in delivering

that personal mandate. Under STV, votes are cast for individual candidates rather than parties, and candidates are elected on the strength of the votes they secure as individuals. This places more power in the hands of voters than under other types of PR system, such as some types of party list, where political parties can have the biggest say over the individual candidate that is eventually elected.

34. On balance, these factors lead the Government to propose the use of STV for elections to the House of Lords. However, all electoral systems have advantages and disadvantages, and the cross-party Committee discussed the case for an open list system under which the voter would have the option of being able to vote for a single individual candidate. The Government recognises that a case can be made for other proportional systems and the arrangements set out in the draft Bill to underpin the use of STV could be applied to an open list system.

How STV would work

35. Under STV, voters are invited to rank candidates on the ballot paper in the order in which they would like them to be elected. Under the version of STV proposed, as long as a first preference is indicated, the vote will be valid – a voter may simply write '1' next to a candidate. After that voters may express preferences for as many or as few candidates as they wish. Voters would not be required to vote for candidates representing only one party: they would be free to vote across parties and for independent candidates. There would be no option to vote for a party instead of an individual candidate.

36. To be elected, a candidate must achieve a target number of votes – known as the 'quota'. The quota is calculated on the basis of the number of votes cast and the number of seats available. The quota, broadly speaking, is the proportion of the total vote that a candidate must achieve to ensure that he or she will at least win the last of the available seats; at that point, he or she has enough votes to be guaranteed election to one of the seats.

37. Candidates need only one more vote than the target (the quota) to be elected – any further votes above this level have no additional bearing on their election. For this reason, when a candidate achieves the target, their 'surplus votes' – i.e. the difference between their total number of votes and the quota – are transferred to other candidates in accordance with the preferences expressed on the ballot papers. In this way, each successful individual candidate is elected only with the votes that they need, and those that they do not need can go on to have an impact on the result.

38. After the transfer of surplus votes from elected candidates to candidates who remain in the contest, a candidate that now achieves the quota is elected. If seats remain unfilled at this point, the candidate with the fewest votes is then eliminated, and their votes are redistributed to the remaining candidates according to the second or later preferences on those ballot papers. Any candidate now meeting the quota is elected. If seats remain, their surplus votes are redistributed, and this process continues until all of the seats have been filled.

Electoral Districts

39. As noted above, PR systems involve the use of constituencies, or districts, electing more than one member. Not every district would need to return the same number of candidates.

40. Since the reformed House of Lords would be elected in thirds, 80 seats would be contested at each election. That is roughly one member for every 570,000 voters. Multi-member 'Electoral Districts' will therefore be much larger than the current Parliamentary constituencies, and closer in size to the 12 regions used as constituencies for elections to the European Parliament.

41. Electoral Districts must have a sufficient number of seats to ensure proportionality (the degree to which the result reflects the votes cast), but not so many seats that it is difficult for voters to make an informed choice between candidates, particularly after the first few preferences.

42. The Government considers it practical where possible to start from the basis of existing boundaries in use for elections in the UK. Local authorities and administrative counties are well understood and have a sense of history and local connection. However, they are too small to be used as Electoral Districts. The twelve 'Nations and Regions' used for elections to the European Parliament will in some cases themselves be too large.

43. The Government therefore proposes that the STV Electoral Districts are formed of the nations, and, within England, groups of administrative counties, taking the existing nine regions as the starting point, but allowing for districts to cross the regional boundaries where necessary to ensure a sufficiently proportional result. This will mean districts comprising around 5 to 7 seats in England. There will be a floor of three seats to ensure a proportional result in Northern Ireland, as is the case for the European Parliamentary elections.

44. The Government considers that an independent committee of experts should be formed to decide which counties should be combined to form Electoral Districts. The committee would also make a recommendation as to the number of members that each constituency should return. The Government believes that the weight of a vote should be broadly equal for voters across the UK. This need not mean districts of the same size, because, unlike the House of Commons, the number of seats in each Electoral District may vary.

45. The committee's Terms of Reference would be consulted during the first part of pre-legislative scrutiny, but the committee will be established and set a deadline that will allow for their recommendations to form part of the final Bill introduced into Parliament.

Equally weighted votes

46. It would be necessary to check periodically that the districts finally agreed by Parliament continued to result in a broad equality in the potential weight of a vote across the country reflecting patterns of electorate distribution. The Government proposes

that the Electoral Commission would conduct a periodic review after every third election to the reformed House of Lords – that is, after each full electoral 'cycle'. If necessary, the Commission would make a recommendation that restored equality as far as possible between the districts. This would be done by ensuring the ratio of voters to representatives was as nearly as possible the same in all districts, using the Sainte-Laguë formula, widely accepted as the fairest way of conducting distributions of this kind. The relevant Minister would be required to present this to Parliament in the form of secondary legislation, requiring the approval of both Houses. This process is similar to that already used for the European Parliamentary elections.

47. Reviewing districts in this way would be more cost effective and simpler to implement, without compromising the principle of equality in the weight of a vote. It also reflects the decision to use counties as a building block. This proposal would mean that the Electoral District boundaries would not be re-drawn once they had been initially set, it would be the number of members per district which would change.

Women in Parliament

48. There is widespread agreement that the balance between men and women members in Parliament needs to be improved. Research suggests that the choice of proportional representation should facilitate the election of women to the reformed House of Lords. However, parties also have an important role to play in ensuring that Parliament reflects the society that it serves.

49. Reform of the House of Lords is therefore an opportunity to consider how to increase the participation of women in Parliament. The political parties and the Government should consider how to achieve this.

Franchise

50. The franchise for elections to the reformed House of Lords would reflect that for Westminster Parliamentary general elections.

British, resident Irish and qualifying Commonwealth citizens would therefore be eligible to vote in elections to the reformed House of Lords, as would those entitled to vote in Parliamentary elections whilst overseas. Voters would be entitled to vote in the Electoral District containing the address in respect of which they are registered to vote in a Parliamentary constituency.

51. The Government proposes that all members of the reformed House of Lords should be entitled to vote in both House of Commons and reformed House of Lords elections. Peers who presently sit in the House of Lords are disqualified from voting in Parliamentary elections on the basis that, as they are able to make representations directly in Parliament, there is no case for them to vote to elect representatives. The Government therefore proposes that, since these reforms would end the automatic link between a peerage and membership of the second chamber, the disqualification from voting in UK Parliamentary elections by virtue of a peerage should be lifted completely (it has already been lifted for hereditary peers who are not members of the House of Lords). Peers (who are not otherwise disqualified from voting) would therefore be able to vote in elections both to the reformed House of Lords and to the House of Commons with effect from the first set of elections to the House of Lords, which will take place on the same day as elections to the Commons.

Vacancies

52. It is the Government's intention that vacancies in the reformed House of Lords should not be left open until the end of the departing member's term, as this could mean that voters were underrepresented for significant periods of time. However, unlike in the House of Commons, vacancies created by elected members of the reformed House of Lords would not be filled through by-elections. This is partly due to the fact that it would be necessary to replace members elected through a proportional system with a candidate elected on a majoritarian basis, and also because holding

by-elections across larger Electoral Districts has the potential to result in significant costs.

53. Instead, the Government proposes that an elected member would be temporarily replaced by a substitute member until the next election. Under the STV system, if the departing member stood for election from a particular party, the substitute would be the candidate from the same party in that Electoral District, who, at the point the final seat in that district was awarded, had achieved the highest number of votes (whether first preferences or transferred votes) at the most recent election without gaining a seat. If this person does not take up the position, then the offer would revert to the person from that party with the next highest number of votes; should there be no further candidates eligible from that party, the seat would go to the person outside that party who gained the highest number of votes without being elected. In the event that an independent member vacated his or her seat, the substitute membership would be offered first to the person, of any party or none, that achieved the highest number of votes without being elected. If no person takes up the position of substitute member, the vacancy would be left open until the next election.

54. The substitute member appointed through this process would hold the seat until the next election to the reformed House of Lords. If the original member's term had been due to conclude at that election, then the seat would be contested at that election in the normal way. If, however, the original member's term had been due to continue beyond that election for a further one or two electoral periods then an additional seat would be contested in the relevant Electoral District. The additional seat would be awarded last, to the candidate who would otherwise have had the highest number of votes without gaining a seat. This elected replacement would then serve a shortened term of one or two electoral periods, as the case may be, until the end of the original member's term. This arrangement would ensure that the size of the reformed House of Lords would remain consistent, since the size of each electoral cohort would remain the same.

Statutory Appointments Commission

55. The House of Lords Appointments Commission (HOLAC) was established in 2000 to recommend individuals for appointment as non-party political peers and to vet nominations for life peers, including those nominated by the UK political parties. Since 2001 HOLAC has made recommendations on merit and against set criteria which include personal qualities of integrity, independence and the highest standards of public life.

56. If the reformed House of Lords is to contain appointed members, the Government proposes to establish an Appointments Commission on a statutory basis which would recommend 20 people for appointment at the same time as elected members are returned and people to replace appointed members who leave the chamber during their term. The Commission would be accountable to Parliament, as its work would be overseen by the Joint Committee on the House of Lords Appointments Commission.

57. The Commission would be a body corporate and all its powers would be set in statute. It would set its own criteria and process of appointment but it would be under a statutory duty to publish the criteria of appointment and the details of the appointment process.

58. It is expected that appointed members would bring a non-party political perspective to the work carried out by the reformed House of Lords.

59. The Government proposes that the current arrangement on recommendations is to remain unchanged. The Commission would make nominations to the Prime Minister. Appointments would be made by The Queen on the recommendation of the Prime Minister.

Commissioners

60. The Queen would appoint seven commissioners, including a Chair, to the statutory Appointments Commission. Appointments to the Commission would be based on merit.

61. The Government proposes that members of the House of Commons and Ministers should not be eligible for appointment

as Commissioners. This would follow the long-held principle that it is not right for members of one House of Parliament to be involved in the business of the other (exclusive cognisance).

62. However, the Government considers that it is important that the Commission should have access to firsthand knowledge of how the second chamber works. We propose that there should be no ban on former and current members of the House of Lords or the reformed House of Lords serving as Commissioners.

63. The Commissioners would be appointed for a single non-renewable ten-year term. A long term for Commissioners with no prospect of renewal would enable a high degree of independence in the exercise of their functions.

64. Following Addresses from both Houses of Parliament, it would also be possible for Commissioners to be removed from their role by The Queen on certain grounds.

The Joint Committee on the House of Lords Appointments Commission

65. The Joint Committee on the House of Lords Appointments Commission would oversee the work carried out by the Commission. The Committee would be composed of members of both Houses. In the case of the reformed House of Lords, members could be elected, appointed or transitional members. Although the Joint Committee would consist of members of both Houses, its appointment by statute means that it would not be a committee of Parliament.

66. In particular the Joint Committee would approve the Commission's income and expenditure; it would lay the Commission's annual report before Parliament, review and consequently approve the Code of Conduct of the Appointments Commission. It would be modelled on the Speaker's Committee for the Electoral Commission.

Ministers

67. The Government proposes that Ministers may be drawn from elected members of the reformed House of Lords and, in

the transitional period, both elected members and transitional members. This would ensure that Government business in the reformed House of Lords would be managed by members belonging to the same political party that had formed the Government.

68. The Prime Minister should also be able to appoint a limited number of people to serve as Ministers who would be members of the reformed House of Lords only for the duration of their appointment. The draft Bill makes provision for the detailed arrangements to implement this to be set out in secondary legislation, though the Government is open to including this in the Bill itself.

Transition

69. The Government proposes a process of transition to the reformed House of Lords. During this period, some of the current members of the House of Lords would work alongside new elected and appointed members of the reformed House of Lords. The Government recognises that this would help the reformed House of Lords work effectively during this period.

70. The draft Bill sets out one option for the transitional period. However, the Government remains open to views on the exact process of transition. Other possible options are discussed below.

Option 1 set out in the draft Bill

71. The aim is to reduce the number of current members in parallel with the introduction of new elected and appointed members of the reformed House of Lords over three elections. This would provide a gradual handover from the old to the reformed House. By the time of the third election, the chamber would comprise only those members, apart from the Bishops, who have been either elected or appointed to sit in the reformed House of Lords.

72. Existing members of the House of Lords, except Bishops, who are selected to remain in the reformed House of Lords through a transitional period are to be known as transitional

members. Within the limits set out in the draft Bill, it would be for the House of Lords to determine the procedures for selecting members to sit in the first and second transitional periods. Transitional members would not be replaced if they leave the reformed House of Lords.

First transitional period

73. The first transitional period would begin with the first election to the reformed House of Lords. 80 members would be elected and 20 members would be appointed by the statutory Appointments Commission for terms of three electoral periods. If the House were wholly elected, 100 members would be elected at this time.

74. At the beginning of the first transitional period, the maximum number of transitional members who may be selected would be two thirds of the existing peers. This would ensure that, during the passage of the Bill through Parliament, the maximum number of transitional members would be known. It would also allow the House of Lords to make the arrangements for selection of transitional members in advance of the first election to the reformed House of Lords, including the making of standing orders. This follows the system for the departure of hereditary peers following the House of Lords Act 1999.

75. In order to be eligible for selection, a peer would have to be entitled to receive a writ of summons to attend the House of Lords immediately before dissolution of the last Parliament before the first election to the reformed House of Lords.

76. These members would have to be selected prior to the beginning of the first transitional period.

Second transitional period

77. At the time of the second election, a further 80 members would be elected and 20 would be appointed. If the House were wholly elected, a further 100 members would be elected at this time.

78. In order to be eligible for selection as transitional members for the second transitional period, members would have to

be transitional members immediately before the dissolution of the Parliament of the first transitional period. The maximum number of transitional peers who would be selected would be one half of the maximum number who may be selected for the first transitional period. The selected members would remain as transitional members for the whole of the second transitional period. The selection would have to be made prior to the beginning of the second transitional period.

79. At the time of the third election, all the transitional members would leave.

80. There are two other options for the transitional process on which the Government would welcome the views of the Joint Committee.

Option 2

81. This option would allow all those eligible, and who chose to do so, to remain in the reformed House of Lords until the dissolution of Parliament immediately prior to the third election. No selection process to determine which peers are to remain in the chamber would be needed. Up until the third election former members of the House of Lords would probably continue to form a majority of the reformed House.

82. Their knowledge of the work of the House of Lords would be retained as new members joined. However, this would lead to a chamber with a very large membership, comprising all those members of the House of Lords eligible to remain plus 200 new members after the second election. This could result in a chamber of nearly 1,000 members, unless this is reduced through resignation or retirement, as well as death.

Option 3

83. A third option would be to reduce the size of the reformed House of Lords to 300 members at the time of the first election. This would mean that the advantages of a smaller House could be realised immediately and would make clear that the House of Lords had been reformed.

84. 200 of the existing members of the House of Lords would remain at the time of the first election to the reformed House of Lords. They would be joined by 100 new members.

85. At the time of the second election to the reformed House of Lords the number of former members of the House of Lords would be further reduced to 100. This would mean that after the second election there would be 100 members who were formerly peers in the House of Lords and 200 new members.

86. All remaining former members of the House of Lords would leave immediately before the third election to the reformed House of Lords.

Hereditary Peers

87. There would be no reserved places for hereditary peers in the reformed House of Lords, although hereditary peers could be selected to remain as transitional members. They could also stand for election or be considered for appointment to the reformed House of Lords.

88. The House of Lords Act 1999 provided for a system of by-elections which allowed hereditary peers to enter the House solely by virtue of their peerage. The system was established to ensure that the number of hereditary peers in the House of Lords remained at 90. On the death of a hereditary peer a by-election would be held allowing hereditary peers to seek entry to the House of Lords.

89. The Government proposes that there should be no further by-elections after the start of the transitional period. The draft Bill, therefore, repeals the House of Lords Act 1999.

90. The Earl Marshal and the Lord Great Chamberlain are the two hereditary offices of state. Both are presently held by hereditary peers. However, these office holders would not need to sit in the reformed House of Lords to fulfil their duties as members of the Royal Household.

Church of England Bishops

91. Currently, the Lords Spiritual – the 2 Archbishops and 24 Bishops of the Church of England – have reserved places in the

House of Lords. They do not sit for life, but only for their period as an Archbishop or Bishop of a diocese. Although historically they sit as independent members of the Lords they are widely regarded as representatives of the Church of England.

92. The Government proposes that in a fully reformed second chamber which had an appointed element there should continue to be a role for the established Church. However, in line with proposals for a reduction in the size of the second chamber, the Government proposes that the number of reserved places for Church of England Archbishops and Bishops should also be reduced, from 26 to a maximum of 12.

93. The Government proposes that transitional arrangements should also apply to the Bishops to allow a gradual reduction to take place. The Government believes that this arrangement would allow the Bishops to continue to contribute effectively to the reformed House of Lords.

94. The Archbishops of Canterbury and York and the Bishops of London, Durham and Winchester hold a seat in the House of Lords as of right under the Bishoprics Act 1878. The Government proposes that they should be entitled to occupy reserved places in the reformed second chamber throughout the transitional period and in the fully reformed chamber for as long as they hold that named office. If one of these Archbishops or Bishops were to leave that office, then he would be replaced in the reformed House of Lords by the new holder of that office.

95. The other 7 places would be reserved for Bishops of dioceses in England. These Bishops would be selected to sit in the reformed House of Lords by the Church of England.

First transitional period

96. Presently, in addition to the holders of the five named offices, there are 21 Church of England Bishops entitled to sit in the House of Lords, in order of seniority. It would be for the Church to select up to 16 of these 21 Bishops to remain in the House of Lords during the first transitional period. These members would

have to be selected from those in the House of Lords who, immediately before the dissolution of Parliament before the first election, would be entitled to sit as Bishops in the House of Lords.

Second transitional period

97. At the time of the second election to the reformed House of Lords, it would be for the Church to select a maximum of 11 of the Bishops to remain throughout the second (and final) transitional period. They would be selected only if they had been in the reformed House of Lords immediately before the dissolution of the Parliament of the first transitional period.

98. At the time of the third election to the reformed House of Lords, it would be for the Church of England to select up to 7 of these Bishops to sit in the chamber.

Fully reformed chamber

99. For each subsequent electoral period, a maximum of 7 serving Church of England Bishops could be selected by the Church to sit in the reformed House of Lords. They would be able to be selected from those Bishops who were sitting in the reformed House of Lords at that time or serving Church of England Bishops not in the chamber, but they would not be the holder of a named office.

100. The Church would not be obliged to fill any of the places reserved for Bishops at the start of each transitional or electoral period. If however it chose to fill any of these seats, and a vacancy subsequently arose among them, the Church would be able to fill the vacancy only if not to do so would cause the number of Bishops (excluding holders of a named office) to fall below 7. The Church would be able to select any serving Bishop, except a named office holder, to fill the vacancy.

101. A vacancy would arise if a Bishop becomes one of the named office holders or ceases to be a Bishop, or resigns from the reformed House of Lords. If, at any time, one of the Bishops in the reformed House of Lords became the Bishop of a different diocese, he would continue to hold a reserved place.

102. The Bishops who would remain in the reformed House of Lords after the end of the transitional period would have the same speaking and voting rights as other members of the reformed House of Lords.

103. The Bishops would continue to sit in the reformed House of Lords on a different basis from other members. Currently, Bishops sit in the House of Lords by virtue of their being serving office holders within the Church of England. They attend on a rota basis as their episcopal duties allow. They are also subject to the Church's terms and conditions on remuneration and discipline. Therefore in the transitional period, and in a fully reformed chamber, the Government proposes that:

• Bishops would not be entitled to a salary or pension in the reformed House of Lords;
• Bishops would be exempt from the tax deeming provision;
• Bishops would be entitled to claim allowances under the scheme administered by the IPSA[19] for members of the reformed House of Lords;
• They would be subject to the disqualification provision;
• They would not be subject to the serious offence provision and those on expulsion and suspension as it is anticipated that such members would be subject to the disciplinary procedures established by the Church of England.

Remuneration

104. The overall cost of the reformed House of Lords will depend to a significant degree on the pay and pensions of members, and their allowances (including staffing allowances). However, the number of members will be reduced to only 300 members, less than half its current size.

19   IPSA = Independent Parliamentary Standards Authority.

105. The draft Bill includes provisions on salaries and allowances for all members of the reformed House of Lords (excluding Bishops).

106. Current members of the House of Lords do not receive a salary. They are, however, entitled to non-taxable allowances to cover expenses incurred while conducting their parliamentary duties. Certain members of the House of Lords are remunerated due to the additional positions held. These are the Lords Speaker, the Chairman of Committees, the Principal Deputy Chairman and Government Ministers.

107. The Government proposes that, in a reformed House of Lords, members would be entitled to a taxable salary as they would be full time Parliamentarians. It is also proposed that they would be entitled to receive a pension and allowances for expenses incurred in carrying out their parliamentary duties.

108. The Government proposes that members of the reformed House of Lords would be subject to the same independent regulatory regime as the House of Commons as provided by the IPSA.

109. The draft Bill provides for salaries to be paid to transitional members. The final decision on whether this was appropriate would be taken in the light of the transitional scheme and therefore the number of transitional members.

Salaries

110. The Parliamentary Standards Act 2009 (PSA 2009), as amended by the Constitutional Reform and Governance Act 2010 (CRAG Act 2010), made provision for MPs' salaries to be set and paid by the IPSA. The Government proposes that salary arrangements of members of the reformed House of Lords should be broadly similar to those which apply to members of the House of Commons.

111. The Government proposes that the IPSA should set and pay not only salaries of members of the House of Commons but also those of the members of the reformed House of Lords. The

Government considers that the level of salary for a member of the reformed House of Lords should be lower than that of a member of the House of Commons but higher than those of members of the devolved legislatures and assemblies. This would recognise that they would have responsibilities for UK-wide legislation but would not have constituency duties. However, it will be for the IPSA to set the level of salaries.

112. The IPSA would have freedom to make arrangements for the setting, payment and review of salaries and would have the duty, after the first determination, to consult a specific set of people and bodies in order to determine the level of pay.

113. A general review of salaries of the reformed House of Lords would be carried out in the first year after each House of Lords election and at any other time the IPSA considers it appropriate. It is also proposed that the IPSA would have the additional power to delegate its function of reviewing a salary determination to the Senior Salaries Review Body (SSRB).

Allowances

114. The Government proposes that members of the reformed House of Lords should be entitled to claim allowances for costs incurred while conducting their parliamentary duties.

115. It is also proposed that the allowances scheme would be set and run by the IPSA. The regime provided by the PSA 2009 as amended by the CRAG Act 2010 imposes on the IPSA the duty to revise and review allowances for members of the House of Commons at every qualifying general election.

116. The Government proposes that the IPSA's role in administering allowances would also be extended to the reformed House of Lords with reviews conducted after every reformed House of Lords election and whenever the IPSA considers it appropriate.

Governance

117. The Government proposes that the governance arrangements for the IPSA should be amended to take account of the fact that

it would be dealing with the reformed House of Lords as well as the House of Commons.

Pensions

118. Currently, only Ministers and a small number of other office holders in the House of Lords receive a pension. The Government proposes that the pensions provisions for all transitional, elected and appointed members (but not Bishops) of the reformed House of Lords should mirror those available for members of the House of Commons. These provisions are not set out in the draft Bill. They would however be included in the Bill introduced into Parliament.

119. The Report of the Committee on Standards in Public Life: *MPs' Expenses and Allowances: Supporting Parliament, Safeguarding the Taxpayer*, published in November 2009, recommended that the IPSA determine MPs' pensions and oversee their administration. The CRAG Act 2010 enacted this recommendation, although it has not yet been brought into force. The Act also made provision for the continuation of the Parliamentary Contributory Pension Fund (PCPF) out of which MPs' pensions, and those of Ministers and other office holders, are currently paid. It is intended that the provisions will be brought into force by 2012.

120. The Government proposes to extend the IPSA's remit to include members of the reformed House of Lords who are not already paid a pension out of the PCPF. The IPSA would therefore be required to make a pension scheme similar to the MPs' scheme provided for in the 2009 Act, containing provisions on the application of assets of the PCPF for the provision of members' pensions. The Act already provides for a separate Ministers' pension scheme for Ministers and other office holders (including members of the House of Lords who are already entitled to a pension). The Act requires this to be made by the Minister for the Civil Service.

121. When setting the appropriate pension levels the IPSA would consult the Senior Salaries Review Body and other relevant bodies.

122. As currently provided by the PSA 2009, a yearly Exchequer contribution would be paid into the Fund out of money provided by Parliament. The amount of the contribution would be calculated in accordance with the recommendations of the Government Actuary, which would report every three years.

123. The administration of the PCPF, including overseeing investment decisions, is entrusted to 10 trustees under the PSA 2009. The Government intends to consult the current trustees of the PCPF about the transitional arrangements which would be necessary to ensure continuity and fair representation on the board under its proposals.

124. The changes would be carried out in the context of the reform of pension provision in the wider public sector in the light of the findings and recommendations of the Independent Public Service Pension Commission chaired by Lord Hutton.

Tax

125. Members of the reformed House of Lords would consider legislation that affects all aspects of life in the UK, including policies with significant public expenditure and therefore tax consequences. It is only right that members should be liable to pay the same tax as the vast majority of people in the UK. The requirement which already exists for all members of the House of Lords and all MPs to be resident, ordinarily resident and domiciled for tax purposes would therefore be extended to the members of the reformed House of Lords.

126. The draft Bill provides for a deeming provision which would apply to all members (except the Bishops) so that they would be liable to pay UK tax on the same basis as the majority of the population, regardless of actual tax status. Members would be deemed resident, ordinarily resident and domiciled (ROD) for the purposes of income tax, capital gains tax and inheritance tax. There would be an exception, during the transitional period, for any transitional members who are temporarily disqualified from sitting and voting because they hold judicial offices.

127. The provision would apply for the whole of each tax year in which the person is a member, from the start of the tax year in which membership commences, to the end of the tax year in which membership ceases.

128. The provision would make members liable to pay UK tax on their domestic and foreign income when it arises, subject to any relevant Double Taxation Agreements, for the whole of their period of office. Those who die while a member would be deemed ROD on their death and would be subject to normal UK inheritance tax provisions.

Expulsion or suspension for misconduct

129. The draft Bill provides a power for the reformed House of Lords to make standing orders which allow it to suspend or expel any member (except the Bishops).

130. Under the power, the reformed House of Lords could make provisions broadly mirroring the sanctions available to the House of Commons in respect of misconduct by MPs, however it would not be restricted to doing so.

131. Although the House of Lords currently has a power to suspend a member, this is limited to the remainder of the Parliament within which the power is exercised. The Government proposes an enhanced power of suspension that does not have this limitation.

132. Expulsion would result in permanent loss of membership. By contrast, if a member was suspended, the individual would not lose his or her membership but would not be entitled to sit and vote for the period of the suspension. The member would lose his or her entitlement to receive writs of summons to attend the reformed House of Lords, and his or her rights under any previously issued writ of summons would no longer be exercisable.

133. As a suspended individual would continue to be a member, he or she would continue to be deemed resident, ordinarily resident and domiciled in the UK under the deeming provision on tax status.

Resignation

134. The Government proposes that all members of the reformed House of Lords should have the right voluntarily to relinquish their membership at any time. We recognise that there are many unforeseen circumstances which may prevent members fulfilling an initial commitment to serve for a full term.

135. Appointed or elected members who resign would be replaced in accordance with the draft clauses on filling vacancies, so that their numbers are maintained at a constant level.

136. Transitional members, including those who resign, would not be replaced, however, because the rate of resignation is unlikely to be high enough to conflict with the overall aim of gradual removal of these members from the second chamber.

137. A member would resign by giving written notice to the Clerk of the Parliaments. They would cease to be a member of the reformed House of Lords on signing the written notice.

Recall

138. The Government is committed to bringing forward legislation to introduce a power to recall MPs where they have engaged in serious wrongdoing.

139. The Government will also consider whether elected members of the reformed House of Lords should be subject to a similar system.

Disqualification

140. The Government proposes that the disqualification regime for the reformed House of Lords should be similar to that of the House of Commons, to ensure that there is a common standard governing membership of both Houses. The main purpose of the disqualification regime would be to ensure the fitness and propriety of members of the reformed House of Lords.

141. The draft Bill makes provision for the disqualification of persons from being elected or appointed to the reformed House of Lords on the following grounds:

- Age (a minimum of 18 years).
- Nationality (Members are disqualified if they are not a British citizen, a citizen of the Republic of Ireland, or a citizen of a Commonwealth country who does not require leave to enter or remain in the UK, or who has indefinite leave to remain in the UK).
- Holding a disqualifying office (matching the House of Commons regime).
- Insolvency (applying if the person is subject to a bankruptcy restrictions order or undertaking or a debt relief restrictions order or undertaking).
- The person is imprisoned for more than 12 months for an offence committed in the UK or overseas.
- The person has previously been elected or appointed to the reformed House of Lords and has served a full term. This would ensure that members serve a single non-renewable term.

142. A person would be disqualified from being a transitional member on the grounds of nationality, insolvency or imprisonment for a serious offence.

143. In addition, the Government proposes that a person could not be a member of both Houses of Parliament at the same time.

144. The Government proposes that disqualification, due to an insolvency order in relation to a member or due to the serious offence condition being met by a member, could be lifted if:

- The member's membership had come to an end, in the first or second electoral period, and;
- A subsequent reversal of the insolvency order or the quashing of the conviction for a serious offence had taken place.

145. The exception would allow a person to be reconsidered for nomination as a candidate for election or for appointment to the reformed House of Lords for a full term (of three electoral periods).

Disqualification of former members of the reformed House of Lords for election as MPs

146. The Government intends that the second chamber should continue to be a scrutinising and revising chamber, and should therefore attract individuals with different qualities from members of the House of Commons. It recognises however that an elected second chamber may attract the kind of candidates who typically seek election to the House of Commons, who if successful may try to build a political base in the reformed House of Lords with that intention. Appointed members and transitional members could also use their profile in the reformed House of Lords to their advantage in planning to move to the House of Commons.

147. The Government therefore proposes a time restriction to disqualify former members of the reformed House of Lords (except for the Bishops) from being elected to the House of Commons for a specified period of time after they cease to be members.

148. The restriction would bar a member of the reformed House of Lords who completes their term from being elected as a MP at the general election which immediately follows the day they cease to be a member. The former member would remain disqualified until immediately before the earliest date on which it is calculated that a scheduled general election could occur after that election.

149. A member of the reformed House of Lords who ceased membership early would be subject to exactly the same period of disqualification, from the day their membership ceases, so that they would be neither advantaged nor disadvantaged by leaving early.

150. There would be no equivalent time restriction for former MPs who wish to seek membership of the reformed House of Lords.

Ceremonial and the Sovereign

151. Certain ceremonies take place in the House of Lords. Some questions will be matters for the reformed House of Lords, such

as the introduction of new members and the wearing of robes in the presence of the Sovereign. Others are matters for the Crown, such as Royal Commissions for the opening and prorogation of Parliament and, most importantly, The Queen's Speech. The Government proposes similar continuity in ceremonial: once the House of Lords has been reformed, Parliament will comprise The Queen, the reformed House of Lords and the House of Commons. The Queen will continue to open sessions of Parliament in state from the Parliament Chamber, the House of Lords Chamber, as happens in other Commonwealth second chambers. The Earl Marshal and Lord Great Chamberlain will retain their duties but will perform them without being members of the reformed House of Lords. The question as to which member of the reformed House of Lords presents humble Addresses to The Queen will be one for the reformed House of Lords but the duty was performed by the Government Chief Whip (the Captain of the Gentlemen at Arms) when the Lord Chamberlain was not a member of the House of Lords.

Political donations and spending rules

152. The Government anticipates that the regulatory regime covering donations and loans to members of the reformed House of Lords, and expenditure by parties and candidates at elections to the reformed House of Lords, would broadly reflect arrangements for MPs and elections to the House of Commons.

153. At present these controls are set out primarily in the Political Parties, Elections and Referendums Act 2000 ('PPERA', as amended) and the Representation of the People Act 1983. The Government has made clear its intention to pursue a detailed agreement on limiting donations and reforming party funding in order to remove big money from politics. This would result in change to the regulatory framework. The draft Bill therefore does not contain detailed provision on donation and spending rules, since proposals in this area will be developed consistent with wider policy. The Government will set these out in due course.

Conclusion

154. This draft Bill marks the transformation of the House of Lords into a democratically legitimate second chamber. It provides our vision for the reform of the House of Lords. The Government looks forward to the results of the work of the Joint Committee which is undertaking pre-legislative scrutiny of the Bill. We will consider their report carefully, but remain committed to introducing a Bill for enactment in time to provide for the first elections in 2015.

Response to the Proposals

The publication of the government's White Paper was announced in the House of Commons on 17 May 2011 by the deputy prime minister. He briefly described the contents of the draft bill and stated that it 'will now be scrutinised by a Joint Committee composed of 13 Peers and 13 Members of this House'. The Joint Committee was to report early in the following year, and after that the government intended to introduce a full government bill.[20] On the same day, a similar announcement was made in the House of Lords by the chancellor of the Duchy of Lancaster, Lord Strathclyde.[21]

The new White Paper provided further stimulation for debate on the issues. Dr Alan Renwick (Reading University) published a profound analysis of the White Paper, which he in principle welcomed.[22] Neither the issues nor the conclusions were novel, but Dr Renwick's analysis helps us understand the basic problems the reformers faced. The analysis went into depth, explaining the options available and what solutions could be accommodated.

20   *Parliamentary Debates*, House of Commons, vol. 528, 17 May 2011, col. 155.
21   *Parliamentary Debates*, House of Lords, vol. DCCXXVII, 17 May 2011, col. 1268.
22   See Alan Renwick, *House of Lords: A Brief Paper* (London: Political Studies Association, July 2011). A detailed analysis of the White Paper and various responses to it is to be found in *End of the Peer Show* (CentreForum, July 2011).

Dr Renwick did not believe that a largely elected chamber would in any way overturn the primacy of the House of Commons. The Lords would still be 'constrained' by the Parliament Acts. The Lords could nevertheless maintain 'substantial independence' through the appointed element. Here the Single Transferable Vote system would 'facilitate the election of independents'. Yet there were a number of important questions that needed to be answered. Dr Renwick listed some of these in his 'Executive Summary':

(i) Did the current House of Lords 'use its delaying power enough' or did it 'leave governments too readily able to pass legislation without listening to others?'

(ii) 'What would be the effects of establishing the House of Lords as a full-time, salaried chamber?'

(iii) Was there not an insufficient accountability mechanism? Members of the second chamber, once elected, would 'not be subject to re-election and would be free to do as they pleased for fifteen years. This would have advantages in encouraging independence and giving individuals who [were] not professional politicians more reason to seek office. But it would also limit the democratic character of the chamber and [might] allow members who persistently failed to attend to go unpunished'.

(iv) 'What would be the effect of electing members of the House of Lords in very large constituencies of around four million voters? There is good reason to think that such large constituencies would prevent excessive localism. But what would be the effects on the candidates likely to stand, the nature of election campaigns, the power of political parties, and the character of those elected?'

(v) Would not the hybrid membership create problems? The 'specific form of hybridity' as proposed 'is unique and its effects are somewhat uncertain'.

(vi) Should ministers sit in the Upper House? There were 'both advantages and disadvantages in this link to the government'.

(vii) Should the Prime Minister 'have an unconstrained right, as proposed, to appoint *ministerial members* who would retain

membership of the second chamber as long as they remain ministers? Should there not at least be a cap on such appointments,
as previous reform schemes [had] suggested?'

Dr Renwick put forward reasonable arguments and probable answers.

Iain McLean agreed with most of what Dr Renwick had to say, and
emphasized his disagreement with those who thought that an elected
House of Lords 'would cease to be a forum of expertise'.[23]

Dawn Oliver advocated the total abolition of a second chamber.
It would be much cheaper, more representative and efficient to have an
'Independent Scrutiny Commission' instead, to handle legislative scrutiny.[24]

Lord Harries of Pentregarth favoured an elected element within the
House of Lords. That would 'allow better regional representation'.[25]

Baroness D'Souza believed that whole or part election would 'cause
the House to become too similar to the House of Commons, risking a loss
of individual expertise and stronger party political bias'.[26]

23   Iain McLean, 'The Salisbury convention that avoided complete Lords reforms for
     the last century is dead, but achieving any mandate for change that Peers must accept
     remains very difficult' (London School of Economics Blog, 4 July 2011).

24   Dawn Oliver, 'An Independent Scrutiny Commission Could Take Over the
     Constitutionally Valuable Roles that the House of Lords Presently Performs, and
     at Lower cost – Whether We Move to Create an Elected Second Chamber; or
     Reform the Unacceptable Features of the Current House of Lords; or Just Scrap a
     Second Chamber Altogether' (LSE Blog, 6 July 2011). In a separate article Dawn
     Oliver argued that a wholly or partly elected House of Lords would have a negative
     effect on its role. There would be 'increased reliance on party whips', and the number
     of experts would be hugely reduced. See Dawn Oliver, 'The Parliament Acts, the
     Constitution, the Rule of Law, and the Second Chamber', *Statute Law Review*, 23
     December 2011.

25   Lord Harries of Pentregarth, 'The Draft Bill and the Report of the Royal Commission
     on the reform of the House of Lords' (LSE Blog, 11 July 2011).

26   Baroness D'Souza, 'Expertise in the House of Lords is vital and supplied by the cross
     benchers: there is no democratic deficit and so elections are not needed' (LSE Blog,
     13 July 2011).

Stephen MacLean displayed little enthusiasm for an elected second chamber. Having two elected chambers would 'see more policy compromises between the two Houses', and would add to the 'risk of government failure'.[27]

The public discussion in no way interfered with the government's programme of setting up a Joint Committee, as it had all along planned.

The Joint Committee on the Draft House of Lords Reform Bill

The House of Commons appointed the following members to the Joint Committee on 23 June 2011:

Gavin Barwell MP
Tom Clarke MP
Ann Coffey MP
Bill Esterson MP
Oliver Heald MP
Tristram Hunt MP
Eleanor Laing MP
William McCrea MP
Daniel Poulter MP
Laura Sandys MP
John Stevenson MP
John Thurso MP
Malcolm Wicks MP

The House of Lords announced its appointments on 6 July 2011.

27   Stephen MacLean, 'Public Choice Theory and House of Lords Reform', *Economic Affairs*, October 2011.

Baroness Andrews
Tim Stevens, Bishop of Leicester
Lord Hennessy of Nympsfield
Lord Norton of Louth
Lord Richard
Lord Rooker
Baroness Scott of Needham Market
Baroness Shephard of Northwold
Baroness Symons of Vernham Dean
Lord Trefgarne
Lord Trimble
Lord Tyler
Baroness Young of Hornsey

The Joint Committee was to report to both Houses by 27 March 2012. The Committee had the power to 'require the submission of written evidence and documents, to examine witnesses, to meet at any time (except when Parliament is prorogued or dissolved), to adjourn from place to place, to appoint specialist advisers, and to make Reports to both Houses'. It eventually had power to 'agree with the Commons in the appointment of a Chairman.'[28]

The Committee called for both oral and written evidence on the terms of the White Paper. They wanted to know:

(i)   How the draft bill would fulfil its objectives;
(ii) The effect the bill would have on the powers of the House of Lords and the existing conventions governing the relationship between the Lords and the Commons;
(iii) The role and functions the reformed House would have;
(iv) The means of ensuring continued primacy of the House of Commons under any new arrangements;

---

28   Source: *Joint Committee on the Draft House of Lords Reform Bill*, volume I: *Report*, together with appendices and formal minutes (23 April 2012). HL Paper 284-I; HC 1313-I.

(v)　The size of the proposed House and the ratio of elected to non-elected members (from among the draft bill's options);

(vi)　About the Statutory Appointments Commission;

(vii)　The electoral term, retirement, etc.;

(viii)　The electoral system preferred (from among the draft bill's options);

(ix)　Transitional arrangements (again from options given).

(x)　The provisions on bishops, ministers and hereditary peers;

(xi)　Other administrative matters like pay and pensions;

(xii)　Relevant comparisons with other bi-cameral parliaments;

(xiii)　Anything else relevant to the introduction of a largely elected House (for example, the name it should go by, the question of referendum, the applicability of the Parliament Acts, etc.).

The Joint Committee met on 11 July 2011 to elect Lord Richard as chairman. The 'Orders of Reference' were read and the 'Call for Evidence' agreed to. The Committee met again on 12 September, and after deliberation adjourned until 10 October, when it examined the first witness. This was Mark Harper MP, minister for Political and Constitutional Reform. Written evidence had also been received – from 24 different people.

From then onwards, the Committee held its deliberations regularly until the end of February 2012. Mark Harper appeared again before the Committee on 17 October 2011. Distinguished public figures had agreed to give oral evidence on the appointed dates:

- 24 October 2011: Professor Vernon Bogdanor (King's College London); Rt Hon. Peter Riddell (Institute of Government); Professor Dawn Oliver (master treasurer of the Middle Temple).
- 31 October 2011: Dr Meg Russell (Constitution Unit, University College, London); Dr Alan Renwick (University of Reading); Professor Sir John Baker QC, and David Howarth (University of Cambridge).
- 7 November 2011: Mark Harper MP again (minister for Political and Constitutional Reform).

- 14 November 2011: Ms Katie Ghose (Electoral Reform Society); Professor David Denver (University of Lancaster); Professor John Curtice (University of Strathclyde).
- 21 November 2011: Mr Peter Facey, and Ms Alexandra Runswick (Unlock Democracy); Lord Jay of Ewelme, and Mr Richard Jarvis (House of Lords Appointments Commission).
- 22 November 2011: Senator Lee Rhiannon (senator for New South Wales and one of the Australian 'Greens'); Senator the Hon Michael Ronaldson (senator for Victoria, from the Liberal Party); Senator the Hon Ursula Stephens (senator for New South Wales, and from the Labour Party).
- 28 November 2011: Most Rev. and Rt Hon. Rowan Williams (Archbishop of Canterbury); Andrew Copson (chief executive, British Humanist Association); Elizabeth Hunter (director, Theos).
- 5 December 2011: Lord Adonis and Lord Carter of Barnes.
- 12 December 2011: Professor Ian Kennedy, and Dr Andrew McDonald (Independent Parliamentary Standards Authority); Sir Christopher Kelly, and Peter Hawthorne (Committee on Standards in Public Life).
- 19 December 2011: Dr Alan Renwick (reader in Comparative Politics, University of Reading); Professor Iain Mclean (professor of Politics, Nuffield College, University of Oxford).
- 16 January 2012: Damien Welfare, and Daniel Zeichner (Campaign for a Democratic Upper House); Lord Cormack, and Rt Hon. Paul Murphy MP (Campaign for an Effective Second Chamber); Rt Hon. Baroness Hayman.
- 23 January 2012: David Beamish (clerk of the Parliaments); Mr Graham Allen MP (chair, Political and Constitutional Reform Committee); Robert Rogers (clerk of the House); Jacqy Sharpe (clerk of Legislation).
- 30 January 2012: Lord Pannick; Rt Hon. Lord Cunningham of Felling; Rt Hon. Lord Grocott; Rt Hon. David Blunkett MP.
- 27 February 2012: Rt Hon. Nick Clegg MP (deputy prime minister); Mr Mark Harper MP (minister for Political and Constitutional Reform).

The texts of these interviews were later published.[29] The Joint Committee also received written evidence from 105 prominent individuals, as well as from various organizations such as the All-Party Parliamentary Humanist Group, the London Buddhist Vihara, the Democratic Audit, the Electoral Commission, the Fawcett Society, the Federation of Muslim Organizations, the Green Party, the Hansard Society, the Council of the Law Society of Scotland, the Muslim Council of Britain, the National Assembly for Wales, the National Secular Society, North Yorkshire for Democracy, the Northern Ireland Assembly, the Programme for Public Participation in Parliament and the Zoroastrian Trust Funds of Europe. This evidence is also available in print.[30] It tended to be repetitive and it is doubtful whether the Joint Committee became much wiser after hearing or reading all the evidence submitted. But it is worth citing here a few examples from the oral evidence.

On 21 November 2011, for instance, the following gave evidence: Peter Facey (director of Unlock Democracy); Alexandra Runswick (deputy director of Unlock Democracy); Lord Jay of Ewelme (chairman of the House of Lords Appointments Commission). Facey and Runswick were interviewed first and had this to say:[31]

> PETER FACEY: You cannot get expertise through election. Government Ministers should be able to speak in the House of Lords, but they should not be its members. The electoral system should be such as would allow independents to be elected and [which] weakens the power of the party Whip. A directly elected or predominantly elected second Chamber would be more assertive.

---

29 *Ibid.*, volume II: *Oral and associated written evidence* (23 April 2012). HL Paper 284-II; HC 1313-II.

30 *Ibid.*, volume III: *Other written evidence* (23 April 2012). HL Paper 284-III; HC 1313-III.

31 A valuable source is 'Uncorrected transcripts of oral evidence. Minutes of Evidence taken before the Joint Committee on the Draft House of Lords Reform Bill', which Lord Hennessy of Nympsfield so kindly made available to the present author.

ALEXANDRA RUNSWICK: We would rather have a fully elected Chamber.

Then Lord Jay of Ewelme spoke on the role of the Lords Appointments Commission. Its primary role was to 'recommend independent Members of the House of Lords for appointment to the Cross Benches. In line with our published criteria, we recommend people based on their merit and ability to contribute to the work of the House of Lords'. The commission's secondary role was in 'vetting for propriety people who are recommended for peerages, including those put forward by the political parties'.

On 22 November 2011 Lee Rhiannon, Michael Ronaldson and Ursula Stephens, members of the Australian Senate, were interviewed via a video/ telephone link:

> RONALDSON: Our Senate can reject any legislation [...] if you do not have that power I am not sure how your 300 full-time Members are going to be controlled, for want of a better word, when they are there to deal and review the legislation.

> STEPHENS: [The strongest role of the Australian Senate] is often in moderating the Bill or improving the drafting by suggesting amendments that give legislation coherence. [Much of] our work is quite collaborative, consensual and agreeable.

> RHIANNON: [When] I was growing up, the House of Lords did not have a good name for itself among many people in a place like Australia, because you were not elected. When I heard that you were working on reform, I was extremely impressed. I think that it will enhance the democratic process and bring greater confidence to people that they have opportunities to engage with their elected representatives, which is so important.

On 28 November 2011, the Archbishop of Canterbury, the Most Rev. Rowan Williams, addressed the Committee, along with Andrew Copson (the chief executive of the British Humanist Association and Elizabeth Hunter (the director of Theos):

THE ARCHBISHOP: We would accept the need for a proportionate reduction. [A second Chamber should be so composed as to] ensure true and impartial accountability, scrutinising and revising government legislation with a degree of independence not possible in the House of Commons. [It is] doubtfully likely that an entirely elected or almost entirely elected second Chamber [would secure those objectives. An elected second Chamber runs the risk of being] in competition with the first Chamber in terms of legitimacy, especially if the second Chamber is elected by a method, the single transferable vote.

HUNTER: We believe that having religious voices in a reformed second Chamber is well within the logic of the draft Bill.

COPSON: We are against Bishops or any religious representatives *ex officio*, as of right having a place in a reformed House of Lords.

On 5 December 2011 it was the turn of Lord Adonis and Lord Carter of Barnes to appear:

CARTER: To have a mechanism to allow a Prime Minister to appoint Ministers to the second Chamber can bring a level of knowledge and expertise in areas that the electoral system may not necessarily throw up, so one hopes that it augments the skills set in Government. [It may be imprecise, and it] is certainly not democratic, but it is strangely effective, which is a reasonable description of the House of Lords.

ADONIS: I take the view that people who make the law should be elected – period.

On 19 December 2011 the Committee heard Dr Alan Renwick and Professor Iain McLean:[32]

32 The Joint Committee separately received a substantial paper on electoral system options prepared by Dr Alan Renwick and Professor Iain Mclean, 'Electoral System Options' (11 January 2012). Source: *Joint Committee on the Draft House of Lords*

RENWICK: [There are four important points when] we are thinking about the choice between the single transferable vote [STV]
and the open list system. [One is] the degree to which voters can
express a choice or preference among candidates. [The second is]
the degree to which those preferences actually make a difference
to who gets elected from within political parties. [The third is]
the likelihood of electing people who are entirely independent of
political parties. [And the fourth:] diversity within the Chamber
[...] 'you are more likely to get independents – people who are
independent entirely of party – under STV'.

MCLEAN: [STV] is more candidate-centred and open list is relatively more party-centred. [If it were] a matter of concern to ensure
that candidates entirely independent of party were elected, then
STV would probably be more appropriate.

Perhaps the most vivid and realistic approach towards 'speedy action' on
reform of the House of Lords was suggested by Baroness Hayman. She was
examined as witness on 16 January 2012. The size of the House, she said,
was 'unsustainable':[33]

BARONESS HAYMAN: [We are] operating with a size of House
that does not function properly and which I think is indefensible.
We need to do something about the size of the House and I believe
that we could get agreement on that. [It should be] possible to get
agreement on the balance between independent Peers and party-
political Peers in terms of proportion, [and on the] view that the
hereditary principle should not play any part in the future membership, [and thus to end the link between the honours system
and membership of the second Chamber. It would be possible

Reform Bill, volume I: *Report*, together with appendices and formal minutes.
Appendix 6 (23 April 2012). HL Paper 284-I; HC 1313-I.

33   See 'Minutes of Evidence taken before the Joint Committee on the Draft House of
Lords Reform Bill'. Uncorrected transcript of oral evidence, 16 January 2012, pp. 58–9.

to] deal with the issue of time limits for appointments – that is, time limited appointments, and to deal with the establishment and remit of the statutory Appointments and with provisions for retirement and exclusion. [One could start with] a moratorium on new Peers; and, if we did those things and cleared that undergrowth, the issue of whether what you gain in democratic legitimacy from election outweighs what you lose in terms of experience and expertise could be considered, as well as focusing democratic accountability in one place – the clarity that we have at the moment and the complementarity of the two Houses.[34]

The Committee's Report and Its Recommendations

The last interview took place on 27 February 2012, when Nick Clegg and Mark Harper gave witness. The Joint Committee then adjourned until 5 March. At this last meeting a full draft Report was presented by the chairman, Lord Richard. The Joint Committee met on 7, 12, 14, 19, 21 and 26 March 2012 to deliberate on it. Each paragraph of the draft was considered separately and thoroughly gone through. Points were amended where necessary and until agreed to. The Committee divided many times.[35] Finally it

---

34 At this time a variety of proposals appeared in the press. For instance, John Longworth suggested that the appointments process should be strengthened. See 'Our House: Reflections on Representation and Reform in the House of Lords' (*ResPublica*, 29 February 2012); for an interesting analysis of the composition and representation in the House of Lords, see Hugh Bochel and Andrew Defty, 'A More Representative Chamber: Representation and the House of Lords', *Journal of Legislative Studies*, 15 February 2012; on the composition of second chambers throughout the world and how they function, see Meg Russell, 'Elected Second Chambers and their Powers', *Political Quarterly*, 6 February 2012; Beatrice Ferguson warned against such reform as might eventually change the Lords from 'complementation' to 'competition'. See her 'Complementary Reform in the House of Lords?' (*ResPublica* Blog, 8 March 2012).

35 For details, see *Joint Committee on the Draft House of Lords Reform Bill*, volume I: *Report*, together with appendices and formal minutes (23 April 2012), pp. 148–64.

was ordered 'that Report be made by Lord Richard to the House of Lords and by Mr Tom Clarke to the House of Commons'. The Joint Committee then adjourned. Both Houses of Parliament ordered that the Report be printed on 26 March. It was published on 23 April 2012. The Report gave a full analysis of the oral and written evidence, and made recommendations. The Report was not anonymous, and we often find it recorded that the Committee only agreed 'on a majority'.

Here, in brief, are the main recommendations.[36] The Joint Committee agreed:

(i)   that the 'reformed second chamber of legislation should have an electoral mandate provided it has commensurate powers';

(ii)   that 'a reformed House should perform, but not be constrained by, the functions of the present House of Lords';

(iii) that the primacy of the House of Commons should be preserved. (Although some members believed that, following election, the balance of power would shift in favour of the House of Lords, a majority of the Committee did not 'advocate any proposals for making statutory provision to entrench the Commons primacy');

(iv)   that, following any reform, 'the two Houses will need to establish a means of defining and agreeing the conventions governing the relationship between [them], thereafter keeping them under review';

(v)   that the government's proposal for an 80 per cent elected and 20 per cent appointed House was reasonable as a 'means of preserving expertise and placing its mandate on a different footing from that of the Commons'. (Some members preferred a fully appointed House);

(vi)   that a House of 300 members was too small (the Committee favoured a House of 450 members);

(vii) that a form of proportional representation for elections should be used;

36   For details, see *Ibid.*, pp. 97–108.

(viii)   that the government's proposal for non-renewable terms was acceptable;

(ix)   that a 15-year term was plausible;

(x)   that elections to both Houses of Parliament should be held at the same time;

(xi)   that a recall mechanism 'would be an appropriate way to ensure elected members can be held accountable by the electorate in exceptional circumstances';

(xii)   that by-elections should not be used to fill vacant seats;

(xiii)   that it would be 'inappropriate for elected members to involve themselves in personal casework of the kind currently undertaken by MPs on behalf of their constituents';

(xiv)   that the Appointments Commission 'should be placed on a statutory footing';

(xv)   that a reformed House should 'continue to contain Ministers of the Crown to represent the government';

(xvi)   that there should be 'no reserved places for bishops' in a fully elected House (but the Committee agreed, on a majority, with the government's proposal that the number of reserved seats for bishops be set at 12);

(xvii)   that the Appointments Commission, when recommending individuals for appointment, should consider inclusion of the major faiths;

(xviii)   that the House of Lords should itself be 'responsible for establishing the selection of transitional members';

(xix)   that the Independent Parliamentary Standards Authority (IPSA) should determine the level of salary and allowances;

(xx)   that elected members should be subject to the same 'disqualification regime' as members of the House of Commons;

(xxi)   that the new House should use its power 'responsibly' to expel or suspend its members;

(xxii)   that the dispute resolutions should be a matter for the two Houses of Parliament, and not for the courts;

(xxiii)   that the government should submit the constitutional changes to a referendum.

The 'Alternative Report'

An 'Alternative Report' also appeared on 23 April 2012. Its authors had also been members of the Joint Committee.[37] The Alternative Report could not be called a 'minority report' because, according to the rules of the *Companion*, the Select Committees of the House of Lords cannot publish minority reports. The Alternative Report thus had no official binding. The following were its the authors:

> Baroness Andrews
> Tom Clarke MP
> Oliver Heald MP
> Lord Hennessy of Nympsfield
> Eleanor Laing MP
> Tim Stevens, Bishop of Leicester
> Lord Norton of Louth
> Lord Rooker
> Baroness Shephard of Northwold
> Baroness Symons of Vernham Dean
> Lord Trefgarne
> Lord Trimble

All of these people had also signed the Report of the Joint Committee. It is therefore strange that this group should have felt it necessary to issue a separate report. We summarise the intentions of the group.

The report begins with a summary of the Joint Committee's Report, and then highlights areas with which the signatories agree or disagree. The reader is then told that the Joint Committee's Report 'has not proved to be the right or even an adequate vehicle to consider comprehensively further reform of the House of Lords'. Therefore an alternative approach was needed which 'is comprehensive, inclusive, not based around the policy

---

37   *House of Lords Reform: An Alternative Way Forward. A Report by Members of the Joint Committee of Both Houses of Parliament on the Government's Draft House of Lords Reform Bill* (April 2012).

prescriptions of one particular participant in the debate, stands apart from party politics and gives full consideration to the complexity of the issues involved in such a major constitutional change as moving to an elected House of Lords'.[38]

It is difficult to understand why the signatories felt that the Joint Committee had 'not proved to be the right' body to consider reform, after so many experts had made such a valuable contribution to its work. Why was it necessary to set up a new Joint Committee on Conventions, as was suggested by the Alternative Report? Would this not delay reform even further? Moreover, its terms of reference were not only abstract, but repetitive and superfluous.

The authors of the Alternative Report believed:[39]

(i)   that 'a better vehicle for consideration of further reform of the House of Lords would be a Constitutional Convention';

(ii)   that the purpose of such a Constitutional Convention would be 'either to draw up a new constitution, or to modify an existing constitution, or existing constitutional arrangements';

(iii)   that a Constitutional Convention should 'include both the government and parliamentarians, from both Houses of Parliament, but should not be confined to them';

(iv)   that the purpose of the Convention should be 'clear from the beginning: to consider, in depth, the issues involved in further reform of the House of Lords, and to bring forward proposals';

(v)   that the issues involved should include 'the impact on the House of Commons of any reform of the House of Lords, the method of any elections to the House of Lords, including indirect elections, the relationship between the two Houses of Parliament, the impact of reform on the devolved assemblies, and the impact on Parliament';

---

38   *Ibid.*, p. 71.
39   For details see *Ibid.*, pp. 70–89.

(vi)   that a Constitutional Convention 'should be established with the ability to continue, if necessary beyond any changes in government, in order to allow it to concentrate properly on the constitutional and other issues involved in further reform of the House of Lords';

(vii)   that the Constitutional Convention should be 'properly and fully staffed and resourced on a continuing basis until its conclusion';

(viii) that a final report of the Constitutional Convention should be 'put to the people of the United Kingdom in a determinative referendum'.

The Alternative Report repeated the same points that had been the subject of discussion so often in the past. Lord Richard rightly remarked that he saw 'no virtue whatever' in setting up a Constitutional Convention, merely to 'reiterate the differences which already exist and which we all know about'.[40]

Debate in the House of Lords

On 30 April 2012, the Report of the Joint Committee came before the House of Lords, where it received devastating criticism. Lord Richard moved that 'this House takes note of the report from the Joint Committee on the draft House of Lords Reform Bill'.[41] He told the House how the Joint Committee had proceeded with its work and what it had achieved. The Committee had had to consider in detail the bill with its 68 clauses and nine schedules together with a lengthy White Paper. It had heard evidence

40   *Parliamentary Debates*, House of Lords, vol. DCCXXXVI (Part I), 30 April 2012, col.1942.

41   *Ibid.*, 30 April 2012, col. 1938.

from 20 witnesses and had received 227 written submissions of evidence. The Committee had held lengthy sessions, and had been much divided in its deliberations. There had been divisions 'within parties and within the Houses. There was no clearly visible Labour view versus a Conservative view. There was no clear Lords view versus a Commons view. Opinions inevitably differed.'[42] Lord Richard then described the issues on which the members of the Committee had agreed and those on which they had disagreed. There was only one issue on which the Committee had been unanimous – its view that Clause 2 of the Draft Bill was of 'little use and should be discarded'. The Committee felt that this clause was only 'declaratory' and 'risked becoming justiciable'. Lord Richard concluded by defending the work of the Joint Committee: '[We have] produced a better Bill as a result of our deliberations.' He begged to move his motion.

The debate in the Lords lasted for two days.[43] The chancellor of the Duchy of Lancaster, Lord Strathclyde, said that the Joint Committee had 'produced a detailed and comprehensive report which will undoubtedly leave its mark on the Government's final proposals'. There were indeed differences of opinion, but there was only one way to test whether consensus on reform of 'this House exists or can emerge, and that is to introduce a Bill and then to allow Parliament to take a view'.

Baroness Royall of Blaisdon wondered what the government's answer was when it was described as incompetent. Lords reform was an important issue, but the idea that it was the 'most pressing issue facing the country is risible'. Anyway, several members on all sides of the House were 'not in favour of this House having an electoral mandate'. It would be much better for the government to accept that a constitutional change of 'this level of importance' required a referendum. The baroness welcomed the idea of a Constitutional Convention. She supported Lord Steel's bill and the proposals that had been made by Baroness Hayman.

Baroness Scott of Needham Market regretted that the House had become 'more confrontational and less courteous'. Debate was 'more

---

42 *Ibid.*, col. 1939.
43 *Ibid.*, 30 April 2012, cols 1937–2001, 2013–80; 1 May 2012, cols. 2081–2113.

partisan and the majority of votes are cast along party lines. At some point in the future, having a political house with no equivalent electoral mandate is going to cause us a problem.'

Lord Hennessy of Nympsfield maintained that, in every 'generation or so, we take a crack at the question of Lords reform. We throw the particles in the air and hope that, this time, they will fall on a way that paves a path on the road to consensus. Once again, we have failed'. Over those 30 meetings of the Joint Committee, the noble lord confessed, there 'was not a flicker of consensus'. He believed that the 'ingredients of a substantial reform are lying at our feet. Let us pick them up, fashion them into something coherent, something valuable, and let us implement that bundle of reforms before the next general election.'

The Bishop of Leicester contended that the House had before it a bill 'predicated on the encouragement of greater assertiveness by an elected upper House yet one so circumscribed by the electoral proposals and so dependent on the Parliament Act that a reformed upper House would soon either find itself frustrated in its attempts to behave representatively or [would] assert its determination to test the present conventions to breaking point. Either way, the risks are considerable.'

Lord Norton of Louth said the bill was 'fundamentally hampered in two respects. The first was that the Government presented us with a Bill of which we had the detail but for which we had no justification. Assessing the Bill on the Government's own terms is not possible if the Government make no attempt to say what they are.'

Baroness Symons of Vernham Dean regretted that the Draft Bill and White Paper offered a 'misleading prospectus for change'. What was 'not logical or sustainable [was] to argue that Commons primacy and the current relationship between the two Houses will be unchanged'. In an elected House the members would be 'expected to exercise a mandate' on behalf of electors. 'Why should an elected Peer subjugate the wishes of his or her electorate to those of an elected MP? What is the logic of continuing Commons primacy after the Lords is elected?'

Lord Ashdown of Norton-sub-Hamdon argued that it was 'essential now' to elect a second chamber democratically. The fundamental principle of a democratic state was that the 'people's laws should be made by the people's representatives'. The House presently was a 'creature of the Executive', a creature of patronage. There were only 'two ways to get into this place. One is because you are a friend of the Prime Minister, or at least he does not object to you, and the other is because your great-grandmother slept with the king'.

Lord Trefgarne found the last remark 'offensive'. He must, he said, challenge it. He was 'the second Lord Trefgarne; my father was the first Lord Trefgarne. He was a Liberal MP.'

Lord Ashdown retorted: 'He came here by an act of patronage, then, which is the point I was seeking to make.' He was, he said, in favour of a 'fully elected second Chamber'. But it should be 'supported by a referendum'.

The Earl of Sandwich said that he did not see elections to 'this House as a necessary route to legitimacy or democracy. I am among those reformists who value and cherish the traditions of this House and the practices of our revising Chamber as they are now.' However, there were 'positive reforms' that could be enacted following the work done by Lord Steel and Baroness Hayman.

Lord Trimble said that he was committed to the Alternative Report.

Lord Dubs welcomed the fact that the Joint Committee report supported elections, yet he was not happy about being elected once for 15 years. That seemed to 'undermine the basic principle of accountability'. And he was worried about the idea of a Constitutional Convention. That was 'a recipe for long delays'.

Lord Willoughby de Broke said that he was 'grateful to the members of the committee that produced the excellent alternative report', and that he was 'attracted' by the conclusions in this document.

Lord Cormack argued that, at present, the House of Commons and the House of Lords were complementary to each other; but, if 'we had two elected Chambers, they would be in competition with each other. If we were to move to that undesirable state, surely the people must have the ultimate decision. How fatuous to wave the flag of democracy but say, *You can't have a vote on it*. That is the ultimate insult to the British people, and up with that we should not put!'

Lord Grenfell said that he admired 'the extraordinary achievement of the Joint Committee and its chairman'. The 'fruits of nine months' hard work are impressive. As a piece of pre-legislative scrutiny, it fulfils the requirements of rigour, comprehensiveness, focus, careful argument and a clarity that contrasts starkly with the Draft Bill and the White Paper into which it inquired.' Yet the immediate conclusion he drew from reading the report was that the Draft Bill 'as a vehicle for reforming your Lordships' House is not fit for purpose'.

Lord Low of Dalston thought that Lord Steel's bill and other similar proposals would attract widespread support in the House.

Lord Lipsey complained that the Joint Committee had put no costs on its proposals, although Lord Richard had said that 'we will not get a second Chamber for free'. The government, he complained, would not 'tell us' the exact cost for reform. He thought that this was done on purpose, because the costs were so enormous. That too was why the government resisted a referendum. The government knew that 'the chances of the public voting yes to reform will melt like a snowball in the midsummer sun once people understand the bill that they will have to pay for this folly. In this age of austerity, does anyone seriously believe that the public will agree to hand huge chunks of their hard-earned money to a whole new gang of second-rate elected politicians?'

Lord Trefgarne believed 'with complete conviction' that, if 'we move to a wholly or largely elected second Chamber, the new House will straightaway use its existing powers more aggressively and very soon be agitating for more'. The primacy 'will move measurably away from the House of Commons' to the new House.

Lord Brooke of Alverthorpe argued that 'we need a dispute resolution procedure beyond that which has been presented by the Government'.

Lord MacGregor of Pulham Market said that he 'strongly supported' the proposals made by Lord Steel and Baroness Hayman.

Lord Thomas of Gresford said that he opposed a referendum. In Britain we 'do not govern by referenda. We expect our legislators to take on the responsibility of making difficult decisions. A referendum is not an exercise in democracy but a way of passing the buck, which this report proposes to do.' And 'no matter how many people voted for a bad idea, it is still a bad idea'.

Lord Desai maintained that, if we 'want to preserve the primacy of the House of Commons, we must spell out what that primacy consists of and establish it by statute, because nothing can be taken for granted in an unwritten constitution whereby one Parliament can change what another Parliament does'.

The Earl of Clancarty suggested that the possibility of recording abstentions must be considered. This could be done through a Standing Order. That would make Parliament more transparent.

Lord Crickhowell said that there was no consensus about the way to reform the House of Lords. In that situation, it would be 'political madness and deeply unsound constitutional practice' were the government to commit itself to the 'introduction of the same Bill or one closely similar'.

Lord Hoyle wished to put himself 'firmly on the side of reform and an elected House'.

Lord Williamson of Horton had no doubt that the bill would have 'one tremendously important consequence: it would bring to an end the House of Commons' monopoly in democratic legitimacy. That is just the most fundamental change that could happen to the first Chamber of a Parliament.'

The debate on this day went on past 6 p.m., and was resumed the following morning, 1 May 2012, at 10 a.m.

Lord Forsyth of Drumlean spoke first. He wondered whether their lordships remembered Austin Allegro, the 'worst car ever built'. It was 'completely unreliable, it had a totally underpowered engine, and its big selling feature was that it had a square steering wheel. This car was designed by the management for political reasons. They ignored the people who knew about cars and design and it was meant to save British Leyland. It was the management's answer. In fact, they were so convinced that it would save the company that it was nicknamed *the flying pig*.' It seemed to him that 'the Bill, which has been so comprehensively filleted by the Joint Committee' had 'many similarities to the Austin Allegro'. 'Reform', as proposed there, was, he thought, the 'wrong word'. It was actually 'the abolition of this House' and also the 'destruction' of the House of Commons.

Baroness Taylor of Bolton said she would prefer a 'unicameral system to a confrontational system'. She was also against 'proportional representation, which will always lead to post-election deals that no one has voted for'. And if the 'will of unelected Senators outvotes the will of the elected

Senators, how does that enhance democracy?' Also democracy was about 'more than just the vote: it is about accountability. What accountability is there for a Senator who is elected for 15 years and cannot seek re-election? What sanction does the electorate have? It is utter nonsense.'

Lord Tyler thought that the conclusions of the Joint Committee had been 'misinterpreted'. Perhaps a further pre-legislative scrutiny was needed.

Lord Kakkar argued that it would be 'unwise to proceed with the creation of an elected second Chamber unless the important issue of the powers of the two Chambers, how disputes are to be resolved, the potential role that the Supreme Court may play in resolving disputes, and therefore how Parliament may be secured as sovereign in future, are properly defined before a Bill is brought for further scrutiny before this Parliament'.

Lord True believed that election would certainly change the relations between the Houses. An elected member with a mandate 'will not wish to be restrained'; and it was 'equally absurd to say [that an elected peer] would not respond in a representative capacity; of course he would.'

Baroness Andrews explained that 'our disagreements' in the Joint Committee were 'indeed all about principle, not perversity'. The principle concerned the primacy of the House of Commons and the 'positive obligation that MPs have to their electors – that is, the principle and the power of the unique mandate held by Members of Parliament'. It was felt that an electoral mandate 'with commensurate powers rips up these foundations. Who can predict which Chamber would prevail? The result would be a Parliament divided against itself, uncertain of where power might lie and locked into its own internal battles'.

Baroness Young of Hornsey said she remained 'convinced of the principle of election, at least for the majority of the House'.

Lord Hunt of Kings Heath said that he supported an elected House. But this must not be 'at the expense of primacy of the Commons, nor must it threaten gridlock or detract from our role as an effective revising Chamber'.

Lord Wallace of Saltaire suggested that if 'we are to seek consensus, compromise is part of the way that may lead to a consensus'. '[We] cannot 'preserve the current House in aspic; it will continue to change and evolve.' Reform of the House should 'contribute to redressing the balance of power between the Executive and the legislature as a whole'.

Lord Richard wound up what had been a long debate. Various themes, he noted, had been 'explored, and explored and explored. We went down various avenues, and avenues and avenues. I am no wiser at the end of the debate than I was at the beginning, although a great deal of argumentation was displayed.' Personally, he simply wanted to say, 'calmly and quietly', that he rejected the suggestion that:

> The constitution we want in this country is one in which the House of Commons is basically a unicameral legislature and this House merely an advisory House to the Commons. I do not agree with that. I have always believed that this should be a proper, functioning House of Parliament, not merely an advisory council, there to give advice that the Government may in their wisdom or ignorance choose to accept or reject. This is meant to be functioning, legislative House of Parliament. We are a vital part of the legislature and we should never let go of that fact.[44]

Lord Richard then begged to move. This motion was agreed, and the House adjourned.

The government took note of the criticisms voiced and considered suggested improvements to the draft. Some changes were indeed made, and the final text of the bill was now prepared to be introduced in the House of Commons. Later events showed that these changes, though unsatisfactory, were accepted by the House of Commons at first, but that they then so violated the feelings of the Tory MPs that the government was forced to withdraw the bill altogether.

44 *Ibid.*, 1 May 2012, col. 2113.

CHAPTER SEVENTEEN

2012. The Coalition Government's House of Lords Reform Bill

At the House of Lords debate on 30 April 2012, Baroness Miller of Hendon had said that she awaited to 'see whether the Government will be rash enough to introduce the defective House of Lords Reform Bill, which has received absolutely no unequivocal support from the committee set up to consider it'; would it be 'stupid enough to do so'?[1] Lord Crickhowell had expressed himself in a similar tone, saying that it would be 'political madness and deeply unsound constitutional practice' were the government to press on with the bill.[2]

Their fears were soon realized. Ready to be 'rash', 'unsound' and 'stupid', the government went ahead. Its House of Lords Reform Bill – 'To make provision about the membership of the House of Lords; to make provision about the disclaimer of life peerages; to abolish the jurisdiction of the House of Lords in relation to peerage claims; to make other provision relating to peerage; and for connected purposes' – was presented by the deputy prime minister, supported by the prime minister, the first secretary of state, William Hague, the chancellor of the exchequer, George Osborne, the secretary of state for justice, Kenneth Clarke, the secretary of state for Scotland, Michael Moore, Danny Alexander, Sir George Young and Mr Mark Harper. It was to be printed on 27 June 2012 and was introduced in the House of Commons on 9 July by the deputy prime minister, Nick Clegg.[3]

1   *Parliamentary Debates*, House of Lords, vol. DCXXXVI (Part I), 30 April 2012, col. 1992.
2   *Ibid.*, col. 1997.
3   *Parliamentary Debates*, House of Commons, vol. 548(I), col. 24.

Text of the Bill

BILL[4]

To

Make provision about the membership of the House of Lords; to make provision about the disclaimer of life peerages; to abolish the jurisdiction of the House of Lords in relation to peerage claims; to make other provision relating to peerage; and for connected purposes.

BE IT ENACTED by the Queen's most Excellent Majesty, by and with the advice and consent of the Lords Spiritual and Temporal, and Commons, in this present Parliament assembled, and by the authority of the same, as follows:

PART 1
COMPOSITION OF THE HOUSE OF LORDS

1 Composition of the House of Lords

(1) In the first electoral period the House of Lords is to consist of –

    (a) 120 elected members,
    (b) 30 appointed members,
    (c) up to 21 Lords Spiritual,
    (d) any ministerial members, and
    (e) the transitional members for that period.

(2) In the second electoral period the House of Lords is to consist of –

    (a) 240 elected members,
    (b) 60 appointed members,

---

4   House of Lords Reform Bill 52. Our text has left out: Explanatory Notes, Table of Contents; and tables attached to: Clause 31(3), p. 16, Clause 33(3), p. 17, and Clause 55(1).

(c) up to 16 Lords Spiritual,

(d) any ministerial members, and

(e) the transitional members for that period.

(3) In each subsequent electoral period the House of Lords is to consist of –

(a) 360 elected members,

(b) 90 appointed members,

(c) up to 12 Lords Spiritual, and

(d) any ministerial members.

(4) Accordingly, no-one is a member of the House of Lords by virtue of a peerage.

(5) In this Act 'electoral period' means a period which –

(a) begins immediately after the day of a House of Lords election, and

(b) ends with the day of the next House of Lords election.

2 Continued application of the Parliament Acts

(1) The Parliament Acts 1911 and 1949 continue to apply after the beginning of the first electoral period, despite the changes to the House of Lords made by this Act.

(2) The preamble to the Parliament Act 1911 is repealed.

PART 2
ELECTED MEMBERS
House of Lords elections

3 House of Lords elections

(1) A House of Lords election is to be held whenever there is a qualifying House of Commons general election.

(2) The polling day for the House of Lords election is to be the same as the polling day for the qualifying House of Commons general election.

(3) The qualifying House of Commons general elections are –

(a) the first House of Commons general election the polling day for which is on or after 7 May 2015, and

(b) any subsequent House of Commons general election except one whose polling day is within the period of 2 years beginning with the day of the previous qualifying House of Commons general election.

(4) Writs for a House of Lords election are to be sealed and issued –

(a) as soon as practicable after the dissolution, by section 3(1) of the Fixed Term Parliaments Act 2011, of the last Parliament before the election, and

(b) in accordance with the practice in relation to writs for House of Commons general elections; but this is subject to any provision made under section 7 (power to make provision about elections).

(5) In this Act any reference to the day of a House of Lords election is to the polling day for the election determined in accordance with subsection (2).

4 Ordinary elected members and the electoral districts

(1) At each House of Lords election, 120 persons are to be returned as ordinary elected members.

(2) Each of them is to be returned as an ordinary elected member for an electoral district.

(3) The electoral districts are specified in Schedule 1.

(4) Schedule 2 specifies how many of the 120 persons mentioned in subsection (1) are to be returned for each electoral district.

(5) The returning officer for an electoral district must notify the Clerk of the Crown of –

(a) the name of each person returned as an ordinary elected member for that district, and

(b) the return day in respect of each such person.

(6) A person returned at a House of Lords election as an ordinary elected member is such a member for the first 3 electoral periods to occur after the day of that election, excluding –

(a) any period before the return day, and

(b) the dissolution period in the last of those electoral periods.

5 Voting system

(1) At a House of Lords election, an election is to be held in each of the electoral districts.

(2) The election in an electoral district is for the total number of elected members who are to be returned at that election for that district.

(3) That number is –

(a) the number of ordinary elected members specified in Schedule 2 in respect of the district, and

(b) such number of persons as may be required under section 8 to be returned as replacement elected members for the district.

(4) Schedule 3 contains provision about the system of election in Great Britain (which is a list system).

(5) The system of election in Northern Ireland is a single transferable vote system under which –

(a) a vote is capable of being given so as to indicate the voter's order of preference for the candidates for election, and

(b) a vote is capable of being transferred to the next choice –

(i) when the vote is not required to give a prior choice the necessary quota of votes, or

(ii) when, owing to the deficiency in the number of votes given for a prior choice, that choice is eliminated from the list of candidates.

(6) At a House of Lords election –

(a) a person may not be a candidate in more than one electoral district;

(b) an elected member may not be a candidate.

6 Entitlement to vote

(1) At a House of Lords election, a person is entitled to vote in
an electoral district if, on the day of the poll in that district –

(a) the person would be entitled to vote at a House of
Commons election in a parliamentary constituency
wholly or partly comprised in the electoral district, and

(b) the person has a qualifying address.

(2) A person has a qualifying address if –

(a) the address in respect of which the person is registered in
the relevant register of parliamentary electors is within
the electoral district, or

(b) the person's registration in the relevant register of parliamentary electors results from an overseas elector's
declaration which specifies an address within the electoral district.

(3) At a House of Lords election, a person is not entitled to vote
more than once.

(4) References in this section to voting are to voting as an
elector.

7 Power to make provision about elections

(1) The Minister may by order make provision about the conduct of House of Lords elections or other matters relating to
such elections.

(2) In particular, an order under subsection (1) may make
provision –

(a) about the registration of electors;

(b) about the designation of persons as returning officers,
and local returning officers, for each electoral district;

(c) conferring functions on those officers;

(d) about the recovery of charges by those officers in respect of services rendered, or expenses incurred, by them;

(e) requiring local authorities to place the services of their officers or employees at the disposal of returning officers or local returning officers for the purpose of assisting them;

(f) for the combination of polls at House of Lords elections with polls at other elections or at referendums;

(g) about funding and expenditure, in relation to House of Lords elections, of candidates, political parties and other persons (including the provision of free postal services to candidates);

(h) for limiting the number of persons who may be nominated as candidates for election in the name of a party in an electoral district to the number of elected members to be returned for that district in the election;

(i) about the way in which the names of candidates and parties appear on the ballot paper;

(j) for the postponement of the poll in an electoral district due to the death of a candidate or other exceptional circumstances;

(k) for the allocation of seats in Northern Ireland in the case of an equality of votes;

(l) conferring on candidates a right to choose not to be returned as a replacement elected member;

(m) for the allocation of seats where such a choice is made or where more than one replacement elected member is to be returned;

(n) about the questioning of House of Lords elections and the consequences of irregularities.

(3) An order under subsection (1) may –

(a) apply, or incorporate, with or without modifications, any provision of primary or secondary legislation;

(b) modify any provision made by or under the Representation of the People Acts, the Political Parties,

Elections and Referendums Act 2000 or the Electoral Administration Act 2006;

(c) modify any provision of primary or secondary legislation which is a provision relating to a House of Commons election;

(d) modify Part 7 (disqualification);

(e) create criminal offences.

(4) An order under subsection (1) may provide for sums to be charged on, and paid out of, the Consolidated Fund in relation to –

(a) the provision of training relating to functions of returning officers or local returning officers;

(b) the recovery of charges by such officers in respect of services rendered, or expenses incurred, by them;

(c) the provision of free postal services to candidates.

(5) The return of an elected member at a House of Lords election may be questioned only in accordance with provision made under this section (whether by the application or incorporation of Part 3 of the Representation of the People Act 1983 or otherwise).

(6) In this section 'local authority' means –

(a) a county or district council in England;

(b) a London borough council;

(c) the Greater London Authority;

(d) the Council of the Isles of Scilly;

(e) a county or county borough council in Wales;

(f) a council constituted under section 2 of the Local Government etc (Scotland) Act 1994;

(g) a district council constituted under section 1 of the Local Government Act (Northern Ireland) 1972.

Filling vacancies

8 Interim replacement elected members and replacement elected members

(1) This section applies where, before the end of the expected term ('the expected term') of a person returned as an elected member, the Clerk of the Parliaments certifies that –

(a) the return is void, or

(b) the person has ceased to be an elected member, and, accordingly, that the member's seat is vacant.

(2) The seat is to be filled as follows –

(a) subject to subsection (5) and Schedule 4, a person is to be returned in accordance with that Schedule as an interim replacement elected member for the electoral district in question, and

(b) subject to subsection (6), a person is to be returned at the next House of Lords election as a replacement elected member for the electoral district in question.

(3) A person returned under subsection (2)(a) is an interim replacement elected member for the period –

(a) beginning with the day the person is declared to be returned, and

(b) ending with the day of dissolution of the last (or only) Parliament of the electoral period in which the vacancy is certified.

(4) A person returned under subsection (2)(b) is a replacement elected member for the period –

(a) beginning with the day the person is declared to be returned, and

(b) ending at the end of the expected term.

(5) Subsection (2)(a) does not apply if the expected day of the next House of Lords election is within the period of 6 months beginning with the day the certificate under subsection (1) is issued.

(6) Subsection (2)(b) does not apply if the day of the next House of Lords election is after the end of the expected term.

(7) Where subsection (2)(b) applies, the returning officer for the electoral district must notify the Clerk of the Crown of –

(a) the name of the person returned under that provision, and

(b) the day the person is declared to be returned.

(8) When allocating the seats of elected members for an electoral district following a House of Lords election, the seats for any replacement elected members are to be allocated after the seats for the ordinary elected members.

9 The 'expected day' of the next House of Lords election

(1) For the purposes of section 8(5), the determination of the expected day of the next House of Lords election ('the expected day') is to be –

(a) undertaken as at the day specified in the following provisions of this section, and

(b) made in accordance with subsection (5).

(2) The expected day is to be determined as at the day the certificate under section 8(1) is issued ('the day of the certificate'); but this is subject to subsections (3) and (4).

(3) If, on the day of the certificate –

(a) an early House of Commons general election is to take place as provided for by section 2(1) or (3) of the Fixed-term Parliaments Act 2011 ('the 2011 Act'), but

(b) no polling day has been appointed for that election under section 2(7) of that Act,

the expected day is to be determined as at the day after the day that appointment is made.

(4) If a motion under section 2(3)(a) of the 2011 Act (no confidence motion) is passed on or before the day of the certificate but the period mentioned in section 2(3)(b) of that Act ends after that day –

(a) where an early House of Commons general election is to take place as a result of the motion, the expected day is to be determined as at the day after the day on which the polling day for that general election is appointed, and

   (b) otherwise, the expected day is to be determined as at the day after the day a motion under section 2(3)(b) of the 2011 Act is passed.

(5) When determining the expected day, any possibility that the polling day for a House of Commons general election may change is to be disregarded.

10 Vacancies certified in dissolution periods

Where a certificate under section 8(1) is issued in a dissolution period –

   (a) for the purposes of sections 8 and 9 and Schedule 4, the certificate is to be treated as issued on the first day of the electoral period after the one in which it is actually issued, and

   (b) references in those provisions to the 'next House of Lords election' and the 'last House of Lords election' are to be read accordingly.

PART 3

APPOINTED MEMBERS

House of Lords Appointments Commission etc

11 The House of Lords Appointments Commission

(1) There is to be a body corporate known as the House of Lords Appointments Commission (referred to in this Act as 'the Appointments Commission').

   (2) Schedule 5 makes provision about the Appointments Commission.

12 The Speakers' Committee on the House of Lords Appointments Commission

(1) There is to be a committee known as the Speakers' Committee on the House of Lords Appointments Commission (referred to in this Act as 'the Speakers' Committee').

(2) Schedule 6 makes provision about the Speakers' Committee.

Ordinary appointed members

13 Ordinary appointed members

(1) In each electoral period, 30 persons are to be appointed as ordinary appointed members of the House of Lords.

(2) The appointments are to be made by Her Majesty on the recommendation of the Prime Minister.

(3) The Appointments Commission must, during the first 14 days of an electoral period, recommend 30 persons to the Prime Minister for appointment.

(4) The Prime Minister must, as soon as reasonably practicable, recommend each of those persons to Her Majesty for appointment (and may not recommend any other person).

(5) A person appointed under this section is an ordinary appointed member for the electoral period in which the appointment is made and the next 2 electoral periods, excluding –

(a) any period before the day of the appointment, and
(b) the dissolution period in the last of those electoral periods.

Filling vacancies

14 Replacement appointed members

(1) This section applies where, before the end of the expected term of a person ('A') appointed as an appointed member, the Clerk of the Parliaments certifies that –

(a) the appointment is void, or
(b) A has ceased to be an appointed member.

(2) A person is to be appointed as a replacement appointed member of the House of Lords in order to replace A.

(3) The appointment is to be made by Her Majesty on the recommendation of the Prime Minister.

(4) The Appointments Commission must, as soon as reasonably practicable, recommend a person to the Prime Minister for appointment.

(5) The Prime Minister must, as soon as reasonably practicable, recommend that person to Her Majesty for appointment (and may not recommend any other person).

(6) No appointment may be made after the end of A's expected term.

(7) Where –

(a) A's expected term is the period mentioned in section 15(3) (extended term of office), and

(b) the certificate under subsection (1) is issued in the electoral period in which A is appointed, no appointment may be made after the end of that electoral period.

15 Replacement appointed member's term of office

(1) A person ('R') appointed under section 14 in order to replace another person ('A') is a replacement appointed member for the period which –

(a) begins with the day of R's appointment, and

(b) ends at the end of A's expected term.

(2) But if –

(a) that period begins and ends in the same electoral period, and

(b) R has not previously been an elected or appointed member as a result of a previous return or appointment, R is a replacement appointed member for the period mentioned in subsection (3).

(3) That period –

(a) begins with the day of R's appointment, and

(b) ends with the day of dissolution of the last (or only) Parliament of the third electoral period after the electoral period in which R is appointed.

16 Reduction in number of ordinary appointed members to be appointed

(1) This section applies where, at the beginning of an electoral period ('the electoral period'), there are one or more replacement appointed members to whom section 15(2) (extended term of office) applies who were appointed in the previous electoral period.

(2) Section 13(1) and (3) (number of persons to be appointed as ordinary appointed members etc) have effect in relation to the electoral period as if the number of persons mentioned there were reduced by the number of replacement appointed members referred to in subsection (1) above.

Supplementary provision

17 Criteria and procedure for selection

(1) The Appointments Commission is to select persons for recommendation for appointment on the basis of fair and open competition.

(2) In doing so it must take account of –

(a) the principle that, although past or present party political activity or affiliation does not necessarily preclude selection, the role of an appointed member is to make a contribution to the work of the House of Lords which is not a party political contribution,

(b) the desirability of the appointed members collectively reflecting the diversity of the population of the United Kingdom and having a range of experience and expertise,

(c) a person's integrity and commitment to the principles of public life,

(d) a person's ability and willingness to contribute effectively to the work of the House of Lords, and

(e) such other matters as the Appointments Commission considers appropriate.

(3) 'The principles of public life' are the Nolan principles or such other similar principles as may be adopted by the Appointments Commission from time to time.

(4) The Appointments Commission must take whatever steps it considers necessary to ensure that a diverse range of persons is considered for recommendation.

(5) The Appointments Commission may recommend a person for appointment only if the person has declared (at the time or times required by the Commission) that –

(a) the person is aware of the provisions of section 26 (disqualification) so far as they relate to appointed members, and

(b) to the best of the person's knowledge and belief, the person is not disqualified from being an appointed member (whether by virtue of that section or otherwise).

(6) The Appointments Commission must –

(a) prepare a scheme setting out its criteria and procedures (which must comply with subsections (1) to (5)) for selecting persons to recommend for appointment,

(b) review the scheme regularly and revise it as appropriate, and

(c) publish the scheme and any revision to it.

(7) The Minister may by order amend subsection (2) or (3); but that power is exercisable only on, and in accordance with, a recommendation of the Appointments Commission.

18 Withdrawal of recommendations

(1) A recommendation under section 13 or 14 must be withdrawn if, before it is acted upon, it appears to the person who made it that the recommended person is disqualified from being an appointed member.

(2) Where a recommendation is withdrawn, the Appointments Commission must, as soon as reasonably practicable, recommend

another person to the Prime Minister for appointment ('the new recommendation').

(3) For the purposes of this Act (including this section) the new recommendation is to be treated as made –

(a) under section 13(3), where the withdrawn recommendation was made under section 13;

(b) under section 14(4), where the withdrawn recommendation was made under section 14.

(4) For the purposes of subsection (1) –

(a) a recommendation by the Appointments Commission to appoint a person is acted upon when the Prime Minister recommends the person to Her Majesty for appointment;

(b) a recommendation by the Prime Minister to appoint a person is acted upon when the person is appointed by Her Majesty.

PART 4
LORDS SPIRITUAL
Named Lords Spiritual

19 Named Lords Spiritual

(1) A person who holds a named office is a member of the House of Lords for the period for which the person holds that office.

(2) In this Act 'named office' means –

(a) Archbishop of Canterbury,
(b) Archbishop of York,
(c) Bishop of London,
(d) Bishop of Durham, or
(e) Bishop of Winchester.

(3) In this Act 'named Lord Spiritual' means a person who is a member of the House of Lords by reason of holding a named office.

(4) The Secretary General must, as soon as reasonably practicable, notify the Clerk of the Crown of the appointment of a person to a named office.

(5) In this Act the 'Secretary General' means the Secretary General of the General Synod of the Church of England.

Ordinary Lords Spiritual

20 Ordinary Lords Spiritual

(1) For each electoral period the Church of England may select bishops who do not hold a named office to be members of the House of Lords as ordinary Lords Spiritual.

(2) The maximum number that may be selected is –

    (a) for the first electoral period, 16,
    (b) for the second electoral period, 11, and
    (c) for each subsequent electoral period, 7.

(3) The Secretary General must notify the Clerk of the Crown –

    (a) before each electoral period, of the persons selected for that period (or that no persons have been selected before that period), and
    (b) of any selection made during an electoral period, as soon as reasonably practicable after it is made.

(4) A person selected for an electoral period is an ordinary Lord Spiritual for that period, excluding –

    (a) any period before the day of the selection, and
    (b) the dissolution period in that electoral period.

(5) For provision about ordinary Lords Spiritual for the first and second electoral periods, see section 21.

21 Ordinary Lords Spiritual for the first and second electoral periods

(1) Any selection under section 20 for the first or second electoral period must be made before the beginning of that period.

(2) A person may be selected under that section as an ordinary Lord Spiritual for the first electoral period only if, at the beginning of the day of the first House of Lords election, the person is entitled by virtue of being a bishop to receive writs of summons to attend the House of Lords.

(3) In determining whether a person is entitled as mentioned in subsection (2), section 427 of the Insolvency Act 1986 (no entitlement to writs of summons during bankruptcy etc) is to be disregarded.

(4) A person may be selected under section 20 as an ordinary Lord Spiritual for the second electoral period only if the person is an ordinary Lord Spiritual at the beginning of the day of the second House of Lords election.

(5) But if the number of persons eligible for selection under subsection (4) is less than 7, so many persons as will bring the number of ordinary Lords Spiritual for the second election period up to 7 may be selected from among the other bishops who do not hold a named office.

(6) Section 20(4) applies in relation to a person selected under section 20 for the first or second electoral period as if section 20(4)(b) were omitted.

22 Ordinary Lords Spiritual: vacancies

(1) This section applies where, before the end of the expected term ('the expected term') of a person selected as an ordinary Lord Spiritual, the Clerk of the Parliaments certifies that –

(a) the selection is void, or
(b) the person has ceased to be an ordinary Lord Spiritual.

(2) The Church of England may, before the end of the expected term, select another person as an ordinary Lord Spiritual to replace the person mentioned in subsection (1).

(3) The person selected must be a bishop who does not hold a named office.

(4) The Secretary General must notify the Clerk of the Crown of any selection, as soon as reasonably practicable after it is made.

(5) A person selected under this section is an ordinary Lord Spiritual for the expected term, excluding any period before the day of the selection.

(6) In the first and second electoral periods, subsection (2) applies only if there will be fewer than 7 ordinary Lords Spiritual if the person is not replaced.

23 Certain cases in which a person ceases to be an ordinary Lord Spiritual

(1) A person who is an ordinary Lord Spiritual ceases to be an ordinary Lord Spiritual if the person –

    (a) is appointed to a named office, or
    (b) ceases to hold office as a bishop.

(2) A person who is an ordinary Lord Spiritual does not cease to be an ordinary Lord Spiritual by reason of the person becoming the bishop of a different diocese (without being appointed to a named office).

PART 5
MINISTERIAL MEMBERS

24 Ministerial members

(1) Persons may be appointed under this section as ministerial members of the House of Lords.

(2) Appointments are to be made by Her Majesty on the recommendation of the Prime Minister.

(3) A recommendation may be made only for the purpose of facilitating the performance by the recommended person of that person's functions as a Minister of the Crown.

(4) An appointment may be made only at a time when there are fewer than 8 ministerial members who are Ministers of the Crown.

(5) A person appointed under this section is a ministerial member for the electoral period in which the appointment is made and the next 2 electoral periods, excluding –

(a) any period before the day of the appointment, and

(b) the dissolution period in the last of those electoral periods.

PART 6
TRANSITIONAL MEMBERS

25 Transitional members

Schedule 7 makes provision about transitional members.

PART 7
DISQUALIFICATION
Disqualification from membership of House of Lords

26 Disqualification from membership of House of Lords

(1) A person is disqualified from being a member of the House of Lords if –

(a) an insolvency order or undertaking is in force in relation to the person (see section 30),

(b) the serious offence condition is met in relation to the person (see section 32),

(c) the person holds a disqualifying office (see Part 1 of Schedule 8),

(d) the person is under the age of 18 on –

(i) the day on which the person is nominated as a candidate to be an elected member, or

(ii) the day of the appointment or selection, or

(e) the person has previously been an elected, appointed or ministerial member as a result of a previous return or appointment (subject to subsection (6) and section 33).

(2) A person holding an office specified in the first column of the table in Part 2 of Schedule 8 is disqualified from being an elected member for any corresponding electoral district specified in the second column of that table.

(3) A person is disqualified from being an appointed member if the person is an elected member.

(4) A person is disqualified from being a Lord Spiritual or transitional member if the person is an elected or appointed member.

(5) A person is disqualified from being a ministerial member if the person is a member of any other kind.

(6) For the purposes of subsection (1)(e) no account is to be taken of a person having been an elected member as a result of only one previous return if, as a result of that return, the person was –

    (a)   an interim replacement elected member, or
    (b)   a replacement elected member whose expected term began and ended in the same electoral period.

(7) References in this Act to a person being disqualified from being a member of the House of Lords include a person who is incapable of being a member by virtue of –

    (a)   section 3 of the Act of Settlement (nationality), which is qualified by section 29, or
    (b)   section 160 or 173 of the Representation of the People Act 1983 (corrupt or illegal electoral practices) or any corresponding provision of primary or secondary legislation relating to elections or referendums.

27 Effect of being disqualified on return day, day of appointment etc

(1) This section applies where –

    (a)   a person returned as an elected member is disqualified from being an elected member at any time on the return day,

> (b) a person returned as an elected member for an electoral
>   district is disqualified from being an elected member for
>   that district at any time on the return day,
> (c) a person appointed as an appointed or ministerial
>   member is disqualified from being that kind of member
>   at any time on the day of the appointment,
> (d) a person who holds a named office is disqualified from
>   being a Lord Spiritual at the time the person becomes
>   the holder of that named office, or
> (e) a person selected as an ordinary Lord Spiritual or tran-
>   sitional member is disqualified from being that kind of
>   member at any time on the day of the selection or the
>   day on which the person would (apart from this section)
>   become such a member.

(2) The person does not become a member of the House of Lords of the kind in question.

(3) Any return within subsection (1)(a) or (b), appointment within subsection (1)(c) or selection within subsection (1)(e) is void.

28 Effect of becoming disqualified while a member

(1) Where a person who is a member of the House of Lords of a particular kind becomes disqualified from being that kind of member, the person ceases to be a member of that kind; but this is subject to subsection (3).

(2) Where a person who is an elected member becomes disqualified from being an elected member for the electoral district for which the person was returned, the person ceases to be an elected member.

(3) Where a person is disqualified by virtue of –

> (a) section 160 or 173 of the Representation of the People
>   Act 1983 (corrupt or illegal electoral practices), or
> (b) any corresponding provision of primary or secondary
>   legislation relating to elections or referendums, the

person ceases to be a member when required to vacate the person's seat in the House of Lords under the provision in question.

(4) For provision about the resumption of membership in certain cases, see section 43.

29 Nationality of members

(1) Despite section 3 of the Act of Settlement –

- (a) a qualifying Commonwealth citizen or citizen of the Republic of Ireland may be a member of the House of Lords, and
- (b) a Commonwealth citizen may be a transitional member.

(2) 'Qualifying Commonwealth citizen' means a Commonwealth citizen who –

- (a) is not a person who requires leave under the Immigration Act 1971 to enter or remain in the United Kingdom, or
- (b) is such a person but has (or is by virtue of primary or secondary legislation to be treated as having) indefinite leave to remain within the meaning of that Act.

(3) But a person who does not require leave to enter or remain in the United Kingdom by virtue only of section 8 of the Immigration Act 1971 (exceptions to requirement for leave in special cases) is not a qualifying Commonwealth citizen by virtue of subsection (2)(a).

30 Meaning of 'insolvency order or undertaking'

(1) In this Act 'insolvency order or undertaking' means –

- (a) a bankruptcy restrictions order or undertaking (but not an interim order) under –
  - (i) Schedule 4A to the Insolvency Act 1986,
  - (ii) section 56A or 56G of the Bankruptcy (Scotland) Act 1985, or

(iii) Schedule 2A to the Insolvency (Northern Ireland) Order 1989 (S.I. 1989/2405 (N.I. 19)), or

(b) a debt relief restrictions order or undertaking (but not an interim order) under Schedule 4ZB to the Insolvency Act 1986.

(2) References in this section to orders and undertakings include orders made, and undertakings accepted, before this section comes into force.

31 Notification of making of insolvency order etc

(1) A court or sheriff which makes an order listed in subsection (2) in relation to a member of the House of Lords must notify the Speaker of the House of Lords.

(2) The orders are –

(a) a bankruptcy restrictions order or interim order under –
   (i)   Schedule 4A to the Insolvency Act 1986,
   (ii)   section 56A of the Bankruptcy (Scotland) Act 1985, or
   (iii) Schedule 2A to the Insolvency (Northern Ireland) Order 1989, or

(b) a debt relief restrictions order or interim debt relief restrictions order under Schedule 4ZB to the Insolvency Act 1986.

(3) Where a person mentioned in the first column of the following table accepts an undertaking mentioned in the second column made by a member of the House of Lords, the person must notify the Speaker of that House.

[...]

32 Serious offence condition

(1) The serious offence condition is met in relation to a person if –

(a) the person is imprisoned or detained in pursuance of a sentence or order (or would be if the person were not unlawfully at large),

(b) the sentence or order is for imprisonment or detention for more than one year or for an indefinite period, and

(c) the sentence or order was passed or made in respect of an offence for which the person has been convicted.

(2) Any reference in subsection (1) to –

(a) imprisonment or detention includes imprisonment or detention outside the United Kingdom,

(b) a sentence or order includes one passed or made by a court outside the United Kingdom, and

(c) an 'offence' includes any act punishable under the law of a country or territory outside the United Kingdom (however it is described in that law).

(3) References in subsection (1) to offences, convictions, sentences and orders include those occurring before this section comes into force.

33 Exception to disqualification under section 26(1)(e)

(1) This section applies if –

(a) a person is returned as an elected member or is appointed as an appointed or ministerial member,

(b) the person has not previously been an elected, appointed or ministerial member as a result of a previous return or appointment,

(c) before the electoral period in which the person's expected term ends, the person becomes disqualified and accordingly ceases to be an elected, appointed or ministerial member, and

(d) subsequently –

    (i) a qualifying event occurs in relation to the disqualification in question, or

    (ii) a qualifying resolution is passed in respect of that disqualification.

(2) For the purposes of section 26(1)(e) (disqualification because of previous membership) no account is to be taken of the person having been an elected, appointed or ministerial member as mentioned in subsection (1).

(3) A 'qualifying event' means, in the case of a disqualification by virtue of a provision mentioned in the first column of the following table, an event mentioned in the second column.

[...]

(4) In the table, the reference to the annulment of an insolvency order or undertaking is to –

(a) a bankruptcy restrictions order within section 30(1)(a) being annulled on an appeal against the making of the order,

(b) a bankruptcy restrictions order or undertaking within section 30(1)(a) being annulled under –

(i) paragraph 9(3)(a) or 10 of Schedule 4A to the Insolvency Act 1986,

(ii) section 56E(3)(a), 56G(5)(a) or 56J of the Bankruptcy (Scotland) Act 1985, or

(iii) paragraph 9(3)(a) or 10 of Schedule 2A to the Insolvency (Northern Ireland) Order 1989 (S.I. 1989/2405 (N.I. 19)),

(c) a debt relief restrictions order within section 30(1)(b) being annulled on an appeal against the making of the order,

(d) a debt relief restrictions order or undertaking within section 30(1)(b) being annulled by a direction under paragraph 10 of Schedule 4ZB to the Insolvency Act 1986, or

(e) a debt relief restrictions undertaking within section 30(1)(b) being annulled under paragraph 9(3)(a) of Schedule 4ZB to that Act.

(5) A 'qualifying resolution' is a resolution under section 34 or 35 (relief from disqualification etc) in relation to which section 34(5) or 35(6) applies (resolution passed after vacancy certified).

(6) In this section 'corresponding provision' means a corresponding provision of primary or secondary legislation relating to elections or referendums.

Relief from disqualification etc

34 Relief from disqualification: age, disqualifying office or nationality

(1) The House of Lords may resolve that any disqualification incurred by a person on a ground within any of the following provisions is to be disregarded –

    (a) section 26(1)(c) or (d) or (2) (disqualifying office or age);

    (b) section 3 of the Act of Settlement (nationality) as qualified by section 29.

(2) It may do so only if it appears to the House of Lords –

    (a) that on the day on which it is passed –

        (i) in the case of the ground within section 26(1)(d) (age), the person is aged 18 or over, or

        (ii) in any other case, the ground no longer applies (or does not apply), and

    (b) that it is proper to disregard any disqualification so incurred.

(3) The effect of a resolution is, except where subsection (5) applies, that the disqualification is treated as never having been incurred.

(4) For the effect of resolutions in respect of certain elected or appointed members in cases where subsection (5) applies, see section 33.

(5) This subsection applies where a resolution is passed in respect of an elected or appointed member or an ordinary Lord Spiritual after a certificate relating to the person in question has been issued under –

    (a) section 8(1) (elected members: vacancies),

    (b) section 14(1) (appointed members: vacancies), or

    (c) section 22(1) (ordinary Lords Spiritual: vacancies).

(6) A resolution does not –

    (a) affect any proceedings on an election petition, or

    (b) enable the House of Lords to disregard any disqualification which has been established in such proceedings.

(7) 'Election petition' means –

    (a) an election petition presented in pursuance of Part 3 of the Representation of the People Act 1983 as applied by or incorporated in an order under section 7 or under paragraph 11 of Schedule 4 (powers to make provision about elections or the return of interim replacement elected members), or

    (b) any procedure under such an order which is similar to such a petition.

35 Relief from disqualification: serious offence condition

(1) The House of Lords may resolve that any disqualification incurred by a person under section 26(1)(b) (serious offence condition) by virtue of a sentence or order given or made outside the United Kingdom is to be disregarded.

(2) It may do so only if it appears to the House of Lords that it is proper to disregard any disqualification so incurred.

(3) The effect of a resolution is, except where subsection (6) applies, that the disqualification is treated as never having been incurred.

(4) Where that subsection applies, in relation to any time after the passing of the resolution the person is treated as not disqualified by virtue of the sentence or order.

(5) For the further effect of resolutions in respect of certain elected or appointed members in cases where subsection (6) applies, see section 33.

(6) This subsection applies where a resolution is passed in respect of an elected or appointed member or an ordinary Lord Spiritual after a certificate relating to the person in question has been issued under –

(a) section 8(1) (elected members: vacancies),

(b) section 14(1) (appointed members: vacancies), or

(c) section 22(1) (ordinary Lords Spiritual: vacancies).

(7) A resolution does not –

(a) affect any proceedings on an election petition, or

(b) enable the House of Lords to disregard any disqualification which has been established in such proceedings.

(8) 'Election petition' has the same meaning as in section 34.

Disputes

36 Jurisdiction of Privy Council as to disqualification

(1) A person may apply to Her Majesty in Council for –

(a) a declaration that a person purporting to be a member of the House of Lords of a particular kind is, or has at any relevant time been, disqualified from being a member of that kind by virtue of –

(i) section 26(1)(c) or (d) of this Act, or

(ii) section 3 of the Act of Settlement as qualified by section 29 of this Act, or

(b) a declaration that a person purporting to be an elected member for an electoral district is, or has at any relevant time been, disqualified under section 26(2) from being an elected member for that district.

(2) 'Relevant time' means –

(a) any time on or after the return day,

(b) any time on or after the day of the appointment,

(c) any time on or after the time the person becomes the holder of a named office, or

(d) any time on the day of selection as an ordinary Lord Spiritual or transitional member or any time on or after the day the person becomes (or purportedly becomes) that kind of member.

(3) An application under this section must be made in accordance with such rules as Her Majesty may by Order in Council prescribe.

(4) Section 3 of the Judicial Committee Act 1833 (reference to the Judicial Committee of the Privy Council of appeals to Her Majesty in Council) applies to an application under this section as it applies to an appeal to Her Majesty in Council from a court.

(5) The person in respect of whom the application is made is to be the respondent.

(6) Where an application is made under this section, the applicant must give such security for the costs of the proceedings as the Judicial Committee may direct.

(7) The amount of the security may not exceed £5,000.

(8) The Minister may by order substitute a different amount for the amount for the time being specified in subsection (7).

(9) No declaration is to be made under this section in respect of a person in relation to a ground if –

(a)   in the case of an elected member, the ground subsisted at any time on the return day and an election petition is pending or has been tried in which the person's disqualification on that ground is or was an issue, or

(b)   a resolution of the House of Lords under section 34 requires that any disqualification incurred by the person on that ground is to be treated as never having been incurred.

(10) 'Election petition' has the same meaning as in section 34.

37 Power to direct an appropriate court to try issues of fact

(1) For the purpose of determining any issue of fact arising on an application under section 36, the Judicial Committee may direct the issue to be tried in the appropriate court.

(2) Where the application is in respect of a person purporting to be an elected member for an electoral district, 'the appropriate court' is, according to where the electoral district is situated –

(a) the High Court in England and Wales,

(b) the Court of Session, or

(c) the High Court in Northern Ireland.

(3) In the case of any other application, 'the appropriate court' is such of the courts mentioned in subsection (2) as the Judicial Committee considers appropriate.

(4) Where a direction is given under subsection (1), the decision of the appropriate court is final.

Disqualification from sitting or voting

38 Holders of certain judicial offices disqualified from sitting or voting

(1) A transitional member within paragraph 3 of Schedule 8 (holders of disqualifying judicial offices) is disqualified from sitting or voting in the House of Lords or a committee of the House of Lords.

(2) Subsection (1) does not affect any entitlement of the transitional member to receive a writ of summons to attend the House of Lords, but any such writ is subject to that subsection.

Restrictions on membership of the House of Commons

39 Members of the House of Lords disqualified from being MPs

In section 1(1) of the House of Commons Disqualification Act 1975 (disqualification for membership of the House of Commons) for paragraph (za) substitute –

'(za) is a member of the House of Lords;'.

40 Bar on standing for election to both Houses at the same time

(1) A person may not be both –

(a) a candidate at a House of Lords election to be an elected member for an electoral district, and

(b) a candidate at the relevant House of Commons general election to be the Member of Parliament for a parliamentary constituency.

(2) The relevant House of Commons general election is the House of Commons general election the polling day for which is the same as the day of the House of Lords election.

(3) Amend the Representation of the People Act 1983 as follows.

(4) In section 65A(1A) (making false statements in candidate's consent to nomination a corrupt practice) –

(a) omit the 'or' after paragraph (b), and

(b) after paragraph (c) insert 'or (d) a statement that he is not a candidate at a House of Lords election the day of the poll for which is to be the same as the day of the poll for the election to which the consent relates.'

(5) In paragraph 8(3) of Schedule 1 (declarations to be made by candidate on consenting to nomination for election) after paragraph (c) insert –

'(d) shall state that he is not a candidate at a House of Lords election the day of the poll for which is to be the same as the day of the poll for the election to which the consent relates.'

41 Restriction on former members being elected as MPs

(1) A former member of the House of Lords is disqualified from being elected to the House of Commons at an election if the day of the poll is in the disqualification period.

(2) The disqualification period is the period of 4 years and 1 month beginning with the day on which the person ceased (or last ceased) to be a member of the House of Lords.

(3) This section does not apply in relation to membership of the House of Lords as a Lord Spiritual.

PART 8
GENERAL PROVISION ABOUT MEMBERSHIP
Writs of summons

42 Writs of summons

(1) A person who is a member of the House of Lords is entitled to receive a writ of summons to attend the House of Lords in relation to each Parliament which meets while the person is a member.

(2) This is subject to any provision made by or under this Act or other primary legislation.

(3) No person is entitled to receive a writ of summons otherwise than under subsection (1).

(4) A writ of summons issued to any of the following has no effect –

    (a) a person whose return as an elected member is void;

    (b) a person whose appointment as an appointed or ministerial member is void;

    (c) a person whose selection as an ordinary Lord Spiritual or transitional member is void;

    (d) a named Lord Spiritual within section 27(1)(d) (disqualified when becomes the holder of a named office).

(5) Where a person ceases to be a member of a particular kind, any writ of summons issued to the person by virtue of being that kind of member has no further effect.

Certification of vacancies etc

43 Certification of vacancies etc

(1) In this section 'certificate' means a certificate under –

    (a) section 8(1) (elected members: vacancies),

    (b) section 14(1) (appointed member: vacancies), or

    (c) section 22(1) (ordinary Lords Spiritual: vacancies).

(2) The issue by the Clerk of the Parliaments of a certificate is to be in accordance with standing orders of the House of Lords.

(3) The standing orders may provide that, in specified cases, where at any time the Clerk of the Parliaments becomes aware of matters which, in the opinion of the Clerk, justify the issuing of a certificate, a certificate may not be issued until after the end of such period beginning with that time as the standing orders provide.

(4) As soon as reasonably practicable after issuing a certificate, the Clerk of the Parliaments must give a copy of the certificate to the Clerk of the Crown.

(5) As soon as reasonably practicable after receiving a certificate, the Clerk of the Crown must give a copy of it to –

(a) in the case of a certificate under section 8(1), the returning officer for the electoral district in question;

(b) in the case of a certificate under section 14(1), the Appointments Commission;

(c) in the case of a certificate under section 22(1), the Secretary General.

(6) A disqualified person who has ceased to be a member of the House of Lords under section 28 (effect of becoming disqualified while a member) may resume membership if a qualifying event occurs in respect of the disqualification.

(7) But subsection (6) –

(a) does not entitle a person to resume membership after the Clerk of the Parliaments has issued a certificate relating to the person, and

(b) does not affect section 173(6) of the Representation of the People Act 1983 or any corresponding provision.

(8) 'Qualifying event' and 'corresponding provision' have the same meanings as in section 33.

Expulsion, suspension and resignation

44 Expulsion and suspension

(1) Standing orders of the House of Lords may make provision under which the House of Lords may by resolution –

(a)   expel a member of the House of Lords, or

(b)   suspend a member of the House of Lords for the period specified in the resolution.

(2) A person expelled by virtue of this section ceases to be a member.

(3) A person suspended by virtue of this section remains a member during the period of suspension, but during that period the person –

(a)   is not entitled to receive writs of summons to attend the House of Lords, and

(b)   despite any writ of summons previously issued to the person, is disqualified from sitting or voting in the House of Lords or a committee of the House of Lords.

(4) A resolution passed by virtue of subsection (1) must state that, in the opinion of the House of Lords, the conduct giving rise to the resolution –

(a)   occurred after the relevant time, or

(b)   occurred before the relevant time and was not public knowledge before that time.

(5) 'The relevant time' means –

(a)   in the case of an elected member, the beginning of the polling day for the election at which the person was returned;

(b)   in the case of an appointed or ministerial member, the beginning of the day of the appointment;

(c)   in the case of a named Lord Spiritual, the time at which the person became the holder of the named office in question;

(d)   in the case of an ordinary Lord Spiritual or a transitional member, the beginning of the day of the selection.

45 Resignation

(1) A person who is a member of the House of Lords other than a named Lord Spiritual may at any time resign from being a member by notifying the Clerk of the Parliaments.

(2) The notice of resignation must be signed by the person and two witnesses.

(3) On receipt of the notice, the Clerk of the Parliaments must do the following as soon as reasonably practicable –

(a) sign a certificate of receipt, and

(b) send a copy of the certificate to the person and the Clerk of the Crown.

(4) The person ceases to be a member of the House of Lords on signature of the certificate.

Pay, allowances etc

46 Pay and allowances

(1) In the Parliamentary Standards Act 2009, after section 7 insert –

Pay and allowances for members of the House of Lords[5]

7A Pay of members of the House of Lords

(1) Elected, appointed and ministerial members of the House of Lords are to be paid.

(2) Pay is payable by the IPSA, on a monthly basis in arrears.

(3) The IPSA must make a determination as to the level of pay under this section. For more about determinations, see sections 7B and 7C.

(4) The amount of a member's pay for a month is the amount calculated in accordance with that determination in respect of the member for that month.

(5) In a Parliament, no payment is to be made to a member before the member has made and subscribed the oath required

---

5   What follows is a long passage to insert into the Parliamentary Standards Act 2009. It has been italicised for clarity.

by the Parliamentary Oaths Act 1866 (or the corresponding affirmation).

(6) The IPSA's duty to pay a member is subject to anything done in relation to the member in the exercise of the disciplinary powers of the House of Lords.

(7) A person who is being paid a salary under the Ministerial and other Salaries Act 1975 is not entitled to pay under this section.

7B Determination of pay of members of the House of Lords

(1) This section is about determinations under section 7A(3).

(2) A determination must ensure that there is a relation-ship between –

(a) the amount of a member's pay for a month, and
(b) the participation of the member in the work of the House of Lords in that month.

(3) A determination may –

(a) make provision about what counts as participation in that work

for these purposes,

(b) make different such provision for different cases, and
(c) make provision about the way in which the participa-tion of members is to be ascertained.

(4) A determination must ensure that the amount of a mem-ber's pay in any 12 month period does not exceed the amount of an MP's salary for that period.

This limit does not apply where the member receives higher pay in that period by virtue of subsection (6).

(5) For the purposes of subsection (4) an MP's salary for a period is the amount payable under section 4 in respect of that period to a member of the House of Commons who does not fall within section 4A(2).

(6) A determination may provide for higher pay for members who hold an office or position specified for the purposes of this subsection in a resolution of the House of Lords.

(7) A determination made by virtue of subsection (6) may make different provision for different offices, positions or other cases (and may include exceptions).

(8) A determination may include a formula or other mechanism for adjusting pay from time to time.

(9) A determination may have retrospective effect.

7C Determination of pay: duty to review and procedure
(1) This section is about determinations under section 7A(3).

(2) The IPSA must review the current determination (and make a new determination as appropriate) –

(a) in the first year after each House of Lords election (other than the first House of Lords election);
(b) at any other time it considers appropriate.

(3) In reviewing a determination (and before making the first determination) the IPSA must consult –

(a) the Review Body on Senior Salaries,
(b) persons appearing to the IPSA to represent persons likely to be affected by the determination or the review,
(c) the Minister for the Civil Service,
(d) the Treasury, and
(e) any other person the IPSA considers appropriate.

(4) After making a determination, the IPSA must publish in a way it considers appropriate –

(a) the determination, and
(b) a statement of how it arrived at the determination.

(5) If the IPSA reviews the current determination but decides not to make a new determination, it must publish in a way it considers appropriate a statement of how it arrived at that decision.

(6) The IPSA may delegate to the Review Body on Senior Salaries its function of reviewing a determination (but not its function of deciding whether or not to make a new determination).

7D House of Lords allowances scheme
(1) Allowances are to be paid by the IPSA, in accordance with the House of Lords allowances scheme, to the following kinds of members of the House of Lords –

  (a) *elected members,*
  (b) *appointed members,*
  (c) *Lords Spiritual, and*
  (d) *ministerial members.*

(2) In this Act 'the House of Lords allowances scheme' means the scheme prepared under this section as it is in effect for the time being.
(3) The IPSA must –

  (a) *prepare the scheme;*
  (b) *review the scheme regularly and revise it as appropriate.*

(4) In preparing or revising the scheme, the IPSA must consult –

  (a) *the Speaker of the House of Lords,*
  (b) *the Committee on Standards in Public Life,*
  (c) *the Leader of the House of Lords,*
  (d) *any committee of the House of Lords nominated by the Speaker of the House of Lords,*
  (e) *members of the House of Lords,*
  (f) *the Review Body on Senior Salaries,*
  (g) *Her Majesty's Revenue and Customs,*
  (h) *the Treasury, and*
  (i) *any other person the IPSA considers appropriate.*

(5) The Speaker of the House of Lords must lay the scheme (or revision) before the House of Lords.
(6) The IPSA must publish in a way it considers appropriate –

(a) the scheme (or revision), and

(b) a statement of its reasons for adopting that scheme (or making that revision).

(7) The scheme (or revision) comes into effect on the day specified in the scheme (or revision).

(8) The scheme may, for example –

(a) provide for allowances to be payable in respect of specified kinds of expenditure or in specified circumstances;

(b) provide for allowances to be payable only on specified conditions (such as a condition that claims for allowances must be supported by documentary evidence);

(c) impose limits on the amounts that may be paid.

(9) The scheme may not provide for an allowance to be payable to an elected member in respect of expenditure incurred in connection with maintaining an office in the electoral district for which the member was returned.

(10) The scheme may provide for allowances to be payable in connection with a person's ceasing to be a member of the House of Lords; and in relation to any such allowances, references in this Act to a member of the House of Lords include a former member of the House of Lords.

(11) Any duty of the IPSA to pay an allowance to a member is subject to anything done in relation to the member in the exercise of the disciplinary powers of the House of Lords.

7E Dealing with claims under the scheme
(1) No allowance is to be paid to a member of the House of Lords under the House of Lords allowances scheme unless a claim for the allowance has been made to the IPSA.

(2) The claim must be made by the member (except where the scheme provides otherwise).

(3) On receipt of a claim, the IPSA must –

(a) determine whether to allow or refuse the claim, and

(b) if it is allowed, determine how much of the amount claimed is to be allowed and pay it accordingly.

(4) The House of Lords allowances scheme may include –

    (a) further provision about how claims are to be dealt with;

    (b) provision for deducting repayable amounts from allowances payable under the scheme or pay under section 7A;

    (c) provision about how such deductions, and deductions under paragraph 5 or 12 of Schedule 4, are to be made.

A 'repayable amount' is an amount which a member (under section 9(8) or otherwise) has agreed to repay, in respect of an amount paid to the member under the House of Lords allowances scheme that should not have been allowed.

(6) The scheme may provide for an allowance to which a member is entitled under the scheme to be paid to another person at the member's direction; and references in this Act to the payment of an allowance to a member are to be read accordingly.

(7) The IPSA must publish such information as it considers appropriate in respect of –

    (a) each claim made under or by virtue of this section, and

    (b) each payment of an allowance by the IPSA under or by virtue of this section.

(8) The IPSA must publish the information at times it considers appropriate and in a way it considers appropriate.

(9) The IPSA must determine procedures to be followed by the IPSA in relation to publication of the information, and in doing so must consult –

    (a) the Speaker of the House of Lords,

    (b) the Leader of the House of Lords,

    (c) the House of Lords Committee for Privileges and Conduct,

    (d) the Compliance Officer, and

    (e) any other person the IPSA considers appropriate.

7F Review of determination under section 7E
(1) This section applies if –

> (a) *the IPSA determines under section 7E(3) that a claim is to be refused or that only part of the amount claimed is to be allowed, and*
>
> (b) *the member (after asking the IPSA to reconsider the determination and giving it a reasonable opportunity to do so) asks the Compliance Officer to review the determination (or any altered determination resulting from the IPSA's reconsideration).*

(2) The Compliance Officer must –

> (a) *consider whether the determination (or the altered determination) is the determination that should have been made, and*
>
> (b) *in light of that consideration, decide whether or not to confirm or alter it.*

(3) The Compliance Officer must give the IPSA a statement of any decision under subsection (2)(b), and may include a statement of the Compliance Officer's findings about the way in which the IPSA has dealt with the claim.

(4) The IPSA must make any payments or adjustments necessary to give effect to the Compliance Officer's decision; but it must not do so until –

> (a) *it is no longer possible for there to be a relevant appeal, and*
>
> (b) *all relevant appeals have been withdrawn or determined.*

(5) A relevant appeal is –

> (a) *an appeal under subsection (6) brought before the end of the period mentioned in subsection (7), or*
>
> (b) *a further appeal in relation to the Compliance Officer's decision which –*

(i) is brought before the end of the usual period for bringing such an appeal, and

(ii) is an appeal against the determination of an appeal which was itself a relevant appeal.

(6) The member may appeal to the First-tier Tribunal against a decision of the Compliance Officer under subsection (2)(b).

(7) The appeal must be brought before the end of the period of 28 days beginning with the day on which notice of the decision is sent to the member (unless the Tribunal directs that it may be brought after the end of that period).

(8) The appeal is by way of a rehearing.

(9) On an appeal under subsection (6) the Tribunal may –

(a) allow the appeal in whole or in part, or

(b) dismiss the appeal.

(10) If the Tribunal allows the appeal (in whole or in part) it may –

(a) order the IPSA to make any payments or adjustments necessary to give effect to that decision;

(b) make any other order it thinks fit.

(11) If the Tribunal dismisses the appeal it may make any other order it thinks fit.

(12) The Compliance Officer must notify the IPSA of the Tribunal's decision (and the result of any further appeal).

7G Information and guidance for members of the House of Lords

(1) The IPSA must –

(a) prepare guidance for members of the House of Lords about –

(i) pay under section 7A (including what counts as participation in the work of the House for those purposes), and

> (ii) *making claims under the House of Lords allow-*
> *ances scheme;*
> (b) *review the guidance regularly and revise it as*
> *appropriate;*
> (c) *publish the guidance in a way the IPSA considers*
> *appropriate;*
> (d) *provide to any member on request such further advice*
> *about pay or making claims as the IPSA considers*
> *appropriate.*

(2) *The IPSA must provide to members of the House of Lords –*

> (a) *details of any general information or guidance about*
> *taxation issues published by HMRC that it considers*
> *they should be aware of, and*
> (b) *any other general information or guidance about taxa-*
> *tion issues that it considers appropriate (consulting*
> *HMRC for this purpose as it considers appropriate).*

(3) *'Taxation issues' means –*

> (a) *issues about the taxation of pay under section 7A and*
> *allowances payable under the House of Lords allow-*
> *ances scheme, and*
> (b) *any other issues about taxation arising in connection*
> *with that pay or those allowances.*

(4) *'HMRC' means Her Majesty's Revenue and Customs.*

47 Power to require IPSA to consider pension scheme

(1) Where this section applies, IPSA must prepare and publish a report on whether there should be a House of Lords pension scheme.

(2) This section applies if an order has been made by the Minister under this section and, before it is made, a draft of the order has been laid before Parliament and approved by a resolution of each House.

(3) 'House of Lords pension scheme' means a scheme which provides for the payment of pensions or other benefits to or in respect of persons with service as elected, appointed or ministerial members.

(4) An order under this section –

(a) must require the report to be completed by a specified date;

(b) may provide that, in preparing the report, IPSA must consider specified proposals or other specified matters;

(c) may provide that, in preparing the report, IPSA must not consider specified proposals or other specified matters;

(d) may require IPSA to consult specified persons or bodies in connection with the preparation of the report. "Specified" means specified in the order.

48 Tax status of members

(1) A person who is a member of the House of Lords for any part of a tax year is to be treated for the purposes of income tax, capital gains tax and inheritance tax as resident, ordinarily resident and domiciled in the United Kingdom for the whole of that tax year.

(2) For the purposes of this section a person is to be treated as becoming a member of the House of Lords when (having received a writ of summons to attend the House of Lords) the person makes and subscribes to the oath required by the Parliamentary Oaths Act 1866 (or the corresponding affirmation).

(3) For the purposes of this section a person is to be treated as ceasing to be a member of the House of Lords –

(a) when the Parliament to which the writ relates is dissolved, or

(b) (if earlier) when the person ceases to be a member of the House of Lords.

(4) In relation to a transitional member, in subsection (1) the reference to any part of a tax year excludes any part of the year

during which the member is disqualified from sitting or voting in the House of Lords under section 38 (holders of certain judicial offices).

(5) This section applies in relation to –

(a) the tax year in which the first meeting of the House of Lords in the first electoral period takes place, and

(b) subsequent tax years.

(6) 'Tax year', in relation to inheritance tax, means a year beginning on 6 April and ending on the following 5 April.

PART 9
MISCELLANEOUS AND GENERAL
Parliamentary privilege

49 Parliamentary privilege

Nothing in this Act –

(a) affects the application of any enactment or rule of law preventing the freedom of speech and debates or proceedings in Parliament being impeached or questioned in any court or place out of Parliament, or

(b) otherwise affects the scope of the exclusive cognisance of Parliament.

Peerages

50 Peers not disqualified from voting or from membership

(1) A person who holds a peerage is not by virtue of that peerage disqualified from voting at elections to either House of Parliament.

(2) A person who holds a peerage is not by virtue of that peerage disqualified from membership of either House of Parliament.

51 Power to disclaim life peerage

(1) A person who holds a life peerage may at any time disclaim that peerage by notifying the Lord Chancellor.

(2) The notice of disclaimer must be signed by the person and two witnesses.

(3) On receipt of the notice, the Lord Chancellor must do the following as soon as reasonably practicable –

(a) sign a certificate of receipt, and

(b) send a copy of the certificate to the person.

(4) The disclaimer takes effect on signature of the certificate.

(5) The disclaimer divests the person (and any spouse or children of the person) of all right to or interest in the peerage and all titles, rights, offices, privileges and precedence attaching to it.

(6) The Lord Chancellor must –

(a) keep a register containing the particulars of any disclaimer of a peerage under this section, and

(b) make arrangements under which the public may inspect the register.

(7) In this section 'life peerage' means a peerage under the Life Peerages Act 1958 or the Appellate Jurisdiction Act 1876.

52 Peerage claims

(1) Any peerage claim is to be made to Her Majesty in Council.

(2) A claim under this section must be made in accordance with such rules as Her Majesty may by Order in Council prescribe.

(3) Section 3 of the Judicial Committee Act 1833 (reference to the Judicial Committee of the Privy Council of appeals to Her Majesty in Council) applies to a claim under this section as it applies to an appeal to Her Majesty in Council from a court.

(4) The Judicial Committee may require an applicant to give such security for the costs of the proceedings as the Judicial Committee may direct.

(5) The jurisdiction of the House of Lords in relation to peerage claims is abolished.

(6) 'Peerage claim' includes a claim to a peerage in abeyance.

General

53 Consequential, transitory and transitional provision and savings

(1) Schedule 10 contains minor and consequential amendments (including the repeal of provisions which are spent or obsolete).

(2) The Minister may by order make such provision modifying any provision of primary or secondary legislation as the Minister considers necessary or expedient –

  (a) in consequence of any provision made by virtue of section 7 (power to make provision about elections),

  (b) in consequence of the amendment made by paragraph 1(2) of Schedule 10 (amendment to the definition of "parliamentary election" in the Interpretation Act 1978), or

  (c) in consequence of any other provision made by or under this Act.

(3) Where the provision mentioned in subsection (2)(a) is made by virtue of section 7(3)(d) (power to modify Part 7), the reference in subsection (2) to primary legislation includes this Act.

(4) An order under subsection (2)(b) may not modify any provision of primary or secondary legislation passed or made after the Session in which this Act is passed.

(5) Schedule 10 is subject to provision made by virtue of –

  (a) subsection (2)(a) or (b), or

  (b) section 7.

(6) Schedule 11 makes transitional and transitory provision and savings.

(7) The Minister may by order make such other transitional and transitory provision and savings as the Minister considers necessary or expedient in connection with the commencement of any provision made by this Act.

54 Orders and directions

(1) Orders made by a Minister of the Crown under this Act are to be made by statutory instrument.

(2) A statutory instrument containing an order under any of the following provisions may not be made unless a draft of the instrument has been laid before and approved by a resolution of each House of Parliament –

(a) section 7 (power to make provision about elections);
(b) section 17(7) (power to amend the matters the Appointments Commission must take into account);
(c) section 53(2) (power to make consequential provision);
(d) paragraph 11 of Schedule 4 (power to make provision about the return of interim replacement elected members);
(e) paragraph 16 of Schedule 9 (power to transfer staff etc to IPSA).

(3) Any other statutory instrument made under this Act, except one containing only an order made under a provision listed in subsection (4), is subject to annulment in pursuance of a resolution of either House of Parliament.

(4) Those provisions are –

(a) section 59 (commencement);
(b) paragraph 4 of Schedule 2 (implementation of Electoral Commission's recommendation);
(c) paragraph 9 of Schedule 8 (power to amend disqualifying offices).

(5) Orders made by a Minister of the Crown under this Act (except one under section 59) and Orders in Council under this Act may –

(a) make different provision for different cases, purposes or areas;
(b) make provision which applies generally or subject to specified exemptions or exceptions or only in relation to specified cases;
(c) make supplementary, incidental, consequential, transitional, transitory or saving provision.

(6) Section 26 of the Welsh Language Act 1993 (power to prescribe Welsh version) applies in relation to an order under section 7 or under paragraph 11 of Schedule 4 as it applies in relation to Acts of Parliament.

(7) A direction under a provision of this Act may be varied or revoked by a further direction under that provision.

(8) This section does not apply to an order made under section 47 (power to require IPSA to consider pension scheme).

55 Meaning of the 'expected term' of a member

(1) In this Act the 'expected term' of a member of a description in the first column of the following table is the term for which the person would be a member if the person were a member for the term provided for by the provision specified in the second column of that table.

(2) Where –

(a) a person is returned as an elected member, appointed as an appointed or ministerial member, or selected as an ordinary Lord Spiritual, but

(b) the return, appointment or selection is void, the person's expected term is to be determined as if it were not void.

56 Interpretation

(1) In this Act –

'appointed member' means an ordinary appointed member or replacement appointed member;

'the Appointments Commission' has the meaning given by section 11(1);

'bishop' means the bishop of a diocese of the Church of England that is wholly or partly in England;

'Clerk of the Crown' means Clerk of the Crown in Chancery;

'dissolution period' means a period –

(a) beginning immediately after the day of dissolution of the last (or only) Parliament of an electoral period, and

(b) ending at the end of that electoral period;

'elected member' means an ordinary elected member, interim replacement elected member or replacement elected member;

'electoral period' has the meaning given by section 1(5);

the 'expected term' of a member has the meaning given by section 55;

'insolvency order or undertaking' has the meaning given by section 30;

'IPSA' means the Independent Parliamentary Standards Authority;

'Lord Spiritual' means a named Lord Spiritual or ordinary Lord Spiritual;

'the Minister' means the Lord President of the Council or the Secretary of State;

'Minister of the Crown' has the same meaning as in the Ministers of the Crown Act 1975;

'modify' includes amend, repeal or revoke (and related terms are to be read accordingly);

'named Lord Spiritual' has the meaning given by section 19(3);

'named office' has the meaning given by section 19(2);

'Nolan principles' means the seven general principles of public life set out in the First Report of the Committee on Standards in Public Life (Cm 2850);

'peerage' means –

(a) a hereditary peerage (including the principality of Wales and the earldom of Chester),

(b) a peerage under section 1 of the Life Peerages Act 1958, or

(c) the dignity conferred by virtue of appointment as a Lord of Appeal in Ordinary, and "peer" is to be read accordingly;

'primary legislation' means –

(a)   an Act of Parliament,
(b)   an Act of the Scottish Parliament,
(c)   an Act or Measure of the National Assembly for Wales, or
(d)   Northern Ireland legislation; and, subject to any express provision to the contrary, includes such Acts, Measures or legislation whenever passed or made;

'registered party' means a party registered under Part 2 of the Political Parties, Elections and Referendums Act 2000;
'the return day', in relation to an elected member of any kind, means the day the person was declared to be returned as that kind of elected member;
'secondary legislation' means an instrument made under primary legislation; and, subject to any express provision to the contrary, includes an instrument whenever made;
'Secretary General' has the meaning given by section 19(5);
'the Speakers' Committee' has the meaning given by section 12(1).

(2) Any reference in this Act to the 'day' of a House of Lords election is to be read in accordance with section 3(5).

(3) A requirement or power under this Act to notify is a requirement or power to give notice in writing.

(4) Any provision of this Act as to the term for which a person is a member of the House of Lords of a particular kind is subject to the person ceasing to be a member of the House of Lords before the end of that term by virtue of any provision made by or under this Act or other primary legislation.

57 Financial provisions

There is to be paid out of money provided by Parliament –

(a) any expenditure incurred by a Minister of the Crown by virtue of this Act, and

(b) any increase attributable to this Act in the sums payable under any other Act out of money so provided.

58 Extent

(1) This Act extends to England and Wales, Scotland and Northern Ireland.

(2) But an amendment, repeal or revocation by this Act has the same extent as the provision to which it relates.

59 Commencement

(1) Sections 54 to 60 come into force on the day on which this Act is passed.

(2) The other provisions of this Act come into force on such day as the Minister may by order appoint.

(3) Different days may be appointed for different purposes.

60 Short title

This Act may be cited as the House of Lords Reform Act 2012.

Schedules

SCHEDULE 1
ELECTORAL DISTRICTS

1 The electoral districts for House of Lords elections are –

(a) the districts listed in the first column of the following table, which comprise the areas specified in the second column,

(b) Scotland,

(c) Wales, and

(d) Northern Ireland.

2 In the second column of the table, a reference to an area is –

(a) except in the case of Greater London and the Isles of Scilly, a reference to the county of that name, and

(b) a reference to the area as it is for the time being.

3 A change in a specified area has effect only in relation to elections occurring after that change.

Name of electoral district	Area included
East Midlands	Derby
	Derbyshire
	Leicester
	Leicestershire
	Lincolnshire
	Northamptonshire
	Nottingham
	Nottinghamshire
	Rutland
Eastern	Bedford
	Cambridgeshire
	Central Bedfordshire
	Essex
	Hertfordshire
	Luton
	Norfolk
	Peterborough
	Southend-on-Sea
	Suffolk
	Thurrock
London	Greater London
North East	Darlington
	Durham
	Hartlepool
	Middlesbrough
	Northumberland
	Redcar and Cleveland
	Stockton-on-Tees
	Tyne and Wear

North West	Blackburn with Darwen
	Blackpool
	Cheshire East
	Cheshire West and Chester
	Cumbria
	Greater Manchester
	Halton
	Lancashire
	Merseyside
	Warrington
South East	Berkshire
	Brighton with Hove
	Buckinghamshire
	East Sussex
	Hampshire
	Isle of Wight
	Kent
	The Medway Towns
	Milton Keynes
	Oxfordshire
	Portsmouth
	Southampton
	Surrey
	West Sussex
South West	Bath and North East Somerset
	Bournemouth
	The City of Bristol
	Cornwall
	Devon
	Dorset
	Gloucestershire
	North Somerset
	Plymouth
	Poole
	Somerset
	South Gloucestershire

	Swindon
	Torbay
	Wiltshire
	Isles of Scilly
West Midlands	Herefordshire
	Shropshire
	Staffordshire
	Stoke-on-Trent
	Telford and Wrekin
	Warwickshire
	West Midlands
	Worcestershire
Yorkshire and the Humber	The City of Kingston upon Hull
	The East Riding of Yorkshire
	North East Lincolnshire
	North Lincolnshire
	North Yorkshire
	South Yorkshire
	West Yorkshire
	York

SCHEDULE 2
ALLOCATION OF ORDINARY ELECTED MEMBERS

Initial allocation of ordinary elected members for House of Lords elections

1 The number of ordinary elected members that are to be returned for each electoral district at a House of Lords election is set out in the following table –

Name of electoral district	Number of ordinary elected members
East Midlands	9
Eastern	11
London	14
North East	5
North West	14

South East	16
South West	11
West Midlands	11
Yorkshire and the Humber	10
Scotland	10
Wales	6
Northern Ireland	3

Review of allocation of ordinary elected members after every third House of Lords election.

2 (1) In each review period, the Electoral Commission must –

(a) carry out a review of the number of ordinary elected members that are to be returned for each electoral district at a House of Lords election, and

(b) send a report of its conclusions to the Minister.

(2) 'Review period' means the period of 12 months which begins with the day after the day of every third House of Lords election.

(3) In carrying out a review, the Commission must consider whether the arrangements then in place achieve the same result as the allocation method set out in paragraph 3.

(4) If those arrangements do not achieve the same result as that method, the Commission must include in its report a recommendation specifying the number of ordinary elected members that should be returned for each electoral district at a House of Lords election in order to achieve the result produced by that method.

(5) The report must be published by the Commission and laid before Parliament by the Minister.

3 (1) The allocation method referred to in paragraph 2(3) is as follows.

(2) The number of ordinary elected members to be allocated between the electoral districts is 120.

(3) Three ordinary elected members are to be allocated to each electoral district.

Name of electoral district / Number of ordinary elected members

(4) Each subsequent ordinary elected member is to be allocated, in turn, to the electoral district for which the following formula gives the largest number – $E/2N+1$ where – E is the number of electors in an electoral district, and N is the number of ordinary elected members already allocated to that district.

(5) Where the number given by sub-paragraph (4) is the same for two or more electoral districts, the ordinary elected member is to be allocated to the electoral district for which E is smaller or smallest.

Implementation of Electoral Commission's recommendation

4 (1) This paragraph applies where a recommendation is made under paragraph 2(4).

(2) As soon as may be after the publication of the report, the Minister must –

(a) consult the Electoral Commission, and
(b) having done so, lay before Parliament a draft of an order giving effect to the recommendation by amending any of the numbers specified in the table in paragraph 1.

(3) Where –

(a) the Commission has made a recommendation under paragraph 2(4) (but no draft under sub-paragraph (2) has been laid in relation to the recommendation),
(b) the Commission notifies the Minister that the recommendation is to have effect with specified modifications, and
(c) the Commission submits to the Minister a statement of the reasons for those modifications; the draft under sub-paragraph (2) is to give effect to the recommendation with those modifications.

(4) If the draft under sub-paragraph (2) is approved by a resolution of each House, the Minister must make an order in the terms of the draft.

(5) For the purposes of sub-paragraph (4) an order is made in the terms of a draft order if it contains no material changes to the provisions of the draft order.

(6) Where an order under this paragraph makes consequential, transitional or saving provision by virtue of section 54(5), that provision may modify this Act or secondary legislation made under it.

Meaning of 'electors' in a district

5 (1) This paragraph applies for the purposes of paragraph 3.

(2) A person is an 'elector' in an electoral district if –

(a) the person's name appears on the relevant day in the register of parliamentary electors for a constituency which is wholly or partly comprised in the electoral district, and
(b) the person has a qualifying address.

(3) A person has a qualifying address if –

(a) the address in respect of which the person is registered in the relevant register of parliamentary electors on the relevant day is within the electoral district, or
(b) the person's registration in the relevant register of parliamentary electors on the relevant day results from an overseas elector's declaration which specifies an address within the electoral district.

(4) 'Relevant day' means the most recent 1 December before the beginning of the review period in question.

SCHEDULE 3
VOTING SYSTEM IN GREAT BRITAIN

Introduction

1 This Schedule contains provision about the system of election at a House of Lords election, in electoral districts in Great Britain.

Party lists

2 (1) A single registered party that has been nominated for an election in an electoral district may, in accordance with provision

made under section 7, submit a list of candidates standing for election in that district in the name of the party (a 'party list').

(2) At a House of Lords election, a person may not be on more than one party list.

How votes may be cast

3 (1) A vote may be cast for –

   (a) a party which has submitted a party list for the election in the electoral district in question,
   (b) a candidate on such a list (a 'party candidate'), or
   (c) a candidate who is not on such a list (an 'independent candidate').

(2) A vote for a party candidate is treated for the purposes of paragraph 4 as a vote for the candidate's party.

Allocation of seats to parties or independent candidates

4 (1) The allocation of seats in an electoral district to parties and independent candidates is to be undertaken in the following way.

(2) The first seat is to be allocated to the party or the independent candidate with the largest number of votes.

(3) The second and subsequent seats are to be allocated in the same way, except that the number of votes given for a party to which one or more seats have already been allocated is to be divided by the number of seats already allocated to that party plus one.

(4) Fractions are to be taken into account for the purposes of sub-paragraph (3).

(5) In allocating the second or any subsequent seat there is to be disregarded –

   (a) any votes given for a party to which there has already been allocated a number of seats equal to the number of candidates on its party list, and
   (b) any votes given for an independent candidate to whom a seat has already been allocated.

Allocation under paragraph 4: special rules for cases involving equality of votes

5 (1) If, on the application of paragraph 4(2) or on any application of paragraph 4(3), the largest number of votes is the number of votes of two or more parties, the provision in question applies to each of them (so they are each allocated a seat).

(2) However, if sub-paragraph (1) would mean that more than the full number of seats for the electoral district were allocated, paragraph 4(2) or (3) does not apply until the number of votes for each of those parties is increased by one.

(3) If, after that, the application of paragraph 4(2) or (3) together with subparagraph (1) would mean that more than the full number of seats were allocated, the returning officer must decide by lots between the parties to whom sub-paragraph (1) would otherwise require seats to be allocated.

(4) In this paragraph references to a party include an independent candidate.

Allocation of party candidates to the seats allocated to the party

6 (1) Seats allocated in an electoral district to a party are to be allocated to its candidates in the following order –

  (a) qualifying candidates, in order of the votes given for each candidate (largest number of votes first);
  (b) other candidates, in the order in which they appear on the party list.

(2) A candidate is a 'qualifying candidate' if the number of votes given for the candidate is at least 5% of the number of votes given for the party as determined for the purposes of paragraph 4(2).

(3) As between qualifying candidates with an equal number of votes, seats are to be allocated in the order in which they appear on the party list.

SCHEDULE 4
INTERIM REPLACEMENT ELECTED MEMBERS
PART 1

INTRODUCTION

Application of Schedule

1 This Schedule applies where, under section 8(2)(a), a person is to be returned as an interim replacement elected member in order to fill the seat of another person ('E').

2 In this Schedule –

Part 2 applies where the relevant electoral district is in Great Britain;

Part 3 applies where the relevant electoral district is Northern Ireland;

Part 4 contains supplementary provisions.

Interpretation

3 In this Schedule –
'independent candidate' –

(a) in relation to an electoral district in Great Britain, is to be read in accordance with Schedule 3;
(b) in relation to the electoral district of Northern Ireland, means a person who stood when elected otherwise than in the name of a party;

the 'nominating officer', in relation to a party, means the person registered as the party's nominating officer under section 24 of the Political Parties, Elections and Referendums Act 2000;
'party candidate' –

(a) in relation to electoral districts in Great Britain, is to be read in accordance with Schedule 3;
(b) in relation to the electoral district of Northern Ireland, means a person who stood when elected in the name of a party;

'party list' is to be read in accordance with Schedule 3;

'the previous elected member' means –

(a) E, unless E was an interim replacement elected member;

(b) if E was an interim replacement elected member, the person who was last returned as an ordinary elected member or replacement elected member at a House of Lords election to fill E's seat;

'the relevant electoral district' means the electoral district for which E was returned as an elected member;

'the returning officer' means the returning officer for the relevant electoral district.

PART 2
ELECTORAL DISTRICTS IN GREAT BRITAIN

Procedure for filling vacancy

4 (1) The returning officer must take such steps as the officer considers reasonable to contact the person determined under paragraph 5, to ask that person to –

(a) make the necessary declaration (see paragraph 10), and

(b) deliver it to the officer.

(2) If the procedure under sub-paragraph (1) (including that procedure undertaken by virtue of this sub-paragraph) is unsuccessful in respect of a person, the procedure must be repeated.

(3) On the second or any subsequent application of sub-paragraph (1), any person in relation to whom the officer has already taken steps under subparagraph (1) in respect of the vacancy is a 'disregarded person' for the purposes of paragraph 5.

(4) The procedure in sub-paragraph (1) is unsuccessful in respect of a person if –

(a) within such period as the returning officer considers reasonable, the officer decides that the steps which the officer has taken under that sub-paragraph to contact the person have been unsuccessful,

(b) within such period as the returning officer considers reasonable, the officer has not received the necessary declaration made by the person, or

(c) the person states in writing that the person is not willing or able to make the necessary declaration.

Person to be contacted

5 (1) If the previous elected member was a party candidate, the person to be contacted is –

(a) the person on the relevant party list who, in accordance with paragraph 6 of Schedule 3, would be allocated a seat first, or

(b) if there is no person on that list (or there is no such list), the person to whom a seat would have been allocated at the last House of Lords election if, in the relevant electoral district, there had been an additional seat to allocate.

(2) 'The relevant party list' is the party list submitted at the last House of Lords election for the relevant electoral district by the party for which the previous elected member stood when elected.

(3) If the previous elected member was an independent candidate, the person to be contacted is the person to whom a seat would have been allocated at the last House of Lords election if, in the relevant electoral district, there had been an additional seat to allocate.

(4) For the purposes of applying paragraph 6 of Schedule 3 (allocation of party candidates to party seats) by virtue of sub-paragraph (1) or (3) any disregarded person is to be disregarded.

(5) For the purposes of applying paragraph 4 of Schedule 3 (allocation of seats to parties or independent candidates) by virtue of sub-paragraph (1)(b) or (3) there is to be disregarded –

(a) any votes given for a party where all of the candidates on its party list are disregarded persons, and

(b) any votes given for an independent candidate who is a disregarded person.

(6) 'Disregarded person' means –

   (a) any person who was returned as an elected member at the
        last House of Lords election or who has been so returned
        since then, including any person whose return is void,
   (b) any party candidate in respect of whom the nominating
        officer of the party in question has given notice, before
        the returning officer first takes steps under paragraph
        4(1) in relation to the vacancy, that the party candidate
        is to be disregarded for the purposes of this Schedule, or
   (c) any person who the returning officer knows has died.

(7) A person to whom section 33 applies (disqualified person:
change in circumstances) who would otherwise fall within
sub-paragraph (6)(a) is to be treated as not falling within that
provision.

Return of person as interim replacement elected member

6 (1) This paragraph applies where, in response to a request to a
person under paragraph 4(1), the returning officer receives the
necessary declaration made by the person.

   (2) The returning officer must (subject to sub-paragraph
(5)) –

   (a) declare the person to be returned as an interim replace-
        ment elected member for the relevant electoral district,
        and
   (b) if the person was a party candidate, declare that the
        person is so returned in the name of the party in question.

Paragraph (b) does not apply in respect of a party that is not a
registered party on the date the necessary declaration is made.

   (3) The declaration under sub-paragraph (2) must –

   (a) be in writing, and
   (b) specify the date on which it is made.

(4) The returning officer must –

(a) give public notice of the declaration, and

(b) give a copy of it to the Clerk of the Crown.

(5) Where –

    (a) the returning officer takes steps under paragraph 4(1) in relation to a person ('A'),

    (b) the officer then takes steps under that provision in relation to another person ('B'), in respect of the same vacancy, and

    (c) the returning officer then receives the necessary declaration made by A; the receipt of that necessary declaration does not count for the purposes of this paragraph unless and until the procedure in paragraph 4(1) is unsuccessful in respect of B.

Procedure where vacancy not filled

7 (1) This paragraph applies if –

    (a) there is no person in relation to whom the returning officer may take steps under paragraph 4(1),

    (b) the procedure under that provision is unsuccessful in respect of each person in relation to whom steps are required to be taken, or

    (c) E's seat has not been filled under this Schedule by the end of the day of dissolution of the last (or only) Parliament of the electoral period in which the vacancy is certified.

(2) The returning officer must notify the Clerk of the Crown that E's seat has not been filled under this Schedule.

(3) No person is to be returned under section 8(2)(a) to fill E's seat.

PART 3
ELECTORAL DISTRICT OF NORTHERN IRELAND

Procedure where the previous elected member was a party candidate

8 (1) This paragraph applies where –

(a) the previous elected member was a party candidate, and

(b) the relevant party is a registered party.

(2) The returning officer must ask the nominating officer of the relevant party to nominate, within the period of 28 days beginning with the day of the request, a person to be returned as an interim replacement elected member.

(3) If, within that period, the returning officer receives –

(a) a nomination made and signed by the nominating officer of the relevant party, nominating a person who is not disqualified from being an elected member, and

(b) the necessary declaration made by the person nominated,

the returning officer must declare the nominated person to be returned as an interim replacement elected member for Northern Ireland.

(4) The declaration must –

(a) be in writing, and

(b) specify the date on which it is made.

(5) The returning officer must –

(a) give public notice of the declaration, and

(b) give a copy of it to the Clerk of the Crown.

(6) 'The relevant party' means the party for which the previous elected member stood when elected.

Procedure where vacancy not filled

9 (1) This paragraph applies if –

(a) paragraph 8 applies but paragraph 8(3) (return of person) does not apply, or

(b) paragraph 8 does not apply (for example, because the previous elected member was an independent candidate).

(2) The returning officer must notify the Clerk of the Crown that E's seat has not been filled under this Schedule.

(3) No person is to be returned under section 8(2)(a) to fill E's seat.

PART 4
SUPPLEMENTARY

The necessary declaration

10 (1) For the purposes of this Schedule a person makes 'the necessary declaration' if the person makes and signs a declaration that –

(a) states the person's date of birth,

(b) states the date on which the declaration is made,

(c) gives the person's consent to being returned as an interim replacement elected member for the relevant electoral district,

(d) declares that the person is aware of the provisions of section 26 (disqualification) so far as relating to elected members, and

(e) declares that to the best of the person's knowledge and belief, the person is not disqualified from being an elected member (whether by virtue of that section or otherwise).

(2) The declaration must also give the person's consent to being returned as an interim replacement elected member in the name of the party in question if –

(a) the person was a party candidate, or

(b) the relevant electoral district is Northern Ireland.

(3) Sub-paragraph (2) does not apply in respect of a party that is not a registered party on the date the necessary declaration is made.

Power to make provision about return of interim replacement elected members

11 (1) The Minister may by order make provision about the return of interim replacement elected members.

(2) The order may, in particular, make provision about the questioning of the return of an interim replacement elected member and the consequences of irregularities.

(3) The order may –

(a) modify this Schedule (other than this paragraph), but only if the modification relates to a procedural matter;

(b) apply, or incorporate, with or without modifications, any provision of primary or secondary legislation;

(c) create criminal offences.

(4) The return of an interim replacement elected member may be questioned only in accordance with provision made under this paragraph (whether by the application or incorporation of Part 3 of the Representation of the People Act 1983 or otherwise).

SCHEDULE 5
THE HOUSE OF LORDS APPOINTMENTS
COMMISSION

The Commissioners

1 (1) The Appointments Commission is to consist of seven members ('Commissioners') appointed by Her Majesty.

(2) One of the Commissioners ('the chair') is to be appointed by Her Majesty to chair the Appointments Commission.

(3) Her Majesty's powers under sub-paragraphs (1) and (2) are exercisable on the recommendation of the Prime Minister.

(4) The Prime Minister is to select persons for recommendation on merit on the basis of fair and open competition.

(5) A Minister of the Crown may not be appointed as a Commissioner.

(6) If a Commissioner becomes a Minister of the Crown, that person ceases to be a Commissioner.

Terms and conditions: general

2 (1) Subject to the provisions of this Schedule, the chair and the other Commissioners hold office in accordance with the terms and conditions of their appointment.

(2) Those terms and conditions are to be determined by the Speakers' Committee.

Term of office

3 (1) The chair and the other Commissioners are to be appointed for a fixed term of 10 years.

(2) A person who ceases to hold office as the chair also ceases to hold office as a Commissioner.

(3) A person may not be appointed as a Commissioner more than once.

Resignation

4 (1) The chair may resign from office by notifying the Prime Minister.

(2) The other Commissioners may resign from office by notifying the chair (or, if the office of chair is vacant, the Prime Minister).

Removal from office

5 (1) Her Majesty may remove the chair, or any of the other Commissioners, from office on an address of both Houses of Parliament.

(2) A motion for an address under sub-paragraph (1) may be made (in either House) only if the Speakers' Committee has reported to the House that it is satisfied that one or more of the removal conditions is met.

(3) The removal conditions are –

(a) that the person is absent from 3 successive meetings of the Appointments Commission without its approval;

(b) that the person has been convicted (anywhere in the world) of an offence (committed anywhere);

(c) that an insolvency order or undertaking comes into force in relation to the person (see section 30);

(d) that the person is unfit or unable to carry out the functions of the office.

(4) In sub-paragraph (3)(b) 'offence' includes any act punishable under the law of a country or territory outside the United Kingdom (however it is described in that law).

(5) For the purposes of sub-paragraph (3)(c), subsection (2) of section 30 (inclusion of pre-commencement undertakings and orders) does not apply.

Remuneration

6 (1) The terms and conditions on which a person is appointed as the chair or as one of the other Commissioners may provide for the Appointments Commission –

    (a) to pay remuneration and allowances to the person;
    (b) to make provision for a pension to or in respect of that person.

(2) The Appointments Commission must make the payment or provision accordingly.

Code of conduct

7 (1) The Appointments Commission must prepare, and may from time to time revise, a code of conduct for the chair and the other Commissioners.

    (2) The code must in particular –

    (a) incorporate the Nolan principles or such other similar principles as may be adopted by the Appointments Commission from time to time, and
    (b) include provision about the disclosure of interests by the chair and the other Commissioners.

(3) The Appointments Commission must submit the code (or revision) to the Speakers' Committee.

    (4) The code (or revision) does not come into effect until it is approved by the Speakers' Committee.

Powers

8 The Appointments Commission may do anything (except borrow money) which is calculated to facilitate the carrying out of its functions or is incidental or conducive to the carrying out of those functions.

Committees etc

9 (1) The Appointments Commission may establish committees, and any committee may establish sub-committees.

(2) All members of a committee or sub-committee must be Commissioners.

(3) The Appointments Commission may delegate functions, other than the functions listed in sub-paragraph (5), to a committee or to one of the Commissioners.

(4) A committee may delegate functions (including functions delegated to it) to a sub-committee or to one of the Commissioners.

(5) The functions which the Appointments Commission may not delegate are –

(a) the preparation of a scheme under section 17(6) (criteria and procedure for selection);

(b) the making of recommendations under section 17(7) (recommendations to the Minister to amend the criteria);

(c) the selection of persons to recommend to the Prime Minister for appointment;

(d) the making of recommendations under sections 13(3) and 14(4) (recommendations for appointment);

(e) the withdrawal of recommendations under section 18;

(f) the appointment of a chief executive under paragraph 11(1).

Procedure and proceedings

10 (1) The Appointments Commission may determine its own procedure and the procedure of its committees and sub-committees (including quorum).

(2) The validity of proceedings of the Appointments Commission or a committee or sub-committee is not affected by –

(a) a vacancy among its members, or

(b) a defect in the appointment of a member.

Staff

11 (1) The Appointments Commission must appoint a chief executive.

(2) The Appointments Commission may appoint other staff.

(3) The chief executive and other staff are to be appointed on terms and conditions determined by the Appointments Commission, having regard to the desirability of keeping them broadly in line with those applying to persons employed in the civil service of the State.

Interim staff

12 (1) The chair of the Speakers' Committee may appoint a person to act as chief executive until the first appointment under paragraph 11(1) takes effect.

(2) A person acting under sub-paragraph (1) may incur expenditure and do other things (including appointing staff) in the name and on behalf of the Appointments Commission –

(a) before the membership of the Commission is first constituted in accordance with paragraph 1, and
(b) after that, until the Commission determines otherwise.

(3) A person's powers under sub-paragraph (2) are exercisable subject to any directions given to the person by the chair of the Speakers' Committee.

(4) The chair of the Speakers' Committee may, until the membership of the Appointments Commission is first constituted in accordance with paragraph 1, appoint other persons to the Commission's staff.

Staff pensions

13 (1) In Schedule 1 to the Superannuation Act 1972 (kinds of employment to which a scheme under section 1 of the Act may apply), at the end of the list of 'Royal Commissions and other Commissions' insert – 'House of Lords Appointments Commission'.

(2) The Appointments Commission must pay to the Minister for the Civil Service the sums determined by the Minister in respect of any increase attributable to this paragraph in the sums payable out of money provided by Parliament under that Act.

Delegation to staff

14 (1) Any of the following may delegate any function (except one listed in paragraph 9(5)) to any of the Appointments Commission's staff –

the Appointments Commission;
a committee or sub-committee;
a Commissioner;
the chief executive.

(2) The functions that may be delegated under sub-paragraph (1) include any function that has been delegated to the body or person in question.

Delegation and contracting out of superannuation functions

15 (1) Section 1(2) of the Superannuation Act 1972 (delegation of functions relating to civil service superannuation schemes by Minister for the Civil Service to another officer of the Crown etc.) has effect as if the reference to an officer of the Crown other than a Minister included a reference to the Appointments Commission's chief executive.

(2) Any administration function conferred on the chief executive under section 1(2) of that Act (in accordance with sub-paragraph (1)) may be carried out by, or by employees of, any person authorised by the chief executive.

(3) 'Administration function' means a function of administering schemes made under section 1 of that Act.

(4) Under sub-paragraph (2) the chief executive may authorise a person to carry out administration functions –

(a) to their full extent or to a specified extent;
(b) in all cases or in specified cases;
(c) unconditionally or subject to specified conditions.

(5) An authorisation under sub-paragraph (2) –

    (a) is to be treated for all purposes as given by virtue of an order under section 69 of the Deregulation and Contracting Out Act 1994 (contracting out of functions of Ministers and office-holders);

    (b) may be revoked at any time by the Appointments Commission or the chief executive.

Status

16 (1) The Appointments Commission, its members and its staff are not to be regarded –

    (a) as the servants or agents of the Crown, or

    (b) as enjoying any status, immunity or privilege of the Crown.

(2) The Appointments Commission's property is not to be regarded as property of, or property held on behalf of, the Crown.

Funding

17 (1) The Appointments Commission's expenditure is to be paid out of money provided by Parliament.

(2) For each financial year other than its first, the Appointments Commission must prepare an estimate of its use of resources and submit it to the Speakers' Committee.

(3) The Speakers' Committee must review the estimate and decide whether it is satisfied that the estimate is consistent with the efficient and cost-effective performance by the Appointments Commission of its functions.

(4) If not so satisfied, the Speakers' Committee must make such modifications to the estimate as it considers necessary for achieving that consistency.

(5) Before deciding whether it is satisfied or making modifications, the Speakers' Committee must consult the Treasury and have regard to any advice given.

(6) After the Speakers' Committee has reviewed the estimate and made any modifications, its chair must arrange for the estimate to be laid before the House of Commons.

(7) If the Speakers' Committee does not follow any advice given by the Treasury, or makes any modifications to the estimate –

(a) it must prepare a statement of its reasons, and
(b) its chair must arrange for the statement to be laid before the House of Commons.

Accounts and accounting officer

18 (1) The Appointments Commission must keep proper accounting records.

(2) The Appointments Commission must, for each financial year, prepare accounts in accordance with directions given to it by the Treasury.

(3) The Treasury may, in particular, give the Appointments Commission directions as to –

(a) the information to be contained in the accounts and how it is to be presented,
(b) the methods and principles in accordance with which the accounts are to be prepared, and
(c) any additional information that is to accompany the accounts.

(4) The Appointments Commission's chief executive is its accounting officer.

Audit

19 (1) As soon as reasonably practicable after the end of each financial year, the Appointments Commission must submit its accounts for that year to –

(a) the Comptroller and Auditor General, and
(b) the Speakers' Committee.

(2) The Comptroller and Auditor General must –

(a) examine and certify the accounts, and
(b) arrange for a copy of the certificate and the accounts, together with a report on them, to be laid before Parliament.

Reports

20 (1) As soon as reasonably practicable after the end of each financial year, the Appointments Commission must –

    (a) prepare a report about the performance of its functions during that year, and

    (b) give a copy of it to the chair of the Speakers' Committee.

(2) The Speakers' Committee must consider the report.

(3) When the Speakers' Committee has considered the report, its chair must arrange for the following documents to be laid before Parliament –

    (a) a copy of the report, and

    (b) a copy of any statement produced by the Committee setting out its views on the report.

(4) Where a statement within sub-paragraph (3)(b) is laid before Parliament, the chair of the Speakers' Committee must give a copy of the statement to the Appointments Commission.

(5) When the report has been laid, the Appointments Commission must publish it and any statement received under sub-paragraph (4).

Documentary evidence

21 (1) A document purporting to be duly executed under the seal of the Appointments Commission or signed on its behalf –

    (a) is to be received in evidence, and

    (b) unless the contrary is proved, is to be taken to be executed or signed in that way.

(2) But this paragraph does not apply in relation to a document signed in accordance with the law of Scotland.

Disqualification

22 (1) In Part 2 of Schedule 1 to the House of Commons Disqualification Act 1975 (bodies of which all members are disqualified), at the appropriate place insert – 'The House of Lords Appointments Commission'.

(2) In Part 2 of Schedule 1 to the Northern Ireland Assembly Disqualification Act 1975 (bodies of which all members are disqualified), at the appropriate place insert – 'The House of Lords Appointments Commission'.

Freedom of information

23 In Part 6 of Schedule 1 to the Freedom of Information Act 2000 (other public bodies and offices which are public authorities), the entry for 'The House of Lords Appointments Commission' is to be treated as a reference to the Appointments Commission.

Public records

24 In Schedule 1 to the Public Records Act 1958 (definition of public records) at the appropriate place in Part 2 of the Table at the end of paragraph 3 insert – 'The House of Lords Appointments Commission'.

Interpretation

25 In this Schedule 'financial year' means –

(a) the period beginning with the day on which the Appointments Commission is established and ending with the next 31 March, and

(b) each successive period of 12 months.

SCHEDULE 6
THE SPEAKERS' COMMITTEE ON THE HOUSE OF LORDS APPOINTMENTS COMMISSION

Members

1 (1) The Speakers' Committee is to consist of the following –

(a) the Speaker of the House of Commons;

(b) the Speaker of the House of Lords;

(c) a Minister of the Crown with responsibilities in relation to constitutional matters who is a member of the House of Commons;

(d) four members of the House of Lords who are not Ministers of the Crown;

(e) four members of the House of Commons who are not Ministers of the Crown;

(f) the person who chairs the relevant committee of the House of Lords;

(g) the person who chairs the relevant committee of the House of Commons.

(2) Members of the Speakers' Committee are to be appointed –

(a) for the purposes of sub-paragraph (1)(c), by the Prime Minister,

(b) for the purposes of sub-paragraph (1)(d), by the House of Lords, and

(c) for the purposes of sub-paragraph (1)(e), by the House of Commons.

(3) The Speakers' Committee is to select one of its members to chair it.

(4) For the purposes of sub-paragraph (1)(f) and (g), the relevant committee of the House of Lords or the House of Commons is the committee of that House concerned with constitutional matters, so far as relating to membership of the House of Lords.

(5) Any question arising under sub-paragraph (4) is to be determined by the Speaker of the House in question.

Term of office of members

2 (1) In this paragraph 'appointed member of the Speakers' Committee' means a member appointed under paragraph 1(2).

(2) Except as provided by this paragraph, an appointed member of the Speakers' Committee is a member of the Speakers'

Committee for the remainder of the Parliament in which the person is appointed.

(3) If an appointed member of the Speakers' Committee who is a member of the House of Lords ceases to be a member of that House, that person ceases to be a member of the Speakers' Committee.

(4) If an appointed member of the Speakers' Committee who is a member of the House of Commons ceases to be a member of that House, that person ceases to be a member of the Speakers' Committee.

(5) If an appointed member of the Speakers' Committee within paragraph 1(1)(d) or (e) becomes a Minister of the Crown, that person ceases to be a member of the Speakers' Committee.

(6) An appointed member of the Speakers' Committee ceases to be a member of the Speakers' Committee if another person is appointed in that person's place.

(7) An appointed member of the Speakers' Committee may resign from the Speakers' Committee by notifying the Committee.

(8) An appointed member of the Speakers' Committee may be reappointed (more than once).

Procedure

3 (1) The Speakers' Committee may establish sub-committees.

(2) The functions of the Speakers' Committee under paragraph 17 of Schedule 5 (review of Appointments Commission's estimates) are to be exercised by a sub-committee which does not include any member of the House of Lords.

(3) Subject to that, the Speakers' Committee may determine its own procedure and the procedure of its sub-committees (including quorum).

(4) The validity of proceedings of the Speakers' Committee or a sub-committee is not affected by –

(a)   a vacancy among its members, or

(b)   a defect in the appointment of a member.

SCHEDULE 7
TRANSITIONAL MEMBERS

Transitional members for first electoral period

1 (1) A person is a transitional member for the first electoral period if –

   (a) before the beginning of that period, the person is selected as a transitional member for that period, and

   (b) at the beginning of the day of the first House of Lords election, the person is a peer who is entitled to receive writs of summons to attend the House of Lords.

(2) The maximum number of persons who may be selected under this paragraph is two thirds of the number of peers who, at the beginning of 27 June 2012, were entitled to receive writs of summons to attend the House of Lords.

   (3) If the number given by sub-paragraph (2) is not a whole number, it is to be rounded up to the nearest whole number.

Transitional members for second electoral period

2 (1) A person is a transitional member for the second electoral period if –

   (a) before the beginning of that period, the person is selected as a transitional member for that period, and

   (b) at the beginning of the day of the second House of Lords election, the person is a transitional member.

(2) The maximum number of persons who may be selected under this paragraph is one third of the number of peers who, at the beginning of 27 June 2012, were entitled to receive writs of summons to attend the House of Lords.

   (3) If the number given by sub-paragraph (2) is not a whole number, it is to be rounded up to the nearest whole number.

Selection of transitional members

3 (1) The selection of persons under paragraph 1 or 2 is to be made in accordance with standing orders of the House of Lords.

(2) The standing orders may make provision for persons to be selected in any way (for example, by election or by reference to decisions made by political parties or other groups of members).

(3) The standing orders may in particular –

(a) make provision about a person's eligibility for selection;

(b) make provision under which the selection of a person is void.

(4) Anything required or permitted to be done by standing orders under this paragraph may be done when the House of Lords is adjourned, or Parliament is prorogued or dissolved; but this is subject to any provision made in the standing orders.

(5) A person may be selected under paragraph 1 in accordance with standing orders made in anticipation of this paragraph being enacted or coming into force.

Supplementary provisions

4 In determining for the purposes of paragraph 1 or 2 whether a peer is entitled to receive writs of summons to attend the House of Lords, section 427 of the Insolvency Act 1986 (no entitlement to writs of summons during bankruptcy etc) is to be disregarded.

5 (1) Any question as to –

(a) the maximum number of persons who may be selected under paragraph 1 or 2, or

(b) whether a person has been selected under paragraph 1 or 2,

is to be determined by the Clerk of the Parliaments.

(2) A certificate of the Clerk's decision signed by the Clerk is conclusive.

6 Where the selection of a person as a transitional member is void, no other person is to be selected to replace that person.

7 Where a person ceases to be a transitional member, no other person is to be selected to replace that person.

SCHEDULE 8
PERSONS DISQUALIFIED FROM MEMBERSHIP
OF THE HOUSE OF LORDS
PART 1
DISQUALIFYING OFFICES

Meaning of 'holding a disqualifying office' etc

1 (1) A person holds a disqualifying office if the person is of a description falling within any of the following paragraphs of this Part of this Schedule.

(2) But in relation to membership as a transitional member, a person holds a disqualifying office only if the person is the Comptroller and Auditor General.

Persons with functions relating to Parliament, elections etc

2 A person who is any of the following –
the Comptroller and Auditor General;
the Parliamentary Commissioner for Administration;
the Public Standards Commissioner for Scotland;
a member of IPSA;
the Compliance Officer for IPSA;
a member of the Electoral Commission;
a member of the Boundary Commission for England;
a member of the Boundary Commission for Scotland;
a member of the Boundary Commission for Wales;
a member of the Boundary Commission for Northern Ireland;
a member of the Local Government Boundary Commission for England;
a member of the Local Government Boundary Commission for Scotland;
a member of the Local Government Boundary Commission for Wales;
a Local Government Boundaries Commissioner appointed under section 50 of the Local Government Act (Northern Ireland) 1972;

an electoral registration officer appointed under section 8 of the Representation of People Act 1983;

a returning officer under section 25(1) of the Representation of the People Act 1983 and any deputy returning officer appointed by such a returning officer;

the Chief Electoral Officer for Northern Ireland;

a whole-time officer appointed under section 14A(1) of the Electoral Law Act (Northern Ireland) 1962 (assistants to Chief Electoral Officer);

a returning officer or local returning officer designated by virtue of provision made under section 7.

Holders of certain judicial offices

3 A person who is any of the following –

judge of the Supreme Court;

judge of the Court of Appeal in England and Wales;

judge of the High Court of Justice in England and Wales;

Circuit judge;

district judge in England and Wales;

District Judge (Magistrates' Courts) (but not a Deputy District Judge (Magistrates' Courts)) in England and Wales;

judge of the Court of Session, or Temporary Judge appointed under the Law Reform (Miscellaneous Provisions) (Scotland) Act 1990;

Chairman of the Scottish Land Court;

Sheriff Principal or Sheriff (other than Honorary Sheriff) appointed under the Sheriff Courts (Scotland) Act 1907, or Temporary Sheriff Principal or part-time sheriff appointed under the Sheriff Courts (Scotland) Act 1971;

Stipendiary Magistrate in Scotland;

judge of the Court of Appeal in Northern Ireland;

judge of the High Court in Northern Ireland;

county court judge or deputy county court judge in Northern Ireland;

district judge in Northern Ireland;

district judge (magistrates' courts) or deputy district judge (magistrates' courts) in Northern Ireland;

judge of the Court Martial Appeal Court;

judge of the Upper Tribunal;

judge of the First-tier Tribunal (including an adjudicator appointed under section 5 of the Criminal Injuries Compensation Act 1995 by the Scottish Ministers);

Chief or other Social Security Commissioner (not including a deputy Commissioner);

Chief or other Child Support Commissioner for Northern Ireland or deputy Child Support Commissioner for Northern Ireland;

Chief or other Social Security Commissioner for Northern Ireland or deputy Social Security Commissioner for Northern Ireland;

Adjudicator to Her Majesty's Land Registry.

Civil servants

4 (1) A person employed in the civil service of the State.

(2) For this purpose it does not matter whether the person is employed full-time or part-time or whether the person is employed in an established capacity or not.

Members of the regular armed forces

5 (1) A member of the regular forces (within the meaning of the Armed Forces Act 2006) other than –

(a) a person recalled to service,

(b) a person who holds an emergency commission, or

(c) a person within sub-paragraph (2) who does not for the time being hold an appointment in the naval, military or air force service of the Crown.

(2) A person is within this sub-paragraph if the person –

(a) is an Admiral of the Fleet, a Field Marshal or a Marshal of the Royal Air Force, or

   (b) has previously been appointed to any of the following roles –
     (i)   Chief of the Defence Staff;
     (ii)   Vice Chief of the Defence Staff;
     (iii) Chief of the Naval Staff;
     (iv) Chief of the General Staff;
     (v)   Chief of the Air Staff.

Police officers

6 A person employed as a full-time constable by –

   (a) a police force maintained by a local policing body,
   (b) the Police Service of Scotland, or
   (c) a police force maintained by the Northern Ireland Policing Board.

Members of foreign legislatures

7 A member of the legislature of a country or territory other than Ireland that is outside the Commonwealth.

Ambassadors etc

8 An ambassador, high commissioner, or permanent representative to an international organisation, representing Her Majesty's Government in the United Kingdom.

PART 2
OFFICES DISQUALIFYING FOR PARTICULAR ELECTORAL DISTRICTS

Office:

Member of Her Majesty's Commission of Lieutenancy for the City of London

Electoral District:

The electoral district which includes the City of London

Office:

Her Majesty's Lord-Lieutenant or Lieutenant for Greater London

Electoral District:

Any electoral district which includes the whole or part of Greater London

Office:

Her Majesty's Lord-Lieutenant or Lieutenant for a county in England and Wales

Electoral District:

Any electoral district which includes the whole or part of the area for which the holder of the office is appointed

Office:

Her Majesty's Lord-Lieutenant or Lieutenant for an area in Scotland

Electoral District:

Any electoral district which includes the whole or part of the area in which the Lord-Lieutenant holds office or in which the Lord-Lieutenant or Lieutenant discharges the functions of that office

Office:

Her Majesty's Lord-Lieutenant or Lieutenant for the city of Aberdeen, Dundee, Edinburgh or Glasgow

Electoral District:

Any electoral district which includes the whole or part of the city in which the Lord-Lieutenant holds office or for which the Lieutenant is appointed

Office:

Her Majesty's Lord-Lieutenant or Lieutenant for a county or county borough in Northern Ireland

Electoral District:

Northern Ireland

Office:

Governor of the Isle of Wight

Electoral District:

The electoral district which includes the Isle of Wight

Office:

The High Sheriff of Greater London

Electoral District:

Any electoral district which includes the whole or part of Greater London

Office:

The High Sheriff of a county in England and Wales

Electoral District:

Any electoral district which includes the whole or part of the area for which the holder of the office is appointed

PART 3
POWER TO AMEND SCHEDULE

9 (1) If each House of Parliament resolves that this Schedule (other than this paragraph) should be amended in a particular way, Her Majesty may by Order in Council amend the Schedule in that way.

(2) A resolution under sub-paragraph (1) may provide that the amendments are to apply –

(a) to all members,
(b) to a specified description of member, or
(c) to all members other than members of a specified description.

SCHEDULE 9
PAY AND ALLOWANCES
PART 1
AMENDMENTS TO THE PARLIAMENTARY
STANDARDS ACT 2009

Introduction

1 Amend the Parliamentary Standards Act 2009 as follows.

Section 2: application of the Act to the House of Lords

2 Omit section 2 (nothing in the Act affects House of Lords).

Section 3: IPSA etc

3 In section 3(5) (Speaker's Committee for IPSA) for 'Speaker's' substitute 'Speakers'.

Section 3A: IPSA's general duties

4 In section 3A(2) (general duties of IPSA) after 'members of the House of Commons' insert 'and members of the House of Lords'.

Section 5: MPs' allowances scheme

5 In section 5(4)(d) and (5) (MPs' allowances scheme) after 'Speaker' insert 'of the House of Commons'.

Section 9: investigations

6 (1) Amend section 9 (investigations) as follows.

(2) In subsection (1)(a) the words from 'a member' to the end become paragraph (a), and (b); after that paragraph insert –
'or (b) a member of the House of Lords may have been paid an amount under the House of Lords allowances scheme that should not have been allowed.'

(3) In subsections (6)(b), (7) and (8)(a) for 'MPs' allowances scheme' substitute 'relevant allowances scheme'.

(4) In subsection (10)(a) the words from 'to a member' to the end become paragraph (a), and (b); after that paragraph

insert – ', and (b) to a member of the House of Lords, include a former member of the House of Lords.'

(5) After that subsection insert – '(11) In this section the "relevant allowances scheme" means –

(a) in relation to an investigation under subsection (1)(a), the MPs' allowances scheme, and

(b) in relation to an investigation under subsection (1)(b), the House of Lords allowances scheme.'

Section 9A: procedures etc

7 (1) Amend section 9A (procedures to be followed in investigations etc) as follows.

(2) In subsection (5)(a) for 'section 6A(3)' substitute 'sections 6A(3) and 7F(3)'.

(3) In subsection (6) after paragraph (c) insert –

'(ca) the Speaker of the House of Lords,

(cb) the Leader of the House of Lords,

(cc) the House of Lords Committee for Privileges and Conduct,'

Section 9B: enforcement

8 In section 9B (enforcement) after subsection (2) insert – '(3) The Compliance Officer may provide to the House of Lords Commissioner for Standards any information connected with an investigation under section 9 or action taken under Schedule 4 which the Compliance Officer considers may be relevant to the work of the House of Lords Commissioner for Standards.'

Section 10: offence of providing false or misleading information for allowances claims

9 (1) Amend section 10 (offence of providing false or misleading information for allowances claims) as follows.

(2) After subsection (1) insert – '(1A) A member of the House of Lords commits an offence if the member –

(a) makes a claim under the House of Lords allowances scheme, and

(b) provides information for the purposes of the claim that the member knows to be false or misleading in a material respect.'

(3) In subsection (2) after subsection (1) insert 'or (1A)'.

Section 10A: relationships with other bodies etc

10 (1) Amend section 10A (relationship with other bodies) as follows.

(2) In subsection (1) after paragraph (a) insert – '(aa) the House of Lords Commissioner for Standards;'.

(3) In subsection (3) after 'House of Commons' insert 'or the House of Lords'.

(4) In subsection (4) –

(a) after 'a member of the House of Commons' insert 'or a member of the House of Lords', and

(b) in paragraph (b) after 'the House of Commons' insert 'or the House of Lords'.

(5) In subsection (5) –

(a) the words from 'to a member' to the end become paragraph (a), and

(b) after that paragraph insert ', and (b) to a member of the House of Lords, include a former member of the House of Lords.'

Section 12: interpretation

11 (1) Amend section 12 (interpretation) as follows.

(2) In subsection (1) –

(a) after the definition of 'the Compliance Officer' insert – '"the House of Lords allowances scheme" has the meaning given by section 7D(2);', and

(b) after the definition of 'the Leader of the House of Commons' insert – '"the Leader of the House of Lords" means the Minister of the Crown who is for the time being designated as Leader of the House of Lords by the Prime Minister;'.

(3) After subsection (4) insert – '(5) In this Act –

(a) references to the House of Lords Committee for Privileges and Conduct are to the committee or committees of the House of Lords concerned with the conduct of members of the House of Lords,

(b) references to the person who chairs that Committee are, where there is more than one such committee, to the persons who chair those committees, and

(c) references to the House of Lords Commissioner for Standards are to the officer of the House of Lords responsible for investigations into the conduct of members of the House of Lords.

(6) Any question arising under subsection (5) is to be determined by the Speaker of the House of Lords.'

Schedule 1: IPSA

12 (1) Amend Schedule 1 (IPSA) as follows.

(2) In paragraph 1(4) and (5) for 'the House of Commons' substitute 'either House of Parliament'.

(3) In paragraph 2 –

(a) in sub-paragraphs (1) and (2) for 'the House of Commons' substitute 'both Houses of Parliament',

(b) in sub-paragraph (3) for 'only with the agreement of the Speaker' substitute –
'(a) in the House of Commons, only with the agreement of the Speaker of the House of Commons, and
(b) in the House of Lords, only with the agreement of the Speaker of the House of Lords'.

(c) in sub-paragraph (4) omit 'by the Speaker' and after 'competition' insert 'by the Speaker of the House of Commons and the Speaker of the House of Lords', and

(d) in sub-paragraph (5) – (i) for 'Speaker' substitute 'Speakers', and (ii) for 'Speaker's' substitute 'Speakers'.

(4) In paragraph 3(2) for 'the Speaker' substitute 'the Speaker of the House of Commons and the Speaker of the House of Lords'.

(5) In paragraph 5(1) and (2) for 'the Speaker' substitute 'the Speaker of the House of Commons and the Speaker of the House of Lords'.

(6) In paragraph 18

(a) in sub-paragraph (1) after paragraph (c) insert –
'(d) section 7A (payment of House of Lords pay) except subsection (3) of that section,
    (e) section 7D(1) (payment of House of Lords allowances), and
    (f) section 7E (dealing with House of Lords allowances claims) except subsection (9) of that section.', and

(b) in sub-paragraph (2) after paragraph (aa) insert – '(ab) section 7A(3) and 7B and 7C (determination of level of House of Lords pay), (ac) section 7D(3) and (4) (preparing and revising House of Lords allowances scheme), (ad) section 7E(9) (determining procedures for publication of allowances claims)'.

(7) In paragraph 20(4) –

(a) after paragraph (a) (but before the 'and') insert – '(aa) paying pay under section 7A',

(b) in paragraph (b) after 'MPs' allowances scheme' insert 'and the House of Lords allowances scheme', and

(c) in the text after that paragraph, after 'function' insert 'of calculating the amount of pay for a member of the House of Lords,'.

(8) In paragraph 22 –

- (a) in sub-paragraph (2) for 'Speaker's' substitute 'Speakers', and
- (b) in sub-paragraphs (6) and (7) after 'Speaker' insert 'of the House of Commons'.

(9) In paragraph 25 –

- (a) in sub-paragraph (1) omit 'and the Speaker must lay before each House of Parliament',
- (b) after that sub-paragraph insert –

    '(1A) The IPSA must send the report to the Speaker of the House of Commons and the Speaker of the House of Lords.

    (1B) The Speaker of the House of Commons must lay the report before the House of Commons, and the Speaker of the House of Lords must lay the report before the House of Lords.', and
- (c) in sub-paragraph (2) for 'the Speaker lays' substitute 'the Speakers lay'.

(10) In paragraph 27(2) –

- (a) in paragraph (b), for ', and' substitute 'of the House of Commons,', and
- (b) after paragraph (c) insert –

    '(d) the Leader of the House of Lords,
    (e) the Speaker of the House of Lords, and
    (f) the House of Lords Committee for Privileges and Conduct.'

(11) In paragraph 29(2) omit the definition of 'the Speaker' (and the 'and' before it).

Schedule 2: Compliance Officer for IPSA

13 In paragraph 8 of Schedule 2 (Compliance Officer's annual report) –

- (a) in sub-paragraph (2) for ', who must lay it before each House of Parliament' substitute 'and the Speaker of the House of Lords',

(b) after that sub-paragraph insert – '(2A) The Speaker of the House of Commons must lay the report before the House of Commons, and the Speaker of the House of Lords must lay the report before the House of Lords.', and

(c) in sub-paragraph (3) for 'the Speaker lays' substitute 'the Speakers lay'.

Schedule 3: Speaker's Committee for IPSA

14 (1) Amend Schedule 3 (Speaker's Committee for IPSA) as follows.

(2) In the heading to the Schedule, for 'Speaker's' substitute 'Speakers''.

(3) In paragraph 1 –

(a) for 'Speaker's' substitute 'Speakers'',

(b) in paragraph (d) for 'five' substitute 'three',

(c) omit 'and' at the end of that paragraph,

(d) after that paragraph insert –

'(da) the Speaker of the House of Lords,

(db) the Leader of the House of Lords,

(dc) the person who chairs the House of Lords Committee for Privileges and Conduct,

(dd) three members of the House of Lords who are not Ministers of the Crown, appointed by the House of Lords, and', and

(e) in paragraph (e) for 'the House of Commons' substitute 'each House of Parliament'.

(4) After that paragraph insert – '1A The Committee is to select one of its members to chair it.'

(5) In paragraph 2(1) –

(a) after paragraph 1(d) insert 'or (dd)', and

(b) in paragraph (b) after 'House of Commons' insert 'or a member of the House of Lords (as the case may be)'.

(6) In paragraph 2A –

(a) in sub-paragraph (2) for 'only with the agreement of the Speaker of the House of Commons' substitute –

'(a) in the House of Commons, only with the agreement of the Speaker of the House of Commons, and

(b) in the House of Lords, only with the agreement of the Speaker of the House of Lords.',

(b) in sub-paragraph (3) for 'the Speaker' substitute 'the Speaker of the House of Commons and the Speaker of the House of Lords', and

(c) in sub-paragraph (8) –

(i) after 'Speaker of the House of Commons' insert 'and the Speaker of the House of Lords', and

(ii) for 'Speaker' substitute 'Speakers'.

(7) In paragraph 3 –

(a) for sub-paragraph (1) substitute –

'(1) The Committee may establish sub-committees.

(1A) The functions of the Committee under paragraph 22 of Schedule 1 (review of IPSA's estimates) are to be exercised by a sub-committee of the Committee which does not include any member of the House of Lords.

(1B) Subject to that, the Committee may determine its own procedure and the procedure of its sub-committees (including quorums).', and

(b) in sub-paragraph (2) after 'Committee' insert 'or a sub-committee'.

Schedule 4: enforcement

15 (1) Amend Schedule 4 (enforcement) as follows.

(2) In paragraph 1 –

(a) in sub-paragraph (1)(a) for 'section 9' substitute 'section 9(1)(a) or a member of the House of Lords under section 9(1)(b)',

(b) in sub-paragraphs (1)(b) and (3) after 'MPs' allowances scheme' insert 'or the House of Lords allowances scheme', and

   (c) in sub-paragraph (8) the words from 'to a member' to the end become paragraph (a), and after that paragraph insert – ', and (b) to a member of the House of Lords, include a former member of the House of Lords.'

(3) In paragraph 5 –

   (a) in sub-paragraph (3) for 'The' substitute 'Where the repayment direction was given following an investigation under section 9(1)(a), the', and

   (b) after that sub-paragraph insert –

    '(3A) Where the repayment direction was given following an investigation under section 9(1)(b), the IPSA may recover the amount by making deductions from –

     (a) any pay payable to the member under section 7A;

     (b) any allowances payable to the member under the House of Lords allowances scheme.'

(4) In paragraph 6 –

   (a) in sub-paragraph (1) after 'member of the House of Commons' insert 'or a member of the House of Lords', and

   (b) in sub-paragraph (6) the words from 'to a member' to the end become paragraph (a), and after that paragraph insert ', and (b) to a member of the House of Lords, include a former member of the House of Lords.'

(5) In paragraph 7(5) for 'the House of Commons' substitute 'each House of Parliament'.

   (6) In paragraph 12 –

   (a) in sub-paragraph (3) for 'The' substitute 'Where the penalty was imposed following an investigation under section 9(1)(a), the', and

   (b) after that sub-paragraph insert –

    '(3A) Where the penalty was imposed following an investigation under section 9(1)(b), the IPSA may recover the amount by making deductions from –

(a) any pay payable to the member under section 7A;

(b) any allowances payable to the member under the House of Lords allowances scheme.'

(7) In paragraph 13(b) after '12(3)' insert 'or (3A)'.

PART 2
TRANSFER SCHEMES

16 (1) The Minister may by order provide –

(a) for the employment of persons of a specified description who are employed in connection with matters relating to allowances for members of the House of Lords to be transferred to IPSA by a scheme,

(b) for specified property, rights and liabilities which subsist wholly or mainly for the purposes of the House of Lords to be transferred to IPSA by a scheme, and

(c) for specified documents and information held by or on behalf of the House of Lords (or an officer or committee of the House of Lords) to be transferred to the Compliance Officer or IPSA.

(2) A scheme made by virtue of sub-paragraph (1) is to be made by the Minister with the consent of the Speaker of the House of Lords.

SCHEDULE 10
MINOR AND CONSEQUENTIAL AMENDMENTS
PART 1
CHANGE TO THE DEFINITION OF 'PARLIAMENTARY ELECTION'

Amendments to the Interpretation Act 1978 (c. 30)

1 (1) Amend Schedule 1 to the Interpretation Act 1978 (words and expressions defined) as follows.

(2) For the definition of 'Parliamentary Election' substitute –

'"Parliamentary election" means a House of Commons election or an election to the House of Lords.'

(3) At the appropriate place insert – '"House of Commons election" means the election of a Member of Parliament to serve in the House of Commons for a constituency; and references to a general election or a by-election, in the context of the House of Commons, are to be construed accordingly.'

(4) At the appropriate place insert – '"Election to the House of Lords" means the election in an electoral district at a House of Lords election of persons to serve as elected members of the House of Lords for that district.'

(5) In consequence of the amendment made by sub-paragraph (2), references in the following provisions to a parliamentary election (however expressed) include an election in an electoral district at a House of Lords election –

paragraphs 21(1) and 37(1) of Schedule 12 to the Local Government Act 1972 (c. 70);

sections 13B, 13BA and 47(1) of the Representation of the People Act 1983 (c. 2);

section 20(1) of the Representation of the People Act 1985 (c. 50);

section 65(6) of the Local Government Finance Act 1988 (c. 41);

paragraph 2 of Schedule 2 to the Northern Ireland Act 1998 (c. 47);

section 22(5)(a) of the Political Parties, Elections and Referendums Act 2000 (c. 41);

sections 42(2), 44(5) and 69(9)(a) of the Electoral Administration Act 2006 (c. 22);

section 1(1)(a) of the Northern Ireland (Miscellaneous Provisions) Act 2006 (c. 33);

sections 104(8) and 106(5) of the Equality Act 2010 (c. 15).

Specific modifications of Acts of Parliament

2 (1) In the Acts or, as the case may be, the provisions of the Acts listed in subparagraph (2), for the words in the first column (in each place) substitute the words in the corresponding entry in the second column –

Old words	*New words*
'parliamentary election'	'House of Commons election'
'parliamentary elections'	'House of Commons elections'
'parliamentary or local government election'	'House of Commons or local government election'
'parliamentary or local government elections'	'House of Commons or local government elections'
'parliamentary general election'	'House of Commons general election'
'parliamentary general elections'	'House of Commons general elections'
'parliamentary by-election'	'House of Commons by-election'

A reference falls within the first column regardless of whether any of the words in question starts with a capital letter.

(2) The Acts or provisions of Acts are –

section 4(4) of the Agricultural Marketing Act 1958 (c. 47);
section 219(6) of the Local Government Act 1972 (c. 70);
paragraph 1(3) of Part 5 of Schedule 1 to the Ministerial and other Salaries Act 1975 (c. 27);
section 108(1) of the Judicature (Northern Ireland) Act 1978 (c. 23);
section 142(1) of the Senior Courts Act 1981 (c. 54);
the Representation of the People Act 1983, except sections 13B, 13BA and 47(1);
the Elections (Northern Ireland) Act 1985 (c. 2);
the Representation of the People Act 1985, except section 20(1);
the Parliamentary Constituencies Act 1986 (c. 56);
section 2(1) of the Elected Authorities (Northern Ireland) Act 1989 (c. 3);

section 264(1) of the Taxation of Chargeable Gains Act 1992 (c. 12);

sections 12(4) and 12A(4) of the Scotland Act 1998 (c. 46);

section 12(1) and (2) of, and Schedule 4 to, the Representation of the People Act 2000 (c. 2);

sections 9HE(3) and 44(3) of the Local Government Act 2000 (c. 22);

the Political Parties, Elections and Referendums Act 2000 (c. 41), except section 22(5)(a);

section 4 of, and the Schedule to, the Elections Act 2001 (c. 7);

sections 6(5A), 7(3) and 8(2) of the European Parliamentary Elections Act 2002 (c. 24);

section 67(2) of the Finance Act 2003 (c. 14);

sections 34(1), 44(8) to (11) and 46(3)(a) of the Electoral Administration Act 2006 (c. 22);

section 13(5)(d) of the Government of Wales Act 2006 (c. 32);

sections 13B(3)(b), 223B(3)(b) and 223D(7)(b) of the National Health Service Act 2006 (c. 41);

section 4(5) of the Parliamentary Standards Act 2009 (c. 13);

section 15(1) of, and paragraph 2(8) of Schedule 1 to, the Constitutional Reform and Governance Act 2010 (c. 25);

section 11(1)(a) of the European Union Act 2011 (c. 12);

sections 54(1) and (5) and 58(7) of the Police Reform and Social Responsibility Act 2011 (c. 13); the Fixed-term Parliaments Act 2011 (c. 14).

(3) This paragraph applies only in so far as the reference is in the context of an election to the Parliament of the United Kingdom.

(4) This paragraph does not apply if the reference is amended by any of the following provisions of this Schedule.

3 In the following provisions for 'general election' (in each place) substitute 'House of Commons general election' –

paragraph 3(3)(a) of Schedule 1 to the House of Commons (Administration) Act 1978 (c. 36);

paragraph 2(3)(a) of Schedule 1 to the National Audit Act 1983 (c. 44);

section 24(2) of the Inheritance Tax Act 1984 (c. 51);

section 170(3) of the Criminal Justice and Public Order Act 1994 (c. 33).

4 (1) Amend the Representation of the People Act 1983 as follows.

(2) In section 31 (polling districts at local government elections) –

(a) in subsection (3) for 'parliamentary' (in each place) substitute 'House of Commons', and

(b) after subsection (3) insert – '(3A) For the purposes of subsection (3) – "House of Commons polling district" means a polling district designated for the purpose of House of Commons elections under section 18A; "House of Commons polling place" means a polling place designated for such a district under section 18B.'

(3) In the following for 'parliamentary' substitute 'House of Commons' –

(a) the heading immediately before section 49;

(b) the heading to section 68;

(c) section 73(3).

(4) In section 202(1) (general provisions as to interpretation) –

(a) omit the definition of 'parliamentary election petition',

(b) at the appropriate place insert – '"House of Commons election petition" means an election petition questioning a House of Commons election or return;',

(c) omit the definition of 'parliamentary elections rules', and

(d) at the appropriate place insert – '"House of Commons elections rules" means the House of Commons elections rules in Schedule 1 to this Act;'.

(5) In the Appendix of Forms at the end of Schedule 1, in the form of writ –

    (a) for 'general election' (in each place) substitute 'House of Commons general election', and

    (b) for 'Member to serve in Parliament' substitute 'Member of Parliament to serve in the House of Commons'.

(6) In that Appendix, in the form of nomination paper for 'Parliament' substitute 'the House of Commons'.

5 In the heading to section 5 and to section 15 of the Representation of the People Act 1985 for *'parliamentary'* substitute *'House of Commons'.*

General modifications of other legislation

6 (1) In so far as is appropriate in consequence of the amendment made by paragraph 1(2), a reference (however expressed) in primary or secondary legislation, or in an instrument or other document, to an expression in the first column is to be read as a reference to the expression in the corresponding entry in the second column –

Old expression	*New expression*
'parliamentary election'	'House of Commons election'
'parliamentary general election'	'House of Commons general election'
'parliamentary by-election'	'House of Commons by-election'
'parliamentary election petition'	'House of Commons election petition'
'parliamentary elections rules'	'House of Commons elections rules'

(2) This paragraph applies only –

    (a) in so far as the reference is in the context of an election to the Parliament of the United Kingdom, and

    (b) if the legislation is passed or made, or the instrument or document is issued, before paragraph 1 comes into force.

(3) This paragraph does not apply if the reference –

    (a) is in an Act of Parliament,

    (b) is in the short title of other primary legislation,

    (c) is in the title of secondary legislation, or

    (d) is contained in the amendment made by paragraph 23 to the Sex Discrimination (Northern Ireland) Order 1976 (S.I. 1976/1042 (N.I.15)).

Supplementary

7 (1) Where legislation (A) which is passed or made before paragraph 1 comes into force amends other legislation (B), the amendments are to be treated for the purposes of this Part as part of legislation B and not part of legislation A.

(2) That is the case whether or not the amendments are in force; and where they are not in force, legislation B is to be treated for the purposes of this Part as including both the text which is in force and the amended text.

(3) Sub-paragraphs (1) and (2) are subject to express provision to the contrary.

PART 2
OTHER MINOR AND CONSEQUENTIAL AMENDMENTS

House of Lords Precedence Act 1539 (c. 10)

8 Omit section 1, sections 3 to 8, and section 10 of the House of Lords Precedence Act 1539 (seating in the House of Lords and the Privy Council).

Bill of Rights (1 Will. & Mar. Sess. 2 c. 2)

9 In section 1 of the Bill of Rights (acceptance of the Crown etc) for 'House of Peers in the presence of the lords and commons' substitute 'House of Lords in the presence of the members of the House of Lords and the members of the House of Commons'.

Union with Scotland Act 1706 (c. 11) and Union with England Act 1707 (c.7)

10 The Union with Scotland Act 1706 and the Union with England Act 1707 have effect subject to this Act.

Parliamentary Privilege Act 1737 (c. 24)

11 In section 4 of the Parliamentary Privilege Act 1737 (claims on behalf of the Crown not to be subject to parliamentary privilege) –

    (a) for the words from 'peer or lord' to 'House of Commons of Great Britain' substitute 'member of the House of Commons or House of Lords', and

    (b) after 'by or upon any such' insert 'suit'.

Parliamentary Privilege Act 1770 (c. 50)

12 In section 1 of the Parliamentary Privilege Act 1770 (legal proceedings against members of either House of Parliament) –

    (a) in the heading, for '*peers*' substitute '*members of the House of Lords*', and

    (b) for 'peer or lord of Parliament of Great Britain' substitute 'member of the House of Lords'.

Union with Ireland Act 1800 (c. 67)

13 (1) Amend Article the Fourth of the Union with Ireland Act 1800 as follows.

    (2) Omit –

    (a) the paragraph beginning 'That any person holding' (which provides that peers of Ireland may be MPs),

(b) the paragraph beginning 'That it shall be lawful' (power
to create and promote peers of Ireland), and the paragraph beginning 'That if any peerage shall' (provision
about peerages in abeyance etc).

(3) In the paragraph beginning 'That when his Majesty' (which
provides for the issue of a proclamation) –

(a) for 'commons' or 'Commons' (in each place) substitute
'members of the House of Commons', and

(b) for 'lords spiritual and temporal and' substitute 'members of the House of Lords and the'.

(4) In the final paragraph (which makes provision about the
rights and privileges of peers of Ireland and Great Britain etc)
omit the words from ', the right and privilege of sitting in the
House of Lords' to the end.

Act of Union (Ireland) 1800 (c. 38)

14 (1) Amend Article Fourth of the Act of Union (Ireland) 1800
as follows.

(2) Omit –

(a) the paragraph beginning 'That any person holding'
(which provides that peers of Ireland may be MPs),

(b) the paragraph beginning 'That it shall be lawful' (power
to create and promote peers of Ireland), and

(c) the paragraph beginning 'That if any peerage shall' (provision about peerages in abeyance etc).

(3) In the paragraph beginning 'That when his Majesty' (which
provides for the issue of a proclamation) –

(a) for 'commons' or 'Commons' (in each place) substitute
'members of the House of Commons', and

(b) for 'lords spiritual and temporal and' substitute 'members of the House of Lords and the'.

(4) In the final paragraph (which makes provision about the
rights and privileges of peers of Ireland and Great Britain etc)

omit the words from ', the right and privilege of sitting in the House of Lords' to the end.

Parliamentary Oaths Act 1866 (c. 19)

15 (1) Amend the Parliamentary Oaths Act 1866 as follows.

(2) In section 3 (time and manner of taking Parliamentary oath) for 'House of Peers' (in both places) substitute 'House of Lords'.

(3) In section 5 (penalty for voting or sitting without taking oath) –

(a) for 'House of Peers' (in both places) substitute 'House of Lords',

(b) omit 'as a peer', and

(c) after 'High Court' insert 'and in addition to such penalty, shall cease to be a member of that House'.

Forfeiture Act 1870 (c. 23)

16 In section 2 of the Forfeiture Act 1870 (persons convicted of treason disqualified from membership of Parliament) for 'either House of Parliament' substitute 'the House of Commons'.

Bishoprics Act 1878 (c. 68)

17 The Bishoprics Act 1878 is repealed.

Welsh Church Act 1914 (c. 91)

18 In section 2 of the Welsh Church Act 1914 (ecclesiastical corporations and bishops) omit subsections (2) and (3).

Life Peerages Act 1958 (c. 21)

19 In section 1 of the Life Peerages Act 1958 (power to create life peerages carrying right to sit in House of Lords) omit –

(a) paragraph (b) of subsection (2) (and the 'and' before it),

(b) subsection (4), and

(c) in the heading 'carrying right to sit in the House of Lords'.

Peerage Act 1963 (c. 48)

20 (1) Amend the Peerage Act 1963 as follows.

(2) In section 1(2) (instruments of disclaimer) omit from 'and no such instrument' to the end.

(3) Omit section 4 (Scottish peers entitled to receive writs of summons).

(4) Omit section 6 (peeresses in own right entitled to receive writs of summons).

Equal Pay Act (Northern Ireland) 1970 (N.I. c. 32)

21 In section 1A(b) of the Equal Pay Act (Northern Ireland) 1970 (definition of 'political office') after '1958', insert 'the office of an appointed member of the House of Lords,'.

Recess Elections Act 1975 (c. 66)

22 (1) Amend the Recess Elections Act 1975 as follows.

(2) In section 1 (issue of warrants by Speaker for making out writs) –

(a) in subsection (1)(a) omit 'or become disqualified as a peer for membership of the House of Commons',

(b) in subsection (2), in paragraph (a) of the definition of 'certificate of vacancy' omit ', become disqualified as a peer for membership of the House of Commons', and

(c) in that subsection, in the definition of 'disqualifying office' –

(i) omit from ', other than' to 'Northstead', and

(ii) at the end insert 'other than –

(a) the office of steward or bailiff of Her Majesty's three Chiltern Hundreds of Stoke, Desborough and Burnham or of the Manor of Northstead, or

(b) the office of member of the House of Lords.'

(3) In Schedule 1 (certificate of vacancy) omit '[that Member of Parliament has become disqualified as a peer for membership of the House of Commons;]'.

Sex Discrimination (Northern Ireland) Order 1976 (S.I. 1976/1042 (N.I. 15))

23 (1) Amend the Sex Discrimination (Northern Ireland) Order 1976 as follows.

(2) In Article 13A(3)(b) (offices to which Article 13B does not apply) after '1958,' insert 'the office of an appointed member of the House of Lords,'.

(3) In Article 43A(4) (selection of election candidates) after 'Article' insert – '(a) "parliamentary election" has the same meaning as in Schedule 1 to the Interpretation Act 1978; (b)'.

Senior Courts Act 1981 (c. 54)

24 In section 142(1) of the Senior Courts Act 1981 (selection of judges for trial of election petitions) for 'members of the House of Lords' substitute 'transitional members of the House of Lords'.

British Nationality Act 1981 (c. 61)

25 In Schedule 7 to the British Nationality Act 1981 (consequential amendments) in the entry relating to the Act of Settlement (see section 47 of the Constitutional Reform and Governance Act 2010), at the end insert – 'Nothing in this entry applies in relation to membership of the House of Lords.'

Representation of the People Act 1983 (c. 2)

26 (1) Amend the Representation of the People Act 1983 as follows.

(2) In section 7B(7)(a) (declaration of local connection) omit 'by a person who is as a peer subject to a legal incapacity to vote at parliamentary elections or'.

(3) In section 15(5)(a) (service declaration) omit 'by a person who is as a peer subject to a legal incapacity to vote at parliamentary elections, or'.

(4) In section 160(4) (persons reported personally guilty of corrupt or illegal practices) –

(a) in paragraph (a) at the end of sub-paragraph (ii) (but before the 'or') insert '(iia) being a member of the House of Lords (whether an elected member or otherwise)', and

(b) in paragraph (b) for 'or holding any such office, shall vacate the seat or office' substitute 'a member of the House of Lords, or the holder of an elective office, shall vacate the seat in the House of Commons or the House of Lords or the elective office'.

(5) In section 173 (incapacities on conviction of corrupt or illegal practice) –

(a) in subsection (1)(a) at the end of sub-paragraph (ii) (and after the 'or' insert '(iia) being a member of the House of Lords (whether an elected member or otherwise), or',

(b) in subsection (1)(b) for 'or holding any such office, shall vacate the seat or office' substitute 'a member of the House of Lords, or the holder of an elective office, shall vacate the seat in the House of Commons or the House of Lords or the elective office',

(c) after subsection (7) insert – '(7A) If a person convicted of a corrupt or illegal practice is a member of the House of Lords, the person shall (in addition to being subject to the incapacities mentioned in subsection (1)(a) above) be treated as a person suspended by virtue of section 44 of the House of Lords Reform Act 2012 for the period of suspension specified in subsection (8) below.',

(d) in subsection (8) after '(7)' insert 'and (7A)', and

(e) in subsection (9) for 'or (7)' substitute ', (7) or (7A)'.

Repatriation of Prisoners Act 1984 (c. 47)

27 (1) Amend the Schedule to the Repatriation of Prisoners Act 1984 (operation of certain legislation in relation to the prisoner) as follows.

(2) In paragraph 7 –

    (a) after '1981' insert 'or section 32 of the House of Lords Reform Act 2012', and

    (b) after 'Commons' insert 'or the House of Lords'.

(3) In the heading immediately before paragraph 7 after '1981' insert 'and the House of Lords Reform Act 2012'.

Representation of the People Act 1985 (c. 50)

28 (1) Amend the Representation of the People Act 1985 as follows.

    (2) Omit section 3 (extension of the franchise for European Parliamentary elections to peers resident outside the UK).

    (3) In section 27(2) (interpretation) for 'to 3' substitute 'and 2'.

Insolvency Act 1986 (c. 45)

29 (1) Amend the Insolvency Act 1986 as follows.

    (2) In section 426A (disqualification from Parliament: England and Wales) –

    (a) in subsection (1) omit paragraphs (b) and (c),

    (b) omit subsection (4),

    (c) in subsections (5) and (6) omit 'or the House of Lords', and

    (d) in the heading for '*Parliament*' substitute '*House of Commons*'.

(3) In section 427 (disqualification from Parliament: Scotland and Northern Ireland) –

    (a) omit subsection (1)(a),

    (b) in subsection (1)(c) for 'either House' substitute 'that House',

    (c) omit subsection (3),

    (d) in subsection (5) omit 'lord of Parliament or' and 'to the Speaker of the House of Lords or, as the case may be', and

    (e) in the heading for '*Parliament*' substitute '*House of Commons etc*'.

Local Government Finance Act 1988 (c. 41)

30 In section 65(7) of the Local Government Finance Act 1988 (owners and occupiers) for the words from 'shall' to the end substitute –

> '(a) in the case of a House of Commons election, is to be construed in accordance with section 24 of the Representation of the People Act 1983;
> (b) in the case of an election to the House of Lords, is to be construed in accordance with provision made under section 7 of the House of Lords Reform Act 2012;
> (c) in the case of a local government election, is to be construed in accordance with section 35 of the Representation of the People Act 1983.'

Caldey Island Act 1990 (c. 44)

31 In section 1(3) of the Caldey Island Act 1990 (elections) for 'parliamentary polling district' substitute 'polling district for the purpose of House of Commons elections'.

Ministerial and other Pensions and Salaries Act 1991 (c. 5)

32 (1) Amend the Ministerial and other Pensions and Salaries Act 1991 as follows.

(2) In section 4 (grants on ceasing to hold ministerial and other offices) –

> (a) after subsection (3A) insert –
> '(3B) The annual amount of the salary paid to a person in respect of the office of Chairman of Committees of the House of Lords or Deputy Chairman of Committees of the House of Lords is the difference between –
> (a) the total amount paid to the person under section 7A of the Parliamentary Standards Act 2009 for the period of 12 months ending at the material time, and

  (b) the total amount that would have been paid to the
person for that period if the determination under section 7A(3) of that Act had not provided for higher
pay for members holding that office.', and
 (b) in subsection (6)(d) for 'a salary' substitute 'pay'.

(3) Omit section 5 (allowances for certain office holders in House
of Lords).

 (4) Omit section 8(2) (financial provision relating to section 5 allowances).

Trade Union and Labour Relations (Consolidation) Act 1992 (c. 52)

33 In section 72(4) of the Trade Union and Labour Relations
(Consolidation) Act 1992 (restriction on use of funds for political objects) in the definition of 'political office' for 'member of
Parliament,' substitute 'Member of Parliament, elected member
of the House of Lords,'.

Disability Discrimination Act 1995 (c. 50)

34 In section 4C(5)(b) of the Disability Discrimination Act 1995
(offices to which sections 4D and 4E do not apply) after '1958,'
insert 'the office of an appointed member of the House of Lords,'.

Reserve Forces Act 1996 (c. 14)

35 In section 125(a) of the Reserve Forces Act 1996 (absence for
voting) after 'Member of Parliament,' insert 'an elected member
of the House of Lords'.

Juries (Northern Ireland) Order 1996 (S.I. 1996/1141 (N.I. 6))

36 In Schedule 3 to the Juries (Northern Ireland) Order 1996 (persons excusable from jury service as of right), for the entry relating
to peers and peeresses substitute 'Members of the House of Lords.'

Race Relations (Northern Ireland) Order 1997 (S.I. 1997/869 (N.I 6))

37 In Article 72ZA(10)(b)(ii) of the Race Relations (Northern
Ireland) Order 1997 (definition of 'political office') after '1958,'
insert 'the office of an appointed member of the House of Lords,'.

Scotland Act 1998 (c. 46)

38 (1) Amend the Scotland Act 1998 as follows.

(2) In section 16(1) (disqualification from membership of Scottish Parliament) for the words from 'because' to the end substitute 'because the person is disqualified from being elected to the House of Commons by section 41 of the House of Lords Reform Act 2012 (temporary disqualification of former members of the House of Lords).'

(3) In section 126(1) (interpretation) in the definition of 'parliamentary' omit ', elections'.

(4) In section 127 (index) in the entry relating to 'parliamentary' omit ', elections'.

(5) In Section B3 of Part 2 of Schedule 5 (reserved matters) after 'House of Commons,' insert 'the House of Lords,'.

Northern Ireland Act 1998 (c. 47)

39 In section 36(6) of the Northern Ireland Act 1998 (disqualification from membership of Northern Ireland Assembly) for the words from 'that' to the end substitute 'that the person is disqualified from being elected to the House of Commons by section 41 of the House of Lords Reform Act 2012 (temporary disqualification of former members of the House of Lords).'

Fair Employment and Treatment (Northern Ireland) Order 1998 (S.I. 1998/3162 (N.I. 21))

40 In Article 20A(10)(b)(ii) of the Fair Employment and Treatment (Northern Ireland) Order 1998 (definition of 'political office') after '1958,' insert 'the office of an appointed member of the House of Lords,'.

House of Lords Act 1999 (c. 34)

41 The House of Lords Act 1999 is repealed.

Representation of the People Act 2000 (c. 2)

42 Omit paragraph 4 of Schedule 2 to the Representation of the People Act 2000 (which substituted section 3 of the Representation of the People Act 1985).

Political Parties, Elections and Referendums Act 2000 (c. 41)

43 (1) Amend the Political Parties, Elections and Referendums Act 2000 as follows.

(2) In section 5(2) (duty of Electoral Commission to report on elections) after paragraph (a) insert '(aa) a House of Lords election;'.

(3) In section 7(2) (Electoral Commission to be consulted on changes to electoral law) after paragraph (e) insert –

'(ea)   an order under section 7 of the House of Lords Reform Act 2012 (power to make provision about House of Lords elections);

(eb)   an order under paragraph 11 of Schedule 4 to that Act (power to make provision about return of interim replacement elected members);'.

(4) In section 8(3) (certain powers exercisable only on the Electoral Commission's recommendation) after paragraph (d) insert '(e) the making of orders under section 7 of the House of Lords Reform Act 2012 so far as relating to the variation of any financial limit set by a previous order under that section relating to the election expenses of candidates.'

(5) In section 22(2) (parties to be registered in order to field candidates at elections) after 'region' (in each place) insert 'or district'.

(6) In section 54(8) (permissible donors: definition of 'electoral register') omit paragraph (c) (and the 'or' before it).

(7) In section 64 (exemptions from weekly donation reports during general election periods) –

(a) in subsection (1) for 'covers the general election in question' substitute –

> (a) covers the House of Commons general election in question, and
> (b) where the polling day for that election is the same as the polling day for a House of Lords election, covers that House of Lords election',

(b) in subsections (2) to (5) for 'particular general election' (in each place) substitute 'particular election',

(c) in subsection (3) –

> (i) for 'parliamentary elections' substitute 'House of Commons general elections or House of Lords elections (as the case may be)', and
> (ii) for 'general election in question' (in each place) substitute 'election in question',

(d) in subsection (9) –

> (i) for 'general election' substitute 'House of Commons general election', and
> (ii) for 'parliamentary election rules' substitute 'House of Commons elections rules', and

(e) after that subsection insert –

> '(10) For the purposes of this section and section 65 a registered party shall be taken to have a candidate at a House of Lords election if any statement published in connection with the election under any corresponding rule contains the name of a candidate standing in the name of the party.
> (11) A "corresponding rule" means any provision made by an order under section 7 of the House of Lords Reform Act 2012 (power to make provision about elections) which corresponds to the rule mentioned in subsection (9).'

(8) In section 65(8) (submission of donation reports to Commission) for 'Section 64(9) applies' substitute 'Section 64(9) to (11) apply'.

(9) In section 71R(1) (exemption from weekly transaction reports during general election periods) for 'covers the general election in question' substitute –

'(a) covers the House of Commons general election in question, and

(b) where the polling day for that election is the same as the polling day for a House of Lords election, covers that House of Lords election'.

(10) In section 71S(9) (submission of transaction reports to Commission) for 'section 64(9)' substitute 'section 64(9) to (11)'.

(11) In section 72(6) (campaign expenditure) at the end insert 'except that it does not include an election to the House of Lords'.

(12) In section 85(6) (controlled expenditure by third parties) at the end insert 'except that it does not include an election to the House of Lords'.

(13) Omit section 141(b) (which amended section 3 of the Representation of the People Act 1985) (and the 'and' before it).

(14) In section 143(11) (details to appear on election material) at the end of the definition of 'election material' insert 'except that references in that provision to a relevant election are to be read as also including an election to the House of Lords'.

(15) In paragraph 1(8) of Schedule 7 (control of donations to individuals and members associations) after paragraph (a) insert '(aa) elected member of the House of Lords;'.

House of Commons (Removal of Clergy Disqualification) Act 2001 (c. 13)

44 (1) Amend the House of Commons (Removal of Clergy Disqualification) Act 2001 as follows.

(2) In section 1 (removal of clergy disqualification) omit –

(a) subsection (2), and
(b) subsection (3)(a) (and the 'and' after it).

(3) Omit Schedule 1 (consequential amendments).

European Parliamentary Elections Act 2002 (c. 24)

45 (1) Amend the European Parliamentary Elections Act 2002 as follows.

(2) In section 8 (persons entitled to vote) –

(a) in subsection (1) for 'any of subsections (2) to (5)' substitute 'subsection (2) or (5)', and
(b) omit subsections (3), (4) and (7).

(3) In section 10(2) (disqualification from membership of European Parliament) –

(a) for paragraph (a) substitute '(a) he is a member of the House of Lords',
(b) omit paragraph (b),
(c) omit the 'or' after paragraph (c), and
(d) after paragraph (d) insert ', or (e) he is disqualified from being elected to the House of Commons by section 41 of the House of Lords Reform Act 2012 (temporary disqualification of former members of the House of Lords).'

(4) In paragraph 6(1) of Schedule 1A (periodic reviews of distribution of MEPs) in the definition of 'relevant register' omit paragraph (c) (but not the 'and' after it).

Employment Equality (Sexual Orientation) Regulations (Northern Ireland) 2003 (S.R. 2003 (N.I.) No. 497)

46 In regulation 12(10)(b)(ii) of the Employment Equality (Sexual Orientation) Regulations (Northern Ireland) 2003 (definition of 'political office') after '1958,' insert 'the office of an appointed member of the House of Lords,'.

Constitutional Reform Act 2005 (c. 4)

47 In section 137 of the Constitutional Reform Act 2005 (parliamentary disqualification) omit subsections (3) to (5).

Electoral Administration Act 2006 (c. 22)

48 Omit paragraph 17 of Schedule 1 to the Electoral Administration Act 2006 (which amended section 3 of the Representation of the People Act 1985).

Government of Wales Act 2006 (c. 32)

49 In section 17(1) of the Government of Wales Act 2006 (disqualification from membership of Welsh Assembly) for the words from the second 'is' to the end substitute 'is disqualified from being elected to the House of Commons by section 41 of the House of Lords Reform Act 2012 (temporary disqualification of former members of the House of Lords).'

Employment Equality (Age) Regulations (Northern Ireland) 2006 (S.R. 2006 (N.I.) No. 261)

50 In regulation 13(10)(b)(ii) of the Employment Equality (Age) Regulations (Northern Ireland) 2006 (definition of 'political office') after '1958,' insert 'the office of an appointed member of the House of Lords,'.

European Parliament (House of Lords Disqualification) Regulations 2008 (S.I. 2008/1647).

51 The European Parliament (House of Lords Disqualification) Regulations 2008 are revoked.

Equality Act 2010 (c. 15)

52 In Schedule 6 to the Equality Act 2010 (excluded offices) after paragraph 3 insert –

> *'Appointed members of the House of Lords*
> 4 The office of an appointed member of the House of Lords is not a personal or public office.'

Constitutional Reform and Governance Act 2010 (c. 25)

53 (1) Amend the Constitutional Reform and Governance Act 2010 as follows.

(2) In the heading to Part 4 (tax status of MPs and members of the House of Lords) omit 'AND MEMBERS OF THE HOUSE OF LORDS'.

(3) In section 41 (tax status of MPs and members of the House of Lords) omit –

(a)   subsections (1)(b) (and the 'or' before it), (5), (6), (8)
      (b) (and the 'and' before it) and (10), and

(b)   in the heading '*and members of the House of Lords*'.

(4) Omit section 42 (tax status of members of the House of Lords: transitional provision).

(5) Omit section 52(3)(b) (commencement of section 42).

(6) In Schedule 5 omit paragraph 2 (which amended section 2 of the Parliamentary Standards Act 2009).

Budget Responsibility and National Audit Act 2011 (c. 4)

54 In section 12 of the Budget Responsibility and National Audit Act 2011 (status of office of Comptroller & Auditor General etc) omit subsection (3).

European Union Act 2011 (c. 12)

55 In section 11 of the European Union Act 2011 (persons entitled to vote in referendum) omit subsections (1)(b) and (2).

Fixed-term Parliaments Act 2011 (c. 14)

56 In section 3(3) of the Fixed-term Parliaments Act 2011 (dissolution of Parliament) for the words from 'the writs' to the end substitute –

'(a) the writs for the House of Commons general election sealed and issued (see rule 3 in Schedule 1 to the Representation of the People Act 1983), and

(b) the writs for any relevant House of Lords election sealed and issued (see section 3(4) of the House of Lords Reform Act 2012).

A "relevant House of Lords election" is a House of Lords election which has the same polling day as the polling day for the general election.'

SCHEDULE 11
TRANSITIONAL AND TRANSITORY PROVISION AND SAVINGS

Section 41: restriction on former members being elected as MPs

1 For the purposes of section 41 (restriction on former members being elected as MPs) a person's membership of the House of Lords on or before the day of the first House of Lords election is to be disregarded.

Section 44: expulsion and suspension

2 (1) This paragraph applies in the case of a member of the House of Lords if section 44 (expulsion and suspension) comes into force after what would (apart from this paragraph) be 'the relevant time' in relation to that member as determined under subsection (5) of that section.

(2) In the case of that member, 'the relevant time' for the purposes of section 44 means the time that section comes into force.

Section 46: saving for pay and allowances for transitional members

3 Nothing in the amendments made by section 46 (pay and allowances), or in any other provision of this Act, affects the power of the House of Lords to provide by resolution for pay or allowances for transitional members.

Section 50: removal of disqualification on peers voting at elections to either House

4 (1) This paragraph applies if section 50(1) (peers not disqualified from voting) comes into force before the day of the first House of Lords election.

(2) In this paragraph –

(a) 'relevant peer' means a peer who, immediately before the coming into force of section 50(1), is by virtue of that peerage disqualified from voting at elections to the House of Commons, and

(b) 'interim period' means the period beginning with the day on which that provision comes into force and ending immediately before the day of the first House of Lords election.

(3) Section 50(1) does not remove the disqualification of a relevant peer from voting as an elector –

(a) at an intervening House of Commons election,

(b) at an intervening election to the European Parliament by virtue of section 8(2) of the European Parliamentary Elections Act 2002 (entitlement to vote as a parliamentary elector), or

(c) at an intervening referendum under the European Union Act 2011 by virtue of section 11(1)(a) of that Act (entitlement to vote as a parliamentary elector).

(4) An 'intervening' election or referendum is an election or referendum the day of the poll for which occurs during the interim period.

(5) In relation to a relevant peer, any disqualification which is preserved by subparagraph (3) is to be disregarded for the purposes of –

(a) section 4(1)(b) of the Representation of the People Act 1983 (entitlement to be registered as a parliamentary elector), and

(b) section 1(1)(b)(i) of the Representation of the People Act 1985 (entitlement to vote as an overseas elector) in so far as that provision relates to legal incapacity to vote on the relevant date (within the meaning of that section).

5 (1) In relation to a relevant peer, sections 1 and 2 of the Representation of the People Act 1985 (conditions as to qualification as an overseas elector) have effect with the following modifications.

(2) In section 1(3) and (4)(b) any reference to a register of parliamentary electors includes –

- (a) any register of local government electors in Great Britain, and
- (b) any register of local electors in Northern Ireland, which was required to be published on any date before the day on which section 50(1) comes into force.

(3) In section 1 after subsection (4) insert –
'(4A) The third set of conditions is that –

- (a) he was last resident in the United Kingdom at a time before the day on which section 50(1) of the House of Lords Reform Act 2012 comes into force and within the period of 15 years ending immediately before the relevant date,
- (b) he was by reason only of being the holder of a peerage incapable of being included in any register of parliamentary electors in force on the last day on which he was resident in the United Kingdom, and
- (c) the address at which he was resident on that day was at a place that is situated within the constituency concerned.'

(4) In section 2(4) –

- (a) omit the 'and' after paragraph (b),
- (b) after paragraph (c) insert 'and (d) in the case of the third set of conditions, specify the address in the United Kingdom at which he was resident,', and
- (c) for 'either set' substitute 'any set'.

(5) 'Relevant peer' has the same meaning as in paragraph 4.

Section 50: removal of disqualification on peers being elected as members of either House

6 (1) This paragraph applies if section 50(2) (peers not disqualified from membership of either House of Parliament) comes into force before the day of the first House of Lords election.

(2) In this paragraph 'relevant peer' means a peer who, immediately before the coming into force of section 50(2), is by virtue of that peerage disqualified from membership of the House of Commons.

(3) Section 50(2) does not remove the disqualification of a relevant peer from membership of the House of Commons as a result of being elected at a House of Commons election the day of the poll for which occurs before the day of the first House of Lords election.

Schedule 5: former House of Lords Appointments Commission

7 In Part 6 of Schedule 1 to the Freedom of Information Act 2000 (other public bodies and offices which are public authorities), the entry for the Appointments Commission includes a reference to the body known as The House of Lords Appointments Commission which was established before this Act was passed.

Schedule 8: Police Service of Scotland

8 At any time before the coming into force of section 6 of the Police and Fire Reform (Scotland) Act 2012 (establishment of the Police Service of Scotland), paragraph 6(b) of Schedule 8 is to be read as a reference to a police force within the meaning of the Police (Scotland) Act 1967.

Schedule 9: consultation provisions relating to pay and allowances

9 (1) This paragraph applies in relation to –

    (a) IPSA's first determination under section 9A(1) and (5) of the PSA 2009 of procedures relating to members of the House of Lords;

(b) the first guidance and the first scheme prepared by IPSA under paragraph 2 of Schedule 4 to that Act in relation to members of the House of Lords;

(c) the first specification of matters by IPSA under paragraph 8 of that Schedule in relation to members of the House of Lords;

(d) the first guidance prepared by IPSA under paragraph 9 of that Schedule in relation to members of the House of Lords.

(2) Section 9A(6) of that Act applies as if paragraphs (a) to (c) were omitted.

10 The amendments made to section 9A(6) of the PSA 2009 by paragraph 7(3) of Schedule 9 do not affect the validity of anything which –

(a) has been determined, specified or prepared under that section or any of the other provisions of that Act to which section 9A(6) is relevant, and

(b) has effect immediately before those amendments come into force for the purpose of the provision in question.

11 The amendments made to paragraph 27(2) of Schedule 1 to the PSA 2009 by paragraph 12(10) of Schedule 9 do not affect the validity of the publication scheme which –

(a) has been adopted by IPSA under section 19 of the Freedom of Information Act 2000, and

(b) has effect immediately before those amendments come into force.

Schedule 9: membership of IPSA and the Speakers' Committee for IPSA

12 (1) The amendments made to Schedule 1 to the PSA 2009 by paragraph 12(2) to (4) of Schedule 9 do not affect a person holding office as a member of IPSA by virtue of an appointment made before the amendments come into force.

(2) The amendments made to Schedule 3 to the PSA 2009 by paragraph 14 of Schedule 9 do not affect a person holding office as a member of the Speakers' Committee for IPSA by virtue of an appointment made under paragraph 1(e) of that Schedule before the amendments come into force.

Schedule 10: saving in relation to the Bishoprics Acts 1878

13 The repeal of the Bishoprics Act 1878 by paragraph 17 of Schedule 10 does not affect the continued operation in relation to that Act of the saving at the end of Part 2 of Schedule 1 to the Statute Law Repeals Act 1973 (which continues in force Orders in Council and schemes made under certain repealed Acts or Church Assembly Measures).

Schedule 10: donations and loans etc to elected members

14 (1) Sub-paragraph (2) applies if paragraph 15A of Schedule 7 to the PPERA 2000 (which is inserted by section 59(3) of the EAA 2006) has been brought into force in relation to the holders of all relevant elective offices before paragraph 43(15) of Schedule 10 (which adds elected members to the definition of 'relevant elective office' in Schedule 7 to the PPERA 2000) comes into force.

(2) The Minister must not make an order under section 59 bringing paragraph 43(15) of Schedule 10 into force for the purposes of paragraph 15A of Schedule 7 to the PPERA 2000 unless the Minister is informed by the Electoral Commission that they are satisfied that they will receive the information mentioned in paragraph 15A(2) of that Schedule in relation to elected members of the House of Lords.

(3) If paragraph 15A of Schedule 7 to the PPERA 2000 has not been brought into force in relation to the holders of all relevant elective offices before paragraph 43(15) of Schedule 10 comes into force, section 59(4) of the EAA 2006 applies to the bringing into force of paragraph 15A of Schedule 7 to the PPERA 2000 in relation to elected members of the House of Lords.

(4) In this paragraph 'relevant elective office' is to be construed in accordance with Schedule 7 to the PPERA 2000.

15 (1) Sub-paragraph (2) applies if paragraph 16 of Schedule 7A to the PPERA 2000 (which is inserted by paragraph 99 of Schedule 1 to the EAA 2006) has been brought into force in relation to the holders of all relevant elective offices before paragraph 43(15) of Schedule 10 (which adds elected members to the definition of 'relevant elective office' which applies in Schedule 7A to the PPERA 2000) comes into force.

(2) The Minister must not make an order under section 59 bringing paragraph 43(15) of Schedule 10 into force for the purposes of paragraph 16 of Schedule 7A to the PPERA 2000 unless the Minister is informed by the Electoral Commission that they are satisfied that they will receive the information mentioned in paragraph 16(3) of that Schedule in relation to elected members of the House of Lords.

(3) If paragraph 16 of Schedule 7A to the PPERA 2000 has not been brought into force in relation to the holders of all relevant elective offices before paragraph 43(15) of Schedule 10 comes into force, paragraph 102(1) of Schedule 1 to the EAA 2006 applies to the bringing into force of paragraph 16 of Schedule 7A to the PPERA 2000 in relation to elected members of the House of Lords.

(4) In this paragraph 'relevant elective office' has the same meaning as in paragraph 14.

Schedule 10: tax status of members of the House of Lords

16 (1) The amendments made by paragraphs 53(2) and (3) of Schedule 10 apply –

(a) where the first meeting of the House of Lords in the first electoral period ('the first meeting') takes place on the first day of a tax year, in relation to that tax year and subsequent tax years, and

(b) otherwise, in relation to tax years after the tax year in which the first meeting takes place.

(2) Where those amendments apply as mentioned in sub-paragraph (1)(b) –

    (a) in applying section 41 of the Constitutional Reform and Governance Act 2010 to the tax year in which the first meeting takes place, a person's membership of the House of Lords after the dissolution of the last Parliament before the first House of Lords election is to be disregarded, and

    (b) in applying section 48 to that tax year, a person's membership of the House of Lords on or before the day of the first House of Lords election is to be disregarded.

(3) 'Tax year' has the same meaning as in section 48.

General

17 Nothing in any provision of this Act affects the validity of anything begun before the provision comes into force (for any purpose) and completed afterwards.

Interpretation

18 In this Schedule –
    'the EAA 2006' means the Electoral Administration Act 2006;
    'the PPERA 2000' means the Political Parties, Elections and Referendums Act 2000;
    'the PSA 2009' means the Parliamentary Standards Act 2009.

This complex bill was soon to face its fatal moments in the House of Commons.

CHAPTER EIGHTEEN

2012. The House of Lords Reform Bill: Its Fate in the House of Commons

The deputy prime minister, Nick Clegg, introduced the House of Lords Reform Bill in the Commons to be read a second time on 9 July 2012. He had it, he said, in 'command from Her Majesty the Queen to acquaint the House that Her Majesty, having been informed of the purport of the Bill, has consented to place her prerogative and interest, so far as they are affected by the Bill, at the disposal of Parliament for the purpose of the Bill'.[1] This is a routine statement whenever a bill is presented to parliament.

Debate in the Commons

Nick Clegg then moved that the bill be read a second time. He began by explaining why the upper chamber was in need of reform. There were three simple reasons. The first was that 'we believe in democracy. We believe that the people who make the laws should be chosen by the people who are subject to those laws.' The second reason, he said, was that reforms 'will lead to better laws – the Bill is not just about who legislates, but about how we legislate'. The third reason was 'simple practicality'. The House of Lords could not carry on along its current path: 'we need to reform the Lords to keep it functioning and we need to do it soon'. The deputy prime minister then summarized the chief clauses of this long and complicated bill.

1   *Parliamentary Debates*, House of Commons, vol. 548(I), 9 July 2012, cols 24–132.

The shadow secretary of state, Mr Sadiq Khan (Labour) answered for the Opposition. The bill was a bit of mess, he said. But the Labour Party remained very much in favour of reforming the second chamber and would support the bill on second reading. His party recognised that consensus-building was crucial to the success of constitutional change.

Andrew Bridgen (Conservative) intervened to say that the House of Lords was a fine institution. It was not broken, so 'why do we need to fix it?'

Sadiq Khan continued. The deputy prime minister had cherry-picked from the Joint Committee's report, while blindly ignoring its other key recommendations. The government had also dropped any reference to the conventions governing the relationship between the Houses.

Anne Main (Conservative) feared that when the majority of its members were elected, with a small proportion appointed, there would 'be a divided second House some of whose Members will have more power than the others'.

Barry Sheerman (Labour/Co-op) said that one of the things that bothered him was that the reformers who wanted change in the Upper House did not pay attention to the quality of the people who would end up in it, and there was nothing in the bill to 'assure us that the party machines will not control all the people who end up there'.

Sadiq Khan agreed that that was the problem of a list system. Labour wanted a fully elected chamber. In proposing a hybrid chamber the present government would be storing up problems for the future. The hybrid system would inevitably lead to tensions between the different types of members. A key absence from the bill was that there was to be no referendum. That was an error.

The harshest criticism against the bill was voiced by Sir Malcolm Rifkind, one of the senior Conservative leaders. The bill, he maintained, was a 'puny measure'. It was unwelcome and it 'will do more harm than good to our constitutional structure and to the good government of this country'. The bill had to be opposed.

Nadhim Zahawi (Conservative) contended that the bill reflected an obsession with the form rather than the function of the other place.

Margaret Beckett (Labour) said she would prefer the outright abolition of the second chamber, and would not vote for an elected House.

John Thurso (Liberal Democrat) said that he supported the bill.

Alan Johnson (Labour) argued that the bill was a small step 'on the road to a better civilisation that we might arrive at if we could get through some of the very tribal differences'.

Jake Berry (Conservative) complained that the House of Lords was hardly representative, given that two-thirds of its members came from public schools.

Eleanor Laing (Conservative) said that the bill 'before us is standing in the way of measured, necessary reform'.

Bob Stewart (Conservative) argued that when the people 'are elected to the House of Lords, they will say that they have a better democratic right than MPs to speak for them. That will mean a challenge to this Chamber.'

According to Oliver Heald (Conservative), the challenge 'will be not just here in the Chamber but in every marginal constituency'.

Graham Allen (Labour) said that 'we should not fear the liberty and the improvement of the second Chamber. It might actually be the making of the freedom of the first Chamber. It might be one step on the road to having a free and independent legislature that would challenge the power of the Executive.'

Graham Brady (Conservative) complained that 'we spend too much time here pursuing party advantage. To do so in changing our constitution would be not just wrong but contemptible.' The bill must be rejected by any true advocate of reform.

Peter Hain (Labour) believed that the Commons should continue to have the primary representative mandate, with peers discharging their important revising, scrutinizing role.

Oliver Heald (Conservative) said that the bill needed to be looked at again.

Hazel Blears (Labour) thought that the bill was a 'distraction'. It was also 'one of the most cynical deceptions to be inflicted on the people of this country, for deeply partisan reasons'.

Julian Lewis (Conservative) feared that the Liberal Democrats could hold the balance of power in the Upper House. They would hold Parliament to ransom over every issue that suited them.

Harriett Baldwin (Conservative) said that she would not be prepared to support the bill in its current form on third reading.

David Blunkett (Labour) said that he was against the bill and the programmed motion.

Richard Shepherd (Conservative) thought that there were many flaws in the bill. It needed to be debated properly.

Graham Stringer (Labour) believed that the bill would not improve the accountability of the executive, but rather 'set them free to do more of what they want to do while being less accountable'. He would 'abolish the other House, for the simple reason that, in the constitutional position that we are in, it is difficult to improve and democratise it without diminishing ourselves or having a written constitution'.

Jesse Norman (Conservative) believed that the bill would 'transform the Lords into a Chamber competing with the Commons. The result will be gridlock, cronyism and a rise in special-interest politics:' all MPs, Conservative or not, had a constitutional obligation to vote against it.

Ian Austin (Labour) believed that there was no question but that the elected members of the 'second House will claim democratic legitimacy in our constituencies'.

Caroline Dinenage (Conservative) thought the bill contained 'rushed, illogical and poorly constructed proposals which bring no discernible benefit to Parliament or to the nation'.

Tristram Hunt (Labour) said that the tide of time was in favour of democracy and 'we need to accept that'. On those grounds, he would support the motion.

Rory Stewart (Conservative) believed that Britain 'should take the example of the rest of the world by not introducing major constitutional change without either a two-thirds vote or a referendum'.

Steve Brine (Conservative) said that the bill did not hang together intellectually. It was in part 'about coalition politics and, much more, about the internal politics of the Liberal Democratic Party – and that is no reason to take a bulldozer to our constitution'.

Gerald Kaufman (Labour) suggested that the House should vote No in the Division and 'be done with this pernicious threat to what has made the United Kingdom a great democracy'.

Mark Field (Conservative) said that the bill was 'shoddy and poorly drafted'.

Chris Bryant (Labour) argued that the most important problem was the question of powers. He did not want the courts to be able to decide on a row between this House and the other House. The best way to 'proceed would be to have a concordat between the two Houses that forms part of our Standing Orders which requires that there can be no change in our House without the agreement of the House of Lords and no change in the House of Lords without the agreement of the House of Commons'.

Charles Kennedy (Liberal Democrat) spoke strongly in favour of the Coalition proposals.

George Howarth (Labour) argued that the only way one could do justice to the issues involved was to have a referendum on the subject.

Laura Sandys (Conservative) felt that the bill was a crucial step forward.

Helen Goodman (Labour) supported the idea that 'we have a democratic second Chamber'.

Nicholas Soames (Conservative) believed that the bill would 'inevitably lead to the greater politicisation of the House of Lords, blur the harmonious and distinctive differences between the two Houses and remove the correctly unambiguous democratic mandate that the House of Commons rightly enjoys'.

Frank Field (Labour) wanted to know: 'To what extent does the reform strengthen representative government, and to what extent does it strengthen responsible government?'

John Stevenson (Conservative) welcomed the bill. He acknowledged that it was a compromise, and thought that, in many respects, that was inevitable.

Jim Dowd (Labour) said that 'we should not just tolerate the lowest common-denominator; we should reform Parliament – reform all of it'.

David Tredinnick (Conservative) did not think that this bill was 'in our national interest or Parliament's interest, and it is certainly not in my party's interest'.

Anne McGuire (Labour) hoped that, as the discussion went on in the Commons, the government 'will have time to reflect and will knock some sense into the head of the Deputy Prime Minister'.

Angie Bray (Conservative) said that she could not stop herself thinking that 'we are being asked to support the dismantling of a crucial part of our constitution for a short-term fix'. She simply could not do that.

Tom Greatrex (Labour/Co-op) said that there were 'big issues' in the bill that 'we need to get right. We need enough time to get them right if the bill is to have any chance of taking us forward'.

Nadhim Zahawi (Conservative) thought that if 'we are really to fix Parliament, we must give it the tools to legislate better. Let us strengthen the role of Select Committees and give more time for Back-Bench business.'

Ian Lucas (Labour) said that it was a bad bill, 'badly drafted, badly drawn and based on a compromise that is not working'.

Dan Byles (Conservative) thought that the bill 'will not make the upper House accountable'.

Angela Smith (Labour) said that the debate had shown that the House did not wish to give the bill 'a swift passage into law'. Rather it wanted 'thoroughly to scrutinise and improve' it and make it 'fit for presentation to the electorate in a referendum'.

The parliamentary secretary, David Heath, summed up the debate, arguing that the government felt that this measure was long overdue, and the polls showed that the British public wanted it. The bill 'puts into effect the modest proposition that those who make our laws should be elected by our People'. He therefore commended it to the House.

The debate was adjourned at 10 p.m. to be resumed on 10 July 2012. The leader of the House of Commons, Sir George Young, opened the debate at 4.39 p.m., asking that the bill be read a second time.[2] The government, he said, remained 'committed to making progress on Lords reform'. 'With Second Reading behind us we will then consider how best to take this agenda forward and how best to secure progress through the House for reforms that have the backing of this House. The Government will move a timetable motion before we make progress in the autumn, in accordance with the rules of the House.'

---

2   *Ibid.*, 10 July 2012, cols 188–279.

Angela Eagle (Labour) asked whether, if the bill passed its second reading, the government would then confirm that they intended to bring 'forward immediately a motion to commit the Bill to debate on the Floor of the House', and with no guillotine. '[We] must have time to debate this Bill and scrutinise it adequately.'

The leader of the House responded that he hoped to tell members more about the government's proposals at the proper time.

Bernard Jenkin (Conservative) said that whatever moral authority the bill had, it had now lost.

George Young disagreed. If the House gave the bill a majority on second reading, the government was perfectly entitled to make progress with it.

Jesse Norman (Conservative) pointed out that the 'very substantial opposition' from within the Conservative party should be 'perfectly clear and reflected in the record'.

George Young again disagreed. He defended the clauses of the bill. He hoped that the back-benchers on both sides of the House would 'see the Bill for what it is: a serious attempt at long last to strengthen Parliament's ability to hold the Government to account'. He commended the bill to the House.

Angela Eagle (Labour) stated that the Labour party was committed to an elected second chamber, and that was why the Opposition would support the bill on second reading. But that made it 'absolutely imperative' that all parts of the bill were effectively scrutinized in the Commons. She believed that on major constitutional issues, by convention and by right, the British people had the final say in a referendum. It followed that the Opposition believed there should be a referendum on an elected second chamber.

Gareth Johnson (Conservative) opposed the principle of an elected second chamber. The details of the bill were also wrong.

Ann Coffey (Labour) argued that it was not about the power and privilege of the House of Commons versus the power and privilege of the Lords: 'it is about improving the way in which we fulfil our role as representatives of the public. It must ultimately be about the people we serve.'

Stephen Lloyd (Liberal Democrat) agreed that the bill was not perfect and that it was a compromise. The bill needed some improvements, which, he hoped, would be implemented in committee.

Jamie Reed (Labour) asked the last speaker how he and his party colleagues responded to the prime minister's 'tacit approval for the Conservative Back-Bench rebellion' against the bill.

This question annoyed Stephen Lloyd so much that he retorted: 'It is interesting to look at the coalition between Blair and Brown in your 13 years, which was internecine every week. I take no lessons on that from Opposition Members.'

Mr Speaker intervened: 'Order. The House is lapsing into improper use of language;' to which Stephen Lloyd had to back down, replying: 'Thank you, Mr Speaker; I stand corrected and apologise.'

Jack Straw (Labour) reminded the House that members had voted 'decisively in March 2007 for an 80% or a 100% elected second Chamber and against all other alternatives.' 'I then chaired the cross-party working group,' he continued, 'which worked hard and constructively to develop detailed proposals for reform. The Deputy Prime Minister has taken that work forward.' There was one major point that he thought was missing. Although the deputy prime minister had made 'many points of considerable substance [...] I have to say that on the referendum issue he was, at the very best, treading water.'

Simon Hart (Conservative) said that he did not want a democratic House of Lords. He wanted 'objectivity, expertise, experience and wisdom, all qualities that we are told so often that we do not have in this House'. He did not want members of the House of Lords to be 'subject to the electoral and party pressures to which we may be subject here'.

Karl Turner (Labour) said that he 'absolutely' supported reform, but he was keen on reforming the Lords 'to the full and having a completely elected second Chamber'. The bill did not offer anything like that.

Penny Mordaunt (Conservative) feared that the bill would challenge the primacy of the Commons. The fact was that the progenitors of the bill had 'tied a chain around one of the central pillars of our constitution and are pulling at it for all they are worth, cheerfully telling us, as the marble begins to crack, that its removal will not bring down the entire edifice. I will not be party to that; I will not support this Bill.'

Nigel Dodds (Democratic Unionist Party) and Richard Harrington (Conservative) said that they would vote against the bill.

David Miliband (Labour) urged all parties to support the bill. The issue before the House was not whether the proposals were perfect, but whether the proposals improved on an unelected and unaccountable House of Lords, and the 'current indefensible set of arrangements'. The bill was not about 'neutering the Commons'; it was about 'bringing our democracy into the 21st century'.

Julian Sturdy (Conservative) suggested that, if 'we are to embark on this delicate and historic matter, we must do so properly. Many members who are concerned about these initial proposals need the opportunity and time to debate them. We should either take our time and get it right, or not do it all.'

Frank Dobson (Labour) said that the bill did not look at what was wrong with Parliament as a whole. One needed to look radically at how 'we improve our performance. Then we need to consider, once we have done that, whether we need a second Chamber, and if so, what its functions can be.'

Julian Lewis (Conservative) thought that the bill would be the 'end' of the House of Lords as a 'place where laws are fine-tuned', and he urged 'all colleagues to reject it'.

Tom Clarke (Labour) and Conor Burns (Conservative) believed that the bill was not the right bill.

Mark Durkan (Social Democratic and Labour Party) said that he, like others, would criticize 'many aspects' of the bill and hoped to see them 'amended and changed if it were to make progress'.

Edward Leigh (Conservative) argued that what was right for the country was to 'retain the system of an elected House of Commons and a revising Chamber that does an excellent job of improving legislation. We must leave it alone and defeat this Bill tonight.'

Mike Gapes (Labour/Co-op) said that there was no opportunity for him to vote for a 'reasoned amendment'. Therefore he felt forced, for the first time in twenty years, to go against his party's whip, and vote against the bill.

Bernard Jenkin (Conservative) believed that any attempt to force through a constitutional bill of such significance and controversy would represent an abuse of Parliament.

Stuart Bell (Labour) contended that the bill was in 'purgatory and limbo, and it will not survive in its present form'.

Rory Stewart (Conservative) argued that constitutional change must happen only through a referendum.

Barry Sheerman (Labour/Co-op) felt that there was no need for an elected Lords 'filled with party apparatchiks similar to those down here'. The danger of the bill was not that 'the other place will get stronger and flex its muscles and that we will become weaker; my concern is that it will simply become a pale and timid shadow of this place.'

Stephen Dorrell (Conservative) said that the question for the Commons was extremely simple: to elect or not to elect. 'I am in favour of election.'

Thomas Docherty (Labour) said that the 'hard reality' was that this was a bad bill, but he intended to vote for it.

Robert Walter (Labour) believed that the present House of Lords was on balance doing a good job, so no change was necessary.

Geoffrey Robinson (Labour) complained that 'we have a dog's breakfast of a Bill'.

Andrew Griffiths (Conservative) thought that 'we all accept that there are people in the other place we would perhaps not choose, but they continue to do a good job'. But if the Commons adopted the bill it would be 'at our peril'.

Rushanara Ali (Labour) said that it was vital that 'we do everything we can to ensure that the House of Lords reform ensures democracy and is fit for this century'.

Geoffrey Clifton-Brown (Conservative) looked forward to the government's 'withdrawing this bad Bill altogether'.

Graeme Morrice (Labour) argued that it was 'imperative that we take our time to consider the detail carefully, and make decisions that will last and best serve the people of the United Kingdom'.

Robin Walker (Conservative) thought that 'we should be seeking reforms that build on the strengths of our second Chamber, broaden its horizons, and eliminate its weaknesses. What we should not do is press on with creating an elected second Chamber without recognising what the consequences would be.'

Michael McCann (Labour) argued that the present second chamber was preferable any day of the week to 'an ill-thought-out plan that seeks to introduce constitutional change for cynical political advantage'.

Richard Drax (Conservative) thought that the Upper House worked, and it worked well. It 'isn't broke, but may I suggest that we fix it very gently?'

Mark Lazarowicz (Labour/Co-op) said that the bill was in danger of being a measure that did not have the 'kind of support that would be required'. It should be improved, to 'make it more radical and democratic. We should make these changes during the course of the bill's passage through this House.'

Alan Cairns (Conservative) feared that the reforms 'will undermine the independence of the other place and its Members, and lead to constitutional deadlock between the two Houses'.

William Bain (Labour) encouraged all members of the House to support the second reading of the bill. Now was 'the time for action'.

Nick de Bois (Conservative) said that he was not prepared to rush legislation on a major constitutional issue.

Wayne David (Labour) feared that the government's proposals would result in the two chambers of Parliament 'being locked in endless conflict, resulting in government grinding to a halt'. That was not in the 'interests of democracy'.

The parliamentary secretary, Mark Harper, wound up the debate. Speaking in support of the bill, he said that its main proposal was 'very simple: that those who make the laws should be elected'. He commended the bill to the House.

The question was put, 'that the Bill be now read a Second time'. The House divided: Ayes 462, Noes 124. The question was accordingly agreed to and the bill went forward to a further hearing. It is, however, interesting to note who the 'Noes' in this division included: Conservatives, 88; Labour, 23; Democratic Unionist Party, 8; Labour/Co-op, 3; Independent, 1, and Liberal Democrat, 1.

So far, the Commons had voted overwhelmingly in favour of the bill; but it had yet to pass two more hurdles, the Committee stage and the third reading. And it was here that the government began to lose confidence.

The Conservative back-benchers were threatening open revolt. They would block the bill by introducing numerous amendments, thereby protracting it for weeks. That, as the deputy prime minister, declared, was a situation the government could not afford to face – and it could become much worse: it might meet with defeat in both Houses of Parliament. So the decision was made to withdraw the bill.

The Bill Withdrawn

To this effect, Nick Clegg made a statement in the House of Commons on 3 September 2012. Members of the House welcomed the statement with a loud 'Hooray!'[3] This reaction did not please Nick Clegg. He was not, he said, as 'happy about that as Members sitting behind me'. He blamed Labour members for the dismal fate of the bill. They had delivered 'lofty speeches' in support of reform, but would not even tell the government 'how many days they wanted in the timetable motion to make that lofty rhetoric a reality'.[4] He thought that history 'will judge the Labour party very unkindly indeed'.

Jack Straw, the Labour leader, dismissed these remarks as a sign of lack of courage on Mr Clegg's part: the deputy prime minister's reliance on timetabling problems will be seen as a tawdry excuse for a lamentable failure of political will'. He should have known that controversial constitutional bills could be got through the House either by 'informal agreement or, if necessary, by subsequent guillotining'.[5]

Ben Bradshaw (Labour) was more specific. He said that the deputy prime minister ought to admit that his 'new friends in the Tory party have never been serious about Lords reform, and that on this, as on the

---

3   *Parliamentary Debates*, House of Commons, vol. 549, 3 September 2012, col. 35.
4   *Ibid.*, col. 37.
5   *Ibid.*, col. 38.

alternative vote referendum, he has been badly let down by his friend the Prime Minister'.[6]

Nick Clegg retorted. The government would never have been forgiven if it had decided to 'soldier on valiantly for months and months, getting into the trenches on this, when there are so many other things to be getting on with'.[7] But he affirmed his conviction that if Labour members had 'decided to back us on the timetable motion, all that ink and paper would not have gone to waste'.[8]

Perhaps Simon Hughes (Liberal Democrat) was nearer the truth, however, when he said that the bill had to be 'withdrawn, because, although both coalition parties clearly signed up to delivering it, at the end of July there was an unholy alliance between Conservatives opposed to an elected second Chamber and the Labour party, which says that it is in favour, but absolutely refused to deliver the meat'.[9]

The deputy prime minister regretted that this had happened. The government, he said, had been 'extraordinarily pragmatic and flexible' in its approach. It had made 'a barrage of changes to the measure to try to secure cross-party support'. It had also 'clearly signalled' that it was prepared to change the bill further to 'make it more acceptable to as many people as possible in all parties, as long we retained the principle, in some shape or form, that the British people, not party leaders, would have a say in who on earth actually sits in the House of Lords'.[10] Nick Clegg had failed to convince the House. He felt indeed distressed about it all. But this did not mean that he would turn his back 'on the real world'. The system was as 'it is, at least for a while longer, and we will continue to operate in it'.[11]

6 *Ibid.*, col. 41.
7 *Ibid.*, col. 42.
8 *Ibid.*, col. 44.
9 *Ibid.*, col. 43.
10 *Ibid.*, col. 51.
11 *Ibid.*

Announcement in the House of Lords

On 8 October 2012, the House of Lords was informed by its leader, Lord Strathclyde, that the government had decided to withdraw the House of Lords Reform Bill.[12] This statement was made in answer to a 'Private Notice Question' by Lord Wakeham. Lords reform, Lord Strathclyde said, was 'now a matter for future Parliaments'. He could also confirm that the government would not be 'able to deliver Lords reform during this Parliament'. This seemed to him 'extraordinary, given that more than 70% of the House of Commons voted in favour of the Bill at Second Reading'.

Baroness Royall of Blaisdon welcomed the fact that the Coalition had 'finally come to its senses and abandoned what was a bad Bill' anyway. But, she said, to 'lambaste Labour for the Bill's failure is a bit rich'.[13] It was also regrettable that the deputy prime minister appeared, 'in a fit of pique, to have ruled out' any reforms before the next election.

Lord Cormack said that there were many people in this House who were 'delighted that the Government came to their senses on this issue'.[14]

Baroness Hayman thought that there were two areas of consensus that had emerged from the debate on the government's bill. First, that the 'Bill for elections to this House was not deliverable', and secondly that there was an urgent need for substantive reforms in the House.[15]

Lord Elystan-Morgan contended that it 'will be the verdict of history that the proposed reform failed because it was fundamentally and fatally flawed'.[16]

Lord Strathclyde wound up this short debate, stating that he did not think that the bill *was* 'fatally flawed'. But he felt that there 'will be no

---

12 *Parliamentary Debates*, House of Lords, vol. DCCXXXIX, 8 October 2012, col. 825.
13 *Ibid.*, col. 825.
14 *Ibid.*, col. 826.
15 *Ibid.*, col. 827.
16 *Ibid.*, col. 828.

further progress until the House of Commons understands the full implications of an elected House being more independent, stronger and able to hold it and the Government to account'.[17]

17   *Ibid.*, col. 828.

CHAPTER NINETEEN

2014. Dan Byles' House of Lords Reform Act 2014 and Two By-Elections

An attempt to recapitulate all the many proposals to reform the House of Lords would be exceeding the bounds of reason. However, certain conclusions drawn from the foregoing study of attempted reforms might prove to be of some value.

The foremost argument that appears to be relevant is that long and complicated bills are destined to fail. Only short bills with one, two or at the most three clauses are likely to win consensus in both Houses of Parliament. Thus reform must come by stages. The collapse of the government's bill of September 2012 should teach us this lesson: long bills are doomed to fail.

A short bill has more chances, and it seems to be in this spirit that Baroness Hayman and Lord Steel of Aikwood have been thinking since the 2012 débâcle.

On 15 May 2013 Baroness Hayman introduced a bill to 'make provision for permanent leave of absence from the House of Lords; to provide for expulsion of members of the House of Lords in specified circumstances; to make provision for the appointment of a Commission to make recommendations to the Crown for the selection of life-peerages; and to restrict membership of the House of Lords by virtue of hereditary peerages'. The bill contained 16 clauses. These included a clause on retirement (that a peer may retire as a member of the House by giving notice in writing; and that retirement may not be rescinded); another on non-attendance (that a peer who did not attend the House during a session should cease to be a member of the House at the end of the session); another on conviction of serious offence (that a peer convicted of a serious offence should cease to be a member of the House); and one clause with several sub-sections on the creation of a commission to recommend life peerages. This bill did not make further progress, perhaps because it had too many clauses.

Then a short bill – the House of Lords Reform (No. 2) Bill – was introduced in the House of Commons by the Conservative MP Dan Byles. On 19 June 2013, he proposed a private member's bill 'to make provision for resignation from the House of Lords; and to make provision for the expulsion of Members of the House of Lords in specified circumstances'. At the time Dan Byles was by no means sure whether he would have the support of the government. Not long ago, on 4 June, the deputy prime minister, Nick Clegg, had said that he saw 'no need for a stand-alone bill' on House Lords reform.[1] But, only a couple of weeks later, he changed his mind. The government, he maintained, had 'no plans for major reforms of the House of Lords in this Parliament', but if there were 'house-keeping' changes for the Lords that required legislation the government was 'willing to look seriously at the case for a package covering both Houses'.[2] Dan Byles' bill was more than a 'house-keeping package'. It involved an important change in the composition of the Lords.

Members of the government appear to have come to the decision that minimal reform would be acceptable to them. No doubt the recommendation made by the Political and Constitution Reform Committee of the House of Commons had influenced them towards this way of thinking. In its report published on 17 October 2013 this Committee had suggested that small-scale reforms were desirable, could be effective and practical and would 'be likely to command a consensus'.[3] There was a positive

---

1   *Parliamentary Debates*, House of Commons, vol. 563, 4 June 2013, col. 1366.

2   *Ibid.*, 9 July 2013, col. 196W.

3   On 17 October 2013 the Political and Constitution Reform Committee of the House of Commons published, *House of Lords Reform: What Next?* (Ninth Report of Session 2013–14, HC 251). The report recommended reforms step by step. It suggested that there should be: no further replacement of hereditary peers in the Lords when they died; measures to remove persistent non-attendees; a moratorium on new peers; fixed-term appointments for new peers; and a retirement age for peers. The Reform Committee appointed by the House of Commons consisted (in October 2013) of the following MPs: Graham Allen (Labour), Christopher Chope (Conservative), Paul Flynn (Labour), Sheila Gilmore (Labour), Andrew Griffiths (Conservative),

government response.[4] Thus, when Byles' bill was given a second reading in the Commons on 18 October 2013, the minister of state, Greg Clark, was able to tell the House that the bill contained 'moderate proposals' and the government was prepared to support them.[5] Emily Thornberry from the Opposition front bench assured the Government that the Opposition would support the bill too. The bill received an unopposed second reading and was scrutinized by a Commons Public Bill Committee on 15 January 2014.[6] Here Dan Byles tabled 27 amendments, mostly technical in nature. to 'tighten the drafting'.[7] All these were agreed to. The bill was then considered on report on 28 February 2014, and given a third reading, that same day.[8]

It subsequently went on to the House of Lords, where it was sponsored by Lord Steel. There, the bill was given a second reading on 28 March 2014. This was indeed Lord Steel's day. It was the sixth time since 2007 that Steel had introduced this kind of bill. Though he had had some success in the

---

Fabian Hamilton (Labour), Simon Hart (Conservative), Tristram Hunt (Labour), Eleanor Laing (Conservative), Andrew Turner (Conservative) and Stephen Williams (Liberal Democrat).

4   The government's positive response was published much later. See *House of Lords Reform: What Next? Government's Response to the Committee's Ninth Report of 2013– 14*, 17 February 20014. HC 1079/2013–14.

5   *Parliamentary Debates*, House of Commons, vol. 568, 18 October 2013, col. 1011.

6   The following were the members of this committee: William McCrea (Chair), William Bain (Lab), Steve Brine (Con), Robert Buckland (Con), Greg Clark (Con), Therese Coffey (Con), Alex Cunningham (Lab), Thomas Docherty (Lab), Andrew George (LB), Jeremy Lefroy (Con), Ian Paisley (DUP), Mark Pawsey (Con), Roy Stewart (Con), Karl Turner (Lab), Stephen Twigg (Lab/Co-op), Alan Whitehead (Lab) and Kate Emms (Committee clerk). After a brief discussion the Committee passed the bill.

7   Warning shots were fired by Meg Russell, but these were mainly overlooked. See her 'The Byles bill on Lords Reform is important: but needs amending if it is not to damage the Lords' (Constitution Unit Blog, 13 February 2014); and 'The Byles/Steel bill – unless amended – holds grave dangers for the Lords' (Constitution Unit Blog, 5 March 2014); see also Dawn Oliver, 'Reform of the Lords – next steps', *Hansard Society News*, 25 March 2014.

8   Jacob Rees-Mogg (Con) and Thomas Docherty (Lab) tabled amendments but, after a short discussion, these were withdrawn.

Lords, he had failed in the Commons. But, on this occasion, the chances looked favourable. Lord Steel paid tribute to Dan Byles for his skill in having piloted the bill through the Commons. Before producing this bill, Lord Steel said, Byles' 'claim to fame was that he rowed across the Atlantic and trekked to the North Pole – not things, that many Members can claim to have done'.[9] Now Byles had created a 'modest' and short bill. In the creation of it, Lord Norton of Louth had been a 'source of good advice and assistance'; therefore, Lord Steel said, he would like to call this bill the 'Norton-Byles-Steel Bill'. Lord Strathclyde and Lord Hill of Oareford had persuaded their cabinet colleagues of the need for these reforms. Lord Steel now hoped that the bill would have an 'untroubled passage'.

The debate on the reforms proposed lasted only two hours. Speaking from the Opposition front bench, Lord Hunt of King's Heath told the House that he had 'come round to the view that we should support small steps taking place on a frequent basis'.[10] Such was the feeling of the whole House. The bill received a second reading on 28 March 2014.

The main reason why the bill had been given an 'untroubled passage' was that, apart from being a 'modest' bill, it had carefully left aside two provisions: (i) the end to hereditary peers' by-elections, and (ii) the appointment of a statutory Appointments Commission. These two matters were still controversial, and Byles had been wise to omit them – at least for the moment.

After a second reading, the bill was committed to a Committee of the Whole House on 6 May. No further amendments were tabled. The Lords Constitution Committee reported that the bill was indeed a measure of constitutional reform, but it raised no concerns.[11] It was given a third reading on 13 May, and received Royal Assent on 14 May 2014.

9   *Parliamentary Debates*, House of Lords, vol. DCCLIII, 28 March 2014, col. 701.
10   *Ibid.*, cols 732–33.
11   For details, see Richard Kelly, *House of Lords Reform (No. 2) Bill*, Parliament Constitution Centre, House of Commons Library, 10 July 2014.

House of Lords Reform Act 2014

The bill was henceforth to be known as the House of Lords Reform Act 2014. Here is the full text:[12]

> An Act to make provision for resignation from the House of Lords; and to make provision for the expulsion of Members of the House of Lords in specified circumstances.
>
> BE IT ENACTED by the Queen's most Excellent Majesty, by and with the advice and consent of the Lords Spiritual and Temporal, and Commons, in this present Parliament assembled, and by the authority of the same, as follows:-
>
> *1 Resignation*
>
> (1) A member of the House of Lords who is a peer may retire or otherwise resign as a member of the House of Lords by giving notice in writing to the Clerk of the Parliaments.
>
> (2) The notice must –
>
> (a) specify a date from which the resignation is to take effect, and
>
> (b) be signed by the peer and by a witness.
>
> (3) At the beginning of that date the peer ceases to be a member of the House of Lords.
>
> (4) Resignation may not be rescinded.
>
> *2 Non-attendance*
>
> (1) A member of the House of Lords who is a peer and does not attend the House of Lords during a Session ceases to be a member of the House at the beginning of the following Session.
>
> (2) A peer 'does not attend the House of Lords during a Session' if, and only if, the Lord Speaker certifies that the peer –

12   House of Lords Reform Act 2014. Elizabeth II c. Chapter 24.

(a) at no time during the Session attended the House, having regard to attendance records kept by officials of the House, and

(b) did not have leave of absence in respect of the Session, in accordance with Standing Orders of the House.

(3) Subsection (1) does not apply to a peer in respect of attendance during a Session if –

(a) the peer was disqualified from sitting or voting in the House, or suspended from its service, for the whole of the Session, or

(b) the House resolves that subsection (1) should not apply to the peer by reason of special circumstances.

(4) Subsection (1) does not apply in respect of attendance during a Session that is less than six months long.

(5) In this section a reference to attendance is a reference to attending the proceedings of the House (including the proceedings of a Committee of the House).

(6) This section applies in respect of attendance during the first Session to begin after its coming into force and subsequent Sessions.

3 Conviction of serious offence

(1) A member of the House of Lords who is convicted of a serious offence ceases to be a member of the House of Lords.

(2) A person 'is convicted of a serious offence' if, and only if, the Lord Speaker certifies that the person, while a member of the House of Lords, has been –

(a) convicted of a criminal offence, and

(b) sentenced or ordered to be imprisoned or detained indefinitely or for more than one year.

(3) It is irrelevant for the purposes of subsection (2) –

(a) whether the offence is committed at a time when the person is a member of the House of Lords;

(b) whether any of the offence, conviction, sentence, order, imprisonment or detention occurs in the United Kingdom or elsewhere; (but see subsection (9)).

(4) The reference in subsection (2) to an offence is only to an offence committed on or after the day on which this section comes into force.

(5) The reference in subsection (2) to a person being sentenced or ordered to be imprisoned or detained indefinitely or for more than one year does not include such a sentence or order where the sentence or order is suspended.

(6) A certificate under subsection (2) takes effect when it is issued.

(7) If a person who has ceased to be a member of the House of Lords in accordance with this section is successful on appeal –

(a) the Lord Speaker must issue a further certificate to that effect, and

(b) on the issue of that certificate, the original certificate under subsection (2) shall be treated for the purposes of this Act as never having had effect.

(8) A person who has ceased to be a member of the House of Lords in accordance with this section 'is successful on appeal' if, and only if, the Lord Speaker certifies that –

(a) the conviction certified under subsection (2)(a) has been quashed, or

(b) the sentence or order certified under subsection (2)(b) has been –

(i) varied so that it is no longer a sentence or order that the person be imprisoned or detained indefinitely or for more than one year within the meaning of subsection (2)(b), or

(ii) replaced with another sentence or order that is not a sentence or order that the person be so imprisoned or detained.

(9) A certificate under subsection (2) in respect of a conviction outside the United Kingdom may be issued only if the House of Lords resolves that subsection (1) should apply; and where the House does so resolve the Lord Speaker must issue the certificate.

4 Effect of ceasing to be a member

(1) This section applies where a person ceases to be a member of the House of Lords in accordance with this Act.

(2) The person becomes disqualified from attending the proceedings of the House of Lords (including the proceedings of a Committee of the House).

(3) Accordingly, the person shall not be entitled to receive a writ to attend the House (whether under section 1 of the Life Peerages Act 1958, by virtue of the dignity conferred by virtue of appointment as a Lord of Appeal in Ordinary, by virtue of a hereditary peerage or as a Lord Spiritual) and may not attend the House in pursuance of a writ already received.

(4) If the person is a hereditary peer who is excepted from section 1 of the House of Lords Act 1999 by virtue of section 2 of that Act, the person ceases to be excepted from section 1 of that Act (and accordingly section 3 of that Act applies (removal of disqualification on voting in parliamentary elections or being an MP)).

(5) If the person is a peer other than a hereditary peer, the person is not, by virtue of that peerage, disqualified for –

  (a) voting at elections to the House of Commons, or
  (b) being, or being elected as, a member of that House.

(6) In relation to a peer who ceases to be a member of the House of Lords in accordance with this Act, any reference in section 1(3) or (4)(b) of the Representation of the People Act 1985 to a register of parliamentary electors is to be read as including –

  (a) any register of local government electors in Great Britain, and
  (b) any register of local electors in Northern Ireland, which was required to be published on any date before the date on which the peer ceased to be a member.

(7) The Standing Orders of the House required by section 2(4) of the House of Lords Act 1999 (filling of vacancies) must make provision requiring the holding of a by-election to fill any vacancy which arises under this Act among the people excepted from section 1 of that Act in consequence of an election.

(8) Subject to section 3(7), a person who ceases to be a member of the House of Lords in accordance with this Act may not subsequently become a member of that House.

5 Certificate of Lord Speaker

(1) A certificate of the Lord Speaker under this Act shall be conclusive for all purposes.

(2) A certificate may be issued on the Lord Speaker's own initiative.

6 Interpretation

(1) For the purposes of this Act a person is a member of the House of Lords if the person is entitled to receive writs of summons to attend that House.

(2) In determining whether a person is so entitled, ignore –

(a) section 2 of the Forfeiture Act 1870 (disqualification on conviction of treason);

(b) sections 426A and 427 of the Insolvency Act 1986 (disqualification on insolvency);

(c) regulation 4 of the European Parliament (House of Lords Disqualification) Regulations 2008 (S.I. 2008/1647) (disqualification where MEP).

(3) In this Act 'peer' includes a person upon whom a dignity has been conferred by virtue of appointment as a Lord of Appeal in Ordinary.

7 Short title, commencement and extent

(1) This Act may be cited as the House of Lords Reform Act 2014.

(2) Sections 1 and 2 of this Act shall come into force at the end of the period of three months beginning with the day on which this Act is passed.

(3) The remaining provisions of this Act shall come into force on the day on which this Act is passed.

(4) This Act extends to England and Wales, Scotland and Northern Ireland.

The House of Lords' Code of Conduct was accordingly amended.[13] The Act marked another turning-point in the process of reform of the Upper House.

Hereditary Peers' By-Elections

At this point, it will not be out of place to refer to two hereditary peers' by-elections which took place in 2014. These by-elections are an indication of the effectiveness of the House of Lords Act 1999.

On 14 February 2014 the death of Lord Moran created a vacancy among the excepted hereditary peers sitting in the House of Lords. The clerk of the parliaments, David Beamish, notified the House on 28 February that under Standing Order 10, this vacancy had to be filled by means of a by-election. Those eligible to stand were all those hereditary peers whose names were listed in the register of hereditary peers wishing to stand for election as members of the House of Lords, a list which the clerk of the parliaments maintained. All those on this register were being asked to indicate by Friday 21 March 2014 whether they wished to be a candidate in this by-election.[14] The following indicated that they wished to stand: Earl Albermarle, Lord Aldington, Lord Cromwell, Lord Darling, Lord Hacking, Lord Harlech, Viscount Massereene and Ferrard, Lord Monson,

---

13   See *House of Lords, Code of Conduct for Members of the House of Lords; Guide to the Code of Conduct; Code of Conduct for Staff or Members of the House of Lords*, third edition, June 2014. HL Paper 5/2014–15.

14   Source: *House of Lords Journal*: David Beamish, Clerk of the Parliaments, 28 February 2014.

Lord Napier and Ettrick, Lord Russell of Liverpool, Lord Sempill, Earl Temple of Stowe, and Lord Thurlow.

Since Lord Moran had been one of the 28 hereditary peers elected by the Cross-Bench hereditary peers, under Standing Order (2), the voters in the by-election had to be the excepted hereditary peers belonging to the Lords' Cross-Bench group. Twenty-nine were eligible to vote. The clerk of the parliaments notified the electors that, in this by-election, votes would be cast by post. Ballot papers were sent to the electors on 25 March, and these had to be returned to the office of the clerk of the parliaments, either by post or in person, by 5 p.m. on 8 April 2014: ballot papers received after this time would not be counted.

The candidates were invited, but not required, to submit statements in support of their candidature. These statements were not to exceed 75 words and were to be circulated by the House administration to all electors. The Code of Conduct for the by-election was set out by the clerk of the parliaments in the following words:[15]

(i)   Ballot papers will not indicate any qualification or reason why a candidate should be elected.

(ii)   Candidates may not offer hospitality, entertainment or financial inducement to electors intended to influence their votes or likely to have that effect.

(iii)   Candidates may not engage in any activity intended or likely to discredit other candidates in the by-election.

(iv)   Candidates may not solicit votes near the room where the by-election is taking place.

(v)   If the Clerk of the Parliaments suspects, on reasonable grounds, that some material irregularity or improper conduct may have occurred in the electoral process, he may refer the matter to the Committee for Privileges and Conduct. The Committee may, if it thinks fit, recommend the disqualification of a successful candidate if their election appears to

15   *Ibid.*

have been influenced by material irregularity or improper
conduct.

vi) In this code of conduct, 'candidate' includes an agent or
supporter acting on behalf of the candidate.

The Alternative Vote System was used:

> Voters place the figure 1 in the box next to the name of the can-
> didate they most strongly support, the figure 2 against the next
> most favoured candidate, and so on. Voters may cast as many
> or as few votes as they wish. In order to be elected, the success-
> ful candidate must receive at least as many votes as all the other
> candidates put together. In the event of this not happening after
> first preference votes have been allocated, the votes of the candi-
> dates receiving the lowest number of first preference votes will be
> shared out according to the second preference marked on them.
> This will be repeated until one candidate has at least half of the
> total valid votes.[16]

Ballot papers would be invalidated 'if: (i) any number is used more than
once, or (ii) in the opinion of the Returning Officer (the Clerk of the
Parliaments) the ballot paper is illegible or ambiguous'. The count was
conducted by the Electoral Reform Service, and scrutinized by Viscount
Craigavon.

The result of the by-election was announced by the clerk of the parliaments on 9 April. He stated that a total of 27 valid votes had been cast
and there were no spoilt ballot papers. Of the 13 candidates, 6 received
one or more first-preference votes. After 4 transfers of votes, the voting
for the final 2 candidates was as follows: Lord Cromwell, 13; Lord Russell
of Liverpool, 12. The successful candidate was Lord Cromwell.[17]

Another hereditary peers' by-election took place later, in October
2014, after the death of Lord Methuen. He had been elected under Standing

16   *Ibid.*
17   *Ibid.*, 9 April 2014.

Order (9)(2ii), among the '15 peers, elected by the whole House, from among those ready to serve as Deputy Speakers or in any other office as the House may require'. Under Standing Order 10(3), the electorate in this by-election would be the whole House. Accordingly all members of the House of Lords who had taken the path, and who were not subject to statutory disqualification, suspended from the service of the House or on leave of absence were entitled to vote. Those eligible to be candidates were the hereditary peers on the register of hereditary peers wishing to stand for election as members of the House of Lords maintained by the clerk of the parliaments. The deadline for registrations of candidature was 3 p.m. on 11 September. The following fifteen candidates registered to stand in the by-election:[18] Lord Biddulph (Conservative), Lord Cadman (Conservative); Lord Calverley (Cross-Bench); Lord Harlech (Conservative); Lord Kennet (Liberal Democrat); Lord Layton (Conservative); Lord Margadale (Conservative); Viscount Massereene and Ferrard (Cross-Bench); Lord Middleton (Conservative); Lord Napier and Ettrick (Cross-Bench); Earl Oxford and Asquith (Liberal Democrat); Lord Rowallan (Conservative); Lord Somerleyton (Cross-Bench); Earl Stockton (Conservative); and Lord Sudeley (Conservative). The candidates had been invited to indicate their party or group affiliation and to submit candidature statements of not more than 75 words. Lords Biddulph and Cadman did not submit any statement. The rest of the candidates submitted the statements that follow:[19]

> LORD CALVERLEY: Since last sitting, I have been greatly dismayed by the behaviour of a minority of newer members. These individuals have usurped their new found status for their own cupidity, rather than upholding the values of our honourable institution. Their actions have brought 'the House' into disrepute in the eyes of the British Public and the world at large. Should I be successful in this ballot, I would endeavour to help to rectify this shameful situation.

18   *Ibid.*, 15 September 2014.
19   *Ibid.*

LORD HARLECH: I am a farmer, forester, land manager, heavy haulage and plant contractor who also for over 40 years has been a consultant in overseas agricultural reconstruction. Mostly in war zones from Vietnam to the Balkans, Africa and others. You do of course need to have a skill in political dialogue at every level: I and my family having served this country in peace and war for more than seven centuries and from field, dock, warehouse, office ... [The remainder of Lord Harlech's statement was omitted because it exceeded the 75-word limit.]

LORD KENNET: My politics started when I was seven years old, addressing envelopes in Paddington North. I later joined the SDP and the LibDems. Between family, business and arts/cultural interests, I have stood in elections for the LibDems whenever and wherever appropriate, including peers' by-elections since inheriting my title in 2009, and council elections. If elected, I will give the best service I can as a working peer and a dutiful member of your lordships' House.

LORD LAYTON: Professional politicians and civil servants in Westminster and Whitehall lacking 'conventional' work experience, indifferent and incompetent managers exploiting a workforce of people who are fearful for their continued employment, with indifferent and incompetent, self-serving unions doing nothing for their members – the House of Lords is the only place where someone like me, who has encountered and/or fought with all of the above, can be a voice for these people I have worked with and understand.

LORD MARGADALE: I manage various businesses between Wiltshire, Islay and London. They relate mostly to Agriculture and property. I am 56. Rural affairs in UK, European and World contexts need more representation and understanding in Government. I feel strongly that the United Kingdom will be poorer for any break up but the current debate may improve certain circumstances. The Lords as a legislative chamber could well change but must not as a result of knee-jerk political reaction.

VISCOUNT MASSEREENE AND FERRARD: I have a lifelong interest in Politics with a strong tendency to Conservatism because I have felt the results of Socialism have been unsuccessful in practice. I am in favour of the nation recovering political autonomy from the E.U. in which respect I support UKIP a party insufficiently represented in Parliament. If elected I propose to be an active and working member of the Cross-benches.

LORD MIDDLETON: If elected I should commit to regular participation. I served in the Regular and Territorial Army. I run an innovative and award winning agricultural and land management company with a particular interest in sustainable and efficient food production. After chairing the Yorkshire region of the Country Land and Business Association I represented the organisation in Europe as its Vice President in Europe helping to formulate views on CAP and lobbying in Brussels and other member states.

LORD NAPIER AND ETTRICK: I have run my own landscape gardening business, near Cambridge, for 15 years. Being born deaf, I will bring a unique insight to the House. In the most recent survey by 'Action on Hearing Loss', 79% of people reported it was employers' attitudes to deafness which created the major barrier to work, hindering career potential. My empathy with disabilities, for which I would campaign, could be invaluable to the work of the House.

EARL OXFORD AND ASQUITH: My first career was in the British foreign service, largely covering the Soviet Union, Eastern Europe and, in due course, the ex-Soviet states, especially Ukraine. My main experience has therefore been in foreign and defence policy, foreign trade and commercial affairs, with strong connections in Russia, Eastern Europe, the Middle East, Iran and China.

Currently I run an environmental company specialising in soil remediation, decontamination and water conservation.

LORD ROWALLAN: Born 08.03.1947. Married with 4 children & 2 stepchildren & 6 grandchildren. Estate Agent 1971–1992. Farmer 1977–2013. Company Director of several Companies 1970–2013. House of Lords 1995–1999 introduced a Mental Health Bill to House. Chairman Fenwick & Lochgoin Covenanters Trust 1977. Interests: Equestrianism, humanitarian projects, Mental Health issues. FEI International show jumping judge. Judge at London 2012 Olympics – Show jumping.

LORD SOMERLEYTON: A liberal conservative who feels his contribution would be better channelled as a cross-bencher free of party whips. I am an entrepreneur of mixed successes in the food and beverage business; Hot Chip is my current project which I aspire to expand nationally. I also devote time researching pioneering animal welfare projects, re-wilding projects, small scale food production businesses and forestry. Outside of work I hold an interest in the Middle Eastern question.

EARL STOCKTON: B. 10.10.43 as Rt Hon. Maurice Macmillan MP, and Hon. Katherine, DBE. Journalist: Glasgow Herald, Daily Mail, Daily and Sunday Telegraph, BBC, CRTF. Publisher Macmillan Ltd. Charities: St Mary-le-Strand, Book Trade, NPFA, RNIB, RLSBP, Archbishop Tenison's School. Director: CENTEC, Countryside Alliance, Publishers' Association. Candidate Bristol EC 1994; MEP SW 1999–2004; member South Bucks DC 2010; HOL 1986–99; 1984–2014 spoken in 414 constituencies. Interests: Foreign, Defence, Europe, handicapped youngsters, countryside.

LORD SUDELEY: In 1900 4th Lord Sudeley was made bankrupt and lost his seat in the House of Lords because his creditors were allowed to enlarge their claims without their being independently and adequately audited. Sudeley recovered his seat and used it to provide us with guide lecturers for museums. I would like to introduce a Bill to prevent any further creditors from enlarging their claims in the same way.

The deadline for requesting postal votes was 2 October 2014. Ballot papers were posted by the Electoral Reform Services on 6 October. Completed postal ballot papers were to be returned to the clerk of the parliaments either by post or in person by 5 p.m. on 21 October. Voters in person did not need to apply for ballot papers in advance: they could vote in Committee Room 3 from 10 a.m. to 8 p.m. on 21 October. The Alternative Voting System was used. All current members of the House of Lords, a total of 776, were eligible to vote.

A total of 283 valid votes was cast in this election; there were no spoilt ballot papers. The count was conducted by the Electoral Reform Services with the following acting as scrutineers: Viscount Craigavon, Lord Geddes, Lord Shutt of Greetland and Lord Tunnicliffe. The results were as follows:[20]

Candidate	1st preference votes
Lord Biddulph	0
Lord Cadman	0
Lord Calverley	1
Lord Harlech	4
Lord Kennet	29
Lord Layton	1
Lord Margadale	13
Viscount Massereene and Ferrard	6
Lord Middleton	1
Lord Napier and Ettrick	35
Earl Oxford and Asquith	155
Lord Rowallan	0
Lord Somerleyton	6
Earl Stockton	31
Lord Sudeley	1

20   *Ibid.*, 22 October 2014.

Total continuing votes at each stage: 283
Votes needed in order to be elected: 142
    The successful candidate was The Earl of Oxford and Asquith,
having received 155 votes.

The results of the October hereditary peers' by-election give us a revealing picture of the House of Lords' way of thinking. It seems to us very forward-looking. The electors did not seem to be impressed by such candidature statements as made by Lord Calverley: only one voter shared his views. The same holds true for Lord Harlech, who got 4 votes, or Lord Sudeley, who got no votes. Some party loyalty was visible in the case of Lord Kennet (Liberal Democrat) and Earl Stockton (Conservative). But on the whole the preferred candidate was the one who had distinguished himself in the British foreign service and who is indeed an expert in the regions of the world that currently invite our serious attention. Earl Oxford's competent voice in the House of Lords should therefore be most welcome.

We must now return to the next House of Lords reform bill.

CHAPTER TWENTY

2014. A Bill Empowering the House of Lords to Expel or Suspend Members: Baroness Hayman

The passing of the House of Lords Reform Act 2014, which was so concise in its presentation, proves that shorter bills have every chance of success in Parliament. It was perhaps this belief that prompted Baroness Hayman to bring forward her own private member's bill on 5 June 2014 in the House of Lords. The bill read:[1]

> BE IT ENACTED by the Queen's most Excellent Majesty, by and with the advice and consent of the Lords Spiritual and Temporal, and Commons in this present Parliament assembled, and by the authority of the same, as follows:
>
> 1. *Expulsion and suspension of members of the House of Lords*
>
> (i) Standing Orders of the House of Lords may make provision under which the House of Lords may by resolution –
>
> > (a) expel a member of the House of Lords, or
> > (b) suspend a member of the House of Lords for the period specified in the resolution.
>
> (ii) A person expelled by virtue of this section ceases to be a member.
>
> (iii) A person suspended by virtue of this section remains a member during the period of suspension, but during that period the person –
>
> > (a) is not entitled to receive writs of summons to attend the House of Lords,

---

1   HL Bill 7.

(b) despite any writ of summons previously issued to the person, is disqualified from sitting or voting in the House of Lords or a committee of the House of Lords.

2. Effect of ceasing to be a member

Section 4 of the House of Lords Reform Act 2014 (effect of ceasing to be a member) applies where a person is expelled in accordance with section 1 of this Act.

3. Short title, commencement and extent

(i) This Act may be cited as the House of Lords (Expulsion and Suspension) Act 2014.

(ii) This Act shall come into force at the end of the period of three months beginning with the day on which this Act is passed.

(iii) This Act extends to England and Wales, Scotland and Northern Ireland.

Ordered to be Printed, 5 June 2014.

What was the purpose behind this bill? It was, Baroness Hayman argued, 'limited to giving the House of Lords power to provide in its standing orders, both for the expulsion of members and for the suspension of members beyond the term of one parliament. These are obviously very limited disciplinary measures, but I believe necessary ones. And I have some hope that they may go through the Lords quite smoothly and there is potential for support in the Commons.'[2]

Second Reading of the Bill in the Lords

The bill received a second reading on 24 October 2014, and it sailed through the Lords not only 'quite smoothly' but with enthusiastic support from all political parties and groups.

2   Private note to the author, 23 July 2014.

At quarter past two on the afternoon of 24 October, Baroness Hayman moved that her bill be read a second time. Lord Newby (Liberal Democrat) opened the debate stating that he had it 'in command from Her Majesty the Queen to acquaint the House that Her Majesty, having been informed of the purport of the House of Lords (Expulsion and Suspension) Bill, has consented to place her prerogative and interest, so far as they are affected by the Bill, at the disposal of Parliament for the purposes of the Bill'.[3]

Baroness Hayman (Cross-Bench) then rose to express her gratitude to 'all noble Lords who are to speak in our debate today'. Their commitment reflected the seriousness with which the House viewed the issues raised in the bill. It was, she said, a 'brief and straightforward measure', but its brevity did not mean that it was 'insignificant in its content'. Her bill would 'empower the House to make Standing Orders to enable a suspension to be imposed that would run beyond the end of a parliament and during that time the right to receive a writ of summons would be suspended. The House would also be given the power to enact in Standing Orders the ability to expel a Member in circumstances other than the narrow ones set out in the House of Lords Reform Act 2014 – non-attendance or being subject to a prison sentence of more than a year.' The bill was 'enabling, not prescriptive'. It did not 'lay down in detail the circumstances in which these sanctions would be appropriate or specify the processes the House should adopt in its disciplinary proceedings'. The House was lucky to have members 'with significant and judicial experience to guide [it] in the painstaking task of drawing up the appropriate Standing Orders'. That in one sense was 'a lock: getting the Standing Orders right and those being approved by the House, and making sure that we deal fairly and appropriately with the regime'. The second lock was 'the fact that the whole House would again have to agree to a recommendation from the disciplinary committees of the House that such an expulsion should take place'. The baroness hoped that, with 'good will and a little support from the Government', the bill could 'become law, even within the short time available in this Session'. She commended the bill to the House and begged to move.

3   *Parliamentary Debates*, House of Lords, vol. DCCLVI, 24 October 2014, cols 924–40.

Lord Mackay of Clashfern (Conservative) stood to support the bill strongly in both its branches. That was the only correct way to regulate the suspension of members of the House.

Baroness Taylor of Bolton (Labour) agreed that this was a 'short and significant' bill. She hoped that 'measures of this kind can help to restore some confidence that those of us here are keen to put our House in order'. The bill should have 'speedy passage'; she saw 'no reason why it should not'.

Lord Phillips of Sudbury (Liberal Democrat) thought that being in the House was 'an absolute privilege, and there comes with that a commensurate duty to police and regulate with absolute rigour'. He believed that self-reform was 'vital'. It was the 'very least that we can do and it should be the first of many such measures'.

Lord Brown of Eaton-under-Heywood (Cross-Bench) greatly welcomed the bill and 'the logical and highly desirable increments to the powers of the House that it would bring with it'. The bill 'would enable us to provide in Standing Orders for the House to resolve to expel a member permanently or to suspend a member beyond the term of the current Parliament. The precise form and scope of such Standing Orders will, of course, require careful thought.'

Lord Trefgarne (Conservative) supported the 'main thrust of this Bill'. He hoped it would '[become] law.'

Lord Butler of Brockwell (Cross-Bench) added his voice to those who supported the bill. It gave the House 'more flexible powers to determine the circumstances in which Peers can be suspended or expelled'. He saw no reason 'why the Government should not support and facilitate this Bill'. He hoped that the minister would 'be able to tell us that the government will indeed support it. If they do not, I think the only reason can be that they are not willing to facilitate any further reform of the House of Lords until more expansive, more ambitious reforms can be introduced. If that is the attitude of the Government, I deplore it.'

Lord Cormack (Conservative) endorsed what Lord Butler had said entirely. He was delighted to commend the first lord Speaker for introducing the bill. There were only 'four or five months left of this Parliament. There is no time to get through sweeping measures, but there is ample time to get this measure through. There is no reason at all why it should not go through with acclamation this afternoon, without amendment in Committee, and be in another place well before Christmas. I hope that that will happen. If it does, we will collectively be giving all those who care for our constitution and our Parliament a good Christmas present.'

Lord Haskel (Labour) said there were many things 'on which we can agree, and by taking them one at a time we may be able to achieve reform by accretional amelioration' – a phrase Lord Phillips had used in an earlier speech.

Lord Dobbs (Conservative) supported 'the noble Baroness's excellent Bill'. He thought that one fundamental principle 'must guide everything we do: every one of us, individually, no matter how long we have perched here, whatever our plumage and pedigree, is here to serve this House. This House does not exist for our benefit, but we for it. This Bill helps to reinforce that fundamental principle.'

Lord Kerr of Kinlochkard (Cross-Bench) said that it was 'a very brief Bill' and his support for it was 'very strong'. There was 'no reason at all why this very sensible, long-overdue, necessary little reform should not be on the statute book before the end of this Parliament'.

Lord Norton of Louth (Conservative) expressed his agreement with Baroness Hayman that the bill extended 'our current limited powers and brings us into line with the other place'. There was 'clearly a powerful case for bringing us into line with the House of Commons'. It was a 'modest' bill, at least 'in length', but it got 'the balance right'. He saw 'no reason at all why it should not be permitted to proceed to the statute book and do so swiftly'.

Lord Jopling (Conservative) said that it was 'extremely difficult to get a Private Member's Bill through the Commons procedures', especially before a general election; but he hoped it *would* go through, and with government support.

Lord Hunt of Kings Heath (Labour) agreed that it was 'absolutely clear that we need the Government to fully support the Bill and make sure that there is time in the other place for it to go through'.

Lord Wallace of Saltaire (Liberal Democrat) spoke for the government. He said that the government had 'no settled view on the Bill at present'. All he could promise – and 'I do promise – is that I will take back the speeches that have been given around the House and the strong arguments that these are essentially housekeeping measures – although I am not sure that expulsion is entirely a matter of housekeeping'. Time, however, was 'very short'.

Lord Hunt of Kings Heath intervened. That statement was 'disappointing', he said. But perhaps it could be 'taken as a positive response if it actually meant that the Government generally would be prepared to discuss' with the noble baroness whether 'they are prepared to support the Bill'. Could Lord Wallace 'say that the door is at least open to that?'

Lord Wallace replied that he was trying to be 'as positive as' he could. Getting consensus inside the government was 'not always entirely simple and straightforward'. But he assured the House that the government remained 'committed to a broader scheme of reform'.

Baroness Taylor of Bolton reminded the minister that in the 'wash-up at the end of the Parliament it is very often easy to get agreement on measures that are as clear-cut as this one'.

Lord Wallace said that he '[took] that point and will take it back'. He had hoped that, 'with a fixed-term Parliament, there would be much less wash-up than before'. But things seemed to be changing.

Lord Cormack thought that if it was 'less of a wash-up, there is only a very tiny dish'.

Lord Wallace feared that 'some rather larger dishes may yet be introduced, which the Government may wish to try to push through'. The bill the baroness had moved needed to be seriously considered. It was 'quite a substantial extension to the power of the House, in spite of the wonderful phrase that that the noble lord, Lord Phillips, had used – that it was 'intended to be merely an *amelioration*'. However, he was 'very happy to talk further with the noble Baroness, Lady Hayman, and certainly take this back to the Cabinet Office to see what is possible'.

Lord Kerr of Kinlochard intervened to say that the noble lord's tone was 'encouraging but slightly light-hearted. I regard this as a very important Bill. It may be short but if it is carried by acclamation in this House, as it should be; it will be very odd if the Government do not find time for it in the other place.'

Lord Wallace agreed that it was a 'serious matter', and he assured the House that conversations 'will continue off the Floor, as they so often do. We will see what we can do.'

Baroness Hayman ended the debate, offering thanks for the support she had received from all benches of the House and 'for the seriousness with which Members have addressed the Bill'. The debate had given her encouragement to pursue the matter further. She did not think that 'anyone expressed any doubt about the importance and necessity of the Bill'. She believed that 'we can deliver it up in good time for it to become law if the Government give it time in another place'. She hoped that, 'in a short period of time, the Government will reach the conclusion that it is in all our interests to do so'.

The bill was read a second time and committed to a Committee of the Whole House.

The Bill in Committee

The Hayman Bill was examined at the Committee Stage in the House of Lords on 21 November 2014.[4] Baroness Hayman moved Amendment 1 to Clause 1: 'Expulsion and suspension of members of the House of Lords':

> Clause 1, page 1, line 14, at end insert: '(...) Standing Orders under subsection (1) may only make provision in respect of conduct by a member which takes place after the coming into force of this Act'.

She upheld the amendment, stating that this was a simple bill, an 'enabling Bill', dealing with 'a limited but very important issue, which was to ensure that the House had available to it, if the circumstances arose in which they were needed, sanctions and disciplinary measures that the public would expect us to have in those circumstances and which I think there is general agreement that we do not have at the moment'. She believed

4   *Parliamentary Debates*, House of Lords, vol DCCLVII, 21 November 2014, cols 644–51.

that 'we have a dangerous lacuna in our disciplinary proceedings and the Bill sets out to fill it and protect the House in those circumstances'. She begged to move.

Lord Brabazon of Tara (Conservative) said that he was chairman of the Privileges Committee 'during the saga of the first suspensions to take place in the modern era.[5] They were not as simple as all that, because a number of people thought that we should not have been able to suspend noble Lords from the service of the House. We found that we were, but we also found that we were unable to suspend noble Lords beyond the length of a Parliament. In other words, if someone was suspended today, they could be suspended for only five or six months or so, whereas if someone was suspended on 1 June, they could be suspended for five years. The press and the public were rightly unable to understand why we did not have the power to suspend for longer or, indeed, to expel.' The bill appeared 'to deal with that matter extremely well', and he 'very much' supported the bill and the amendment.

Lord Cormack (Conservative) believed the bill was a 'logical extension of the Bill taken through the House of Commons last year by Mr Dan Byles and through this place by my noble friend Lord Steel of Aikwood, who has done so much in this field'. The bill was 'extremely important, dealing with a vital subject, but it is quite literally about keeping the House in the best possible sense'. The Lords, he said, were 'all grateful to the noble Baroness for, at this late stage in the Parliament, seeking to introduce a very short, precise and particular measure, which can certainly pass in the little time left available in this Parliament, given the good will and support of the Government'. He 'very much' hoped that the minister would 'be able not

---

5   As Lord Phillips had pointed out in this same debate, there was at the time 'unparalleled public mistrust' of parliament, partly due to the cash-for-questions and expenses scandals. The suspensions Lord Brabazon refers to here were of two peers caught trying to take cash for amendments. This was in 2009. In 2010, three more peers were suspended in an expenses scandal. (See The *Guardian*, 20 May 2009 and 21 October 2010.) In a wider context, in 2012 the chief of the Royal Bank of Scotland was stripped of his knighthood after the collapse of the bank and ensuing revelations. People asked why peers could not be similarly treated.

only to accept the spirit of the amendment but indicate that the Bill can have a fair wind. It is in the best interests of your Lordships' House that this House should be kept in the best possible way, and the Bill enables us to move in that direction.'

Baroness Flather (Cross-Bench) said she was 'totally in favour of this power being given to us'. She 'utterly' supported the bill. The House 'need[s] these powers to protect all of us who do not cheat or behave badly, because one or two people can make all of us look bad. I hope that we can get on with this and that the Bill passes.'

Lord Finkelstein (Conservative) thought the principle was 'absolutely right, but I just question whether Amendment 1 is really a very good idea'. The amendment 'would make it impossible to deal with that conduct'. In other words, the amendment makes it difficult to deal with some of the worst conduct. To use an entirely hypothetical example,[6] if someone committed perjury in a libel case and it took four years for that perjury to be revealed, in the course of which the Bill was passed, the conduct would no longer fall under the Bill. I wonder whether the amendment is quite what we want.'

Lord Hunt of Kings Heath (Labour) said that the Opposition 'fully' supported the noble baroness in her 'endeavours'. He thought that the bill 'can be fairly assured of passage through your Lordships' House'. The question was, 'when it gets to the Commons, what help will the Government give it? Without Government help, I suspect that it will be very difficult for the Bill to pass, so it is right for me to press the Minister on what the Government's attitude will be.' There was 'an appetite in this House for sensible change'.

Lord Wallace of Saltaire spoke again for the government. The bill, he said had a 'limited and specific purpose and is concerned with the

---

6   This was *not* a hypothetical example. It obliquely referred to the case of Lord Archer, who was convicted in 2000 and imprisoned from 2001 to 2003. He was not the only peer to have been imprisoned around this time. The Labour MP Paul Flynn said it was 'crazy' to have people making laws if they had been in jail for breaking them. See Jim Richard, 'Jailed Peers Set to Face Expulsion', *Politics and Policy*, 2 February 2012.

reputation of Parliament as a whole. We welcome that. The Bill is also concerned with rebuilding public trust in our political institutions.' The bill 'is intended to give the House precautionary powers – powers which are intended to be available but to be rarely, and, one hopes, never, used. We recognise that and the Government also recognise the sentiment around the House on the Bill. We are very happy to work with the noble Baroness to ensure that the amendments are tweaked into a form that would suit. We understand the spirit of the amendments but there are some issues about the exact definition, which we need to clarify. The noble Lord, Lord Finkelstein, raised one example: what do we do if we become aware of past conduct which was egregious but was not previously known? What do we do about past conduct, the effects of which are continuing? The issues of retrospectivity are complicated in this regard and the House will also need to be concerned that we currently have an inherent power of suspension, which may or may not be used with retrospective regard to past conduct. If we were to pass this, we would be limiting the power of suspension that the House currently has. What I can do on behalf of the Government is to say that we would be very happy for Cabinet Office officials and lawyers to discuss between this stage of the Bill and the next, with the noble Baroness and others, how we might reshape these amendments to put them into a reasonable form. The Government are giving the Bill a fair wind in this House. How far we will be able to assist it in the other place is a matter which the Government do not yet need to address and have not yet fully addressed. All Members of this Chamber will know of the complicated internal procedures that the Government need to go through. It will be tight to get the Bill through the other House, given the queue of Private Members' Bills before the next election – although I take the comment from the noble Lord, Lord Hunt, that some of them are not entirely overworked at the moment – but we need not address that issue definitively at present. For the moment, I am very happy to say that the Government will work with the noble Baroness to revise the amendment into a form that would suit the purposes that are intended, and that we have thought through some of the complications about the principle of retrospection, which is a very delicate and important one in the issue of conduct.

After the debate Amendment 1 was agreed and Clause 1 amended. Then Baroness Hayman moved Amendment 2 to Clause 2: 'Effect of ceasing to be a member': 'Clause 2, page 1, line 16, after "4" insert "(2) to (8)".'

Baroness Hayman said that it had been pointed out to her that it 'would be helpful, in spelling out the consequences of expulsion under the Bill that are to mirror those under the Byles Bill – the House of Lords Reform Act 2014 – if I referred not simply to Section 4 of that Act but also to subsections of that Act'. She begged to move.

Lord Wallace of Saltaire assured the House that 'here again the Government are sympathetic to the principle, but there are some technical issues about how the Bill refers to the 2014 Act and how one relates to the other. Again, the Government would be very glad to talk to the noble Baroness between Committee and Report to sort them out and perhaps come back with a different amendment on Report.' He hoped that the noble baroness was 'happy with the Government's response'.

Baroness Hayman responded positively. She would be 'not just happy but very grateful to have the discussions that the Minister suggests. I agree with the Minister that the heavy lifting about getting this right has to be done within the House, with the Committee for Privileges and Conduct looking at the code of conduct and Standing Orders and making sure that we have the appropriate procedures. This is an enabling Bill to allow us to get on and do that meticulous and careful work under its auspices.'

Amendment 2 was agreed and the revised Clause 2 accepted. Clause 3 was also agreed. The bill was returned to the House with amendments for a third reading.[7]

---

7   The bill received its third reading on 7 January 2015, and was sent to the Commons. Here the bill, sponsored by Sir George Young, had its second reading, without debate on 23 January 2015. The bill was then committed to a Public Bill Committee, which debated it on 4 February 2015, to be reported without amendment. The bill has now completed its committee stage and the report stage is expected on 27 February 2015. The bill is likely to receive a safe third reading, and go on to receive Royal Assent.

A Future Undecided (November 2014)

Judging from the mood of unanimity in the Lords debates, one would suppose that the bill should have a smooth passage into legislation without any obstruction. At the point of writing – late November 2014 – it is difficult, however, to speculate on how the government will act. If it has enough good will, it could push through the bill in the Commons before the general election which is to be held early next year (2015). If the bill is made law, it would indeed be an important additional step towards reforming the House of Lords.

Epilogue

It is perhaps incumbent on us to offer a few, if only brief, conclusive remarks. We must once and for all give up the thought of creating a wholly or partly elected second chamber. The system of elections should be completely ruled out. Not only would an elected second chamber become more powerful than it should be, but such a chamber would challenge the primacy of the House of Commons. Further, the very process of introducing various forms of electoral system would make reform more, and not less, complicated. Besides a hybrid system – a partly elected and partly nominated second chamber – would divide the House into two classes: the 'representative' and the 'appointed'. That would hardly be a welcome reform.

There is general accordance in opinion that a second chamber should be a revising chamber. That this element remains effective should be our major concern. The House of Lords has at present sufficient powers to do this job, and it has so far fulfilled its responsibilities most properly. Any major disputes between the two Houses can be resolved by creating joint committees.

Failure to agree on the composition of a second chamber has been the sole cause of delay in reform. The problem of membership should be the domain of an independent Appointments Commission. Only a body of this kind could guarantee the legitimacy of the new House. At the time of writing, the House of Lords is overcrowded: there is hardly room to accommodate all its members. But what is far more out of keeping with the function of the House is that the debating time of each individual is limited to six minutes. This is most unfortunate. Such a limitation could seriously affect the revising function of the House, which is its main purpose. Therefore the membership should be cut, perhaps by introducing a system of compulsory retirement at a certain age and by delaying the appointment of new members.

And then let us not totally eliminate the services of the hereditary peers from the House of Lords. They are part of the Convention. When there is so much talk about minority and ethnic representation in the House, why then disregard that section of the British people who have so richly contributed to the welfare of the nation?

On 24 October 2014, during the debate in the House of Lords on Baroness Hayman's Expulsion and Suspension Bill, members from all political parties, and the cross benches too, confirmed that there were many things on which there was little disagreement among them, and that one way to achieve reform could be by 'accretional amelioration'. This 'wonderful phrase' ought to stand as the guide-line for any future schemes for reform of the House.

We believe that the name 'House of Lords' is an appropriate appellation, derived from the classical Parliament of antiquity. It should not be changed. The House can be thought of as a great work of art, which has developed over centuries. It also symbolizes the vitality of British history. Posterity will never forgive us if we were to destroy what has been the envy of parliamentary democracies all over the world.

Bibliography

I. Archival Sources

The Parliamentary Archives: Houses of Parliament, London:
Reference Code: HL/WHE/1/1/15–16.

Bodleian Library, Oxford:
Conservative Party Papers.

Nuffield College Library, Oxford:
Lord Wakeham Papers.

II. Published Works

Adonis, Andrew, *Modernising Britain's Democracy. Why, What and How. The Case for Change* (Democratic Audit in association with the Scarman Trust, March 1997).
A Future Fair for All (2010).
A House for the Future (Royal Commission on the Reform of the House of Lords, January 2000). Cm 4534.
Aitken, Ian, 'Nix the fix and scrape the lot of them', *Tribune*, 28 January 2000.
Ambitions for Britain (2001).
Amory, Edward Heathcoat, *Lords a' Leaping* (Centre for Policy Studies, September 1998).
An Elected Second Chamber: Further Reform of the House of Lords (14 July 2008). Cm 7438.
An Invitation to Join the Government of Britain (2010).
Baldwin, Nicholas, 'The House of Lords – Into the Future?' *Journal of Legislative Studies*, June 2007.

Baldwin, Nicholas, and Donald Shell (eds), *Second Chambers* (London: Frank Cass, 2001).

Baldwin, Tom, 'Lack of Agreed Blueprint', *The Times*, 20 January 2000.

Bale, Tim, 'Nick Clegg's proposed reforms to the House of Lords is a solution seeking a problem' (London School of Economics Blog, 6 June 2010).

Ballinger, Chris, *The House of Lords 1911–2011. A Century of Non-Reform* (Oxford: Hart Publishing, 2012).

Barnett, Anthony and Peter Carty, *The Athenian option: radical reform of the House of Lords* (Demos, June 1998).

Bell, Stuart, *How to abolish the Lords* (Fabian Society tract, September 1981).

Beloff, Michael, 'The End of the Twentieth Century: The House of Lords, 1982–2000', in Louis Bloom-Cooper, Brice Dickson and Gawin Drewry, *The Judicial House of Lords, 1876–2009* (Oxford: Oxford University Press, 2009).

Biffen, John, 'The Joy of Decent Obscurity', *The Guardian*, 9 May 1988.

Blackburn, Robert, 'House of Lords Reform', *Public Law*, 1988.

Blair, Tony, *A Journey* (London: Hutchinson, 2010).

Blair, Tony, 'The John Smith Memorial Lecture' (Queen Elizabeth II Conference Centre, London, 7 February 1996).

Bochel, Hugh and Andrew Defty, 'A More Representative Chamber: Representation and the House of Lords', *Journal of Legislative Studies*, 15 February 2012.

Bogdanor, Vernon, 'Camera obscure. The contested institution of the Upper House and the unsung virtues of the Wakeham Report', *Times Literary Supplement*, 4 February 2000.

—— 'Why the Lords must face up to change', *Financial Times*, 8 June 1995.

Bradford, Bishop of, 'Against the Grain' (Nick Baines' Blog, 14 March 2010).

Brazier, Rodney, *Constitutional Reform: Reshaping the British Political System* (Oxford: Oxford University Press, 1998).

Britain Forward Not Back (2005).

Carlin, Brendan, 'Lords shake-up sparks North home rule hope', *The Northern Echo*, 21 January 2000.

Carmichael, Paul and Brice Dickson (eds), *The House of Lords. Its Parliamentary and Judicial Roles* (Oxford: Hart Publishing, 1999).

Clarke, K., R. Cook, P. Tyler, T. Wright and G. Young, *Reforming the House of Lords: Breaking the Deadlock* (London: The Constitution Unit, 2005).

Constitutional Reform: A Supreme Court for the United Kingdom, 14 July 2003. CP 11/03.

Conventions of the UK Parliament. Government Response to the Joint Committee on Conventions' Report of Session 2005–06 (December 2006). Cm 6997.

Cornes, Richard, *Single Chamber Parliaments* (London: The Constitution Committee, September 1998).

Cracknell, Richard, *Lords Reform: Background statistics* (Research Paper 98/104, House of Commons Library, 15 December 1998).

Cranborne, Robert, *The Chain of Authority* (London: Politeia, 1997).

—— *The End of the Era of Representative Democracy?* (London: Politeia, 1998).

—— *The Individual, the Constitution and the Tory Party* (London: Politeia, 1996).

Crewe, Emma, *Lords of Parliament: Manners, rituals and politics* (Manchester: Manchester University Press, 2005).

Crowther-Hunt, Lord, 'Abolishing the House of Lords', *The Listener*, 4 December 1980.

Dale, Iain (ed.), *Conservative Party General Election Manifestos, 1900–1997* (London: Routledge, 2000).

——*Labour Party General Election Manifestos, 1900–1997* (London: Routledge, 2000).

——*Liberal Party General Election Manifestos, 1900–1997* (London: Routledge, 2000).

Davies, Michael, 'House of Lords: New ways of working', *The Table*, vol. 71, 2003.

Denham, Lord, 'Time to Reform the Lords' (*The Field*, November 1991).

Desai, Lord and Lord Kilmarnock, *Destiny not Defeat: Reforming the Lords* (Fabian Society, January 1997).

Draft House of Lords Reform Bill. Report, Session 2010–12. Volume I, 26 March 2012. HL Paper 284–1, HC 1313–1.

Drewry, Gavin, *The Judicial House of Lords, 1876–2009* (Oxford: Oxford University Press, 2009).

D'Souza, Baroness, 'Expertise in the House of Lords is vital and supplied by the cross benchers: there is no democratic deficit and so elections are not needed' (LSE Blog, 13 July 2011).

End of the Peer Show (London: CentreForum, July 2011).

Evans, Paul, *Dod's Handbook of House of Commons Procedure* (London: Dod's, 6th edn, 2007).

Ferguson, Beatrice, 'Complementary Reform in the House of Lords?' (ResPublica Blog, 8 March 2012).

Giddy, Pam, 'Citizen', *New Times*, No. 12, February 2000.

Griffith, J.A.G., Michael Ryle and M.A.J. Wheeler-Booth, *Parliament: Functions, Practice and Procedure* (London: Sweet & Maxwell, 1989).

'Hague launches commission on the future of the House of Lords', Conservative Party PN, 13 July 1998.

Hague, William, *Change and tradition: thinking creatively about the constitution* (Centre for Policy Studies, 24 February 1998).

Harries, Lord, 'The Draft Bill and the Report of the Royal Commission on the Reform of the House of Lords' (LSE Blog, 11 July 2011).

Hastings, A.J., 'More Modernisation? Recommendations of the Joint Committee on Parliamentary Privilege of the UK Parliament, 1997–99' *The Table*, vol. 67, 1999.

Hattersley, Roy, 'Devolution to defend the nation against elective dictatorship', *The Independent*, 30 December 1988.

Hazel, Robert, *Commentary on the White Paper: The House of Lords – Completing the Reform* (London: The Constitution Unit, January 2002).

—— *Constitutional Reform and the new Labour government* (London: The Constitution Unit, July 1997).

—— *Reforming the Lords* (London: The Constitution Unit, January 1998).

Heffer, Simon, *The End of the Peer Show? Why the Hereditary System is Wright and Wromantic* (Centre for Policy Studies, December 1996).

—— 'Why they should have left well alone', *Daily Mail*, 21 January 2000.

Here We Stand (Liberal Democrat Federal White Paper No. 6, August 1995).

Heydel-Mankoo, Rafael, 'Lords reform: A century in the making', Part 2 (ResPublica Blog, 9 December 2010).

Hicks, Andrew, *Reforming the Lords: proposals for a peoples' peerage* (The Bow Group, 5 May 1998).

Hoggart, Simon, 'Blurred way ahead for Lords', *The Guardian*, 21 January 2000.

House of Lords Act 1999. Elizabeth II Chapter 34.

House of Lords: Annual Report and Accounts, 1999–2000. HL Paper 104.

House of Lords Bill, 19 January 1999. Bill 34.

House of Lords Reform Act 2014. Elizabeth II Chapter 24.

House of Lords Reform: An Alternative Way Forward. A Report by Members of the Joint Committee of Both Houses of Parliament on the Government's Draft House of Lords Reform Bill, April 2012.

House of Lords Reform: Draft Bill (May 2011). Cm 8077.

House of Lords Reform: First Report of the Joint Committee on House of Lords Reform, 10 December 2002. HL Paper 17, HC 171.

House of Lords Reform: Government Reply to the Joint Committee's Second Report, 16 July 2003. HL Paper 155, HC 1027.

House of Lords Reform: Second Report of the Joint Committee on House of Lords Reform, 29 April 2003. HL Paper 97, HC 668.

House of Lords Reform: What next? Government's Response to the Committee's Ninth Report of 2013–14 (17 February 20014. HC 1079/2013–14).

Howe, Lord, 'If it isn't Broke', *Journal of Legislative Studies*, June 2007.

Irvine, Lord, 'Interview: Lord Irvine of Lairg', *New Statesman*, 6 December 1996.

—— 'Lord Chancellor's Views': Third Worldwide Common Law Judiciary Conference, 5 July 1999. As Delivered. (MS).

Jenkins, Simon, 'Wakeham the Weak', *The Times*, 21 January 2000.

Johnson, Paul, 'How to Settle the Scots, the Welsh and the Lords in One Senatorial Stroke', *The Spectator*, 22 February 1997.

Joint Committee on House of Lords Reform: *First Report* (Ordered by the House of Lords to be printed, 9 December 2002. HL Paper 17. Ordered by the House of Commons to be printed, 10 December 2002. HC 171).

Joint Committee on House of Lords Reform: *Government Reply to the Committee's Second Report.* (Ordered by The House of Lords to be printed, 16 July 2003. HL Paper 155. Ordered by The House of Commons to be printed, 16 July 2003. HC 1027).

Joint Committee on the Draft House of Lords Reform Bill. Volume I (Report, together with appendices and formal minutes, 23 April 2012. HL Paper 284-I; HC 1313-I).

Jones, George, 'How a Great Fixer Failed to Find a Solution', *Daily Telegraph*, 21 January 2000.

Judge, David, ed., *The Politics of Parliamentary Reform* (London: Heinemann, 1983).

Keith, Brendan, 'The Law Lords Depart: Constitutional Change at Westminster', *The Table*, vol. 78, 2010.

Keller, Peter, 'On what the Report Means', *Evening Standard*, 20 January 2000.

Kelly, Richard, *House of Lords Reform (No. 2) Bill* (Parliament Constitution Centre, House of Commons Library, 10 July 2014).

Kelso, Alexandra, *Parliamentary reform at Westminster* (Manchester: Manchester University Press, 2009).

Kennet, Lord, 'Democratic way to replace the Lords', *The Times*, 16 April 1996.

Le Sueur, Andrew, 'From Appellate Committee to Supreme Court: A Narrative', in Louis Bloom-Cooper, Brice Dickson and Gavin Drewry, *The Judicial House of Lords, 1876–2009* (Oxford: Oxford University Press, 2009).

Liberal Democrat Manifesto 2010 (2010).

Linford, Paul, 'North to have a voice in the Lords', *Newcastle Journal*, 21 January 2000.

Linklater, Magnus, 'The Lords Fix that became a Fudge', *Scotland on Sunday*, 23 January 2000.

Lipsey, Lord, 'How I learned to love the unelected House of Lords', *The Independent*, 21 January 2000.

Longworth, John, 'Our House: Reflections on Representation and Reform in the House of Lords' (ResPublica, 29 February 2012).

Lyon, Elizabeth and Anthony Wigram, *Electoral Reform: The House of Lords* (London: Conservative Action for Electoral Reform, 1977).

MacIntyre, Donald, 'With all the dismal caution of an insider, Wakeham stayed well clear of democracy', *The Independent*, 21 January 2000.

MacLean, Stephen, 'Public Choice Theory and House of Lords Reform', *Economic Affairs*, October 2011.

Maitland, F.W., *The Constitutional History of England* (London: Cambridge University Press, 1911).

Make the difference (1997).

Mandelson, Peter and Roger Liddle, *The Blair Revolution. Can New Labour Deliver?* (London: Faber, 1996).

McDonald, Oonagh, *Parliament at Work* (London: Methuen, 1989).

McLean, Iain, *Response to 'Cm 5291': The House of Lords – Completing the Reform* (Oxford: Oxford University Press, 2001).

—— 'The Salisbury convention that avoided complete Lords reforms for the last century is dead, but achieving any mandate for change that Peers must accept remains very difficult' (LSE Blog, 4 July 2011).

McLean, Iain and Vernon Bogdanor, 'Debate: Shifting Sovereignties: Should the United Kingdom have an elected upper house and elected head of state?', *Political Insight*, April 2010.

McLean, Iain, Arthur Spirling and Meg Russell, 'None of the Above: The UK House of Commons Votes on Reforming the House of Lords, February 2003', *Political Quarterly*, 14 July 2003.

Meadowcraft, Michael, *The Politics of Electoral Reform* (London: The Electoral Reform Society, 1991).

Milne, Kirsty, 'Appetite for more change may have been lost', *The Scotsman*, 21 January, 2000.

Mirfield, Peter, 'Can the House of Lords Lawfully be Abolished?', *Law Quarterly Review*, (95), January 1979.

Mitchell, Jeremy and Anne Davies, *Reforming the Lords* (Institute of Public Policy Research, June 1993).

Mount, Ferdinand, 'Reforming the House of Lords', in *The British Constitution Now: Recovery or Decline?* (April 1992).

Moving ahead: towards a citizens' Britain (September 1998).

Nairne, Patrick, 'Reform of the House of Lords', 11 July 2002. MS.

New Labour: because Britain deserves better (1997).

Newland, Robert, *Only Half a Democracy* (London: The Electoral Reform Society of Great Britain and Ireland, 3rd edn 1982).

O'Leary, Brendan, 'Response: Can the Second Chamber Bind the Union Together?', Conference Papers: The Future of the House of Lords, 8 March 2000 (London: The Constitution Unit, April 2000).

Oliver, Dawn, 'An Independent Scrutiny Commission Could Take Over the Constitutionally Valuable Roles that the House of Lords Presently Performs, and at Lower Cost – Whether We Move to Create an Elected Second Chamber; or Reform the Unacceptable Features of the Current House of Lords; or Just Scrap a Second Chamber Altogether' (LSE Blog, 6 July 2011).

—— 'Reform of the Lords – next steps', *Hansard Society News*, 25 March 2014.

—— 'The Parliament Acts, the Constitution, the Rule of Law, and the Second Chamber', *Statute Law Review*, 23 December 2011.

Osmond, John, *Reforming the Lords and changing Britain* (Fabian pamphlet 687, August 1998).

Paget-Brown, Nicholas, *Unfinished Business: Proposals for the Reform of the House of Lords* (Bow Paper, September 1983).

Parker, Andrew, 'Reform Plan that strives to please everyone', *Financial Times*, 21 January 2000.

Partington, Andrew and Paul Bickley, 'Coming off the Bench: The Past, Present and Future of Religious Representation in the House of Lords', *Theos*, 2007.

Peerage Creations, 1958–2000 (London: House of Lords Library. LLN2001/003).

Perry, David, 'Campaign for northern voice in the new Lords', *Edinburgh Evening News*, 22 January 2000.

Plant, Lord, *Co-operating for Change – a Strategy for Constitutional Reform* (Labour Initiative on Co-operation, November 1996).

Plant Report: *Democracy, Representation and Elections. Report of the Working Party on Electoral Systems* (July 1993).

Plant, Raymond and Michael Steed, *PR for Europe. Proposals to change the electoral system of the European Parliament* (London: Federal Trust for Education and Research, 1997).

Porteus, Keith, 'Letter', *The Times*, 22 January 2000.

Press Reaction to the White Paper: The House of Lords: Completing the Reform (London: House of Lords Library. LLN 2001/009).

Press Reaction to the Report of the Royal Commission on the Reform of the House of Lords: A House for the Future (London: House of Lords Library. LLN 200/002).

Proposals for reform of the composition and powers of the House of Lords, 1968–1998 (London: House of Lords Library. LLN 98/004.

Rallings, Colin and Michael Thrasher (eds), *British Electoral Facts, 1832–2006* (Aldershot: Ashgate Publishing Company, 2007).

Rebalancing the Lords, the numbers (London: The Constitution Unit, January 1998).

Rees-Mogg, William, 'The awkward squad', *The Times*, 24 January 2000.

Reforming the House of Lords (Modernising Parliament), January 1999. Cm 4183.

Reforming the Lords: A step by step guide (London: The Constitution Unit, January 1998).

Reform of the House of Lords (Charter 88's policy paper, September 1998).

Religious Representation in the House of Lords (March 2010).

Renwick, Alan, *House of Lords: A Brief Paper* (London: Political Studies Association, July 2011).

Renwick, Alan and Iain Mclean: 'Electoral System Options (11 January 2012)', in *Joint Committee on the Draft House of Lords Reform Bill. Volume I* (Report, together with appendices and formal minutes. Appendix 6, 23 April 2012. HL Paper 284-I; HC 1313-I).

'Representation', *Journal of Electoral Record and Comment*, vol. 33, No. 2, 1995.

Results of Hereditary Peers Party Elections (House of Lords: Press Information, 5 November 1999).

Richard, Ivor and Damien Welfare, *Unfinished Business: Reforming the House of Lords* (London: Vintage, 1999).

Richard, Lord, 'An Institution Past its Sell-by-Date', *The House Magazine*, 30 September 1996.

Riddell, Peter, 'Report Shies Away from the Big Issues', *The Times*, 21 January 2000.

—— *The Unfulfilled Prime Minister: Tony Blair's quest for legacy* (London: Politicos, 2005).

Routledge, Paul, 'Chamber of Horrors', *Daily Mirror*, 21 January 2000.

Runciman, Viscount, 'Labour's plans for reform of Lords', *The Times*, 22 April 1996.

Russell, Earl, 'Is Tony Blair to be lord and master?', *Sunday Telegraph*, 23 January 2000.

Russell, Meg, *An Appointed Upper House: lessons from Canada* (London: The Constitution Unit, November 1998).

—— 'A Stronger Second Chamber? Assessing the Impact of House of Lords Reform in 1999 and the Lessons for Bicameralism', *Political Studies*, 4 November 2010.

—— 'Blair's Bungalow: A feeble mix of symbolic responsibility and synthetic power', *The Times*, 8 November 2001.

—— 'Elected Second Chambers and their Powers', *Political Quarterly*, 6 February 2012.

—— *Reforming the House of Lords* (Oxford: Oxford University Press, 2000).

—— *Reforming the Lords: a step-by-step guide* (London: The Constitution Unit, January 1998).

—— 'The Byles bill on Lords Reform is important: but needs amending if it is not to damage the Lords' (London: The Constitution Unit Blog, 13 February 2014).

—— 'The Byles/Steel bill – unless amended – holds grave dangers for the Lords' (London: The Constitution Unit Blog, 5 March 2014).

Russell, Meg and Meghan Benton, *Analysis of existing data on the breadth of expertise and experience in the House of Lords* (London: The Constitution Unit, March 2010).

Russell, Meg and Robert Hazel, *Next Steps in Lords Reform: Response to the September 2003 White Paper* (London: The Constitution Unit, November 2003).

Russell, Meg and Maria Sciara, *The House of Lords in 2005: A More Representative and Assertive Chamber* (London: The Constitution Unit, February 2006).

—— *The House of Lords in 2006: Negotiating a Stronger Second Chamber* (London: The Constitution Unit, January 2007).

——'Why Does the Government get Defeated in the House of Lords? The Lords, the Party System and British Politics', *British Politics*, 2007.

Sacranie, Iqbal, 'May be forgotten', *Daily Telegraph*, 21 January 2000.

Sandwich, Earl, 'Why aren't Hereditary Peers Working?' *The House Magazine*, 23 December 1999.

Scarman, Lord, 'Power House', *The Guardian*, 6 June 1988.

Settle, Michael, 'Plenty of scope to kick it into the long grass', *The Herald*, 21 January 2000.

Shell, Donald, *House of Lords* (Manchester: Manchester University, 2007).

——'Labour and the House of Lords: A Case Study in Constitutional Reform', *Parliamentary Affairs* (53), 2000.

——'The House of Lords', in David Judge, ed., *The Politics of Parliamentary Reform* (London: Heinemann, 1983).

——'The second chamber question', *Journal of Legislative Studies*, 4, 1998.

Singh, Indajit, 'May be forgotten', *Daily Telegraph*, 21 January 2000.

Single Chamber Parliaments: A Comparative Study. Stage Two (London: The Constitution Unit, September 1998).

Skidelsky, Lord, 'Reform not Revolution', *The Times*, 3 July 1996.

Smith, Nicole, *Reform of the House of Lords* (London: The Constitution Unit, April 1996).

Sparrow, Andrew, 'Future of the Lords', *Daily Telegraph*, 21 January 2000.

Strabolgi, Lord, 'Imposing Limits on the Lords', *The Times*, 7 May 1996.

Straw, Jack, Doug Henderson and Derek Foster, *New Politics, New Britain. Restoring Trust in the Way we are Governed* (The Labour Party, September 1996).

Sudeley, Lord, *The Preservation of the House of Lords* (The Monday Club, April 1991).

Taylor, Russell, *Bibliography on Lords Reform* (House of Lords. Library Notes, 26 April 2012. LLN 2012/014).

Thatcher, Margaret, *The Downing Street Years* (London: HarperCollins, 1993).

The Future of the House of Lords (London: The Constitution Unit, April 2000).

'The House of Lords – A Parliamentary Symposium', *The House Magazine*, 2 October 1990.

The House of Lords Bill 1998/99 (London: House of Lords Library. LLN 99/002).

The House of Lords: Completing the Reform, November 2001. Cm 5291.

The House of Lords: Into the 21st Century? Commoners, July 1993.

The House of Lords: Reform (February 2007). Cm 7027.

The House of Lords. The Report of the Conservative Review Committee (London: Conservative Central Office, March 1978).

The Legislative Process (HC 190, 1997–98).

The Other Place: Second Chambers and the House of Lords (London: Background Paper No. 297, House of Commons Library, 7 September 1992).

The Public General Acts and General Synod Measures, 2005. Part I (London, 2005).

'The Restoration of a Parliament', *The Economist*, 4 November 1995.

The Second Chamber: Continuing the Reform: Public Administration Select Committee's Report, 14 February 2002. HC 494-I.

Tyler, Paul, *Reforming the House of Lords* (London: The Constitution Unit, February 2005).

Tyrie, Andrew, *Reforming the Lords: a Conservative approach* (Conservative Policy Forum No.1, June 1998).

Tyrie, Andrew, George Young and Roger Gough, *An Elected Second Chamber: A Conservative View* (London: The Constitution Unit, July 2009).

Toynbee, Polly, 'The Empty Chamber', *The Guardian*, 21 January 2000.

Vibert, Frank, *Britain's Constitutional Future* (Institute of Economic Affairs, December 1991).

Wakeham, Lord, 'Opening Address: The Royal Commission's Thinking' in *Conference Papers: The Future of the House of Lords, 8 March 2000* (London: The Constitution Unit, April 2000).

Waldron, Jeremy, 'Bicameralism' (Current Legal Problems address, Faculty of Laws, University College, London, 15 March 2012). MS.

Watkins, Alan, 'Wakeham's vision is marred by indecision', *Independent on Sunday*, 23 January 2000.

Watson, Roland, 'Fudge Masterminded by Skilled Operator', *The Times*, 21 January 2000.

Watt, Nicholas, 'Treason: last cry of the Lords', *The Guardian*, 27 October 1999.

Wheeler-Booth, M.A.J., 'The House of Lords', in J.A.G. Griffith, Michael Ryle and M.A.J. Wheeler-Booth, *Parliament: Functions, Practice and Procedure* (London: Sweet & Maxwell, 1989).

White, Michael, 'Dismay at Lords' plan', *The Guardian*, 21 January 2000.

Winetrobe, Barry K., *Aspects of Parliamentary Reform* (Research Paper 97/64, House of Commons Library, 21 May 1997).

——*House of Lords reform: developments since general election* (Research Paper 98/85, House of Commons Library, 19 August 1998).

——*House of Lords 'reform': recent proposals* (Research Paper 97/28, House of Commons Library, 17 February 1997).

——*Lords Reform: Recent Developments* (Research Paper 98/105, House of Commons Library, 7 December 1998).

——*Lords Reform: The Legislative Role of the House of Lords* (Research Paper 98/103, House of Commons Library, 1 December 1998).

—— *Parliamentary Reform: The Commons 'Modernisation' Programme* (Research Paper 97/107, House of Commons Library, 28 October 1997).

—— *The Commons committee stage of 'constitutional' bills* (Research Paper 97/53, House of Commons Library, 20 May 1997).

—— *The Constitution: Principles and Development* (Research Paper 96/82, House of Commons Library, 18 July 1996).

—— *The House of Lords Bill: Lords reform and wider constitutional reform* (Research Paper 99/7, House of Commons Library, 28 January 1999).

—— *The House of Lords Bill: Options for 'Stage Two'* (Research Paper 99/6, House of Commons Library, 28 January 1999).

—— *The House of Lords Bill: 'Stage One' Issues* (Research Paper 99/5, House of Commons Library, 28 January 1999).

Winetrobe, Barry K. and Oonagh Gay, *The House of Lords Bill: Options for 'Stage Two'* (Research Paper 99/6, House of Commons Library, 28 January 1999).

Winterton, George, 'Is the House of Lords Immortal?', *Law Quarterly Review* (95), July 1979.

Work of the committee: first progress report, July 1997 (HC 191).

Wyndham, William, *Peers in Parliament Reformed* (London: Quiller Press, 1998.

You can only be sure with the Conservatives (1997).

Young, Angus, 'Local voices in the Lords', *Hull Daily Mail*, 21 January 2000.

Young, Hugo, 'A Commons revolt might make them think', *The Guardian*, 8 November 2001.

Index

In the references below, the roman numerals i. and ii. refer to Book One and Book Two of this volume. The arabic numbers that follow are the page references within these books.

Note on names in the index. Many of those who moved in aristocratic and high political circles received knighthoods or peerages which entailed some change in name. Though every effort has been made to get names correct in the text of this volume, in the index the simplest forms have been used – with no intention of disrespect. Some individuals may appear twice, under their names before and after receiving a peerage.

Index